PENGUIN BOOKS

Freedom from Fear

Aung San Suu Kyi is the leader of the struggle for human rights
and democracy in Burma. Born in 1945, she is the daughter of
Burma's national hero, Aung San, and was two years old when he
was assassinated, just before Burma gained the independence to
which he had dedicated his life. After receiving her education in
Rangoon, Delhi and at Oxford University, Aung San Suu Kyi then
worked at the United Nations in New York and Bhutan. For
most of the following twenty years she was occupied raising a family
in England (her husband is British), before returning to Burma in
1988 to care for her dying mother. Her return coincided with the
outbreak of a spontaneous revolt against twenty-six years of political
repression and economic decline. Aung San Suu Kyi ('Suu' to her
friends and family) quickly emerged as the most effective and
articulate leader of the movement, and the party she founded went
on to win a colossal electoral victory in May 1990. In July 1989 she
was put under house arrest, and the military junta that now rules
Burma refused for six years either to free her or to transfer power to
a civilian government as it had promised. However, in July 1995
she was suddenly released, to the joy and surprise of her followers.

Aung San Suu Kyi is an honorary fellow of St Hugh's College,
Oxford. In 1990 she was awarded the Thorolf Rafto Prize for
Human Rights in Norway and the Sakharov Prize for Freedom of
Thought by the European Parliament. Nominated by Václav
Havel, the President of Czechoslovakia, who contributed the original
Foreword to this volume, Aung San Suu Kyi was awarded the
Nobel Peace Prize for 1991. In its citation the Norwegian Nobel
Committee stated that in awarding the prize to Aung San Suu Kyi
it wished 'to honour this woman for her unflagging efforts and to

show its support for the many people throughout the world who are striving to attain democracy, human rights and ethnic conciliation by peaceful means'.

Dr Michael Aris, the editor of this book, is Aung San Suu Kyi's husband. He is a Fellow of St Antony's College, Oxford.

AUNG SAN SUU KYI

Freedom from Fear
and other writings

Foreword to the First Edition by Václav Havel
Foreword to the Second Edition
by Archbishop Desmond Tutu

Edited with an Introduction by
Michael Aris

PENGUIN BOOKS

PENGUIN BOOKS

Published by the Penguin Group
Penguin Books Ltd, 27 Wrights Lane, London w8 5tz, England
Penguin Books USA Inc., 375 Hudson Street, New York, New York 10014, USA
Penguin Books Australia Ltd, Ringwood, Victoria, Australia
Penguin Books Canada Ltd, 10 Alcorn Avenue, Toronto, Ontario, Canada m4v 3b2
Penguin Books (NZ) Ltd, 182–190 Wairau Road, Auckland 10, New Zealand

Penguin Books Ltd, Registered Offices: Harmondsworth, Middlesex, England

First published 1991
Published in a new edition with additional material 1995
10 9 8 7 6 5 4 3

Printed in England by Clays Ltd, St Ives plc

In honour of
Bogyoke Aung San

'When I honour my father,
 I honour all those who stand for
 political integrity in Burma.'

Contents

Illustrations

Acknowledgements

These writings by and about my wife Suu were assembled by me in the first fortnight of my second year as Visiting Professor at Harvard University. My colleagues and students have been most indulgent when the project, unconnected with my official duties, intruded into their proper concerns during a very busy time of the academic year. I am most grateful for the moral and practical support they all gave me. I also wish to thank the many friends and colleagues in Oxford and London who encouraged me to plan the book last summer. I am indebted to the four contributors to Part Three who worked to a tight schedule without complaint. Above all, my family in England gave me their most unstinting support, not only in the present task but in the more general one of coping with the personal effect of Burma's long crisis. Suu and I are blessed with two young sons, Alexander and Kim, who have witnessed and participated in much of the crisis with cool heads and a complete understanding of the role their mother has had to take. They shared in producing this book in many ways.

Foreword to the First Edition
by Václav Havel

Aung San Suu Kyi has received the Nobel Peace Prize and has now been internationally recognized for her struggle against tyranny for freedom and dignity. She is a most worthy recipient of the award. She has spoken clearly and consistently. She has refused to be bribed into silence by permanent exile. Under house arrest, she has lived in truth. She is an outstanding example of the power of the powerless. It was my deep honour to nominate her for the Nobel Peace Prize, and I join all those who applaud her selection.

By dedicating her life to the fight for human rights and democracy in Burma, Aung San Suu Kyi is not only speaking out for justice in her own country, but also for all those who want to be free to choose their own destiny. As long as the struggle for freedom needs to be fought throughout the world, voices such as Aung San Suu Kyi's will summon others to the cause. Whether the cry for freedom comes from central Europe, Russia, Africa, or Asia, it has a common sound: all people must be treated with dignity; all people need to hope.

Aung San Suu Kyi cannot be silenced because she speaks the truth and because her words reflect basic Burmese and universal concepts. As she herself writes, 'It is a puzzlement to the Burmese how concepts which recognize the inherent dignity and the equal and inalienable rights of human beings, which accept that all men are endowed with reason and conscience and which recommend a spirit of brotherhood, can be inimical to indigenous values.' The Nobel Peace Prize awarded to this brave woman makes clear that she speaks for all of us who search for justice.

Foreword to the Second Edition
by *Archbishop Desmond Tutu*

Aung San Suu Kyi is free. How wonderful – quite unbelievable. It is so very like when Nelson Mandela walked out of prison on that February day in 1990, and strode with so much dignity into freedom. And the world thrilled at the sight.

The world is exultant, too, at the news of Suu Kyi's release from the six years of house arrest which prevented her from becoming the leader of her beloved country after her National League for Democracy won a landslide victory in the 1990 elections. Freedom, justice and goodness have yet again been vindicated as they were vindicated on the release of Nelson Mandela, whose example of compromise and reconciliation Suu Kyi declared had inspired her: this remarkable woman said that she bore no one malice; she nursed no grudges against those who had treated her so unjustly; she had no bitterness; and she was ready to work for the healing of her motherland, which had suffered so grievously. In revealing this extraordinary magnanimity she was emulating Nelson Mandela, who has left the world awed by his singular lack of bitterness, his magnanimity and his willingness to forgive those who ill-treated him.

How wonderful that Aung San Suu Kyi's first public utterance after her release should be a clarion call to all the major role-players for dialogue and reconciliation!

The way forward will demand people of stature who are ready to compromise for the greater good of all, not those who remain intransigent by demanding all or nothing. The way forward will require persons of integrity, who know that negotiation is the art of how to give and take. People will need to acknowledge the past and the awful things that were done so that there may be contrition, confession and forgiveness.

Without forgiveness there can be no future. Forgiveness is not a nebulous spiritual thing. It is practical politics. Bygones can never be bygones if dealt with lightly. They will never then be bygones, for they will return to haunt us.

The land must be healed and then, when the past has been dealt with adequately, let it be put firmly behind us and let all get on with the business of building a prosperous motherland for all, where freedom and justice and goodness and laughter and joy and compassion will rule supreme.

Introduction *by Michael Aris*

It was a quiet evening in Oxford like many others, the last day of March 1988. Our sons were already in bed and we were reading when the telephone rang. Suu picked up the phone to learn that her mother had suffered a severe stroke. She put the phone down and at once started to pack. I had a premonition that our lives would change for ever. Two days later Suu was many thousands of miles away at her mother's bedside in Rangoon.

After three months helping to tend her mother in the hospital day and night, it became clear to Suu and the doctors that her condition would not improve and Suu decided to bring her back to the family home in Rangoon. The familiar surroundings and the help of a dedicated medical team promised to ensure that her remaining days would be peaceful. When Alexander and Kim's summer terms finished at Oxford we flew out to Rangoon to find the house an island of peace and order under Suu's firm, loving control. The study downstairs had been transformed into a hospital ward and the old lady's spirits rallied when she knew her grandsons had arrived.

In the preceding months the students had begun to take to the streets calling for radical change. They had already met with lethal violence at the hands of the authorities. In one incident forty-one wounded students had suffocated to death in a police van. What ignited the whole country just the day after the boys and I arrived was an extraordinary and unexpected speech given by the man who had ruled Burma since he led a military coup in 1962. On 23 July, Ne Win, the general who had turned civilian, announced to a specially convened congress of his Burma Socialist Programme Party that he was resigning forthwith and that a referendum on Burma's political future would be held. I can still remember watching with Suu the scene in the congress as it was shown on state television. She, like the whole country, was electrified. The people at last had a chance to take control of their own destinies. I think it was at this moment more than any other that Suu made up her mind to step forward. However, the idea had gradually taken shape in her mind during the previous fifteen weeks.

In reality, from her earliest childhood, Suu has been deeply preoccupied with the question of what she might do to help her people. She never for a minute forgot that she was the daughter of Burma's national hero, Aung San. It was he who led the struggle for independence from British colonial rule and from the Japanese occupation. Trained by the Japanese during the Second World War, he and his associates among the legendary 'Thirty Comrades' entered Burma with the invading Japanese army who promised independence. When that promise proved false he went underground to lead the resistance with the Burma Independence Army he had created. He assisted the re-invading Allies, and after the war negotiated with Clement Attlee's Labour government for final independence. But he and practically his entire cabinet in the provisional government were gunned down on 19 July 1947 just a few months before the transfer of power. A jealous political rival masterminded the assassination.

Suu, who was born on 19 June 1945, has only the dimmest recollections of her father. However, everything she has learned about him inclined her to believe in his selfless courage and his vision of a free and democratic Burma. Some would say she became obsessed with the image of the father she never knew. At Oxford she steadily acquired a large collection of books and papers in Burmese and English about him. There is a certain inevitability in the way she, like him, has now become an icon of popular hope and longing. In the daughter as in the father there

seems an extraordinary coincidence of legend and reality, of word
and deed. And yet prior to 1988 it had never been her intention
to strive for anything quite so momentous. When she left Oxford
to care for her mother she had been set on writing a doctoral
thesis on Burmese literature for London University. (A draft
chapter is on this computer disk as I write, and I believe she is
still registered at the School of Oriental and African Studies as
a postgraduate student.) She had also entertained hopes of one
day setting up an international scholarship scheme for Burmese
students and a network of public libraries in Burma.

Nevertheless, she always used to say to me that if her people
ever needed her, she would not fail them. Recently I read again
the 187 letters she sent to me in Bhutan from New York in the
eight months before we married in London on 1 January 1972.
Again and again she expressed her worry that her family and
people might misinterpret our marriage and see it as a lessening
of her devotion to them. She constantly reminded me that one
day she would have to return to Burma, that she counted on my
support at that time, not as her due, but as a favour.

> I only ask one thing, that should my people need me, you
> would help me to do my duty by them.

> Would you mind very much should such a situation ever
> arise? How probable it is I do not know, but the possibility
> is there.

> Sometimes I am beset by fears that circumstances and
> national considerations might tear us apart just when we
> are so happy in each other that separation would be a
> torment. And yet such fears are so futile and inconsequen-
> tial: if we love and cherish each other as much as we can
> while we can, I am sure love and compassion will triumph
> in the end.

Suu wrote me these words, and many like them, just over twenty
years ago. Today she is a prisoner of conscience in her country,

totally isolated from the world. The seeds of her present condition were sown long ago.

So it came as no surprise when Suu told me she was resolved to enter the struggle. The promise to support her decision which I had given in advance so many years ago now had to be fulfilled. Like Suu perhaps, I had imagined that if a day of reckoning were to come, it would happen later in life when our children were grown up. But fate and history never seem to work in orderly ways. Timings are unpredictable and do not wait upon convenience. Moreover, the laws of human history are too uncertain to be used as a basis for action. All that Suu had to draw on were her very finely cultivated sense of commitment and her powers of reason. But she was also blessed and burdened with her unique status as the daughter of the national hero. Although the regime had appropriated his image for their own purposes, his reputation was still inviolate in the hearts of the common people. Moreover Suu had never lost her Burmese identity and values through all the years abroad. Her knowledge of the Burmese heritage, her wonderful fluency in her own language and, very important, her refusal to give up her Burmese citizenship and passport despite her marriage to an Englishman – all these factors conspired with the sad circumstances of her mother's final illness to make her engagement unavoidable.

In the nationwide turbulence which followed Ne Win's resignation on 23 July 1988 and the immediate refusal by his party to agree to a referendum on Burma's future, Suu's house quickly became the main centre of political activity in the country and the scene of such continuous comings and goings as the curfew allowed. Every conceivable type of activist from all walks of life and all generations poured in. Suu talked to them all about human rights, an expression which had little currency in Burma till then. She began to take her first steps into the maelstrom beyond her gates. Alexander, Kim and I were behind her when she addressed a colossal rally at the Shwedagon Pagoda for the first time on 26 August.

Despite all the frenetic activity in her house, it never really lost the sense of being a haven of love and care. Suu is an astonishing person by any standards, and I think I can say I know her after twenty years of marriage, but I shall never quite understand how she managed to divide her efforts so equally between the devoted care of her incapacitated, dying mother and all the activity which brought her the leadership of the struggle for human rights and democracy in her country. It has something to do with her inflexible sense of duty and her sure grasp of what is right and wrong – qualities which can sit as a dead weight on some shoulders but which she carries with such grace.

By the time Suu's mother died on 27 December, nine months after her first stroke, it seemed as if several empires had come and gone. The carnival of mass demonstrations had turned repeatedly to bloodshed as the authorities tried to stem the tide of revolt sweeping the country. I shall not quickly forget the surge of hope and fear, the elation followed by near despair, the prolonged gunfire in the streets and the doves cooing in the garden through it all.

Three heads of state were forced by the people's movement to resign in quick succession, though ultimate power remained vested in the military officers loyal to Ne Win. The army controlled by those officers finally staged a coup on 18 September and brought in their State Law and Order Restoration Council (SLORC). They reiterated the promise of free and fair elections while clearing the streets with gunfire. Suu and her close associates promptly formed their party, the National League for Democracy (NLD).

It was the young people who already belonged to her party who brought order to the milling crowds of thousands who came to attend her mother's funeral on 2 January 1989. Having been forced out of the country some weeks earlier, I was allowed to return to Rangoon to be with Suu when her mother died. I flew in from Bangkok with our sons, whose school terms had again finished. Suu's only surviving brother was even allowed to come from America for the funeral, though he was now an American citizen to whom the authorities would normally deny a visit.

The negotiations and arrangements for the funeral of the widow of the national hero were conducted in exemplary fashion. It was the only occasion when the authorities offered Suu any co-operation, realizing that if they failed in this the consequences might be disastrous. Soldiers, students and politicians combined with Suu to make orderly plans in a way that made everyone realize what the country would achieve if unity could be won under her leadership. But the co-operation of the military was, alas, to prove very short-lived. Suu's growing prestige and popularity seemed to strike at the very heart of all that the army had come to represent. The constant appeals for dialogue and understanding which she issued before and after this occasion all went unheeded.

In the next seven months Suu consolidated her party's strength by touring almost the entire country. The boys and I were back at Oxford by then. Although Suu wrote as often as she possibly could, we were more dependent for news on the press reports than on her letters. We would read in the papers of the official harassment and vilification she endured at the hands of the authorities. The effect of this on the people was opposite to the one intended: the more she was attacked, the more the people flocked to her banner.

With hindsight it is easy to see why she and her party were perceived as the main threat to all the interests vested in the old system. The authorities had counted on the scores of new parties to produce a split parliament which they could dominate in any fashion they pleased. The head of state, General Saw Maung, was on record as saying he expected the next government to be a coalition of many parties. The prospect of a single party sweeping the board went counter to all they hoped for.

I shall not attempt to piece together here Suu's policies, movements and activities in this period. I was not with her and cannot speak from first-hand experience. The task must wait for future historians when time, distance and access to all the sources now hidden enable a dispassionate appraisal. But I do not think they will find cause to suggest that Suu acted with anything but dedication to a selfless cause. She brought overwhelming unity to a spontaneous, hitherto leaderless revolt. She insisted at all times that the movement should be based on a non-violent struggle for human rights as the primary object. She spoke to the common people of her country as they had not been spoken to for so long – as individuals worthy of love and respect. In a prolonged campaign of civil disobedience she flouted a great number of the Draconian measures introduced by the authorities. She wrote countless letters to the authorities complaining of their excesses but with no response. At the same time she constantly begged them to open a proper dialogue – but to no effect at all.

Matters came to a head in July 1989. In the days leading up to the annual Martyrs' Day on the 19th, when the death of her father and his cabinet is traditionally commemorated, Suu had decided to point her finger at the main obstacle to political change. She voiced the belief, shared by many but never spoken in public, that the army was still being controlled by the retired general Ne Win. She expressed the doubt that the ruling junta ever intended to keep their promise of transferring power to a civilian government. When she announced her plan to lead a march to pay tribute to the martyrs, the authorities moved quickly to fill the streets with troops. Faced again with the prospect of terrible bloodshed in Rangoon, Suu called off the march.

Our sons Alexander and Kim had already joined Suu from their schools in Oxford, their third trip since the whole drama began to unfold. I could not come with them because my own father had just died in Scotland. On 20 July I heard the news that Suu had been placed under house arrest. I had absolutely no idea of her condition or that of the boys, but very fortunately I had a valid visa for Burma in my passport. I informed the authorities of my plan to come out to Rangoon right away.

As the plane taxied to a halt at Mingaladon Airport I could see a lot of military activity on the tarmac. The plane was surrounded by troops and as I walked down the gangplank I was quickly identified and escorted away to the VIP lounge. The British Embassy official who had come to meet me was unable to make contact. For twenty-two days I effectively disappeared from sight. Nobody knew what had happened to me. The British press carried stories about how an Oxford don had gone missing. My family in England was extremely worried. The British government and the European Community pressed very hard for consular contact, but to no avail. I had vanished.

The story of what really happened in those three weeks, perhaps the greatest single crisis we have so far had to face as a family, could occupy a whole book, but let me be brief. The very personable military officer who met me at the airport said that if I agreed to abide by the same terms under which Suu had been placed under detention I could stay with her and the boys. Those terms included no contact with any embassy or any person engaged in politics. I was able to say truthfully that I had only come to be with the family and saw no difficulty in abiding by these terms. We drove off from the airport to find the house surrounded by troops. The gates were opened and we drove in. I had no idea what to expect.

I arrived to find Suu in the third day of a hunger strike. Her single demand was that she should be allowed to go to prison with all of her young supporters who had been taken away from her compound when the authorities arrested her. She believed her presence with them in prison would afford them some protection from maltreatment. She took her last meal on the evening of 20 July, the day of her arrest, and for the following twelve days until almost noon on 1 August she accepted only water. On that day a military officer came to give her his personal assurance, on behalf of the authorities, that her young people would not be tortured and that the cases against them would be heard by due process of law. She accepted this compromise, and the doctors who had been deputed to attend her, whose treatment she had hitherto refused, immediately put her on an intravenous drip with her consent. She had lost twelve pounds in weight. I still do not know if the authorities kept their promise.

In all this, Suu had been very calm and the boys too. She had spent the days of her fast resting quietly, reading and talking to us. I was less calm, though I tried to pretend to be. Acting as go-between I had even been brought to a grand meeting in Rangoon

City Hall in front of cameras to present Suu's demands to the Rangoon Command Commander and a room full of officers and through them to the SLORC leadership. At all times I met with nothing but courtesy. Eleven days after Suu ended her fast I was finally escorted to see the British Consul in a military guesthouse. In the presence of SLORC officials I confirmed the whole story of Suu's hunger strike which had already somehow leaked out. Indeed, I later discovered that the story had appeared in the Asia-Pacific edition of *Time* magazine with her picture on the cover.

Suu recovered her weight and strength in the days ahead. The crisis had passed and the tension eased. The boys learned martial arts from the guards. We put the house in order. I made arrangements with the authorities to send Suu parcels from England and to exchange letters with her. Things seemed to be on quite an even keel by the time the Oxford term loomed upon us once again. We left for England on 2 September.

It was the last time the boys were allowed to see their mother. Some days after we arrived in England the Burmese Embassy in London informed me that the boys' Burmese passports were invalid and now cancelled since they were not entitled to Burmese citizenship. All attempts to obtain visas on their new British passports have failed. Very obviously the plan was to break Suu's spirit by separating her from her children in the hope she would accept permanent exile. I myself was allowed to return once more to be with her for a fortnight the following Christmas. It seems the authorities had hoped I would try to persuade her to leave with me. In fact, knowing the strength of Suu's determination, I had not even thought of doing this. Perhaps at that moment they realized I was no longer useful to their purpose.

The days I spent alone with her that last time, completely isolated from the world, are among my happiest memories of our many years of marriage. It was wonderfully peaceful. Suu had established a strict regime of exercise, study and piano which I managed to disrupt. She was memorizing a number of Buddhist sutras. I produced Christmas presents I had brought one by one to spread them out over several days. We had all the time in the world to talk about many things. I did not suspect this would be the last time we would be together for the foreseeable future.

While I was there the authorities brought in papers from her party concerning the elections. She was to sign them if she agreed to stand for election in spite of her incarceration. She did so. But several weeks later it was learnt that the SLORC had contrived to rule that her candidacy was invalid. It made no difference in the end to the election results. On 27 May 1990 the people of Burma went to the polls and voted for the party she had founded and led. In an extraordinary landslide victory the National League for Democracy won 392 of the 485 seats contested, more than 80 per cent. Contrary to expectations, the polling was totally free and fair. The reason why the elections were allowed to take place at all seems to have been because the SLORC even then believed no single party could win. But Suu had always sensed that if a free election did take place, then her party would certainly gain the victory. I am not sure, though, that even she realized the scale such a victory might take. Again she appeared on the cover of *Time* magazine in Asia. The photograph must have been taken during one of her long campaign trips. Her lips are cracked and her eyes sore with dust.

The vote was a personal one for her: often the voters knew nothing about their candidate except that he represented Suu. Locked away for ten months before the elections, her place in the hearts of the Burmese had meanwhile only grown stronger. There is a great irony in this, for she had become the focus of a personality cult which she would have been the first to decry. Loyalty to principles, she had often said, was more important than loyalty to individuals. But she personified in the fullest measure the principles she and everyone else were striving for and so the people voted for her.

In the days which followed there was great expectancy that the ruling junta would release her from detention and announce a timetable to transfer power to the National League for Democracy. Back in Oxford I thought at the very least they might allow the boys and me to visit her again. But it was not to be. I received a final letter from her dated 17 July 1990 in which she asked me for copies of the Indian epics, the *Ramayana* and the

Mahabharata. She commented on the fact that there was much more humour in the Thai and Cambodian depiction of the monkey-king Hanuman than in the original Indian version. Her letter was otherwise concerned with family matters and things she wanted me to send her. It was the last we received from her. Every attempt since then to regain contact has failed.

A great number of people have tried their best to persuade the junta to relent and allow us access to Suu, but so far to no avail. As I write these words it is more than two years since our sons last saw their mother, a year and nearly ten months since I was with her, and a year and nearly two months since she was last able to write to us. The SLORC does its best to conceal the completeness of her isolation, refusing even to call it house arrest but instead 'restricted residence'. They say she is free to rejoin her family at any time, refusing to accept that in spite of her British husband she is wholly Burmese, and that the Burmese people have amply demonstrated that they hold her as their own and as the talisman of their future freedom.

Events have proved her right. The regime appears to have no intention of transferring power in the foreseeable future. There is much official talk of the need for a new constitution before power can be transferred but no timetable has been announced to draw one up. The free elections took place, bestowing a clear mandate – but nothing has happened. Suu is still quite alone.

Suu's writings in this collection fall naturally into two parts: firstly those she completed in Oxford, Kyoto and Simla before her return to Burma in 1988, and secondly a medley of later essays, speeches, letters and interviews resulting from her involvement in the struggle for human rights and democracy in her country. The basic division of the book therefore reflects the fundamental change in her fortunes and those of her country in 1988. I believe, however, that there is an underlying consistency uniting the two parts. It stems from Suu's unchanging concern to understand her inheritance, to communicate that understanding to others and to apply it to her country's problems.

The earlier writings were addressed to several very different readerships. Some may say that to bring them now within the covers of the same book will give it an uneven tone and quality. On the other hand, they faithfully reflect Suu's gift of communicating at various levels. The biographical portrait of her father was written for an historical series on Asian leaders intended for senior high-school students in Australia. It is followed by a very simple and factual account of her country and people aimed at English-speaking schoolchildren throughout the world. By contrast, her comparative study of intellectual developments in Burma and India under colonialism is a sophisticated and innovatory work. Some who work in the field of Burmese studies have told me that it breaks new ground both in its method of approach and in its findings. The final piece of Part One, on the interconnections of literature and nationalism in the period 1910–40, also points to the kind of scholarship Suu was engaged in when fate intruded.

These four pieces were all written by her in the midst of raising a young family on slender means. For many years Suu took on the major responsibilities at home in order to free me for my own research. And she helped me beyond measure in my work too. She encouraged me in a field the world looks on as arcane; she applied her own rigorous gift of logic to my arguments; and her sensitivity opened up many new perspectives – invariably causing me to rethink and reformulate. Since we shared many trips and periods of residence in the Himalayas (in Bhutan, Nepal, Ladakh, Arunachal Pradesh and Himachal Pradesh), she was in a very good position to help me in my writings on the area.

Part Two of this book consists of a selection of miscellaneous documents composed by Suu during her later struggle. Together they convey something of the atmosphere of the whole movement and Suu's quick response to the unfolding political situation. The three opening essays are probably her most reflective and articulated statements on the movement for democracy in Burma, on the universality of human rights and on the codes, principles and customs found in the Buddhist heritage which the Burmese people now take to support and guarantee those rights. The inspiration she derives from her father's role and sacrifice is always implicit when it is not explicit both in these essays and elsewhere. The remaining documents are arranged in chronological sequence from the point when she stepped forward with her first political initiative right through to the events which led up to her house arrest. The reader can follow only a few of her movements between these points in her own words, south to the Irrawaddy delta and north to Kachin State, but there were many other trips all over the country. It should be realized that these sixteen documents form only a minute fraction of all the words she wrote or spoke in this period. Whatever records may survive of her total output, at the moment they lie quite beyond reach. But her voice, long silenced, is heard again in this small selection.

In Part Three I have brought together four contributions by others. The first two are very personal reminiscences of Suu in her 'chrysalis period'. The second two are assessments of her later role. Inevitably there is some degree of overlap and repetition within each pair, but I hope this is compensated by the more rounded picture of Suu which emerges from their sum. I have done my best to avoid influencing the authors in any way, and my role as editor has been confined to adjusting a few points of fact and style. I cannot vouch for the truth of every one of the assertions made about Suu or the events related at first or second hand – simply because I was not present when many of them took place. I believe, however, each author has tried hard to convey the truth.

September 1991

Seventeen days after sending this book to the publishers I received an early telephone call from the Norwegian Nobel Committee telling me of Suu's great award. The following is part of the statement I released in a vain attempt to stem the onslaught of the world's press.

I was informed today that my dear wife Suu has been awarded the Nobel Peace Prize. Many will now for the first time learn of her courageous leadership of the non-violent struggle for the restoration of human rights in her country. I believe her role will come to serve as an inspiration to a great number of people in the world today.

The joy and pride which I and our children feel at this moment is matched by sadness and continuing apprehension. I am not sure if the Nobel Peace Prize has ever been given to someone in a situation of such extreme isolation and peril. It has certainly never before been given to a woman in that condition. Suu is now in the third year of her political detention at the hands of Burma's military rulers. We, her family, are denied any contact whatsoever with her and know nothing of her condition except that she is quite alone. We do not even know if she is still kept in her own house or if she has been moved elsewhere.

It seems the authorities in Burma have many times offered to release her if she accepts going into permanent exile. I know Suu well enough to be sure she will not do this: she is firmly committed to her chosen path, whatever the sacrifice it entails. I think she will therefore only be able to travel to Oslo in December to receive the Nobel Peace Prize in person if the authorities undertake not to prevent her return, even if it is only to resume her solitary detention.

It is my earnest hope and prayer that the Peace Prize will somehow lead to what she has always strived for – a process of dialogue aimed at achieving lasting peace in her country. Selfishly I also hope our family's situation will be eased as a result of this supreme gesture of recognition for her moral and physical courage, and that we may at last be allowed to pay her visits again. We miss her very much.

14 October 1991

From May 1992 to January 1995 our sons and I were able to pay
Suu regular visits while her detention continued. This gave her
the opportunity to issue occasional statements and respond to a
few invitations to compose public speeches, which I and others
then delivered on her behalf. Two of these are included in this
new edition of her writings, along with the transcript of part of
her conversation with Congressman Bill Richardson in February
1994. The collection as it now stands ends, very appropriately,
with the statement Suu read to assembled reporters and journalists on 11 July 1995, the day after her release from nearly six
years of detention. Looking now at the photograph of her taken
then, which I have chosen for the cover, I see again what these
long years have done to her, the wisdom and beauty beyond the
suffering endured. Who can now doubt her love and courage?

Oxford, 12 July 1995

PART ONE

The Inheritance

I

My Father

This work first appeared in the Leaders of Asia series published by the University of Queensland Press in 1984 under the title of Aung San. *A second edition with an introduction by Roger Matthews was published in 1991 by Kiscadale Publications, Edinburgh, with the title* Aung San of Burma: A Biographical Portrait by his Daughter. *The opening paragraph formed the preface to these editions and is dated Oxford, October 1982.*

My father died when I was too young to remember him. It was in an attempt to discover the kind of man he had been that I began to read and collect material on his life. The following account is based on published materials; only in two instances about his personal life have I relied to some extent on what I learnt about him from my family and from people who knew him well. Writing about a person to whom one is closely related is a difficult task, and the author is open to possible accusations of insufficient objectivity. Biographers are inescapably at the mercy of the material at their disposal and of events and insights which shape their judgement. For myself, I can only say that I have tried to give an honest picture of my father as I see him.

Aung San was born at Natmauk, a small township in the dry zone of central Burma, on 13 February 1915, thirty years after the third Anglo-Burmese War had ended the monarchy at

Mandalay and brought the whole country under British rule. The people of Natmauk had a tradition of service to the Burmese kings, and some of Aung San's maternal forebears had achieved high positions in government. His father, U Pha, was of solid farming stock, unworldly, of a somewhat taciturn nature so sparing of words that he had no success in his profession as a pleader (advocate) in spite of a brilliant scholastic record. Much of the burden of providing for the family therefore fell on the mother, Daw Su, an intelligent woman of considerable energy and spirit whose uncle U Min Yaung had led one of the earliest resistance groups against the British until he was captured and beheaded. The memory of the fiery patriot who had refused to be a subject of the *Kalahs* ('foreigners from the West') was a source of great pride and inspiration to his family and to the people of his region.

Aung San, the youngest of six children, has left an unflattering description of himself as a sickly, unwashed, gluttonous, thoroughly unprepossessing child who was so late beginning to speak that his family feared he might be dumb. However, according to those who knew him then, he also had certain lovable traits such as guilelessness, scrupulous honesty and compassion for the poor. Aung San's family had a reputation for intelligence and learning, but while his three brothers started their education early, he refused to go to school 'unless mother went too'. The strong-minded Daw Su was indulgent with her youngest and allowed him to remain at home until he was nearly eight, when he himself decided that he was ready for school. The decision was prompted by the occasion of an elder brother entering the local monastery for the short period of novitiate customary for all Burmese Buddhist boys. Whether it was the attractions of monastic life or of the white 'dancing pony' on which candidates for the novitiate were paraded around the town as part of the ordination ceremonies, Aung San expressed a strong desire to become a novice. His astute mother was quick to seize the opportunity to point out that first he would have to learn to read and write.

Aung San immediately proved to be an outstanding student, hard-working, disciplined and always at the top of his class. He began his schooling at a monastery which also provided the elements of modern education and was thus known as a *lawkatat* ('worldly') school to distinguish it from those institutions which devoted themselves exclusively to the traditional Buddhist teachings. However, English was not taught in the schools of Natmauk, and Aung San was determined to emulate his brothers who had learnt this language, in those days a prerequisite for higher education. Thus he moved at the age of thirteen to the National School at Yenangyuang after a brief hunger strike to gain the consent of his mother, who was reluctant to send her youngest child away from home. At Yenangyaung, Aung San had the good fortune to be in the care of his eldest brother, Ba Win, a teacher in the school, who supervised his education and well-being with a healthy mixture of strictness and common sense. The young boy continued to exhibit his academic prowess and at fifteen he won a scholarship and a prize for standing first in the pre-high-school government examinations held throughout the country in the Buddhist and National Schools.

The National Schools had been founded as a result of the 1920 strike against the Rangoon University Act, which was seen as a move to restrict higher education to a small privileged class. These schools were the crucibles in which a political awareness of their colonial status and a desire to free themselves from it were fired in the hearts of young Burmese. However, the desire to free his country from foreign rule seems to have lodged itself in Aung San's mind well before he arrived at Yenangyaung. He has written that as a small boy he often dreamt of various methods of rebelling against the British and driving them out, and sometimes indulged in fancies of discovering magical means to achieve the same purpose. At the National School he began to take an interest in the speeches of political personalities and to participate in debates. Although the style of his delivery was uninspiring, his conviction and the thoroughness with which he prepared any subject he tackled earned him a reputation for eloquence. He also edited the school journal, but in spite of such extra-curricular activities, he remained awkward and often lost in thought and was considered a strange fellow by his schoolmates. In 1932 he matriculated in the 'A' category with distinctions in Burmese and Pali and went to study at Rangoon University.

The year that Aung San joined the university was the year after the Hsaya San uprising had been suppressed and its leaders executed. This rebellion, which had its roots in the sufferings of the agrarian population, was played down by the British as a mere peasants' revolt led by a superstitious fanatic who wanted to be king. But among the Burmese it aroused greater sympathy than might have appeared from the degree of active involvement. Even those who did not find Hsaya San himself an attractive figure were stirred by the courage and nationalist spirit of the rebels and moved to pity by the harsh reprisals taken by the government.

The Burmese had never become reconciled to foreign domination in spite of the fair measure of success obtained by the pacification policy the British had pursued in the early years of their administration. As the colonial government became firmly established, the superior attitudes adopted by the foreign rulers together with the inadequate concern for the true welfare of the country began to foment the resentment of the people. The early nationalist organizations were devoted to the preservation and purification of the Buddhist religion and traditional Burmese culture, but as the number of modern-educated youth increased, political aspirations began to make themselves manifest. The Young Men's Buddhist Association (YMBA), founded in 1906, was the first body to respond to this political situation and was the organizer of the successful strike against the Rangoon University Act. As the nationalist movement gathered momentum, the YMBA was metamorphosed in 1920 into the General Council of Buddhist Associations (GCBA), which might be called the first national alliance. Burmese nationalism was given a combative impulse by U Ottama, a learned Buddhist monk who roused the patriotic fervour of the nation with his spirited agitations for the freedom of Burma. However, the impetus for a concerted independence movement was diverted by the secession of the 'Twenty-One Party' from the GCBA in 1922, followed by further splits within the associations, which finally resulted in three different factions by the end of the 1920s. The beginning of the 1930s saw Burmese politicians, some of whom had come into prominence by defending the Hsaya San rebels at the government trials, wrangling over the question of whether or not Burma should be separated from India under the British administration. In the meantime, the days of quiescence were running out and a younger generation of nationalists was coming on the scene who would have fewer inhibitions about using militant tactics.

Aung San at eighteen was a raw country lad, dour of expression and untidy of dress, quite out of place among the dapper students of Rangoon University who rather fancied themselves to be the cream of Burmese youth. Moreover, he quickly established his indifference to the disapproval and ridicule of his more sophisticated contemporaries. At the end of a debate in English, organized by the Students' Union during his first term, Aung San rose from the floor to support the motion which had been proposed by his eldest brother, that monks should not participate in politics. This was a case of conviction rather than of family solidarity. Aung San's badly accented, clumsy English and unpolished manner of delivery made his speech practically incomprehensible, raising jeers and catcalls and causing his brother some embarrassment. However, Aung San was not to be intimidated or shouted down. He continued until he had said all he wanted to say, interweaving his inadequate English with Pali words and phrases, ignoring the insults and the rude interjections to stick to Burmese.

This debate set the precedent for many subsequent occasions when he would insist on having his say in English amid the groans and abuse of the audience, and this, together with his moodiness, earned him a reputation for being thoroughly eccentric, even mad. But Aung San was not one to let himself be deterred from any task he set himself by fear of criticism. He recognized the importance of English in the contemporary world and worked hard to improve his command of the language, reading voraciously, listening to others and enlisting the help of a close friend who had had the advantage of studying in an English-medium school. In this way he achieved a proficiency in the language unusual for one of his up-country origins and monastery-school beginnings.

It is worth noting here that the motion Aung San supported in that first debate expressed one of his lasting convictions: that monks should not participate in politics. He was to say in a speech made little more than a year before his death that to mix religion with politics was to go against the spirit of religion itself. He appealed to the *a sangha* (the community of Buddhist monks) to purify Buddhism and 'broadcast it to all the world so that all mankind might be able to listen to its timeless message of Love and Brotherhood till eternity . . . this is the highest politics which you can do for your country and people'.[1]

Aung San, whom popular opinion has often cast in the role of a completely political animal, had a deep and abiding interest in religion. As a student at Yenangyaung, the sorrow of his father's death had filled him with a desire to become a monk. Later, towards the beginning of his university career, he apparently conceived a great admiration for an Italian Buddhist monk, U Lawkanada, and asked his mother's permission to follow the venerable *sayadaw* ('holy teacher') in his missionary work. Permission was refused, but his preoccupation with spiritual matters did not cease. Even after he had entered the world of student politics, which was to absorb him so completely, he wrote to one of his closest friends of his 'pilgrimage in quest of Truth and Perfection' and of his conscious striving after 'sincerity in thought, word and deed'. He also expressed his concern over the 'spiritual vacuum . . . among our youth' and the fear that 'unless we brace ourselves to withstand the tide . . . we will soon be spiritual bankrupts *par excellence*'.[2]

Student Politics and the 'Thakins'

Aung San's involvement in student politics was gradual at first, then rapidly accelerated after 1935. By that time he had started to work with such people as Nu, Hla Pe (later known as Let Ya), Rashid, Thein Pe and Kyaw Nyein. It was with these young men who were to become well-known figures in the Burmese independence movement that Aung San wielded the student body into a political force of some reckoning. They began by attempting to penetrate the ranks of the hitherto conformist Students' Union, and although initially they had little success (only Kyaw Nyein and Thein Pe were elected at the first attempt), their spirited nationalism and hard work soon paid dividends. The mood of the university was also shifting. Active patriotism was in the air. By the academic year 1935–6 the group of young nationalists had captured all the major posts of the Students' Union, and Aung San, who was one of those elected to the executive committee, also became the editor of the union magazine.

It was the publication in the union magazine of the article 'Hell Hound at Large' which indirectly helped to trigger off the far-reaching university strike of 1936. The article was taken to be a scurrilous attack on a university official, and the authorities demanded the name of the author from Aung San, who refused on the grounds that it would be against journalistic ethics. This provided the administration with an excuse to serve the editor with an expulsion notice. As Nu had also been expelled very recently for his abrasive criticism of the principal, indignation ran high among the students. They decided to call a strike. It was the time of the university examinations, which made the decision a serious one and gave it much publicity. The sympathies of the newspapers and the country were immediately with the strikers, and this, together with the impressive organization and discipline, brought them vividly to the attention of the older politicians, who suddenly became aware of the potency of student power. The government was forced to consider the grievances of the strikers seriously, and the eventual outcome was the retirement of the high-handed principal, the forming of a committee to look into the amendments the students wanted incorporated into the University Act, and virtual concession to the less important demands.

The 1936 strike, which was an important landmark in the political development of the young nationalists, made Aung San widely known as a student leader. His prestige grew steadily, and he progressed up the executive posts of the Rangoon University Students' Union as well as the All Burma Students' Union, which had been founded after the strike. By 1938 he had become the president of both bodies. In the meantime, having received his BA degree, he had started to read for a degree in law, partly to enable him to stay on at the university. His honesty, single-mindedness and capacity for work won him considerable respect, albeit reluctant, but he was a difficult personality and stood apart from his more courteous and easy-going colleagues. There was much criticism of his moods, his untidiness, his devastating fits of silence, his equally devastating fits of loquacity and his altogether angular behaviour. He himself admitted that he sometimes found polite, refined people irksome and would long to separate himself from them to live the life of a savage. But his view of savages was the romantic one of pure, honest, healthy beings revelling in their freedom.

In 1938 Aung San left the university to become a member of the Dohbama Asi-ayone ('We Burmese' Organization), a party that had its origins in the Indo-Burmese riots of 1930. Its character was nationalist, young and vigorous, and its leaders were a breed apart from the older politicians who were either not bold enough, not Burmese enough, not radical enough or perhaps simply not young enough for the new generation of educated youth who were passionate to dedicate themselves to the patriotic cause. The Asi-ayone members were not universally popular; there were those who looked down on them as brash young upstarts or feckless trouble-makers and found their use of the prefix *Thakin* affected and objectionable. *Thakin*, which means 'master', was the term by which the British rulers expected to be, and for the most part were, addressed by their Burmese subjects. By appropriating the title for themselves, the young Thakins proclaimed the birthright of the Burmese to be their own masters and gave their names a touch of pugnacious nationalism. Internal friction split the organization into two, and Aung San joined the majority faction led by Thakin Kodaw Hmaing, the 'grand old man of letters and politics', who had originally been a patron of the Asi-ayone. It was this faction which was also chosen by Nu, Hla Pe, Thein Pe and two others who had not been among the student leaders but who were to play prominent roles in Burmese politics, Than Tun and Soe. Aung San soon became the general secretary of the Dohbama Asi-ayone and later drafted its manifesto.

During 1938–9 momentous events occurred which were collectively known as the Revolution of 1300 (the year according to the Burmese calendar, which begins its New Year in mid-April). There was the march of the Yenangyaung petroleum workers, the march of the peasants on Rangoon to demand agrarian reforms, the student protests in which Aung Gyaw was mortally wounded in a police baton charge, the consequent school strikes all over the country, communal riots between the Burmese and the Indian Muslims, the labour strikes, the Mandalay demonstrations in which seventeen people died under police fire, and the fall of the government of Prime Minister Ba Maw. All these combined to create a ferment of unrest such as the nation had not known and speeded up the tempo of nationalist activities. But even amid such stirring events, those two scourges of Burmese politics, factionalism and jealousy, began to cast their shadow. The desire to claim the distinction for being the more effective, the most patriotic, the best was to seize groups and individuals and lead to recriminations and bitterness.

Aung San was one of the few considered above faction and jealousy. He had leftist leanings and was a founder member and general secretary of a group started in 1939 which some describe as a Marxist study group and some call the first Burmese communist cell. But Aung San was not fanatical in his belief in communism or any other rigid ideology. He found much to attract him in the broad range of socialist theories, but his real quest was always for ideas and tactics that would bring freedom and unity to his country. In 1939, soon after the outbreak of the war in Europe, seeing that 'Colonialism's difficulty is Freedom's opportunity', he helped to found the 'Freedom Bloc', an alliance of Ba Maw's Sinyetha Party, the Dohbama Asi-ayone, the students and some individual politicians. Ba Maw was made the *anashin* (literally 'lord of power') and Aung San the general secretary of the bloc, which Nu has dubbed the 'brainchild of Thakin Aung San'. The message of the Freedom Bloc to the nation was that the people should support the British war effort only if they were promised independence at the end of the war; if the British government was not prepared to make such a declaration, the people should oppose the war effort strenuously. The authorities responded by making large-scale arrests of nationalists; by the end of 1940 many of the Thakin leaders and Ba Maw were in gaol. A warrant for Aung San's arrest was also issued, but he received a timely warning and disappeared.

Alliance with the Japanese

Aung San had been contemplating the necessity for an armed struggle for some time. Yet in spite of the dreams of his childhood, he had not always ruled out the possibility of achieving independence through constitutional means. As a university student he had considered taking the civil-service examinations and perhaps following the example of Indian politicians, whom he admired for their educated conduct of politics as well as for their patriotism. It has also been said that after he had become a well-known student leader he wrote to the professor of English at Rangoon University that he was a 'peaceful revolutionary'. However, the tide of events in Burma caused him to change his views. He has described his thinking in 1940 thus:

> Personally though I felt that international propaganda and assistance of our cause was necessary. The main work, I thought, must be done in Burma which must be the mobilization of the masses for the national struggle. I had a rough plan of my own – a country-wide mass resistance movement against British imperialism on a progressive scale ... co-extensive with international and national developments in the form of series of local and partial strikes of industrial and rural workers leading to a general and rent strike finally, also all forms of militant propaganda such as mass demonstrations and people's marches leading finally to mass civil disobedience, also economic campaign against British imperialism in the form of boycott of British goods leading to the mass non-payment of taxes, to be supported by developing

guerrilla action against military and civil and police out-posts, lines of communications, etc., leading finally to the complete paralysis of the British administration in Burma when we should be able along with the developing world situation to make the final and ultimate bid for the capture of power. And I counted then upon the coming over of the troops belonging to the British government to our side – particularly the non-British sections. In this plan I also visualized the possibility of the Jap invasion of Burma – but here I had no clear vision (all of us at that time had no clear view in this respect though some might now try to show themselves, after all the events, to have been wiser than others).[3]

Aung San admitted that this was a 'very grand plan of my own' which did not appeal to many of his comrades, partly because of 'our petit-bourgeois origin' which made 'several of us hesitant before any decisive action even though we might think and talk bravely', partly because they were impatient at the idea of the 'seemingly prolonged difficult work of arousing the masses' and partly because 'most of us even though we might talk about mass action and mass struggle were not so convinced of its efficacy'. However, Aung San persisted in the view that it would be necessary to try to get hold of arms to enable the nationalists to carry out guerrilla action, and finally it was decided that one of their number should go outside Burma to seek aid and weapons. 'And as I was the only one leading an underground existence,' he wrote, 'I was chosen for the task.'[4]

In August 1940 Aung San and another Thakin, Hla Myaing (later known as Yan Aung), left Burma on the ship *Hai Lee* and reached the international settlement of Kulangsu at Amoy in China. For a few months they were stranded there, vainly trying to establish contact with the Chinese communists. The communist contacts did not materialize, but they were approached by a Japanese agent and flown out to Tokyo to meet Colonel Keiji Suzuki, an officer of the Japanese army who was to become famous as the head of the Minami Kikan, a secret organization whose task would be to 'aid Burmese independence and to close the Burma Road'.[5]

Contact between Burmese politicians and the Japanese was not an entirely new development. Saw, who had replaced Ba Maw as Prime Minister, was reputed to have made his fortune from Japanese funds, and Ba Maw had also sought the aid of the Japanese against the Freedom Bloc. Yet another veteran politician and one-time minister in the Ba Maw government, Thein Maung, had visited Japan, sponsored the Japan–Burma Friendship Association and met Suzuki on the latter's visit to Burma in mid-1940. It was through this contact that the Japanese had managed to locate the two Thakins in Amoy. The members of the Freedom Bloc were now divided over whether or not they should accept Japanese help, the communists (of whom Soe, Ba Hein, Than Tun and Thein Pe were pre-eminent) especially opposing the idea of co-operation with fascist Japan. Aung San, however, took the pragmatic view that they should accept help from any quarter that offered it and see how the situation developed. However, as his own words indicated, he does not seem to have thought out the consequences clearly.

In Tokyo, Aung San and Suzuki established a kind of mutual understanding, but there seem to have been reservations on both sides. While Suzuki respected Aung San for his honesty and patriotism, he thought that 'his political thinking was not so mature',[6] a not altogether unjustified criticism at that time, for Aung San himself has written that he and his comrades had invited the Japanese invasion 'not by pro-fascist leanings, but by our native blunders and petit-bourgeois timidity'. He had been apprehensive on his way to Japan, and although he was relieved to find on arrival that it was 'not so bad', he still had misgivings. While admiring the patriotism, cleanliness and self-denial of the Japanese people, he objected to the 'barbarity' of some of their militarist views and was somewhat shocked by their attitude towards women.[7]

Aung San came back to Burma in February 1941 disguised as a Chinese seaman. He brought an offer from the Japanese which the Burmese understood to be one of arms and money to support an uprising. There would also be military training for a select group of young men who would have to be smuggled out of the country. Aung San himself did not remain long in Burma but went back to Japan with Hla Pe and three others, the vanguard of the group that was to be known as the 'Thirty Comrades'. The selection of these thirty, who were to become the core of the Burma Independence Army, was decided partly by availability, which precluded those nationalists who were in gaol, and partly by a desire to appease contending factions within the Thakin Party, which sowed the seeds for future dissension.

On Hainan island, where the thirty received strenuous military training, Aung San, Hla Pe, Tun Ok and Aung Than (later known as Setkya) were selected to specialize in high command and administration. Tun Ok, who represented one faction of the Thakin Party, was chosen as the 'political leader' of the group, but it was Aung San who emerged as the unmistakable leader not just of the Thirty Comrades but of the Burma Independence Army when it was created. Although Aung San was slight and not particularly robust, he proved to be a soldier of great skill and courage, able to bear much hardship. And for all the charges of 'poor at human relations' which had been levelled against him, it was he who rallied the men when their bodies and spirits flagged, showed special concern for the youngest ones and counselled self-restraint when feelings ran high against either camp life or the Japanese. For in spite of the respect and even affection that many of the young trainees conceived for some of their instructors, the Burmese found certain Japanese attitudes highly objectionable, and friction began to develop between the two races even before the invasion of Burma at the end of 1941.

The Burma Independence Army (BIA), a force comprising the trainees of the Hainan camp, Thai nationals of Burmese origin and members of the Minami Kikan, was officially launched in Bangkok in December 1941. Suzuki was the commanding officer with the rank of general; Aung San, as chief of staff, was made a major-general. The members of the fledgling army took an oath of loyalty, and the officers adopted valorous-sounding Burmese names, transforming Suzuki to Moegyo ('Thunderbolt') and

Aung San to Teza ('Fire'). Others of the Thirty Comrades who
were to become well known by their names included such men as
Let Ya, Setkya, Zeya, Ne Win, Yan Naing and Kyaw Zaw.
'Major-General Teza', however, was to revert to the name by
which he had been known to the country as a student and
Thakin leader, and it was as *Bogyoke* (General) Aung San that he
was to be idolized as the hero of the people.

The march of the BIA into Burma alongside the Japanese
troops was an occasion of great pride and joy to the Burmese,
who felt that at last their national honour had been vindicated.
But already Aung San and some of his comrades knew that there
was trouble ahead. He has left on record that while still in
Bangkok he tried to arrange for the nationalists in Burma to
organize independence so that the Japanese would be confronted
with the accomplished fact. Failing that, the masses were to be
mobilized and underground activities initiated to prevent the
invaders from consolidating their position. However, Burma was
in disarray and most of her politicians were in prison, so neither
of the plans was practicable, and the Japanese occupied the
country. The story of the Japanese occupation is one of disillusion,
uncertainty and suffering. Those who had believed they were
about to gain freedom from the British were shattered to find
themselves ground under the heels of their fellow Asians instead.
The soldiers of Nippon, whom many had welcomed as liberators,
turned out to be worse oppressors than the unpopular British.
Ugly incidents multiplied daily. *Kempei* (the Japanese military
police) became a dreaded word, and people had to learn to live
in a world where disappearances, torture and forced labour
conscription were part of everyday existence. In addition, there
were the ravages of both Allied and Japanese bombings, the
shortages of wartime, the informers, the clashes between different
temperaments and cultures, the inevitable misunderstandings between people without a common language. There were of course
Japanese who lived in accordance with the principles of justice
and humanity and who befriended the Burmese, but their positive
contributions were lost beneath the welter of militarist racism.

The members of the Minami Kikan who felt honour-bound to

give Burma her promised independence seem to have been unhappy with the way the situation had developed. Suzuki had in
fact set up a central government of Burma with Tun Ok as the
head soon after Rangoon had fallen to the Japanese in March
1942. But that government was short-lived, for as the occupation
of the country proceeded, the Japanese military administration
took over and Burma began to be treated more and more like a
piece of conquered territory. The position of the Burma Independ
ence Army was uncertain and unenviable. Its ranks had been
swelled rapidly by eager recruits who had joined it on its march,
and these new soldiers had yet to be trained and disciplined into
effective troops. Aung San had not been given command of his
men; he was simply Suzuki's senior staff officer, while Suzuki
himself seems to have been having difficulties with the military
administration over the role he and the BIA were to play in the
future of Burma. On the part of Aung San and his comrades
there was a growing feeling that the BIA commands should be
transferred to Burmese officers. Let Ya has described a dramatic
scene in which he, Aung San and several others of the Thirty
Comrades confronted Suzuki over the matter. The outcome was
Aung San's appointment as commander-in-chief of the BIA, with
Let Ya as the chief of staff.

Aung San had no illusions either about his position or about
the plight of the country. He concentrated on strengthening and
disciplining the army, aware that the struggle for independence
was far from over. He also tried to keep the BIA away from party
politics and from interfering in civil administrative matters, but
he must have known that it was already too late to keep politics
out of any army that had been created with politicians at its core.
In July 1942 Suzuki left Burma and the BIA was reorganized as
the Burma Defence Army with Aung San as the commander-in-
chief bearing the rank of colonel. However, there were Japanese
military 'advisers' attached to the new army at every level and
the actual powers of the Burmese officers were heavily circum-
scribed. In August the commander of the Japanese forces in
Burma, General Iida, inaugurated the Burmese administration
and Ba Maw was appointed Chief Administrator. On the surface

it seemed as if the government of Burma had passed to her people; in fact it was the entrenchment of Japanese military rule.

Resistance

Aung San and his comrades had suffered great physical hardship on their march with the BIA, and as malaria and exhaustion caught up with them, many of them landed in hospital. The Rangoon General Hospital, where Aung San and a number of his colleagues found themselves, was run by a group of dedicated doctors and nurses trying to provide medical care against great odds. Aung San was celebrated for his stern looks and impenetrable moods, which, together with his growing reputation as a hero, made him an object of awe to the junior nurses, who hardly dared approach him. He therefore came under the care of the senior staff nurse, Ma Khin Kyi, an attractive young woman of great charm whose dedication to her work of healing had won the respect and affection of patients and colleagues alike. She handled Aung San with firmness, tenderness and good humour. The formidable commander-in-chief was thoroughly captivated. His shyness and sense of mission had kept him away from women, and he was strait-laced to the extent that when, in Tokyo, Suzuki had offered him a woman, presumably out of a sense of Japanese courtesy, he was deeply shocked and wondered if the older man were trying to 'demoralize' him. But Aung San knew what he wanted, and he was nothing if not straightforward. After a brief courtship, he and Ma Khin Kyi (later known as Daw Khin Kyi) were married on 6 September 1942.

It has been said that 'Daw Khin Kyi, in marrying Aung San, married not a man only but a destiny'.[8] And Aung San had married a woman who had not only the courage and warmth he needed in his life's companion but also the steadfastness and dignity to uphold his ideals after he was gone. Theirs was a successful union, and the soldiers who had not been entirely happy at the idea of their adored young commander getting married were soon won over. Marriage brought out the gentler traits in Aung San's character, and he proved to be a loving

husband and father. To have by his side an understanding
companion who was able to share his hard and dangerous life
undoubtedly strengthened him for the momentous tasks that lay
ahead.

In March 1943 Aung San was promoted to the rank of major-
general and invited to Japan to be decorated by the Emperor.
The delegation to Tokyo was led by Ba Maw and, beside Aung
San, included two eminent Burmese statesmen, Thein Maung
and Mya. The Japanese Prime Minister, General Tojo, had
already announced in January that Burma would soon be declared an independent state, and the Burmese party came back
carrying a document that said, in Aung San's laconic words,
'that Burma would be granted independence on 1 August 1943,
and that we were to conclude certain treaties and so forth'. He
did not take it terribly seriously. On 1 August, Burma was duly
declared a sovereign independent nation and a co-equal member
of the Greater East Asia Co-Prosperity Sphere. Ba Maw was
appointed head of state with the title of *Adipati* ('Great Lord') as
well as Prime Minister, while Aung San became the War Minister.
The Japanese tried various tactics to render the Burmese forces,
renamed the Burma National Army (BNA), ineffectual, first
scattering them around the country, then concentrating them in
a few places, trying to make contact between the War Ministry
and the troops difficult. Aung San was unperturbed. He agreed
to everything the Japanese suggested, keeping his own counsel,
and made his plans.

It must have been around the time he came back from Tokyo
that Aung San summoned a few of his army officers, including
Let Ya, Zeya, Ne Win and Kyaw Zaw, to discuss the timing of
the resistance. The officers recommended waiting until things
were better organized, and it seems that Aung San agreed reluct-
antly only after he had discussed the matter with Than Tun,
who also expressed the opinion that the time was not yet ripe.
Other communists, in particular Soe and Thein Pe, had been
preaching resistance against the Japanese even before the retreat
of the British had released them from prison. With the advance of
the Japanese army they had both gone underground, and Thein

Pe, after a brief meeting with Aung San and Ne Win at Shwebo, made his way to India to try to contact the British troops. By November 1943 plans for the resistance had gone far enough for a Major Seagrim, who was hiding in the hills of Burma trying to organize a force of irregulars, to report to India that 'a certain Aung San of the Burma Defence Army was planning to turn his forces against the Japanese when opportunity presented itself'.[9] Meanwhile, Aung San had to allay Japanese suspicions until preparations for the resistance were completed, but he made bold public pronouncements which told the people that their present 'independence' was a counterfeit and that the struggle for the real thing was yet to come.

Towards the end of 1942 clashes had broken out between irresponsible elements among the BIA and the Karens, one of the main ethnic groups within the country, leading to much bloodshed and racial strife. Aung San had always laid great importance on good relations between the different races of Burma, knowing that it was essential for the unity of the nation. In the 'Blue-Print for Burma' which he had drawn up for Suzuki in 1940, he had already stressed the need to 'bridge all gulfs now existing through British machinations between the major Burmese race and the hill tribes, Arakan and Shan State, and unite those all into one nation under the same treatment'.[10] The conflict between the Karens and the Burmese greatly troubled him. Throughout the latter part of 1943, he, Than Tun and Let Ya laboured to bring about peace and understanding between the two races. Their concerted efforts were rewarded; the Karens learnt to trust the Burmese leaders to the extent that a Karen battalion was added to the Burmese army.

Another burning problem Aung San had to resolve was the enmity that was steadily growing between the communists and the socialists of the Burma Revolutionary Party. The communist leaders were Soe (who continued his underground existence throughout the Japanese occupation), Than Tun (who had become the Minister for Forests and Agriculture) and Ba Hein, while Kyaw Nyein and Ba Swe were two of the most prominent and active socialists. Aung San worked hard to bring the two

sides together. Such a conciliation was made more urgent by the
fact that the political differences had seeped into the army and
were threatening its solidarity and therefore the chances for a
successful resistance. Moreover, Soe had been disseminating propaganda harmful to the BNA in the course of his anti-fascist
campaign, creating much resentment within the ranks and anger-
ing Aung San himself. After months spent in exchanging views,
Aung San had a secret meeting lasting several days in August
1944 with Soe, Than Tun and Ba Hein. Aung San's proposal for
an anti-fascist organization was discussed, and a draft manifesto
for the organization and a plan for concerted action approved.
Soon after, a meeting was arranged between the communist
leaders and members of the Burma Revolutionary Party, at
which Aung San read out a proclamation in Burmese entitled
'Rise Up and Attack the Fascist Dacoits', officially launching the
Anti-Fascist Organization (AFO). Soe was the political leader,
Than Tun the general secretary, also in charge of liaison with the
Allied forces, and Aung San the military leader. There were at
the time some younger officers in the BNA who were impatient
for action and frustrated by the reticence of Aung San, who
limited his circle of conferees to a few Thakin leaders and senior
army officers. The younger officers were planning a resistance
campaign of their own. On discovering this, Aung San resolved
the situation by giving them specific roles to play within the
AFO movement.

Once the internal forces were united, it only remained to see
what kind of terms could be arranged with the Allied forces
before finalizing plans for the resistance. Aung San and the AFO
leaders had decided to rise against the Japanese with or without
external help, but there were obvious practical advantages to be
gained from co-operating with the increasingly victorious Allied
forces. In the event, no clear understanding had been reached
with the British by the time the resistance started on 27 March
1945, when Burmese troops throughout the country rose up
against the Japanese. Ten days previously, Aung San had taken
part in a ceremonial parade in Rangoon at the end of which he
and his men had marched out of the capital for 'manoeuvres'.

Slim's Fourteenth Army had already crossed the Irrawaddy north of Mandalay, and Than Tun had left for Toungoo to try to rendezvous with a British army officer. The resistance was soon in full spate. On 15 May, Aung San, accompanied by a staff officer, went to meet Slim at the latter's headquarters. In the interview that followed, Aung San took a bold line, introducing himself as the representative of the provisional government of Burma and demanding the status of an Allied commander. But while trying to get the maximum concessions out of the British officer, he showed himself to be realistic, co-operative and disarmingly honest, winning Slim's liking and respect. In the latter's words, 'The greatest impression he made on me was one of honesty. He was not free with glib assurances and he hesitated to commit himself, but I had the idea that if he agreed to do something he would keep his word.'[11]

After the meeting between Aung San and Slim, the Burmese and the Allied troops joined in the operations against the Japanese army, which rapidly crumbled. By 15 June a victory parade was held in Rangoon at which the Burmese army participated alongside the units representing British Empire and Allied forces. The resistance against the Japanese was over. It had been the finest hour of the Burmese nationalists when ideological differences and personal considerations had been put aside for a common cause. In August 1945 the AFO was expanded to include organizations and individuals representing a broad spectrum of social and political interests and renamed the Anti-Fascist People's Freedom League (AFPFL).

Negotiations with the British

The decision of the British to accept the offer of the AFO to fight the Japanese alongside the Allied forces had been due to the political acumen of Lord Mountbatten, Supreme Allied Commander, South-East Asia. The government in exile set up in India after the 1942 British retreat from Burma was dominated by civil servants who had lived through times when the young nationalists had challenged their authority and disrupted their administration. These officials of the former administration were against any form of co-operation with the AFPFL, and during the period of military administration immediately following the British reoccupation of Burma, they wanted to declare the AFPFL illegal and arrest Aung San as a traitor. Mountbatten, who was in a position to be more objective, saw that to achieve a peaceful settlement in Burma it would be essential to win the co-operation of the man the people had come to regard as their deliverer. The British civil servant who headed the military administration and who was so out of touch with the mood of the Burmese people was soon replaced by Major-General Hubert Rance, a professional soldier.

An immediate problem that Aung San had to resolve was the future of the Burmese army, which had been renamed the Patriotic Burmese Forces (PBF). The difficulties of feeding and equipping the troops were becoming acute. After the Allied victory, Aung San had agreed at a meeting with Mountbatten that those men of the PBF who were willing should be absorbed into the Burma army under British command. The details of this agreement were worked out and finally settled in September 1945 at the Kandy meeting between the Allied Command and a Burmese delegation which included Aung San, Let Ya and Than Tun. On the way to Kandy, some members of the delegation had met with Thein Pe during the stop-over in Calcutta to discuss the question of Aung San's future. One view was that the coming political struggle needed him, that 'he was the only man who could forge a united front of the nationalist forces and give the leadership'. The other view, put forward by the communists with the exception of Thein Pe, was that Aung San should give up politics and remain in the army because he did not possess all the qualities of a political leader, his human relations were poor, and he was not skilful in political tactics. Let Ya, who strongly believed that Aung San was the national leader Burma needed to unite the forces in the 'final struggle', understood the suggestion of the communists to mean that 'they wanted to have the political field all to themselves, with Bogyoke out of the way but giving them indirect support, when they should need it'.[12] Aung San listened to both views and made his own decision: he would leave the army and devote himself to the struggle for independence on the political front.

The years 1945–7 saw the emergence of Aung San as a strong leader and an able statesman who had the confidence as well as the love of the people, disproving beyond doubt the criticisms of those who had wanted him to remain in the army. In May 1945 the British government had declared its future policy towards Burma in the form of a White Paper. This provided for a period of three years' direct rule by the Governor and, in due course, elections and the restoration of a Burmese Council and Legislature, which were no more than what had been established under the 1935 Burma Act. Only after the Council and Legislature had been restored would there be a step forward: the drafting of a constitution by all parties which would eventually provide the basis on which Burma would be granted dominion status. However, the hill and frontier areas would be excluded from this arrangement unless the people of these 'excluded areas' specifically expressed the desire to be amalgamated with the rest of Burma.

The terms of the White Paper were totally unacceptable to the AFPFL, as Aung San and Than Tun made clear to Sir Reginald Dorman-Smith, the returning Governor of Burma, even before the end of the military administration. The leaders of the AFPFL explained that theirs was the party that represented the country and that they should therefore be allowed to form a national provisional government to replace the military administration. Dorman-Smith was not lacking in good intentions, but he, like many of the civil servants surrounding him, was unable to grasp the fluid and complicated political climate of post-war Burma. He had difficulty in believing that the AFPFL had the popular support of the country, and although he could not fail to see that Aung San was the most important figure in Burma at the time, he seemed reluctant to accept the fact. Moreover, he was handicapped by an understandable desire to reward those elder Burmese politicians who had remained loyal to his government throughout the war, unable or perhaps unwilling to see that they no longer had a place in the political arena of the new Burma. Churchill's imperialistic refusal to consider the 'liquidation of the British Empire' did not help, while his successor, Attlee, finding it difficult to 'evaluate the various trends of opinion' in Burma, was slow to formulate a clear-cut policy.

Civil government was restored to the country in October 1945 when Dorman-Smith arrived back in Rangoon, emphasizing that Burma's battle for freedom was over. This, however, was not the view of Aung San and the AFPFL, who had not dismissed the possibility of further armed conflict should the British government fail to give them the independence they wanted on their own terms. The first clash came over the composition of the Governor's Council. The AFPFL insisted that seven of the eleven seats be filled by their nominees and attached other demands which were calculated to turn the Council into the national provisional government for which they had asked in the first place. Not unexpectedly, the British government refused, and Dorman-Smith appointed to the Council and to the Legislature people he considered moderates but who included some politicians seen by many Burmese as sycophants or self-seeking traitors to the nationalist cause. In January 1946 Aung San was elected president of the AFPFL by acclaim, and he set out to mobilize the country behind the league in its contest with the British administration.

In spite of the Kandy agreement, there were substantial numbers of PBF veterans who had not joined the Burma army. Aung San gathered these ex-servicemen together with new recruits to form the People's Volunteer Organization (PVO). The men of the PVO wore uniform and drilled openly; and although it was officially a welfare organization engaged in reconstruction activities, the PVO's potential as the military arm of the AFPFL made the government highly uneasy. Aung San countered the complaints of the Governor with some finesse and produced a statement in which he laid out the aims of the PVO, including 'to co-operate with and help government authorities and other organizations and the public in general in the suppression of crimes and in the maintenance of law and order in the country'.[13]

Dorman-Smith did not know what to make of it. He was

unequal to the task of handling Aung San and the AFPFL, unable to make up his mind about the Burmese leader, oscillating between high praise and puzzled misgivings. Aung San gave indications that he would prefer to achieve independence without resorting to an armed struggle, which would exacerbate the already severe hardships of the people. At the same time he made it evident that he would not refrain from violence should it be necessary for the freedom of Burma. In the large public meetings he addressed, as well as on such emotionally charged occasions as the funeral of peasants killed by police fire during a procession, Aung San showed himself capable of keeping the massive crowds quiet and controlled, even while he denounced the policies of the British administration and exhorted the country to greater exertions for the cause of independence.

Yet Dorman-Smith and his advisers were reluctant to accept that they needed Aung San's co-operation for a peaceful settlement and wondered if they could not set up other parties to test the power of the AFPFL. There were certainly politicians willing to take up the challenge, men of whom it could perhaps be said, as an English writer said of the Governor's Councillors, that the difference between them and the AFPFL lay not so much in their independence policies as in the rivalry for power. Moreover, Aung San's rise to national leadership and the great love and reverence, verging on worship, that he inspired in the people had aroused intense jealousy in some quarters. Just when Dorman-Smith was casting around for possible alternatives to the AFPFL and some of his advisers were clamouring for the arrest of Aung San on the grounds of sedition, Tun Ok, who was serving on the Council, brought an accusation of murder against Aung San. During the advance of the BIA, a village headman had been tried by court martial on charges of pro-British activities, cruelty and corruption, and the sentence of death had been carried out by Aung San. Tun Ok said he had been a witness throughout the proceedings and offered to give evidence should a trial take place.

The government was divided over whether Aung San should be immediately arrested. Some British civil servants recommended the arrest, urging that it would 'clear the air', avert a possible rebellion and cause little trouble, as the people would soon forget Aung San. The Inspector-General of Police demurred, pointed out that a general pardon for war offences was under consideration and judged that the arrest of the leader of the AFPFL and the PVO was more likely to spark off a rebellion than to prevent one. The Commander-in-Chief Burma Command supported the police view, expressing his opinion that Aung San was 'too sensible' to start a rebellion. In addition, there were reservations about acting on the word of Tun Ok, whose motives were suspect and who had published a book in which he had written proudly of the violent deeds he had committed during the Japanese occupation, uncompelled by force of duty. Dorman-Smith decided to discuss Tun Ok's charges directly with Aung San, who accepted full responsibility, explaining that sentence of death had been carried out in accordance with the findings of the court martial.

The Governor was once again in a state of indecision, torn between admiration for Aung San's honesty and 'moral courage', and contemplation of the political advantages that might possibly be gained from putting away on a charge of murder the man who was the chief adversary of his administration. Perhaps fortunately, the government at Whitehall reserved the right to decide what course of action should be taken in the matter. In April 1946, while on a visit to Singapore, Dorman-Smith received a cable directing him to arrest Aung San. The Governor flew back to Rangoon immediately to carry out the instructions. Just before the warrant could be served, another cable arrived rescinding the order.

This episode further corroded the already uncertain authority of the administration, whose every move was known to the AFPFL through their numerous supporters in the government departments. Word soon went out that although the British were eager to put away Aung San, they did not dare to touch him. Dorman-Smith tried to salvage the situation, at last admitting to London that the White Paper was unworkable and suggesting new approaches which would be acceptable to the AFPFL. But it was too late. In June 1946 amoebic dysentery sent the worried Governor back to England; before the end of July, Attlee had decided to replace Dorman-Smith with Major-General Rance. It was a happy choice, for Rance had come to know the Burmese situation well during his term as head of the military administration and was on good terms with a number of AFPFL leaders, including Aung San.

Achieving Independence

While the change of Governor did not change the policies of the AFPFL, it represented a change in the approach of the British government, and thus independence politics entered a new phase. The old Governor's Council was dissolved, and in September 1946 Aung San was appointed Deputy Chairman of the new Executive Council with the portfolios of defence and external affairs. The rest of the eleven-man Council included five more members of the AFPFL. As it assumed collective responsibility (although in name an advisory body to the Governor), the Executive Council became in fact the long-agitated-for national provisional government. Aung San viewed the new developments with cautious optimism. It was not yet the end of the struggle, as he pointed out at a protest meeting against the White Paper, which had not been officially discarded. He warned the people not to imagine that his acceptance of office meant the end of all problems and outlined the tasks that still lay before them. He emphasized the importance of their support to him and the AFPFL, and added a personal note about himself with that frankness and simplicity which endeared him to his countrymen.

> At this time I am a person who is very popular with the public. But I am neither a god, wizard or magician. Only a man. Not a heavenly being, I can only have the powers of a man. I am very young. The responsibility I now bear is that of standing at the very head to carry the burdens of the whole country. I do not consider that I have all the qualifications necessary to bear that burden. Also many people know that I am short tempered. That is my nature. When I am busy and harassed, I get short tempered. I shall try to

correct that as much as possible. But you must also be
patient. I too will be patient and if you will build up your
strength to an even greater height than that which you
have displayed today and support us in what we are doing
for you, we shall be able to do more to achieve the independence and the public welfare that we want ... That is why I
would like to ask the people once more to stand firm and
resolute.[11]

The people did stand firm and resolute behind Aung San, but
he was not free from opposition. More than from the political
parties that tried to challenge the position of the AFPFL, troubles
came from within the organization itself. Although there were
few individual defections, the communists had been working to
strengthen their own party all the while they were ostensibly
united behind the AFPFL front. Personal differences and ideological clashes had led to a split between the 'red' communist
faction of Soe and the 'white' communist faction of Than Tun
and Thein Pe in March 1946, and the militancy of the 'red'
communists had made them illegal under the Unlawful Associations Act in July. Than Tun remained the general secretary of
the AFPFL and Thein Pe was made a member of the new
Council, but the 'Thein–Than' communists tried to place
obstacles in the way of Aung San's negotiations as Deputy Chairman of the Executive Council to end the general strike that had
been launched before the arrival of Rance.
Although the attempt to prevent the settlement of the strike
failed, it had been only one part of a campaign which had been
going on for some time to subvert the authority of Aung San and
the AFPFL. Such a situation could not remain long unresolved.
The socialist Kyaw Nyein displaced Than Tun as the general
secretary of the AFPFL, and the communists were expelled from
the league in October, a move ratified by the league's General
Congress the following month. In the speeches explaining the
expulsion, Aung San denounced the communists for seeking to
wreck the unity of the country, for putting their own party above
the cause of Burma's independence and for following the dictates

of the Indian Communist Party blindly without considering whether their methods were suited to the Burmese situation. Thein Pe, who resigned from the Executive Council, retaliated by declaring that Aung San and his colleagues had become more reformist than revolutionary. 'They have surrendered to British duplicity,' he said. 'They are deplorably weak-kneed in their dealings with the Governor. And they are intolerant of criticism.'[15]

Although the communists and the AFPFL parted company, Aung San, who greatly desired leftist unity, retained his attachment to Marxist socialism and to individuals within the Communist Party. He had tried to reconcile the 'red' and 'white' factions, and after the expulsion of the Thein–Than group from the AFPFL it seemed he contemplated an amalgamation of the PVO and the socialists to form a Marxist League. The new Executive Council also lifted the ban on Soe's communists, but they were inflexibly committed to the path of armed revolution and once again had to be declared illegal in January 1947. Many of the communists, both 'red' and 'white', and in particular ex-PBF servicemen, retained a deep regard for Aung San, who for his part did not seem to have ruled out entirely the possibility of a reconciliation right up to the end of his life. But he would allow no ideology to come before the cause of Burmese freedom and unity.

In December 1946 the AFPFL accepted the invitation of the British government to come for talks to discuss the steps that would be necessary to constitute Burma a sovereign independent nation. The delegation which left for London early in the New Year was headed by Aung San and included several Councillors, politicians and civil servants. At a press conference during the stop-over at Delhi, Aung San stated that they wanted 'complete independence'; there was no question of dominion status. He also said in reply to a query of the press that they had 'no inhibitions of any kind' about contemplating 'a violent or non-violent struggle, or both' if the demands of the Burmese were not satisfactorily met. He concluded that while he hoped for the best, he was prepared for the worst.[16] This was no more than what he had said in greater detail in his New Year's speech just before he left

Burma. He had spoken frankly of his inclination to believe that the British wished to make a peaceful settlement, which he himself would greatly prefer to armed revolution, but asked the people to be ready for a struggle 'outside of the law' if the necessary agreements were not reached. Aung San and the AFPFL had in fact made arrangements for arms to be gathered and for the PVO to be kept in a state of readiness in case the talks with the British government should fail.

Aung San's part in the discussions which resulted in the 'Aung San–Attlee Agreement' was described by Tin Tut, an independent Councillor and member of the delegation to London, as follows:

> He sought the immediate transfer, actual and legal, of responsibility for the government of Burma to a Burmese Government pending the election of a constituent assembly and the framing of a new constitution. The legal transfer he did not obtain but the actual transfer he obtained in effect though the transfer would be based on convention. It was a formula which could be twisted by his political opponents into a failure of the Burmese Mission which he led. He was firm in his minimum demands though with the heavy responsibility of knowledge that a revolution might result from that firmness. He was statesmanlike in the acceptance of the substance of what the Burmese people desired, a clear and short road to freedom with immediate actual responsibility for the government of their own country. Having accepted that compromise he put its implications plainly before his people and led them to work the settlement, pledging himself boldly that if his lead was followed, full political independence would be attained within a year. This was no light pledge for he staked on that conviction his political career, his honour and his life. He thereby proved to the full of his capacity for leadership.[17]

Two members of the Burmese delegation refused to sign the agreement – Saw, the former prime minister, and Ba Sein of the

Dohbama Asi-ayone, who had shared with Tun Ok the leadership
of the minority Thakin faction after the 1938 split. On getting
back to Burma, Saw and Ba Sein joined Ba Maw and Paw Tun,
another former prime minister, to form the National Opposition
Front, claiming that Aung San had gone over to the imperialists
for the sake of holding office.

Aung San was not unduly troubled by the accusations of his
political opponents and plunged straight into negotiations with
ethnic-minority groups within the country. The agreement
reached with the British had left the future of the frontier areas to
the decision of their people. A conference to settle the issue had
been scheduled to be held at Panglong in February, a matter of
days after the delegation's return to Burma. The Panglong Conference, which produced an agreement acknowledging that freedom would be 'more speedily achieved by the Shans, the Kachins
and the Chins by their immediate co-operation with the Interim
Burmese Government',[18] was the culmination of Aung San's
mission to unite the diverse races of Burma, which had begun
with the Thakins' wartime efforts for racial harmony. Again in
the words of Tin Tut, 'It was his [Aung San's] personality no less
than his directness and candour that won him his victories on the
field of negotiations, and his greatest achievement in that field
was the complete confidence he had inspired among the frontier
races and other minorities.'[19]

Immediately after the Panglong Conference, Aung San went on
a gruelling tour of the country, campaigning for the AFPFL in the
forthcoming elections in April. A unique relationship had grown
up between the Burmese public and their young leader, who had
just turned thirty-two. Everywhere Aung San went, vast crowds
braved the dust and heat to come to look, to listen, to demonstrate
their solidarity with 'our Bogyoke', the word originally used to
indicate his military rank transformed into a term of deep reverence
and affection. Aung San was not a fine orator; his speeches could
be monotonously technical, rambling and very long, but the
people listened with quiet respect, matching their moods to his,
delighting as much in his blunt admonitions as in his rare jokes.
The public meetings were always peaceful, well-disciplined affairs.

Aung San was constantly searching for ideas and tactics that would provide the answers to the problems of Burmese independence and unity, and he carried the people with him in his search. He was not afraid to change his mind if the needs of the times warranted it. He would explain his views and motives openly to the public and ask for their support. But he made no facile promises of easy victories or Utopian vistas, pledging only that he would act honourably by his country, give of his best to the cause of Burmese unity and freedom, and lead the people to those twin goals if they would place the strength of their united will behind him and the AFPFL. The people of Burma responded by returning in the elections an overwhelming majority of AFPFL candidates, only a handful of seats going to the independents and the communists. The 'Saw–Sein–Maw' group had boycotted the elections, knowing that there would be certain defeat for them. Allegations of undue pressure were made against the AFPFL, but the findings of the election tribunals indicated that the results had been a fair reflection of the people's choice.

The final phase of Aung San's life saw him developing daily in political maturity and statecraft, his innate ability and sense of responsibility coming into full play as he faced the challenges of nation-building. It was during this period that he won the respect of many erstwhile British adversaries, one of whom wrote:

> Aung San was to develop statesmanlike qualities which showed that his character could grow with events. For the last ten months of his life he was virtually prime minister, realizing, for the first time, the size of his country, the plurality of its races and the complexity of its problems; the volume of work told on his health and at times he was out of his depth but he was man enough to acknowledge it, winning the respect of the British administrators with whom he was now in daily contact. His assassination deprived his country of the one man who might have been able to enforce discipline on his followers in the lawless years that lay ahead.[20]

At the beginning of June, Aung San convened a series of conferences at the Sorrenta Villa in Rangoon, to plan a programme of rehabilitation for the country. In his inaugural address he underlined the most pressing issues, emphasized the need for practical and flexible approaches, cautioned against over-ambitious projects and mentioned the importance of deciding priorities. He also warned of the futility of wasting time and energy attacking and blaming imperialism for all the ills of the nation now that power was back in the hands of her people, for he was fully aware that the weapons used to fight imperialism were not always the right tools for preserving and developing an independent nation. Aung San looked ahead to the time when Burma would take her rightful place in the family of nations and saw that true nationalism would have to be 'an essential complement to true internationalism'.

Never hesitant to speak the truth, painful or otherwise, Aung San in his last public speech on 13 July 1947 exhorted the Burmese people to mend their ways, urging them to cultivate discipline, perseverance and self-sacrifice and to remember that it would take years of toil before the benefits of independence could be savoured to the full. With his honesty and capacity for self-assessment, Aung San was also conscious of the need to remedy his own shortcomings, as he admitted to friends. What had been tolerated in a young student revolutionary would not be seemly in the leading statesman of the nation; there were rough edges to be smoothed, that inconvenient temper to be curbed and social niceties to be observed, however tedious.

Plans for the official transfer of power proceeded apace. The AFPFL laid down their independence policy at a convention in May, and a committee was formed to draft the constitution of the independent sovereign republic which was to be known as the Union of Burma. As the goal for which he had laboured so arduously came within reach, Aung San appeared relaxed and mellowed, visibly different from the tight-jawed young military commander who had led his army through the resistance against the Japanese. There was about him an air of quiet assurance, almost of serenity. But there was also a deep weariness. He spoke of his desire to leave politics once independence had been achieved, to devote himself to his family and writing. But it was not to be. On 19 July, during a meeting of the Executive Council, Aung San, together with six other Councillors, including his eldest brother, Ba Win, a senior member of the civil service and a young aide, were assassinated by uniformed men who burst into the unguarded conference chamber with machine guns.

The assassins escaped, but they were quickly traced to the home of Saw. The former prime minister was a man of large ambitions who had not been able to accept the rise to national leadership of Aung San, whom he was wont to describe as a 'mere boy'. Shortly before Saw had joined the Burmese delegation to London, he had been shot and wounded in the eye by men dressed in khaki. There were those who surmised that Saw had believed Aung San's PVO members to have been responsible for the shooting and therefore sought revenge. But the trial would reveal that the instructions had been for the whole Executive Council to be destroyed, and it seems that Saw had sought the death of Aung San and his colleagues in the strange belief that once they had been removed, he would become the head of the Burmese government. He was found guilty of abetment and sentenced to death.

Although Aung San had died, the independence to which he had dedicated his life came to his country. Nu, the most senior member of the AFPFL left alive, completed the final negotiations, and on 4 January 1948 the independent Union of Burma was born.

It would perhaps be appropriate to quote here the words of Frank N. Trager, an American scholar of modern Burmese history:

> It is a distortion of history to account for events solely in terms of the actions of a great man, and to the extent that these pages imply that, they evidence such distortion. But, given the conditions in Burma, it seemed proper to examine

the record for the twelve years beginning when the Thakins first achieved political office, to the dawn of independence in January 1948, in terms of the ambient leadership of Aung San.[21]

The converse of this is also true, for Aung San's life can be studied only against the backdrop of the Burmese independence movement, even if such an approach neglects much of his personal side. But since the time he had entered student politics in his early twenties, his existence had been inextricably bound up with the struggle for independence, and he was not one to adopt a public image different from his private character. The total picture is one of a young man of great integrity and strong character who led his country to independence with single-mindedness and a high sense of purpose. Accusations of ruthless ambition, unreasonableness and duplicity have been made by some political opponents and by those who saw his fight against the foreign rulers of his country as 'treachery'. Such charges have been evaluated against a consideration of the record of his actions and achievements. As long as he believed that another was better able to provide the leadership, he had accepted subordinate positions readily, assuming the central role only when it became clear that he was the one man who could unite the country and lead it to freedom. In the words of Kyaw Nyein, who had been a close political associate since his student days, 'leadership was not given to Aung San, he earned it by his many qualities'.[22] Aung San was subject to moods and emotional outbursts, but his personal feelings and inclinations were never allowed to interfere with the collective decisions taken in the interests of independence politics. At each stage of the struggle, he worked in consultation with close political associates, accepting justified criticism and delegating responsibility when it seemed best. He would not tolerate self-seekers, irresponsible actions or dereliction of duty which threatened the independence cause. He believed in the principles of justice and democracy, and there were times he deferred to colleagues when he might better have trusted his own judgement. As head of the Executive Council, he did not impose his views on others; decisions were reached after free and full discussions. He was not infallible, as he freely acknowledged, but he had the kind of mind that did not cease expanding, a capacity for continuous development.

Aung San's appeal was not so much to extremists as to the great majority of ordinary citizens who wished to pursue their own lives in peace and prosperity under a leader they could trust and respect. In him they saw that leader, a man who put the interests of the country before his own needs, who remained poor and unassuming at the height of his power, who accepted the responsibilities of leadership without hankering after the privileges, and who, for all his political acumen and powers of statecraft, retained at the core of his being a deep simplicity. For the people of Burma, Aung San was the man who had come in their hour of need to restore their national pride and honour. As his life is a source of inspiration for them, his memory remains the guardian of their political conscience.

Notes

1 Aung San, *Burma's Challenge*, in J. Silverstein (ed.), *The Political Legacy of Aung San*, Cornell University Southeast Asia Program, Data Paper 86, Ithaca, NY, 1972, p. 55.
2 Aung San, letters to Tin Aung *c.* 1935, extracts quoted in Tin Aung, 'My Recollections of Bogyoke Aung San', *Guardian* (Rangoon), August 1971, p. 15.
3 Aung San, *Burma's Challenge*, pp. 45–6.
4 Ibid., p. 46.
5 Izumiya Tatsuro, *The Minami Organ*, trans. Tun Aung Chain, Rangoon, 1981, p. 26.
6 Keiji Suzuki, 'Aung San and the Burma Independence Army', in Maung Maung (ed.), *Aung San of Burma*, The Hague, 1962, p. 58.
7 Aung San, *Burma's Challenge*, pp. 46–7.
8 Maung Maung, 'Aung San's Helpmate', in Maung Maung (ed.), *Aung San of Burma*, p. 117.
9 Papers of Eric Battersby, extract quoted in Maurice Collis, *Last and First in Burma, 1941–1948*, London, 1956, p. 205.
10 Aung San, 'Blue-Print for Burma', in Silverstein (ed.), *The Political Legacy of Aung San*, p. 14.

11 Sir William Slim, *Defeat into Victory*, London, 1956, p. 519.
12 Let Ya, 'The March to National Leadership', in Maung Maung (ed.), *Aung San of Burma*, p. 52. See also Thein Pe, 'A Note from My Diary', ibid., pp. 85–6.
13 Aung San, 'Statement of General Aung San, Commander, PVO, May 8, 1946', in Silverstein (ed.), *The Political Legacy of Aung San*, p. 30.
14 Aung San, speech delivered at the protest meeting against the White Paper, 29 September 1946, in *Bogyoke Aung San Meigun Mya* ('The Speeches of *Bogyoke* Aung San'), Rangoon, 1971, p. 140.
15 Aung San, speeches delivered to explain why the communists had to be expelled from the AFPFL, 20 and 28 October 1946, in *Bogyoke Aung San Meigun Mya*, pp. 142–59. Thein Pe, quoted in 'Burmese Communists Bid for Success in General Elections', *New Times of Burma*, 30 October 1946.
16 Quoted in Maung Maung (ed.), *Aung San of Burma*, pp. 104–5.
17 Tin Tut, 'U Aung San of Burma: A Memoir', *Burma Review*, 25 August 1947, p. 12.
18 'The Panglong Agreement', reproduced in Maung Maung, *Burma's Constitution*, The Hague, 1961, Appendix III, p. 229.
19 Tin Tut, 'U Aung San of Burma', p. 12.
20 F. S. V. Donnison, 'Unifier of Burma', in Maung Maung (ed.), *Aung San of Burma*, p. 148.
21 Frank N. Trager, *Burma – from Kingdom to Republic*, New York, 1966, p. 89.
22 Kyaw Nyein, 'He Made a Dream Come True', in Maung Maung (ed.), *Aung San of Burma*, p. 146.

2

My Country and People

This work, intended for a juvenile readership, was published in 1985 by Burke Publishing Company, London, with the title of Let's Visit Burma. *The author also wrote on the Himalayan kingdoms of Nepal and Bhutan in the same series.*

Burma is one of those countries which seem to have been favoured by nature. Its soil is rich, producing rice and other food crops in abundance. There are vast forests containing a large variety of trees from which valuable timber is extracted.

The ground yields petroleum and many minerals and precious stones including rubies, sapphires and jade. The rivers and streams are full of fish; and from the sea along Burma's coastline come not just seafood but some of the world's loveliest pearls. It is therefore not surprising that Burma has been described as a golden land, an eastern paradise of untold riches. But of course no country on earth is a real paradise and, for all its natural wealth, Burma is not among the rich nations of the world today. It is nevertheless an extremely beautiful country peopled by many different races. It is from the Burmese people, who form the biggest racial group, that the name of the country is derived.

Burma has an area of 676,552 square kilometres (261,218 square miles). To the north is China, to the west India and Bangladesh and to the east Thailand and Laos. The coastline of the Indian Ocean forms a natural boundary to the south. Roughly diamond shaped, Burma is often compared to a kite with a tail trailing along one side.

The main river of Burma is the Irrawaddy which flows from the Kachin Hills in the north and follows a southerly course for over two thousand kilometres (more than one thousand miles) until it reaches the ocean. Two other rivers of importance are the Chindwin and the Salween. The Chindwin flows down from the north-west and joins the Irrawaddy in central Burma. The Salween comes from a source in the mountains of Tibet and finds its way across the Shan plateau in eastern Burma down to the sea.

In the north of Burma are mountains which might be called the tail-end of the eastern Himalayas. The peaks do not rise to the great height of the mountains further west, but on the border with Tibet is Khakhaporazi, reaching 5,887 metres (19,314 feet). Along the north-west border run the Paktai Hills and the Naga Hills. In the west are the Chin Hills, and trailing to the south is the Arakan Yoma (*yoma* is a Burmese term for a ridge of mountains). The Pegu Yoma is another chain of mountains which begins in central Burma and extends down to the Irrawaddy delta.

In the eastern part of the country lies the Shan plateau, a broad tableland averaging between 900 and 1,200 metres (3,000 and 4,000 feet) above sea level.

The plains areas of Burma may be roughly divided into the dry zone in the heart of the country, the coastal lands (Arakan in the west and the long 'tail' of Tenasserim in the south-east) and the lush delta of the Irrawaddy.

Administratively, the country is divided into seven states and seven divisions. The seven states represent the homelands of the seven main racial groups, besides the Burmese, who make up the nation: the Chins, Kachins, Karens, Kayahs, Mons, Arakanese (Rakhines) and Shans.

On the whole the climate of Burma is hot and tropical, although the Shan plateau is more temperate. In parts of the Kachin and Chin states, it can be very cold. The monsoon winds, which bring heavy rains for six months of the year, are the most important factor in the seasonal cycle of the country. Instead of spring, summer, autumn and winter, there is the rainy season (from about the middle of May to the middle of October), the cool season (from the end of the rains until about the latter half of February) and the hot season. The rainfall in an average year varies between about 500 centimetres (200 inches) along the coastlands to between 50 and 115 centimetres (25 and 45 inches) in the dry zone. The temperature also varies across the country but in many parts it rises above 38 degrees Celsius (100 degrees Fahrenheit) during the hot season. The months of December and January are pleasant in the plains, with average temperatures between 21 and 26 degrees Celsius (70 and 80 degrees Fahrenheit). On the Shan plateau and in the hill areas it is much colder and there are places where the temperature can fall to freezing point.

The capital of Burma is Rangoon, a port city on the delta. 'Rangoon' is an English corruption of the Burmese name Yangon, which means 'End of Dangers'. This was the name given by King Alaungpaya in 1755 to the town built to house the army with which he vanquished enemy forces in the south. A town known as Dagon had once flourished on the site of Rangoon, but by the time of King Alaungpaya it had dwindled to the size of a mere hamlet. Rangoon gained importance as a port town in the eighteenth and nineteenth centuries; and, after Burma fell to the British in 1885, it became the capital of the country.

The last capital of the Burmese kings was at Mandalay in central Burma. Mandalay is not, however, a very old city as it was founded only in 1857 by King Mindon. The name is taken from a sacred hill near by. According to tradition, the Lord Buddha had prophesied more than two thousand years earlier that a great city would be founded at the foot of the hill. (The Lord Buddha was a north Indian prince whose teachings were to form the basis of one of the world's great religions, Buddhism.) Mandalay has a special place in the hearts of the Burmese, and remains a symbol of the proud days when Burmese kings ruled the country. Unfortunately, the palace of Mandalay was destroyed during the Second World War. Only the walls are left and a few of the gates, topped by graceful pavilions of carved wood. However, there remain other monuments of considerable interest even though not of any great age. Also around Mandalay are the sites of older royal capitals, Ava and Amarapura.

Moulmein might be termed the third city of Burma. Situated on the Tenasserim coast, it was built up by the British to become the chief town in the territory they acquired in Burma after the first Anglo-Burmese War in 1825. Although it was later displaced by Rangoon as the chief town, Moulmein remained an important urban centre. It is a lively town of brilliant tropical sights, smells and tastes. A popular Burmese saying points out its chief attraction and indicates the outstanding characteristics of the inhabitants of the other two main cities of Burma:

> Moulmein for food,
> Mandalay for conversation,
> Rangoon for ostentation.

Burma is mainly an agricultural country. Its climate and soil, particularly in the rich Irrawaddy delta, are well suited to rice cultivation. At one time Burma exported more rice than any other country in the world. Even today, more than 40 per cent of the country's export earnings come from the sale of rice. But it is not merely an export crop. For the people of Burma, rice is the staple food, taken at every main meal. Even in those hill areas where it does not grow so abundantly, the people like to have at least one meal of rice a day.

In the plains of Burma which produce the major rice crops, the wet method of cultivation is used. The fields are kept flooded, either by the rains or, in the drier areas, through a system of irrigation. Sprouting rice seeds are sown in 'nursery' fields in April. After about a month, the seedlings – then about 30 centimetres (12 inches) tall – are transplanted by hand. This is a long, exhausting job, usually undertaken by women. A scene often associated with the Burmese countryside is that of long rows of women bent over flooded rice fields. Songs and dances are based on the transplantation of rice which plays such an important part in the life of the country. The rice is harvested towards the end of the year, again mostly by hand. Modern techniques and farm machinery have been introduced, but traditional methods still prevail.

The most common method of rice cultivation in the hill areas of Burma is that of 'slash and burn', or shifting cultivation. A plot of land is prepared by cutting down and burning the trees and the scrub. Rain falling on the burnt vegetation enriches the soil on which the rice is planted. After a few years when the soil is exhausted, the plot is abandoned and another one chosen and cleared. The practice of cultivating rice and other food crops in terraced fields is also found in some of the hill areas but it is not as common as the slash-and-burn method.

The forests of Burma are one of the country's biggest sources of wealth. There are different types of forests, found in many parts of the country. The most important are the mixed deciduous forests which include teak, pyinkado and padauk among the many varieties of valuable trees. The strength, durability and lack of shrinkage of teak make it one of the most valued woods of the world. Its many uses include shipbuilding, house-building and the making of furniture. Pyinkado is also known as ironwood because of its hardness and strength. It is mainly used for heavy construction work. Padauk has been described as the best all-round utility timber in Burma next to teak. But it means more to the Burmese than just a good wood-producing tree. The blossoms of the padauk, bright yellow and sweetly scented, herald the coming of the rains after months of intense heat. The brave beauty of the flowers which last for only a short time is a popular theme in Burmese poems and songs.

Burma's principal crops apart from rice are sugar-cane, groundnuts, pulses, maize and sesame. Millet, tobacco, cotton and rubber are also produced in considerable quantities. There is a great range of fruit and vegetables in Burma, each season bringing different varieties. Mangoes, bananas, durians, custard apples, mangosteens, water-melons and pineapples are some of the tropical fruits which grow abundantly in Burma. The Shan plateau produces oranges, strawberries, avocado pears and other fruit which need a more temperate climate. Tea is one of the most important crops in the northern part of the Shan State. The Burmese not only drink a lot of tea, they also eat the leaves in a pickled form. Coffee is grown in the Chin Hills, where fruits like apples, pears and mulberries are also cultivated. There is such a wealth and variety of agricultural products in Burma that it would need a whole book to describe them all.

The mineral products of Burma are also considerable. Coal, petroleum, natural gas, lead, zinc, tin, wolfram and silver are obtained in quantity. Enough petroleum is produced in central Burma to meet the needs of the whole country. Off-shore oil exploration has not yet produced amounts comparable to the output of the traditional oilfields in the Magwe Division, some of which have been worked for many centuries.

Deposits of coal, silver and lead are found in the Shan State. Other minerals are also mined in varying quantities, but it is for its precious gems that the Shan plateau is famous. Burmese rubies are considered the best in the world and the sapphires too are of an excellent quality. There are also semi-precious stones such as spinel, topaz, zircon and tourmaline. Jadeite and some jade come from the Kachin State. Gold has also been obtained from this northern corner of the country but not in amounts large enough to make it an industry. Zinc mines are concentrated in the Tenasserim Division, and the seabed along the Tenasserim coast is the home of Burmese pearls, the culture of which has been greatly developed in recent years.

Burma's main manufacturing industries are cement, cigarettes, fertilizers, soap, salt and cotton yarn. Most of the manufactured goods are for use within the country but some cement is exported. The major export items, however, are the country's agricultural and natural products: rice, pulses, timber, base metals and silver.

The wealth of Burma's natural resources is impressive, but the great fascination of the country lies in its many peoples with their colourful and diverse origins and customs. It is the histories and civilizations of the peoples of Burma which have built up the character of the nation.

A Turbulent History

The history of Burma might be said to have begun with the arrival of the Mon people from Central Asia, probably between

2500 and 1500 BC. The Mons settled in parts of Thailand, along the Tenasserim and on the Irrawaddy delta. Indian influences were strong in the early civilization of the Mons. The most important of these influences was perhaps in the area of religion. From India came Hinduism and Buddhism, both of which made an impact on the Mon civilization. Hinduism is the body of beliefs and social practices which developed into the dominant religion of India thousands of years ago. Buddhism developed later, through the teachings of an Indian prince called Siddartha, who was born around 560 BC. His aim was to help all beings to free themselves from the sufferings of existence. Because he is considered to have rid himself of false beliefs and discovered the path to freedom from suffering, he became known as the Buddha or 'Enlightened One'.

It is generally accepted that the Mons were predominantly Buddhist from early times. There appears to have been a period when the Mons in Burma came under strong Hindu influence and Buddhism declined. However, by the eleventh century, the Mon kingdoms in Pegu and Thaton are known to have been Buddhist.

The second wave of peoples to come into Burma after the Mons were the Tibeto-Burmans from the north. The Burmese, who today form the largest racial group in the country, believe that their early Tibeto-Burman ancestors were the Pyus, the Kanyans and the Theks. Little is known about the Kanyans and the Theks beyond their names. Much more can be said of the Pyus who have left traces of a well-developed civilization. In central Burma the site of an ancient Pyu city has been discovered. This city probably dates back to the beginning of the Christian era. Its name, Beikthano, is a Burmese version of the name of the Hindu god, Vishnu. No Buddhist statues or relics have been found here, but there is reason to believe that a type of Buddhism may have existed side by side with the worship of Vishnu.

Other sites of Pyu cities have been excavated at Halin and Thayekhittaya. These are thought to have flourished in the same period, roughly between the fifth and ninth centuries AD. Halin, like Beikthano, shows no signs of Buddhist statues or relics.

However, Buddhist religious objects have been found in Thayek-hittaya. Near this city also are three pagodas. These are Buddhist monuments usually built to contain sacred relics. There are many different styles of pagoda and the ones at Thayekhittaya are akin to the ones built in India during the Gupta dynasty which ruled from the fourth to the sixth centuries AD.

It is clear that although the Pyus were a Tibeto-Burman people of Mongolian stock, their culture was very similar to that of India. This was a result of Indians coming from the west and establishing their rule over the Pyus. For this reason, Burmese tradition has it that the earliest kings of Burma were of princely Indian blood. According to legend, the first kingdom was founded at a place called Tagaung, long before Thayekhittaya or Beik-thano. There have not yet been enough archaeological finds to support this legend, but new discoveries in the future may shed more light on the early civilization of the Pyus.

The power of the Pyus appears to have declined in the eighth century. In the ninth century, their kingdom was destroyed by raiders from Nanchao in southern China. From this time the Pyus faded away. Perhaps they moved elsewhere or perhaps they were absorbed by the Burmese, who began to make their presence felt at this period. The Burmese were of the same Tibeto-Burman stock as the Pyus. It is not known exactly when they came into Burma or where they lived before they settled in the irrigated areas of the dry zone. However, it is fairly certain that they founded the city of Pagan around AD 850.

The name Pagan spells glory and romance for the Burmese. Today the site of the first capital of the Burmese kings is a sun-baked plain studded with thousands of pagodas, most of them in ruins. There are no traces of palaces or great mansions. The people of Pagan have left only religious monuments as a reminder of their glorious dynasty.

Anawratha, who is believed to have ascended the throne of Pagan in 1044, was the first king to establish Burmese rule over much of the country. He was also the man who did the most to promote Theravada Buddhism among the Burmese. 'Theravada' means 'The Way of the Elders'. This is the name applied to the branch of Buddhism which keeps strictly to the teachings of the Lord Buddha as contained in a collection of writings called the *Tripitaka*. Theravada Buddhism is sometimes called 'Hinayana', meaning 'Small Vehicle', particularly by Buddhists of the Mahayana sect. 'Mahayana' means 'Great Vehicle'. Mahayana Buddhism contains much that is taken from Hinduism and Tantrism, which involves many secret and magic rituals. Mahayana Buddhists tend to believe that their religious practices and attitudes are broader, and therefore greater, than those of the Theravada sect.

There is evidence that both Mahayana and Theravada Buddhism were practised among the Burmese at the time Anawratha became king. It was only after Anawratha's conquest of the Mon kingdom at Thaton, probably between 1054 and 1057, that Theravada Buddhism quickly became the dominant religion. Among the prisoners and rich booty which the victorious Burmese brought back from the Mon country were Theravada monks and religious books. From this time on, the people of Pagan took an increasing interest in religion and became devout Buddhists.

The contacts with the highly civilized Mons contributed greatly towards the development of Burmese culture. Some of the earlier monuments of Pagan were probably built with the help of Mon workmen and artists. It was also during this time that Burmese began to develop as a written language. Making use of an Indian script, it shows many signs of the influence of the Mon language and of Pali, the language of the Buddhist religious texts.

Anawratha's reign has left a lasting impression on Burma. By bringing the central tract of the country, northern Tenasserim, northern Arakan and some of the western Shan principalities under his sway, he first gave shape to a nation with three main racial groups under one rule. Theravada Buddhism, which had taken firm root under his patronage, was to be the major factor in forming the character of Burmese society.

In 1077 Anawratha was succeeded by his son Sawlu, a young man who had inherited little of his father's ability. Fortunately his reign was very brief and the throne passed to Kyansittha. Kyansittha is one of the most romantic and beloved kings in

Burmese history. His parentage is obscure but he seems to have been highly born. He had acquired a reputation as a great general under Anawratha. Towards the end of the king's reign there was a break in the relations between the two men, but Kyansittha never turned against Anawratha. It was only in 1084 that Kyansittha ascended the throne, after defeating a force of Mons who had killed King Sawlu and marched on Pagan.

Kyansittha was not only an outstanding warrior, he was a king who administered the country well and cared for the welfare of his subjects. He also did much to promote the cause of religion. The Ananda temple, the most famous of the monuments of Pagan, was built by him.

Pagan was also fortunate in Kyansittha's successor, his grandson Alaungsithu. But no dynasty can continue to produce strong and able rulers for ever. The thirteenth century brought a decline in the quality of the monarchs as well as the rise of powerful forces outside the kingdom. In the north-east, China had come under the rule of the fierce Mongols; and, to the east, the Shans were gaining strength. In 1287 Pagan was sacked by Mongol troops. After that the kingdom built by Anawratha quickly collapsed. The Mons threw off the rule of Pagan, and the Shans swept into central Burma.

The Shans make up the third of the main racial groups of Burma. They belong to the Thai group of peoples who are the most widely distributed in Indo-China. There appear to have been Thai-Shan settlements along the river valleys of South-east Asia since about the eighth century. According to Shan tradition, their first kingdom was set up by Beinnaka, a descendant of the kings of Tagaung after the fall of that ancient Pyu capital. In fact, the name 'Tagaung' is thought by some to be a Shan word, which would establish a connection between the Burmese and the Shans from the time of the early Pyus. But that is by no means certain. Shans are first mentioned only in Burmese stone inscriptions of the twelfth century.

In the thirteenth century, new waves of Thai peoples fleeing from expanding Mongol power came to settle in the eastern plateau of Burma and in present-day Thailand. The Shans of

Burma fought back against Mongol domination on the one hand and, on the other, started attacking the tottering kingdom of Pagan.

Between the end of the thirteenth century and the first quarter of the sixteenth century, the Shans dominated central Burma. In the early years after the fall of Pagan, there were three kingdoms ruled by Shan princes. However, by the second half of the fourteenth century, only one of them, Ava, remained as a royal capital. Although the rulers of Ava were of Shan stock, Burmese influences remained strong in the kingdom. Burmese literature flowered during the Ava period, and some of the greatest works in the language were produced at this time. The best known of these are poems with religious themes, composed by Buddhist monks. Buddhism had remained a strong force in the country.

The Mons had thrown off Burmese rule when the power of Pagan weakened. By 1287 a kingdom had been founded at Martaban on the Tenasserim coast by Wareru, a Mon-Shan, who had risen from humble beginnings to become the ruler of Lower Burma. Attacks from rising kingdoms in neighbouring Thailand later forced the Mons to abandon Martaban as their capital. They established their new capital in Pegu in 1369.

Pegu was ruled by King Yazadhirit from 1385 to 1423. During his reign, there were repeated wars between the Mons and the kingdom of Ava, ruled by King Minkhaung. The Shan chieftains in the eastern plateau also became involved in the struggles between Pegu and Ava, as did the Arakanese, a people who had founded their kingdom along the western coast of Burma. After the deaths of Yazadhirit and Minkhaung, the fighting between the two kingdoms petered out, especially as Ava was much occupied with trying to keep back ambitious warlike Shan chieftains.

The Mon kingdoms flourished in peace and prosperity for several decades. The fifteenth century produced two great rulers, Queen Shin Saw Bu, who reigned from 1453 to 1472, and King Dhammazedi (1472–92). Both monarchs were devoutly religious and did much to promote the cause of Theravada Buddhism. During their reigns, the Shwedagon pagoda first took on its famous golden magnificence. The Shwedagon stands on a hill in present-day Rangoon. Its name means 'Golden Dagon'. Dagon is the name of the Mon settlement which once existed on the site of Rangoon. The Shwedagon is most sacred and most dear to the people of Burma. There are many legends surrounding the great pagoda. According to tradition, the original monument was built during the lifetime of the Buddha himself. This cannot be verified but there certainly had been a monument there, believed to contain sacred relics of the Lord Buddha, since early times. Stone inscriptions set up by Dhammazedi tell the story of how the pagoda was built up and embellished by successive monarchs of Pegu. The Shwedagon is a lasting memorial to the devotion of the Mons to the Buddhist faith.

In Pegu itself, there are two other famous monuments much revered by Buddhists. These are the Shwemawdaw pagoda and the Shwethalyaung. The second is a huge, beautiful image of the Lord Buddha reclining on his side. It is about 55 metres (180 feet) long and 16 metres (52 feet) high. The Shwemawdaw pagoda is supposed to contain among its sacred relics two hairs from the head of the Lord Buddha. Both the Shwemawdaw and the Shwethalyaung were built before the reign of King Dhammazedi, but he maintained them well and also built other religious monuments.

Burma's first contacts with the West were made during the fifteenth century. Italian merchants were the first to trade with the Mon kingdom but the Portuguese who came later were to play a bigger role in the affairs of Burma. The Portuguese established colonies in India and on the Malay Peninsula during the early years of the sixteenth century. A trading-station was opened at the Mon settlement of Martaban and trade began between the Mons and the Portuguese.

The years of Pegu's stability were also the years of Ava's decline. The kings of Ava were unable to hold out against the Shan chieftains, who interfered more and more in the affairs of the kingdom. As Ava fell into chaos, the power of Toungoo began to rise.

Toungoo was a city some 400 kilometres (250 miles) south of

Ava. Many Burmese had taken refuge there after the fall of Pagan. Throughout the Ava dynasty, Toungoo remained a sanctuary for Burmese wishing to escape from the persecution of some of the Shan kings. In 1486 Minkyinyo came to the throne of Toungoo and Burmese power began to revive.

The Toungoo period is known as the second unification of Burma (the first was under Anawratha of Pagan). Minkyinyo's son, Tabinshwehti (who reigned from 1531 to 1550), succeeded to the throne at only fourteen years of age. But he was a great warrior as well as a considerable statesman. During his reign, the Mon country and much of central Burma came under Burmese rule. Tabinshwehti made his capital at Pegu. He seems to have liked the Mons and to have admired their culture. He spent most of his life waging wars, carrying out repeated campaigns against Thailand. He also led an expedition to the Arakanese kingdom. Many Portuguese were involved in these wars. They served as paid soldiers under the Burmese, the Thais and the Arakanese. They also introduced firearms from Europe.

Tabinshwehti was murdered at the age of thirty-two by one of his Mon subjects. During his last days he had become a drunkard under the influence of a Portuguese favourite. Much of the care of the Burmese kingdom had therefore become the responsibility of Bayinnaung. Bayinnaung means 'Elder Brother of the King', and this was the title Tabinshwehti had conferred on the man who was his best general, his most trusted adviser and also his brother-in-law. At Tabinshwehti's death it seemed for a time as if the young Burmese kingdom would fall to pieces. But Bayinnaung not only managed to hold it together, he built it up to greater size and strength.

Bayinnaung brought the Burmese, the Shans and the Mons under one rule. He also established his overlordship in some of the neighbouring provinces of Thailand. Pegu became a wealthy capital and a well-known trading centre. However, after the death of Bayinnaung, the state began to crumble. He had a number of able successors, but the kingdom was too large for them to be able to retain control. Troubles came from the Thais and the Arakanese. Lower Burma became a battleground for the warring armies.

The country was already exhausted from the wars of Tabin-shwehti and Bayinnaung. Rich ricelands remained untilled and turned to jungle. Without Bayinnaung's strong personality to keep them in check, the Portuguese started playing a more prominent role in the quarrels between the Burmese, the Arakanese and the Thais. At one time De Brito, a Portuguese who had served as a gunner under the king of Arakan, became governor of the port town of Syriam and made a bid to establish his authority over Lower Burma. He was eventually defeated and executed by the Burmese king, but as one trouble was put down, another arose.

The year Ava was burnt down was also the year of the rise of a new Burmese dynasty. Aung Zeya, the headman of a village near Shwebo in central Burma, rallied the Burmese to his standard. He was to become known as Alaungpaya, the first king of the Konbaung dynasty. During a short reign of eight years, he brought the Burmese, the Shans and the Mons once more under one rule. He also extended his powers to some of the outlying provinces of Thailand. The years from 1752 to 1760 brought the third unification of Burma.

The Konbaung dynasty saw ten kings and four capitals: Shwebo, from where Alaungpaya had begun his rise to kingship, Ava, the old capital, Amarapura, founded in 1783, and finally Mandalay, last city of the Burmese kings. The first Konbaung kings were strong and warlike. Arakan was brought into the Burmese kingdom. Manipur and Assam on the Indian border became vassal states. There were also many wars with the Thais. But the old pattern of neighbouring kingdoms fighting for supremacy had been altered by the coming of the Europeans.

During the seventeenth and eighteenth centuries, the Portuguese, the Dutch, the French and the British all scrambled for trading rights and possessions in South and South-east Asia. India came under British domination. It was the era of colonial expansion. Relations between the Burmese and the British were stormy from the beginning. There had been clashes even during the reign of Alaungpaya. However, it was only in 1824 that the first Anglo-Burmese War broke out, over Manipur and Assam. The Burmese could not hold out against the modern military equipment of the British. As a result of the defeat, Burma had to give up its claims to Manipur and Assam. The provinces of Arakan and Tenasserim also had to be surrendered to the British. Relations between the Burmese and the British did not improve and a second war broke out in 1852. The Burmese once again got the worst of it and the whole of Lower Burma fell under British rule. Yet another war broke out in 1885. This one was decisive, for British troops marched on Mandalay and captured the Burmese royal family. Thibaw, the last of the Konbaung kings, was taken away to India; and Burma was made a part of the British Empire.

Building an Independent Nation

British rule brought many changes to Burma. The boundaries of the country were drawn along lines which have remained practically unchanged to the present day. Burma was administered as a province of British India. The rich natural resources of the country were developed and the economy prospered. But British policy also brought in large numbers of Indians and Chinese. These immigrants were hard-working and skilled at business. The new wealth of the country passed into their hands and into those of the British companies rather than to the people of Burma. There was no real contact between the colonial rulers and their subjects.

Pockets of Burmese resistance flared up in different parts of the country after the fall of Mandalay. The British brought in tens of thousands of troops from India to put down the uprisings. They succeeded to a large measure in bringing peace to the countryside. However, the Burmese did not become reconciled to foreign domination. The British found it easier to deal with some of the other racial groups. The Christian missionaries who had come in large numbers also found it easier to convert those peoples of Burma who were not already staunch Buddhists. They were particularly successful with the Karens along the south-eastern tract of Burma. The practice of encouraging the differences between the various racial groups was to have sad consequences for the independent nation of the future.

Burmese nationalism began to gather strength again in the 1920s. It started as a movement to keep the Buddhist religion pure in the face of foreign influences. Later the movement became more political in character. In 1930 there was an uprising of the peasants led by a man called Saya San. The rebellion was quickly stamped out but other nationalist movements continued. In 1937 Burma was separated from India under the British administration. A new constitution came into effect. Under its provisions the people of Burma were given a bigger role to play in the running of their country. But this was not enough to stem the tide of nationalism.

During the 1930s the students of Rangoon University had become prominent in nationalist activities. Some of the student leaders went on to become members of a political organization called the Dohbama Asi-ayone. (Dohbama means 'We Burmese' and Asi-ayone means 'Association'.) They became known as *Thakins* (which means 'masters') because they used this word as a prefix to their names. It was the word the Burmese had to use when addressing their British rulers. The young Thakins wanted to make it clear that the Burmese should be their own masters. Nationalist activities increased and became more militant.

The beginning of the Second World War in 1939 was a turning-point for the Burmese independence movement. Nationalist politicians urged the people not to support British war efforts unless Burma was promised independence at the end of the war. The British government arrested many nationalists. A group of young men left the country secretly to receive military training in Japan. They came to be known as the 'Thirty Comrades'. Japan was a strong and independent nation. Since it had defeated Russia at war in the beginning of the twentieth century, it had been admired by other Asian countries. The Burmese hoped that the Japanese would help them win back their independence. The Burma Independence Army was organized with the Thirty Comrades as the nucleus. In 1941 it marched into Burma with the Japanese. The British were driven out of the country.

Burma was declared an independent nation. In fact, the country had simply exchanged one foreign ruler for another. The occupying Japanese army began to treat the Burmese like a subject people. Burmese people were put in all the key positions of government and administration. In that sense they gained a degree of self-government. But the Japanese had the final authority.

The commander-in-chief of the Burmese army was a young man called Aung San who had been a student leader and one of the Thirty Comrades. Together with other nationalists, he organized a resistance movement against the Japanese. The tide of the war began to turn. British troops came back to Burma and, as the Burmese army had risen against the Japanese, the British and the Burmese now fought on one side. The Japanese were defeated and the war in Burma came to an end in 1945.

However, this was not the end of Burma's struggle for independence. The Burmese did not want the British to come back as their rulers. The strongest opponent of British rule was the Anti-Fascist People's Freedom League (AFPFL), a nationalist party led by Aung San, who had left the army to engage in independence politics. The British gradually had to give in to the demands of the AFPFL, which had won the popular support of the country. But, while agreeing to Burmese demands for independence, the British insisted that the peoples along the frontiers of Burma (the Kachins from the north, the Chins from the north-west and the Shans) should be allowed to decide their own future for themselves. It was thought by some of the British that the frontier peoples would not wish to throw in their lot with the Burmese. However, the Burmese leaders managed to win the confidence of the Shans, Chins and Kachins. They decided to co-operate with the Burmese in the movement for independence. The British had no choice but to hand the government of Burma back to its people.

Before Burma formally became an independent nation, Aung San and six of his ministers were assassinated at a cabinet meeting by gunmen sent by a political rival. Aung San was only thirty-two years old. He is considered the national hero of Burma and the father of the nation.

Burma became an independent republic on 4 January 1948.

U Nu, the most senior member of the AFPFL remaining after the assassinations, became the first Prime Minister. The young nation was immediately faced with grave problems. Burmese communists had worked for independence with the AFPFL, but some of them felt that the cause of international communism came before national interests. They started armed rebellions against the AFPFL government. The People's Volunteer Organization, which had been organized in case it was necessary to fight the British for independence, but which was scheduled to be disbanded, also took up arms. The third group of rebels was the Karen National Defence Organization. In the past there had been clashes between the Burmese and the Karens. Many Karens were Christians and religious differences served to widen the gap between the two peoples. Aung San and other Burmese nationalists had worked hard to bring about better relations. Although they managed to win the trust of some Karens, others refused to believe that it was possible to live in peace under a Burmese government. Some Burmese attitudes have been responsible for the distrust of the Karens. But the British and the missionaries who worked among the Karens must also bear the blame for the division between the two peoples.

On gaining independence, Burma became a parliamentary democracy. The government managed to hold out against the rebellions, and a fair measure of peace was restored. However, the need to keep the rebels in check made the army strong. Many of the top men in the army had been politicians and were inclined to interfere in the government of the country. In 1962 a group of army officers led by Ne Win, the commander-in-chief, overthrew the elected government of U Nu. Since then, Burma has been under army rule, although many officers in high government posts have laid aside their military titles.

Burma under army rule became a socialist republic, guided by the Burma Socialist Programme Party. No other political party is permitted. This and other measures limiting the political liberties of the people are aimed at creating a stable government and a united country. But unity can come only with the willing co-operation of the people. The government of Burma still has to cope with many rebels, prominent among them Karens, Shans and communists. The economy has not been well managed and Burma today is not a prosperous nation. However, with its wealth of natural resources, there is always hope for the future. And that future lies in the hands of its peoples.

The Minority Peoples of Burma

There are a great many peoples in Burma, speaking over one hundred languages. However, each of these peoples belongs to one of three major racial groups, the Mon-Khmers, the Tibeto-Burmans and the Thai-Shans. The seven peoples, apart from the Burmese, who are numerous enough to have separate administrative states marked out for them in the country are the Chins, Kachins, Karens, Kayahs, Mons, Arakanese (Rakhines) and Shans.

The Chins live in the hilly north-western part of Burma. They belong to the Tibeto-Burman racial group. There are many separate tribes and districts among the Chins. This is due to the nature of the area they live in, which does not make for easy communication. The best-known groups, named according to the areas where they live, are the Tidam Chins, the Falam Chins and the Hakha Chins. Some Chin peoples call themselves *Zo-mi*, or *Lai-mi*. Both terms mean 'Mountain People'.

The Chins live by agriculture. They use the slash-and-burn method for planting rice and other food crops. This has led to the clearing of some of the thick forests which covered the Chin Hills. They are skilled at hunting and fishing. Traditionally, domestic animals were reared mainly to be used as sacrifices in religious ceremonies. The mithan, a kind of cow, is particularly valued.

In the old days, all the Chins were spirit-worshippers. Now there are some Christians and Buddhists among them. Among the Tidam and Hakha Chins are some followers of the Pau Chin Hau religion. Pau Chin Hau was born in the Tidam area in 1859 and lived until 1948. He started a religious movement based on the worship of a god known as Pasian. He also invented a script. Originally, the Chins had no written language. Today, apart from the Pau Chin Hau system, there is also a written language using the Roman alphabet.

There are many feasts and festivals among the Chins, differing from area to area: seasonal festivals, agricultural festivals and feasts concerned with the worship of spirits and ancestors. Perhaps the most interesting of them all is the *Khhaung Cawi*. This is a feast given by a man to honour his wife. Up to one hundred mithan may be killed during one of these feasts, which go on for seven days. On the last day, the wife of the host is lifted on to the *khhaung*, a swinging bamboo platform, to scatter gifts. Only a wealthy man could afford such a feast.

In some parts of the Chin Hills, the women tattoo their faces. The patterns vary according to their tribe. Some can be quite elaborate while others are just a few well-placed dots. The most distinctive feature of Chin dress is the woven blanket which is draped around the body. Thick, smooth cotton patterned with broad stripes, these blankets have become a very popular item of bedding for people all over Burma.

The Chins make ornaments of bronze and copper. They are also skilled at weaving mats and baskets from split cane. Some of the finest examples of their craftsmanship can be seen in the carved columns of wood and stone which they raise as memorials to the dead.

The Kachins of Burma are another Tibeto-Burman people. The inhabitants of the Kachin State can be divided into four main language groups – the Jingpaws, Marus, Yaywins and Lisus. Towards the end of the nineteenth century, Christian missionaries developed a written form of Jingpaw, using the Roman alphabet. Because of this, Jingpaw became the most widely known of the languages in the Kachin State. When people speak of Kachins, they usually mean the Jingpaw group. The other groups are not so widely known, partly because their numbers are less.

Most of the Kachins traditionally worshipped spirits, although Christians and Buddhists can now be found among them. There are many spirits, but there is one supreme being who rules over all others, called Karai Kasang. Only live animals are sacrificed to him. These sacrificial animals are allowed to live free and unharmed. Perhaps the most powerful of the other spirits is the *Madai* spirit, from whom the Kachin *duwas* (chieftains) are thought to be descended. It is mainly in his honour that the *manao* feast, the most important celebration among the Kachins, is held. Different types of *manao* feasts are held for different reasons. For example, they may celebrate a victory in battle, mark the occasion of an elderly person's death or be an occasion for inviting the *Madai* spirit to a new territory.

Only *duwas* may sacrifice to the *Madai* spirit. Therefore *manao* feasts may only be given by *duwas*. In any case, the expense of such feasts would be beyond most ordinary people. A great *manao* requires about a year's preparation. Four *manao* columns, painted red, black and white, are set up in a chosen field, together with poles to which the sacrificial animals are tethered. Many little shrines for spirits are built around the field. (Although a *manao* is held chiefly for the *Madai* spirit, sacrifices are made to others as well.)

There is much eating, drinking and dancing during a *manao* feast. A big double-sided drum and a large brass gong boom out the traditional sounds of *manao*. The original *manao* dance imitates birds, with the dancers holding fans which represent the outspread tail of a peacock. The Kachins have many dances in which both men and women take part. There are dances depicting horse-riding, the casting of fishing-nets, the search for scattered cattle. There are also dances for funerals, performed to the sound of cracked gongs.

The Kachins have three kinds of traditional government. The one found mostly in the northern areas is called *gumlao-gumsa*. This is a kind of democracy where each community is ruled according to the will of the majority.

Gumsa is the system most common to the Jingpaw-speaking areas. Here the authority is in the hands of landowning hereditary *duwas*. There are two classes of *duwas* – those who are entitled to one leg of each game animal killed by their subjects and those who are not so privileged. The most highly esteemed *duwas* are those who are descended from a line of youngest sons. Among the Kachins, it is the youngest, not the eldest, who is the heir.

The third system of traditional government among the Kachins is *gumlao*. This may perhaps be described as a revolutionary system of government. It exists in the areas around Hukawng valley, where the people had revolted against the authority of the *duwas* and established a system of electing headmen by popular choice. These revolutions are thought to have taken place some three to four hundred years ago. In some areas, *gumlao* was introduced later. Under the British, some of the *gumlao* areas reverted back the *gumsa* system of hereditary *duwas*.

The Kachins are a handsome people. The men look very dashing in their traditional turbans and baggy trousers, with curved swords dangling at their sides. The women are striking in their costumes heavily decorated with silver ornaments. The Lisus, Marus and Yaywins also have their own different costumes. The Lisu women are considered to be particularly attractive.

The origins of the Karens have been a matter for much discussion. Some Christian missionaries have even thought they might be descendants of a lost tribe of Israel. It was also believed for a long time that the Karens were a Thai-Shan people. However, studies of their languages and social customs have given convincing proof that they belong to the Tibeto-Burman group. There are several different kinds of Karens, such as the Pao, the Sagaw and the Bwe.

The Karens, like the Chins and the Kachins, were traditionally spirit-worshippers. Today there are many Christians among them and some Buddhists. In addition, there are a number of other religious groups which are peculiar to the Karens. One of the most interesting is that which follows the *Leke* faith. This is a kind of Buddhism based on the worship of Maitreya, the Buddha who will next appear in this world. However, unlike other Buddhists, their faith does not include the worship of sacred images, pagodas or monks. Their principal religious monument is a wooden structure without walls. In the centre is a tall pole bearing a sacred umbrella. The people of the *Leke* faith abide by ten rules of conduct which seem to reflect Buddhist ideas.

The religion which has undoubtedly had the greatest impact on Karen life is Christianity. The missionaries who converted the people also gave them schools and education. This enabled many Karens to go on to higher studies and take up modern professions. Karen women have acquired a reputation as excellent hospital nurses. They are also much sought after as nannies.

Like most of the peoples of Burma, the Karens have traditionally lived by agriculture. They are also known as expert foresters. Karens are particularly skilled at capturing and taming wild elephants. They train the elephants to work with heavy logs in the timber camps. Karens depend on patience and perseverance to train the animals. They do not use cruel methods.

Spirit-worship still exists among the Karens. The devout Christians frown upon this. Buddhists are generally more tolerant, but some of them are also strongly opposed to spirit-worship. A traditional Karen occasion where people of different religions can gather together is the 'Shouting Feast', as it is known to the Burmese. This is really arranged for young people in the villages to get to know each other. Two rows of girls sit facing one another and the young men parade between the rows, stripped to their waists, to show that they are healthy and well formed. Later the young men take part in wrestling matches. Then they have a kind of competition of wit and knowledge. It is because these exchanges are usually made loudly and clearly that the Burmese have named the occasion a 'Shouting Feast'.*

Karens are good singers and many of them have beautiful voices. They have their own dances and musical instruments. Their bronze drums, known as 'frog drums' because of the little figures of frogs cast on them, are well known and very valuable.

The Kayah State adjoins the Karen State. It is a beautiful area with hills and many waterfalls. A big hydroelectric project has been set up at the Lawpita Falls. The Kayah people used to be known as Karennis (Red Karens) because of the colour of their costumes. There are a number of different peoples within the

---

* After a campaign trip to the Karen region the author told me there may be a mistake in the common Burmese etymology of Aw-chin, which is usually taken to mean 'Shouting Feast'. An alternative and more likely explanation would focus on the refrain Aw-aw which occurs in these exchanges and which the Burmese have confused for their word 'shout' (aw) [Ed.].

state. Perhaps the best known among them are the Padaung, whose women are often called 'giraffe women'. This is because of their long necks stretched by putting on row upon row of thick brass rings from the time they are about ten, increasing the number over the years. Many of the women wear twenty or more rings.

Situated between the Shans and the Karens, some similarities to both peoples can be seen in the customs and traditions of the Kayahs. Their traditional chieftains are called *saopya* (Shan chieftains are called *saopha*). The area was originally divided under the rule of five *saopyas*, but two of the lines died out before the Second World War. As in the Shan State, these rulers have now surrendered their hereditary rights and privileges.

The 'frog drum', so valued by the Karens, is equally valued by the Kayah people. The music of the drum is only for joyful occasions. There are other musical instruments, including gongs, drums and wind instruments, some made of buffalo horn. Among the songs of the Kayah people are those called *E-yoe*, which have been handed down from generation to generation. They tell of events which have taken place since the beginning of the world. A careful study of the *E-yoe* songs could reveal more information about the origins and history of the people.

Among the Kayah people, as among the Karens, traditional spirit-worship has been replaced to some extent by Christianity and Buddhism. However, the most important festival of the year is the *Kuhtobo* festival, dedicated to the spirit responsible for rain and good weather. In the old days this festival was celebrated at a district level, but since independence it has become a state occasion. The *Kuhtobo* festival is centred on sacrificing to the spirits and raising a sacred pole. It is a time for feasting and joy and takes place around May.

The history and civilization of the Mons have already been discussed in some detail. In spite of the many years of warfare between the two peoples, the Mons and the Burmese have mixed freely and intermarried. Today they are indistinguishable from each other except for the slight and rather attractive accent with which some Mons speak Burmese.

The Arakanese on the western coast of Burma have a long history which can compare with that of the Mons and the Burmese. However, because the area is cut off from the rest of Burma by the Arakan Yoma, the Arakanese have not been so closely involved in the wars of the other two peoples. Powerful kings from central Burma have made their authority felt in Arakan, invading it and demanding tribute. But it was only in the eighteenth century that it was annexed to the Burmese kingdom by King Bodawpaya.

The early peoples of Arakan are something of a mystery. It is thought that they were a mixture of Mongolian and Aryan peoples who had come over from India. Certainly the early kings of Arakan were of Indian stock. There are now several groups of peoples in the Arakan State: Arakanese, Thek, Dainet, Myo, Mramagyi and Kaman. The Arakanese are Tibeto-Burmans and their language is very close to Burmese. In fact, some regard it as archaic Burmese. The languages of some of the other groups show the influence of Bengali. Because of its geographical position, Bengal has played a major part in the history and civilization of Arakan. In the fifteenth century, Bengal helped the Arakanese to resist the power of the kings of Ava. From then on, the kings of Arakan used Islamic titles, although they and the majority of their subjects remained Buddhist. However, there are more people of the Islamic faith to be found in Arakan than anywhere else in Burma.

Despite these Bengali and Islamic influences, however, Arakan has been a predominantly Buddhist region for centuries. According to tradition, Buddhism came to the western coast of Burma during the lifetime of the Buddha. This cannot be verified, but the most famous image of the Buddha made by the Arakanese is thought to date back to the second century AD. This image, the Maha Myamuni, was taken away by King Bodawpaya's son when he conquered Arakan. It is considered one of the most sacred images in the country and is now enshrined in Mandalay. The loss of their great image was a deep sorrow to the Arakanese. There are those who say that the real Maha Myamuni could never have been taken out of Arakan and that it lies hidden somewhere in its jungles.

There are many pagodas and Buddhist temples in Arakan. Many of their religious festivals are Buddhist festivals, similar to the ones celebrated by the Burmese, and there are many similarities between the two peoples. There is, however, one Arakanese custom which is very alien to the Burmese. The Arakanese favour marriage between cross-cousins. (Children of one's mother's brothers or of one's father's sisters are known as cross-cousins.) This is a reflection of Islamic influence.

There are many fine examples of Arakanese literature. A poem by an Arakanese courtier of the fifteenth century, known as the 'Arakanese Princess *E-gyin*' is one of the first examples of the *E-gyin* type of poetry. After Arakan came under British rule in 1826, English became the language of the educated and Arakanese literature declined.

Today one of the greatest attractions of Arakan for people from all over Burma as well as for tourists is its beautiful beaches.

The Shan plateau is looked upon by the Burmese as a beautiful, romantic land. With its temperate climate, lakes and hills, it is certainly a most attractive part of the country. The Shans, as already mentioned, have played a very active part in the history of Burma. There are many different peoples in the area marked out as the Shan State. The majority belong to the Thai-Shan group like the Shans themselves, but there are also those who fall within the Tibeto-Burman and the Mon-Khmer groups. It is estimated that there are twenty-seven major sub-groups, including the Shans, Pa-o, Palaung, Kachin, Intha and Danu. In addition there are thirty-two lesser-known tribes.

Under the kings of Burma there were nine Shan states whose rulers (known as *saophas*) were given the right to use the five symbols of kingship: white umbrella, royal headdress, yak-hair swish, royal slippers and royal dagger. There were also other principalities on the Shan plateau. Under the British there were thirty-seven administrative divisions, the biggest ones ruled by *saophas* and the others under the authority of *myosas* (governors) or *ngwegunmhus* (excise officers). After independence, in 1959, the *saophas* signed an agreement giving up their hereditary rights and privileges.

Of all the minority peoples of Burma, the Shans are probably best known to foreigners today. This is partly because of the size of their territory and partly because parts of the Shan State are included in those areas open to tourists.

The Inle Lake is a great tourist attraction. The people, called Intha, live off the lake, fishing and cultivating gardens on the floating islands produced by a mixture of silt and water weeds. A peculiarly about the Intha boatmen is that they row their boats standing up with one leg hooked around the oar to pull it. Other places which tourists may visit in the Shan State are Taunggyi, the state capital, and Kalaw, a well-known hot-weather resort.

Silk woven at Inle is popular with women all over Burma. Another Shan product known and used everywhere in the country is the woven bag which can be slung over the shoulders. It would be a very unusual Burmese household that did not have one of these colourful bags, for men, women and children all use them. Tea and pickled tea-leaves are also among the chief products exported from the Shan State to the rest of the country.

Within driving distance from Kalaw are the Pindaya caves, a series of caverns which contain many images of the Buddha, of different sizes. It is a strange and awesome place with beautiful images suddenly coming into sight around dark corners.

Spirit-worship is practised by some of the Shans as well as by other peoples on the plateau. Christians are also found among some of the tribal groups. As most of the Shans are Buddhists, their main festivals mark important days of the Buddhist calendar.

In recent years much publicity has been given to the area of the Shan State which falls within the 'Golden Triangle'. This is the name given to the junction where Burma, Laos and Thailand meet. It is an area where opium poppies are grown in vast quantities. One of the most dangerous drugs of today, heroin, is derived from opium. The growing addiction to heroin among people in America and Western Europe has made it very valuable. However, the poor farmers who grow opium poppies do not get rich. It is the people who smuggle heroin in large quantities to the western countries who make large profits. Some of the people who grow opium also become addicted to it. However, as they do not take it in a highly concentrated and refined form, the effects are not as disastrous as among heroin addicts who inject the drug into their bodies. Attempts are being made by several governments to control the opium trade. This is not easy, however, as the 'Golden Triangle' covers difficult terrain, parts of it often overrun by rebels.

Apart from the many indigenous racial groups of Burma, Indian and Chinese immigrants must be mentioned among its minority peoples. Under British rule there was no control on the numbers of Indians and Chinese who came to seek their fortune in Burma. Many Indians left the country during the advance of the Japanese during the Second World War, although some came back after the war was over. Indians and Chinese also left Burma after it became an independent nation. However, there are still large numbers of Indian and Chinese people, particularly in the towns and cities.

Some of the Indians and Chinese have intermarried with the local peoples. For many, Burma is the only home they have ever known and they love it as their own country. There are others whose loyalties to the countries of their origin and to their own people are still strong. In the past there have been serious clashes between the Burmese and the immigrant communities. On the whole, though, they have all lived together peacefully.

The many peoples of Burma make it a fascinating country, rich in variety and tradition. Among them, the Burmese form the majority. It is therefore their habits and customs which have come to be most often associated with Burma.

The Burmese
The one single factor which has had the most influence on Burmese culture and civilization is Theravada Buddhism. In all parts of the country where the Burmese people live there are pagodas and Buddhist monasteries. The graceful tapering shape of a pagoda, painted white or gilded to a shining gold, is a basic part of any Burmese landscape. Burma is often called the 'Land of Pagodas'.

Buddhism teaches that suffering is an unavoidable part of existence. At the root of all suffering are such feelings as desire, greed and attachment. Therefore to be free from suffering it is necessary to be free from those undesirable feelings. This freedom can be obtained by following the Noble Eightfold Path:

Right Understanding
Right Thought
Right Speech
Right Action
Right Livelihood
Right Effort
Right Mindfulness
Right Concentration

This path is also known as the Middle Way, because it avoids two extremes: one extreme is the search for happiness through the pursuit of pleasure, the other extreme is the search for happiness through inflicting pain on oneself. The final goal of a Buddhist is to be liberated from the cycle of existence and rebirth, called *samsara*. Once this final liberation is achieved, one may be said to have attained *nirvana*; this word means 'extinction' and might be explained as Ultimate Reality for all Buddhists.

The teachings of the Buddha are known as the Dharma, and these teachings are generally passed on to ordinary people by the Buddhist monks, collectively known as the Sangha. Therefore, the Buddha, the Dharma and the Sangha are called the 'Triple Gem'. Because the Lord Buddha was a great teacher, the Burmese have a great reverence for all teachers. Parents are also regarded with 'awe, love and respect'. Consequently, the Triple Gem, teachers and parents make up the 'five that must be revered' by Burmese Buddhists.

All good Buddhists undertake to abide by the Five Precepts: not to take life, not to steal, not to commit adultery, not to tell lies, not to take intoxicating drinks. Although the taking of life is considered such an evil that many Burmese will go out of their way to avoid stepping on an insect, there are few who avoid eating meat. This is considered inconsistent by some people. The Burmese would probably argue that the Lord Buddha himself ate meat. The Burmese are a practical people. They have also been described as happy-go-lucky.

As might be expected, many Burmese festivals are based on Buddhist events. Festival days are determined by the Burmese calendar, which is calculated according to the phases of the moon. The full moon days of the month of *Kason* (April/May), *Waso* (June/July) and *Thidingyut* (October/November) are special days for the Buddhists. The full moon day of *Kason* celebrates the birth, enlightenment and death of the Buddha. The Buddha achieved enlightenment – that is, he finally shed all false beliefs and saw through to the ultimate truth – underneath a *bodhi* tree. On the full moon of *Kason*, therefore, people pour offerings of water on *bodhi* trees.

The full moon day of *Waso* also celebrates important events in the life of the Buddha, in particular the first sermon he preached on the truth he had learnt. In addition, this day marks the beginning of the 'Buddhist Lent', which lasts for three months. During this time the monks are not allowed to travel. Many Buddhists observe what are known as the Eight Precepts on all the holy days during Lent. The Buddhist holy days are the day of the dark moon, the eighth day of the new moon, the day of the full moon and the eighth day after the full moon. The Eight Precepts are four of the basic Five Precepts (not to kill, steal, lie or take intoxicating drinks) with the addition of four others: not to commit any immoral acts, not to take any food after twelve noon, not to indulge in music, dancing and the use of perfume, not to sleep in high places. (The last is taken to mean that one should not sleep in a luxurious bed.) Some devout Buddhists keep these eight precepts throughout the three months of Lent. Because it is a time when people should be thinking of their spiritual development, Buddhists should not get married during this period. Marriage brings family life and therefore greater ties and attachments. Thus it is likely to make the achieving of *nirvana* more difficult.

The end of Lent coincides with the end of the monsoon rains in

October. It is a time for happiness and rejoicing. Tradition has it that the Lord Buddha spent one Lent in the *Tavatimsa* heaven to preach to his mother. (His mother had died in giving birth to him and had been reborn in *Tavatimsa*, one of the many Buddhist heavens.) At the end of Lent, he came back to earth and the people of the world welcomed him with lights. In celebration of this, during the three days of the *Thidingyut* festival, pagodas, monasteries and homes are decorated with lights and lanterns. Cities like Rangoon and Mandalay are ablaze with coloured lights, and there are competitions to see which part of the town is the most beautifully decorated. *Thidingyut* is a time for expressing reverence towards older people. Many Burmese visit older friends and relatives to bow down before them and to offer gifts.

There are other Buddhist festivals apart from the ones described above. In addition, many pagodas have their own festival day. One of the most important pagoda festivals is that of the great Shwedagon in Rangoon, which takes place in March. Soaring to a height of almost 100 metres (over 300 feet), covered with layers of solid gold leaf and topped with a hollow gold orb encrusted with many precious gems, the Shwedagon is the most famous landmark in the country. Foreigners come to look at it with curiosity and wonder. For the Burmese it is not just an interesting and beautiful monument, but a very central part of their religious life – and not just on festival days. Every day, an endless stream of people climb up to the Shwedagon from one of its four great stairways (an electric lift has also been installed near one stairway). They buy flowers, incense sticks, gold leaves and candles to offer at the pagoda from the stalls that line the stairs. (These stalls sell a variety of other things apart from religious objects.)

The atmosphere of the Shwedagon is steeped in the religious faith of the people who have worshipped there for generations. Everywhere are the sounds of prayers and the clear ring of prayer gongs. On the platform which surrounds the pagoda are many smaller pagodas, shrines and pavilions. Each person goes to his or her favourite place of worship to pray there and to make offerings. Apart from the main prayer pavilions, the eight planetary posts which mark the days of the week are popular places of worship.

(Each day of the week, together with Rahu – Wednesday night – has its own planet.) People go to the post marking the day of their birth to pray, light candles and incense sticks and to make offerings of flowers and water. In a hot country like Burma, the coolness of water is symbolic of peace.

All Burmese know the day of the week on which they were born. The name given on a person's birth horoscope is decided according to the day of birth. For example, those born on a Monday should have names beginning with the letters *ka*, *hka*, *ga*, *nga*, those born on a Tuesday are given names beginning with *sa*, *hsa*, *za*, *nya*, and so on. Not just horoscope names but also those given by parents are usually chosen according to these rules. The horoscope shows the position of the planets at the time of a person's birth. Astrologers use it to make predictions about the future. This practice is not really in line with the teachings of the Buddha, according to which one's future is decided by one's own actions rather than by the stars.

Another side of Burmese life which is not strictly in accordance with Buddhist teachings is spirit-worship. Like the other peoples of Burma, the Burmese were spirit-worshippers before the arrival of Buddhism. The Burmese use the word *nat* to mean supernatural beings, the good ones who dwell in the various heavens as well as the frightening ones who interfere in the affairs of the human world. Little *nat* shrines can often be seen in Burma, especially under big trees which are believed to harbour spirits. The most powerful of all the *nats* are the *Thonzekhuna Min*, or 'Thirty-Seven Lords'. There are people who take *nat* worship very seriously in spite of their belief in Buddhism. Even those who avoid having anything to do with spirit-worship will not do anything which is known to be offensive to *nats*.

The most important place for *nat* worship in Burma is Mount Popa, an extinct volcano. Mount Popa is considered to be the home of two of the thirty-seven powerful *nats*. A great festival takes place there every year which attracts people from all over the country, *nat* worshippers as well as curious observers.

It is often asked why even educated Burmese can sometimes be found taking part in *nat* worship. Perhaps the answer lies in two aspects of Burmese life. One is the strong hold which old beliefs from the days before Buddhism still have on the minds of the people. The other is the extreme self-reliance which Buddhism demands from the individual. In Buddhism there are no gods to whom one can pray for favours or help. One's destiny is decided entirely by one's own actions. While accepting the truth of this, most people find it difficult to resist the need to rely on supernatural powers, especially when times are hard.

The Burmese may put great importance on their religious life, but that does not stop them from being a fun-loving people. This is particularly obvious during the celebrations for the Burmese New Year, which takes place in April. *Thingyan* is also known as the Water Festival because the last three days of the old year are a time for people to throw water at one another all over the country. This is very refreshing at a time of year when the hot weather is at its worst. The water-throwing can sometimes get too rough, but nobody is supposed to get angry.

Thingyan is also a time when many Burmese boys celebrate one of the most important landmarks of their life. This is the *shinbyu*, when a Buddhist boy enters the monastery for a short time as a novice monk. All Burmese parents see it as their duty to make sure that their sons are admitted to the religious life in this way. The *shinbyu* ceremony can be performed once the boy is old enough to say certain Buddhist prayers correctly, manage the robes of a monk and 'drive away crows from his begging bowl'. This period of novicehood during which boys live the life of monks (although they do not keep all the rules which adult monks must observe) is a good introduction to the religious life. Burmese men like to enter monastic life at least three times during their lifetime: once as a boy, once as a young man and once as an adult.

The *shinbyu* ceremony is a joyful occasion. The candidate for novicehood (*shinlaung*) is usually dressed in princely costume. This recalls the fact that the Buddha was a prince before he gave up his royal position to follow the religious life. The *shinlaung* is paraded through the streets with great ceremony before his head is shaved and he is given the robes of a novice. How simple or elaborate a *shinbyu* ceremony is depends on the inclinations and resources of the family. Often a number of boys take part in a single ceremony. Apart from the *Thingyan* period, the Buddhist Lent is a popular time for *shinbyu* ceremonies.

When brothers are having their *shinbyu*, it is usual for the sisters to have their ears pierced. This gives the girls a chance to dress up as princesses and have their share of fuss and attention. Many see this as an expression of the Burmese belief in the equality of men and women. Although, theoretically, men are considered nobler because only a man can become a Buddha, Burmese women have never really had an inferior status. They have always had equal rights of inheritance and led active, independent lives. Secure in the knowledge of her own worth, the Burmese woman does not mind giving men the kind of respectful treatment that makes them so happy!

A big *shinbyu* ceremony may be accompanied by a *pwe*. *Pwe* is a particularly Burmese word which can mean a festival, feast, celebration, ceremony, gathering or public performance. One common use of the word is to describe a popular entertainment which is a marvellous mixture of dance, drama, music and clowning.

The origins of Burmese dance are considered to go back at least to the Pagan period, judging from old wall paintings and references in stone inscriptions. However, many of the dances performed today owe a considerable amount to Thai influences introduced in the eighteenth century when a son of Alaungpaya brought back many artists from his invasions of Thailand. The movements of both male and female dancers are very graceful, involving beautiful hand gestures and extremely skilled footwork.

Burmese drama, which is a little like western opera with music, singing and much dramatic action, also owes a considerable amount to the tradition of court plays brought back from Thailand in the eighteenth century. Popular dramas such as the *Yamazat*, based on the famous *Ramayana* epic of India, are performed again and again. The nineteenth century produced many fine Burmese dramatists whose works also remain popular to this day.

Dance drama is always accompanied by orchestral music. Burmese musical instruments fall into five categories: bronze instruments, stringed instruments, leather instruments, hollow wind instruments and non-metallic percussion instruments used for keeping time. Burmese orchestral music has a great range, from soft, gentle tunes to the loud, stirring clashes which so often announce the presence of a *pwe*. The leading instrument of the orchestra is the *hsaingwaing*, a circle of twenty one small leather faced drums which are played with amazing virtuosity by the performer, who sits in the centre. Another instrument considered particularly Burmese is the gently curving harp, which is held in the lap of the performer as he plays.

There are many different types of classical Burmese song. To mention a few, there are the *kyo* (meaning string), which is always preceded by little phrases of music on the *hsaingwaing*; and the *bawle*, invented by a princess of the last royal dynasty at Mandalay.

Although classical music is always performed at the much loved *pwes*, modern music showing a strong western influence is increasingly gaining popularity, especially among young people. However, Burmese music and dance have not only strong traditions but also the support and encouragement of the government. There is, therefore, little danger that they will fall into decline, in spite of modern developments.

One form of entertainment which has lost some of its popular appeal is the puppet show. This was first introduced in the late eighteenth or early nineteenth century for the amusement of the royal court. A traditional puppet show has twenty-eight characters, including *nats*, a king, queen, courtiers and various animals and birds. Different kinds of wood must be used to make different characters. There are many other rules, such as the order in which the characters come on stage and the direction from which they emerge. Puppeteering is, therefore, a very specialized art. It is a great pity that the public no longer seem very interested in this fascinating form of entertainment.

Today, the cinema has much appeal for the Burmese. The Burmese film industry began before the Second World War. As in other countries, actors and actresses have many fans. But although successful film stars can make a good living, they do not become as rich as the big stars in the western countries. Traditionally, actors and dancers were considered an inferior class, but these old prejudices are fast disappearing. Television, which was introduced several years ago, is quickly gaining in popularity.

The Burmese are an agricultural people, depending on the land for their living. Even today, in spite of some industries and the many professions open to people in the towns, agriculture is the backbone of the country. The number of those engaged in such professions as medicine, engineering and teaching is increasing all the time. The Burmese have always had a high proportion of people who could read and write. This is due to the custom of sending children to the local monastery for their schooling. Traditionally the monasteries limited themselves to religious teachings, but gradually more and more of them added modern subjects to their teaching programme. Nowadays, with the growth of state education, there are few monasteries serving as schools. However, there are still many Burmese who owe their early education to Buddhist monks.

It has already been mentioned that Burmese writing first began to develop in the Pagan period. Much of the traditional literature was concerned with religious themes. But there is also a considerable body of classical works, mainly verse, which deals with non-religious matters. Before the nineteenth century, the Burmese seem to have preferred poetry to prose. However, since the first novel in Burmese was published at the beginning of the twentieth century, prose writing, especially fiction, has developed greatly. Today, Burmese is a vigorous, continuously developing language.

The Burmese have a great respect for education. There is a popular old saying that riches can vanish as if by magic, but knowledge is a truly precious treasure which nobody can take away. Traditionally, education was seen not just as the acquisition of knowledge but as the development of Buddhist values. The needs of the present age have led to more emphasis on formal qualifications, but parents still place importance on bringing children up as good Buddhists.

The family is very important in Burma. Children are brought up to honour and respect their elders. It is believed that the love and care given by parents are beyond repayment. Burmese are taught that even though the Lord Buddha showed his mother the way to *nirvana*, he did not manage to repay more than a minute portion of what he owed her.

In spite of the strong feelings of family, the Burmese do not have a system of family names. Each individual has his or her own personal name, which is often quite different from those of everybody else in the family. Moreover, women do not change their names on marriage. For example, the father may be called U Thein, the mother Daw Saw Tin, the son Maung Tun Aye and the daughter Ma Khin Khin. *U*, *Daw*, *Maung* and *Ma* are prefixes like 'Mr' or 'Mrs'. In Burma, age is an important factor in deciding which prefix to use. *U* literally means 'uncle' and *Daw* means 'aunt', so these cannot be used for young children. *Maung*, meaning 'younger brother', is suitable for a boy, but when he is older the prefix *Ko* ('older brother') will be used. However, *Ma* ('sister') is the only prefix used for girls. Sometimes it is the person's position that decides which prefix should be used. A young man who has achieved a very important position will be addressed as *U*, while an older man, if his status is low, may still be addressed as *Ko* or *Maung*.

A person's position may decide how much respect is shown to him, but Burmese society has no rigid class system. It is not possible to tell from a person's name or accent whether his father is a manual labourer or a wealthy businessman. Even his appearance is not always an indication of his background, as there is not a great deal of difference in the kinds of clothes people wear. Many of those who are in high positions come from humble homes. A person is judged by his own achievements rather than by his family.

An important part of Burmese life is food. Both Burmese men and women take a lively interest in cooking. The basic item of a Burmese meal is usually rice, taken with what westerners would describe as a 'curry'. However, Burmese 'curries' are not quite the same as the better-known Indian ones. The Burmese use less spices but more garlic and ginger. Fish products are an important part of Burmese cooking. Fish sauce and dried shrimps are used for flavouring. *Ngapi*, a paste of preserved fish with a very strong smell, is taken as a relish at almost every meal. Meat is not eaten in large quantities. A great variety of vegetables are available all the year round and Burmese cooking makes full use of them. It has been said that no tender leaf or shoot is safe from the Burmese.

The number of Indians and Chinese in Burma have added further variety to the food of the country. In the towns there are many restaurants and food stalls. It is quite usual for people to stop by the roadside to have a snack or a meal. Two of the most popular dishes are *mohinga* and *khaukswe*. *Mohinga* is a dish of slightly fermented rice noodles eaten with a thick fish soup. *Khaukswe* simply means noodles, and these can be prepared in many different ways. But the *khaukswe* dish considered most typically Burmese is the one eaten with a kind of chicken stew cooked in coconut milk.

In general, the Burmese do not eat many sweets. Hot, spicy snacks are more to their taste. Fruits often take the place of puddings. As in many other South Asian countries, the mango is very popular. There are many varieties and the Burmese eat them in a number of ways. Small green mangoes are taken with *ngapi* as part of the main meal, or eaten as a snack dipped in salt and chili powder. Larger, slightly underripe mangoes can be made into a curry. But of course there is nothing to compare with a ripe, sweet mango eaten on its own.

Green tea is one of the most usual drinks in Burma. Tea with milk and sugar is also taken, but this is usually brewed in such a way that foreigners do not always recognize it as tea. As Buddhists, the Burmese frown upon alcoholic drinks, but there are strong country liquors made from the juice of the toddy palm. Bottled beer of the western variety is also produced nowadays.

Food is a popular subject of conversation. It is quite usual for friends and acquaintances to ask each other on meeting: 'And what did you have for lunch today?' This constant interest makes Burmese cooking one of the most imaginative and varied in the world.

Both Burmese men and women wear the *longyi*, a long tube of cloth which they wrap around themselves and tuck in at the waist. Men wear western-style shirts with their *longyis* and women wear short, fitted tops. Young girls have now taken to wearing western-style blouses and T-shirts. For formal occasions, men wear collar-less shirts with short jackets and a *gaungbaung* (a kind of turban) on their heads. Chains of sweet-smelling white jasmines coiled around a knot of glossy black hair are one of the most attractive sights. Traditionally, both Burmese men and women kept their hair very long. Men started to cut their hair soon after British rule was established in the country. However, men with large top-knots can still be seen in the villages. Women have continued to keep their hair long, but in recent years it has become fashionable for girls to adopt short, westernized hair-styles.

Burmese women are noted for their fine complexions. It is thought that they owe this in some degree to the use of *thanakha*. This is a paste made by grinding the bark of the *thanakha* tree. It gives the skin protection from the sun and is also thought to have medicinal properties. *Thanakha* is a yellow-beige paste and when applied thickly can make the face look as though it has been smeared with mud. In spite of this, it remains the most important item of a Burmese woman's beauty treatment. Even the arrival of modern cosmetics has not diminished the popularity of *thanakha*.

In Burma, as in many Asian countries, western goods are much sought after. Western ideas and attitudes have also crept in through books, films and foreign visitors. Under the policy of the present government, tourists are only allowed into the country for one week at a time. This goes some way towards keeping out foreign influences and, compared with most South-east Asian countries, Burma has done a much better job of preserving its own culture and traditions. The country is to some extent isolated from the rest of the world through restrictions on Burmese wishing to travel abroad as well as on foreigners wishing to come to Burma. This enforced isolation has resulted in giving things foreign the appeal of 'forbidden fruit' for some Burmese. It also means that in many areas of scientific and technological educa-tion, Burma has fallen behind modern developments.

Whatever attractions western goods and culture may hold for some of the Burmese people, Buddhism is still the greatest influence on their daily lives. Young people who dress in T-shirts and listen eagerly to western-style pop music still visit the pagodas frequently. The religious life of the Burmese is not separated from their social life. Most Burmese gatherings are centred around a religious event. The most common social occasion is perhaps the *hsoongway*, offering of food to monks. Friends will come to help, listen to the sermons and join in the chanting of prayers. It is usual to repeat the Five Precepts and undertake to keep them. On holy days people undertake to keep the Eight Precepts. After the monks have left, friends and family will eat together. It will have been an enjoyable as well as a spiritually rewarding occasion.

By international standards, Burma is not a wealthy country and life is hard for many of its people. But there is still a quality of calmness and serenity which is very precious. For this the Burmese are greatly indebted to their religion.

Burmese Crafts

The only monuments and buildings of any great age in Burma are pagodas and monasteries. This is because the houses of ordinary people and even the palaces of kings were traditionally built from the various woods that are available in such abundance. Wooden buildings cannot survive for very long in the climate of Burma. The Burmese are skilled at working with wood. They use it not just for building but also for many decorative crafts.

Prayer pavilions at pagodas are often decorated with elaborate wood carvings. The Shwenandaw monastery in Mandalay boasts some of the finest carvings. It was originally within the grounds of the Mandalay palace. Fortunately King Thibaw had it moved outside, and thus it escaped when the rest of the palace complex was destroyed during the Second World War. The whole monastery is a feast of wood carvings: scrolls, flowers, animals and supernatural beings are arranged in a profusion of intricate patterns.

Almost every Burmese home has a shrine with one or more images of the Buddha. Often these images are placed on beautifully carved and gilt wooden thrones. Sometimes these thrones are lacquered or decorated with glass and mirror inlay. Gilt with glass inlay, known as *hman-si-shwe-cha*, is a well-known decorative art. Some of the prayer pavilions of the Shwedagon show fine examples of this kind of work.

Images of the Buddha may be made of wood, marble or bronze. Some of the best images come from Mandalay and the surrounding districts. There is a good market for such images, as people are always setting up new shrines or adding to the old ones. Traditionally, the Burmese were not interested in collecting antique images. In fact, some believe that it is unlucky to take into their homes old images which were once in pagodas or monasteries. The value which westerners put on antique goods is changing the attitudes of some Burmese. The smuggling of valuable old images is no longer uncommon. Many smuggled goods are sold over the border in Thailand.

Lacquerware is one of the most popular Burmese crafts. It is generally believed that the technique of lacquer originated in China. It was probably introduced to the Burmese when Anawratha's army brought back Mon craftsman from Thaton. Burmese lacquer is slightly different from the Chinese and Japanese variety in that it is derived from a different species of the lacquer tree, *Melanhorroea usitata*. The sap of the tree is mixed with a special kind of ash and applied to a prepared base of wood, woven bamboo, or bamboo and horsehair. Enough of the mixture is applied to give a smooth surface before layers of coloured lacquer are applied.

There are several types of decorated lacquerware. The most common are incised lacquerware, gold-leaf lacquerware and relief-moulded lacquerware. In incised lacquerware, designs are cut into the surface of an object. These designs are then filled in with coloured lacquer, the most usual colours being red, black, green and yellow. In gold-leaf lacquerware, gold-leaf decorations are applied to a black background. The decorations on relief-moulded lacquerware are made by modelling them in lacquer mixed with sawdust and ash, so that the designs are raised above the surface.

Bowls, trays, betel-nut containers and small decorative boxes are some of the most common items of lacquerware. Larger objects, such as tables and screens, are also made; but these can be very expensive.

The Burmese are skilled silversmiths. The most frequently used item of silverware is the bowl. The slightly pot-bellied shape of the traditional Burmese bowl, which comes in many different sizes, is thought to be based on the begging bowls used by monks. Many of these bowls are embossed with scenes from Buddhist stories or from traditional Burmese court life.

On special occasions the Burmese like to wear their traditional hand-woven silk *longyis*. Those made with wavy or zigzag designs in many colour combinations, called *acheik*, are considered the best fabrics. Of these *acheik*, the most rare and expensive are the ones woven with a hundred spools and therefore called *lun-taya* (*lun* means 'spool' and *taya* means 'one hundred'). The *lun-taya acheik* is thick, heavy and long-lasting. Such *longyis* are often passed down from generation to generation.

A Burmese craft which has practically died out is making embroidered wall hangings. It is thought that the inspiration and technique for these hangings came from India or from the West because of the name, *kalaga*. *Kala* is the Burmese term for foreigners from the West, and *ga* signifies a screen or curtain.

Although wall paintings can be seen in the monuments of Pagan, the Burmese have not really developed painting as a traditional art. Even the illustrations in folding books and manuscripts date back only to about the nineteenth century.

The best examples of Burmese art and crafts can be seen at religious monuments. This is a further indication of the importance of Buddhism in Burma.

A Common Future
In recent years a great deal of emphasis has been placed by foreigners on the rebellions against the Burmese government led

by the Karens and the Shans, and the differences between the peoples of Burma have been pointed out. It has been implied that the nation is not a true union of peoples but an artificial state imposed from above. This record of disunity is not one of which any citizen of Burma can be proud. Nevertheless, there is more reason to be hopeful for the future than might appear to some observers.

There are many ties between the peoples of Burma. The Mon-Khmers, Tibeto-Burmans and Thai-Shans have lived among each other for centuries. The Mons and the Burmese, who were sworn enemies throughout much of their history, have learnt to live together in peace. With the development of mutual understanding and tolerance, the other peoples could also learn to live in harmony.

Burma's borders form a natural boundary for a country rich in peoples and natural resources. In time, both could be developed to create a strong and prosperous nation.

3

Intellectual Life in Burma
and India under Colonialism

First published in 1990 as Burma and India: Some Aspects of Intellectual Life under Colonialism *by the Indian Institute of Advanced Study, Simla, in association with Allied Publishers, Delhi.*

A comparative study of the literature of two different nations can be a hazardous task fraught with the dangers of generalization, oversimplification and the temptation to find contrasts and similarities where none, in fact, exists. On the other hand, the comparative approach offers opportunities to highlight the salient characteristics of a particular tradition as well as to indicate those trends which might be considered the product of the human creative impulse independent of the national setting. Yet the latter also take on forms which are decided by the social and political context in which they were given shape. Thus the treatment of love and religion, two of the most popular themes in the literature of many cultures, can differ not only between different societies but also between different periods in the same society reflecting changing values. Consequently, the study of literature is enhanced by an examination not only of the broader corpus of ideas, beliefs and creative thinking which make up the intellectual life of a society, but also of the political and social factors which have shaped this life.

In the course of the study of Burmese intellectual developments under colonialism, my interest was drawn to intellectual life in other Asian countries which had also gone through the colonial experience. Of these, India presented itself as the most obvious choice for a more detailed comparative study with Burma – the two countries had been ruled as part of the same British administration for several decades; while at the same time each preserved its own distinct character. Burma had been open to cultural influences from India since the early days of her history. Of these influences, the most important was Buddhism, which became so integral a part of the Burmese ethos that it has become common to say: 'To be Burmese is to be Buddhist.' These early cultural and religious Indian imports were selected and adapted by the Burmese in a way which brings out the contrasting value of the two societies. By the time of the British conquest of Burma, cultural influences from India and other neighbours had long since matured, in some cases one might say hardened, into attributes of the distinctive culture of the Burmese. Thus, in comparing the intellectual traditions of the two countries, Buddhist concepts and ideas which had originally come from India could legitimately be treated as particularly Burmese in contrast to the predominantly Hindu attitudes of Indians.

The choice of India as one of the major components in a comparative study of intellectual traditions poses a considerable problem of selection. It would be impossible to give satisfactory attention to all the areas of the subcontinent in several tomes, let alone in one very slim volume. I have, therefore, concentrated on those aspects which seem to offer interesting points of comparison with developments in Burma. It has not been possible to avoid the pitfalls of generalization and oversimplification mentioned earlier, but it is hoped that they might be balanced to some extent by the insights that are afforded by the comparative approach. I would like to make it clear that this study has been made in a speculative spirit; possible interpretations have been put forward without the intention to assert that they are the only plausible ones.

I

The times and circumstances under which India and Burma were incorporated into the British Empire were vastly different. It is

not possible to recount the story of the British conquest of India
with a few precise dates: it was a process which took over two
hundred years, stretching from the time the East India Company
started exercising administrative powers over the settlements
which grew up around their factories until 1858, when Victoria
was proclaimed Queen Empress. British annexation of Burma, on
the other hand, was accomplished in three clear-cut phases spread
out over little more than half a century. The first Anglo-Burmese
War of 1824–6 ended with Arakan and Tenasserim passing under
British rule; the second Anglo-Burmese War of 1852 added the
province of Pegu to the British possessions; and, finally, the third
Anglo-Burmese War of 1885 led to the subjugation of the whole
country and brought an end to the Burmese monarchy.[1] For the
Burmese people it was a sudden and wholly unprecedented break
with a past which had been turbulent and often unhappy, but
which was nevertheless an irrefutable part of the recognized
traditional order.

The annexations, subsequent to the first two Anglo-Burmese
Wars, had touched the pride of the Burmese but not seriously
shaken their confidence. With their home in the central dry zone
of modern Burma, they were, in spite of their Buddhism, a
militant race accustomed to regarding the boundaries of their
kingdom as a variable, dependent on the ability of the individual
monarch. Under powerful kings the Burmese would extend their
sway over the Mons to the south, the Shans to the east and the
Arakanese along the western coastline. On occasions they even
penetrated into Manipur, Assam and Thailand. The last royal
dynasty had been established by the military prowess of its
founder, Alaungpaya, who had wrested control of Lower Burma
from the Mons in 1757, while Arakan had been conquered
during the reign of one of his sons, Bodawpaya, as late as 1789.
Thus, the cession of Tenasserim, Arakan and the Pegu province
to the British could be viewed as part of the waxing and waning
cycle of the Burmese kingdom concomitant with the fortunes of
war. But, as long as the king reigned in his royal capital, the
symbol of Burmese freedom remained intact. As admitted even
by an author who consciously focuses on the positive aspects
of British rule, the people in the province of British Burma

looked to the King in Mandalay with respect and indeed reverence; they were proud that he still ruled but they showed no great anxiety to count among his subjects. The Talaings (Mons), the Arakanese, the Karens and the rest had at first been glad to see the English; as memories of anarchy and extortion faded, they, no doubt, like people in India, began to be less sure. But hardly any native of Burma was pleased by the outcome of the Third Burmese War.[2]

Thibaw, the last king at Mandalay, was one of the least competent monarchs in the history of Burma. He, or at any rate his queen, Supayalat, had instigated many well-known acts of atrocity from a narrow and ferocious impulse towards self-preservation. Nevertheless, their removal roused much patriotic indignation among the Burmese, who lamented the exile of the royal couple in compositions which have passed into the realm of literature as a recognized genre.

Conquest was an entirely new experience for the Burmese. Unlike the people of India, who had been subjected to successive waves of foreign invaders from the north-west since their early history, the Burmese had not known any serious foreign intrusion other than a brief Mongol incursion which had destroyed Pagan in the thirteenth century. Later periods saw the three largest ethnic groups within the confines of the present Union of Burma (the Burmese, the Shans and the Mons) engaged in intermittent wars to establish their supremacy. From these struggles the Burmese emerged as the paramount power by the sixteenth century. But even during the period of Shan ascendency in Upper Burma, the predominant cultural influence had been Burmese, and the Shan monarchs of Ava had become highly Burmanized.

For close on a millennium, the Burmese had been firm in the Buddhist faith which provided a philosophy that could meet the challenges of other religions with supreme confidence. On the secular side, the monarchy, while weak in administration, had proved itself strong in battle often enough to have acquired the reputation of a considerable – one might almost say imperial –

power in South-east Asia. Thus it was that, when the Burmese king considered himself the very equal of the English queen, his assurance was not so patently absurd as it might have appeared to those who viewed the still medieval kingdom from the perspective of a western nation upheld by the technical achievements of the Industrial Revolution. Unfortunately, an indifference to developments in the outside world was a characteristic of the Burmese monarchs, who had traditionally held sway over the country from the land-locked heart of their kingdom.[3] The sum of it was that the outcome of the third Anglo-Burmese War came as a rude shock to the Burmese; they hardly knew how to deal with the novel experience of complete political conquest, soon to be followed by cultural subjugation. For a few months after the fall of Mandalay, the British were undecided as to what they would do with their latest colonial acquisition, but by the beginning of 1886 the die was cast: 'Burma, so radically different from India, by force of circumstances became an appendage of the Indian Empire.'[4]

The last quarter of the nineteenth century was a time when imperial attitudes hardened. The British came to assume the role of first citizens of the world with the unquestioned right to mould the destinies of the less fortunate:

> The British were now exporting to their dominions a kind of package civilization, offered in competition with the local product, and backed by powerful service arrangements. Sometimes this was conscious policy ... More often, though, it was instinctive or even incidental, and was seen by the British, if they saw it at all, simply as an aspect of historical determinism.
>
> The indigenous cultures reacted variously to this assault. Some, like the Hindu and Muslim civilizations of India, yielded but did not break, treating the western culture as a transient phenomenon. Some, like the Burmese, simply took no notice.[5]

To yield without breaking was an attitude, both pragmatic and philosophical, which the people of India had long adopted in their encounters with foreign conquerors. In this sense, they were better equipped than the Burmese to deal with the changes brought about by colonialism. But for the Indians also British rule spelt many unprecedented developments and breaks with the past. Muslim invaders had made India their home and over the centuries had become an integral part of the subcontinent, even though the line of demarcation between them and the Hindus remained strong and vivid. For the British, on the other hand, India was a commercial outpost which, through a series of largely unpremeditated events, became a colonial territory to be ruled by an increasingly complex and impersonalized bureaucracy. It was very rare that any Englishman looked upon India as his home, even if the major part of his life were spent in that country. This feeling of apartness increased in the later half of the nine-teenth century with the development of the steam boat and the opening of the Suez Canal. These made it possible for more English women to come out to India and make English homes for their menfolk, taking them further away from the people of the land they were ruling. But perhaps the single most important event that widened the gulf between the British and the Indians was the conflict of 1857, which the former regarded as the Sepoy Mutiny and the latter now define, as did Marx and Engels, as the First Indian War of Independence. The mutual violence and excess, generated by this conflict, added hostility and suspicion to the sense of aloofness and racial consciousness which were fast developing in the high noon of Victorian imperialism.

The racial factor was perhaps the most conspicuous feature of the relationship between the British and the Indians. The Muslim rulers had behaved with the arrogance of conquerors and in-dulged in bouts of religious persecution, but they had not asserted their superiority over the Hindus in aggressive terms of race and colour. In the words of an Indian journalist:

While colour-consciousness undeniably exists in Indians, its manifestations are not as abrasive or offensive as the colour-consciousness of many European whites towards Africans and Asians . . . In European eyes . . . colour seems to have a special social connotation and, until recently, a special political significance: to be a coloured man was to be politically dependent on the European and to be socially his inferior.[6]

However, there had been a time in the early days of British association with India when the sense of racial superiority was not acute in white people. It had been a time when the length and rigours of the voyage from England to India had forced lone men to spend many years away from their English families, when they were more dependent on the local people for social inter-course, when it was not unknown for an Englishman to establish a long-term liaison with a local woman. It was also an era when the atmosphere of eighteenth-century liberalism prevailed, and ideas and attitudes were imported into India which were to pose serious challenges to many tenets of the Hindu faith. It was these challenges which sparked off the train of intellectual, social and religious speculation and activity that constituted the Indian Renaissance, a movement which was to influence much of Indian thinking and tactics during the years of colonial rule.

India in the nineteenth century has been described as a country 'afflicted with the diseases of discord, disunity, lethargy, infidelity, scepticism, irreligion and false religion, pedantism, slavishness, introversion, rigidity and man's inhumanity to man'.[7] This is perhaps an over-harsh judgement, but there is little doubt that many social practices then accepted in India as an integral part of Hindu mores – such as child marriage, *sati* and rigid caste discrimination – were inimical to humanitarian values and politi-cal progressiveness. It was the recognition of the fact that Hindu-ism was not simply a religion but a social philosophy, pervading the lives of the majority of Indian peoples, which led those men concerned with social reform to interest themselves also in the reinterpretation of ancient Hindu texts.

Rammohun Roy, widely acknowledged as the father of the Indian Renaissance, wrote to a friend: 'the present system of religion adhered to by the Hindus is not well calculated to promote their political interests ... It is, I think, necessary that some changes should take place in their religion at least for the sake of their political advantage and social comfort.'[8]

Born in 1771 to a Brahmin family, Roy possessed the classical attributes of the renaissance man – a questioning mind, a lively intellect, catholic tastes, the courage for innovation and the command of several languages. Moreover, he had considerable financial resources, an undeniable asset for those who would bring about reform. Roy's most significant contribution in the socio-religious realm was the founding of the Brahmo Sabha, a movement which advocated a purified form of Hinduism, based on the Vedas and the Upanisads, theistic but rejecting idolatry, incorporating some of the ethics of the Christian West.

Rammohun Roy set the tone for the Indian Renaissance, which was essentially a search for ways and means of revitalizing the classical heritage of India, so that it could face the onslaught of new and alien forces without losing its individual character or failing to fulfil the demands of a rapidly changing society. Among the men who followed in the wake of Roy to make the renaissance a strong, influential movement spanning the whole of the nineteenth century and spilling into the twentieth were Keshub Chunder Sen, Swami Dayananda, I. C. Vidyasagar, M. C. Ranade, G. K. Gokhale, Sri Ramakrishna and his chief disciple Swami Vivekananda, Aurobindo Ghosh, Bankimchandra Chatterji and, of course, Rabindranath Tagore. For many of these thinkers it was important that the social, religious and political aspects of reform should move together. Some put greater emphasis on one aspect, some on another, while others preferred a balance between all three. But, despite the differences in approach as well as tactics, the underlying purpose tended to be the same: to bring India into harmonious step with modern developments without losing her identity.

While Indian intellectuals were caught up in accelerating attempts to master, absorb and adapt ideas imported from the

West to meet the needs of their own country, the Burmese were still steeped in their traditional ways, lulled into a false sense of security by the military successes of the Konbaung dynasty founded by Alaungpaya. The second half of the eighteenth century and the greater part of the nineteenth century were a period when Burmese literature flourished, traditional forms were elaborated and polished and contemporary imports were adapted into the classical mould. The booty brought back from the victorious campaign against Thailand in 1769 had included works of drama, which introduced a genre that was to gain rapid popularity first among the literati centred on the royal court and later among the Burmese people in general. King Bodawpaya, who came to the throne in 1781, collected Sanskrit texts from India. These imports from India and Thailand were not novel developments but simply the most recent in a traditional process which had used elements from neighbouring cultures to diversify and enrich the Burmese civilization. Thus the spirit of eighteenth-century social liberalism and intellectual scepticism, which had triggered off the renaissance in India, passed by Burma, still proudly attached to her traditions.

An important factor in directing Indian thinkers towards their Hindu heritage had been the work of orientalists such as William Jones, founder of the Asiatic Society of Bengal, and Max Mueller. Both of them placed the study of ancient Sanskrit texts in the domain of high scholarship. Their translations also made it possible for many Indians who had not learnt Sanskrit to become acquainted with their own classical heritage.

In Burma, there had been no similar impulse on the part of the early British administrators to attribute scholastic importance to classical works or even to consider them worthy of great notice. Rangoon College, founded in 1873 as an affiliated body of Calcutta University, did not include Burmese in its curriculum. Pali was taught in the college, but the bulk of Pali literature of Burma belonged to the Buddhist canon which had originated in India. In any case, the greater part of traditional religious scholarship in Burma suffered from the same defects that have been attributed to traditional Indian scholarship:

The field of intellectual enquiry was extremely limited. Since growing up in the ancestors' shadow was the desideratum, a scholar, however eminent, could never think in terms of originality of thinking or of questioning the validity of existing systems or texts. A scholar's sole intellectual preoccupation was exposition and elaboration of those texts or clarification of existing commentaries, which, in the words of an eminent intellectual of today, 'not infrequently became exegesis of exegesis'.[9]

The British conquest of Lower Burma did not provide any external stimulus to encourage the Burmese to review their literary heritage in a new perspective. The king at Mandalay continued to provide patronage for traditional learning, and there was no feeling of immediate threat to the established order. Even after the development of the rice trade in the 1830s had begun to attract large numbers of immigrants from monarchical Burma into British territory,[10] the Burmese felt they could afford to ignore the presence of an alien power.

A prime reason for Burmese complacency was the absence from their society of the crippling inhibitions and harmful practices of Hinduism that had driven some Indians like the 'beer-and-beef' radicals of Hindu College in Calcutta to a total rejection of their religious heritage. The same practices had aroused in others the urge to pursue the path of reform and revitalization of old traditions. Burmese society, imbued with the spirit of Buddhism which 'enjoined nothing at which the reason jibs',[11] was remarkably free from social injustices. It had no rigid caste or class stratification. Women enjoyed rights and privileges which a Victorian lady might well have envied. The practice of the ubiquitous monastery providing at least a basic education for local children had resulted in a high percentage of literacy. There existed alongside the teachings of Buddhism a fund of superstitious and supernatural lore, some of which dated back to the pre-Buddhist era. However, these rarely entailed sinister taboos or practices. In fact, the social life of village Burma – and Burma was fundamentally a land of villages owing allegiance to the king, who, remote in his distant capital, left them to the jurisdiction of a governor or to their own ministration – presented such an idyllic picture that Fielding Hall, an early British administrator, was moved to write:

> In Burma it was only the supreme government, the high officials, that were very bad. It was only the management of state affairs that was feeble and corrupt; all the rest was very good. The land laws, the self-government, the social condition of the people were admirable. It was so good that the rotten central government made little difference to the people, and it would probably have lasted for a long while if not attacked from the outside.[12]

Tilak, who paid a visit to Burma in 1899, was also struck by the social order of Burma, but it only helped to strengthen his view that political action was separate from and more important than social reform:

> All the reforms like absence of caste division, freedom of religion, education of women, late marriages, widow re-marriage, a system of divorce, on which some good people of India are in the habit of harping *ad nauseam* as constituting a condition precedent to the introduction of political reforms in India, had already been in actual practice in the province of Burma. But there was not evident among the Burmese a feeling for their religion, their country or their trade to a degree expected of them. Therefore we can conclude that there is no inherent connection between social reform and national regeneration. Some European writers have sought to advise us to bring about social reform as a preparation for political reform. But it is human nature that this piece of precept should stand suspect till we see with our own eyes what kind of political reform is given to Burma which is socially in a position to deserve it.[13]

Tilak's remark that the Burmese did not have strong feelings for their religion and country can only be explained by the fact that his stay in Burma was so brief. (Later he was sent to prison in Burma for six years, but as he was confined in Mandalay gaol with only the company of an Indian cell mate and European prison officers he never really got to know either Burma or the Burmese.) It is true, however, that the Burmese had little feeling for trade, which had not played a vital part in their traditional economy. That lack was a prime reason for the hold which immigrant groups were to get on commercial interests in the country.

While it could be pointed out that social reform, though not a sufficient cause, might well be a necessary condition for 'national regeneration', Burma certainly presents a situation which demonstrates that a sound social system can go hand in hand with political immaturity. In fact, it could be argued that, because the social system placed no inordinate burden on the lives of the people, it made them more tolerant of the deficiencies of government. The Burmese experience of monarchical administration had bred in them a tendency to live their own lives and keep away from the central administration as far as possible. Arthur Phayre, the Chief Commissioner of British Burma, wrote to the Home Department of the Government of India in 1884:

> The people of British Burma as yet know very little of the British government except as a Police, a Revenue, and a judicial power. They know indeed that the British government has established a milder and a more efficient government than existed before the conquest of the country. But from the comparatively few Europeans who speak the language and from the utter absence of Europeans from the interior of the country, the masses of the agricultural population know nothing of the desire of the British Government to educate and to raise them in the scale of civilization. How is the idea to be imparted to them? How are they to be made aware of the fact? ... I reply then that the only effective way to impress this fact upon them is to establish

one or more Central Schools in each district, which shall be so situated as to be under effective control, that is at the head-quarter station or where a European Officer resides. In time such Schools will spread knowledge and the desire for increased knowledge. They will testify to the people the wish of the British Government that its subjects should be taught. I would not establish these Schools all at once in the district, but gradually as opportunity offered ... The general plan of instruction would be Anglo-Vernacular, that is, English to be more or less the medium of instruction, but Burmese not to be altogether neglected. As the desire to learn English is prominent at the seaport towns, and at various other places, I leave the degree and extent to which the English language is to be taught to be settled by local requirements ...

I have already stated the support that has been given to Village Schools supported by Missionaries. Besides those, as already noted, there are no such schools in the country except the Buddhist Monasteries. I think in time we may be able to improve the education given in those institutions. I know of no other feasible plan for imparting sound education to the agricultural population in the interior.[14]

The above has been quoted at some length not only because it is one of the most cogent expressions of British views on education in Burma, but also because it offers an interesting comparison with the sentiments, embodied in Macaulay's much better-known Minute of 1835, which defended the views of those members of the Committee of Public Instruction of India who were in favour of an educational system dependent on English for higher learning:

We have to educate a people who cannot at present be educated by means of their mother-tongue. We must teach them some foreign language. The claims of our own language it is hardly necessary to recapitulate. It stands pre-eminent even among the languages of the West ... In

India, English is the language spoken by the ruling class. It is spoken by the higher class of natives at the seats of government . . . Whether we look at the intrinsic value of the literature or at the particular situation of this country, we shall see the strongest reason to think that, of all foreign tongues, the English tongue is that which would be most useful to our native subjects . . .

The languages of Western Europe civilised Russia. I cannot doubt that they will do for the Hindoo what they have done for the Tartar . . .

I feel . . . that it is impossible for us, with our means, to attempt to educate the body of the people. We must at present do our best to form a class who may be interpreters between us and the millions whom we govern – a class of persons Indian in blood and colour but English in tastes, in opinions, in morals and in intellect. To that class we may leave it to refine the vernacular dialects of the country, to enrich those dialects with terms of science borrowed from the Western nomenclature, and to render them by degrees fit vehicles for conveying knowledge to the great mass of the population.[13]

It can be seen that Phayre's views on education are at once more modest and more paternalistic. He wanted the Burmese to know that the British government cared for them, that it wished to 'raise them in the scale of civilization'. Things were to be taken slowly; the existing system of monastic education was to be disturbed as little as possible. There was a recognition of the desire for learning English in the seaport towns, where there were large numbers of immigrants and few Burmese. But, still, Burmese was not to be neglected. Phayre sees the establishment of schools as a means for imparting 'sound education'.

The tone of Macaulay's Minute is altogether more grandiose, but at the same time more utilitarian; he also thought in terms of civilizing the natives, but the immediate need was to create a class of people who could help the British to rule India. The emphasis on the greatness of the English language is understandable in the context; but it reflects not only the controversy over the relative merits of English and Sanskrit as mediums of higher learning but also the important position English had acquired in nineteenth-century India. It could already be looked upon as the language of the ruling class, the higher classes. More than a decade before Macaulay composed his Minute, Rammohun Roy had written to Lord Amherst arguing against oriental education: 'The Sanskrit language, so difficult that almost a lifetime is necessary for its acquisition, is well known to have been for ages a lamentable check to the diffusion of knowledge.'[16] Roy himself had been educated in Sanskrit as well as Arabic and Persian; so his advocacy of occidental learning was, therefore, very much a matter of conviction. He had come to English only in his adult life, probably for practical reasons, and he quickly saw that it was the language which would open the doors of intellectual and technical advancement to Indians. Vidyasagar a generation later was another able Sanskrit scholar who also accepted the importance of English in the educational scheme, but as a balancing factor to classical oriental studies and as an aid to the development of the vernacular: 'An elegant, expressive and idiomatic Bengali style required Sanskrit scholars to be well versed in English, language and literature. Mere English scholars were incapable of expressing their ideas in idiomatic and elegant Bengali.'[17] Vidyasagar was a pioneer in recognizing the importance of education in the vernacular, and his efforts in that direction have made him known as the father of modern Bengali prose. He might well be said to have been carrying out Macaulay's injunction to make vernacular languages fit vehicles for spreading popular education.

Phayre acknowledged the central role which the vernacular would have to play in any educational scheme for Burma. In this he could have been influenced by the Education Despatch of 1854, which had admitted the need to encourage vernacular learning in India. However, it is more likely that he recognized that there already existed in Burma a language in which widespread education could be achieved. Burma like India is a land of many racial groups speaking many languages and dialects, but only Burmese could be claimed to have a 'national' character, and no other language could boast quite so extensive a body of literature. As mentioned earlier, even when Shan monarchs had held sway in the heartland, Burmese had remained the dominant language. The territories Phayre was administering in 1864 were the homelands of the Mons and the Arakanese, but the vernacular which he proposed was Burmese. In a Memorandum on Vernacular Education for British Burma dated 1865, he states:

> The Burmese language is the mother tongue of three-fourths of the inhabitants of British Burma. The first plan, therefore, for diffusing Vernacular education among the people must proceed upon the basis of using that language as the medium of instruction. Hereafter the language of other peoples may be used for the same purposes as regards those races.[18]

It should be mentioned here that the Arakanese belong to the larger family of Tibeto-Burmans, and that their language might be defined as an archaic form of Burmese. However, the Mons belong to the Khmer racial group, and their language is distinct from that of the Burmese, although there has been a fair amount of interchange in the course of history. The dominant position of the Burmese language in the south was a legacy of recurrent conquests, in particular of the period when the monarchs of the Taungu dynasty had made Pegu their capital for close on a century.[19]

Traditionally, the Buddhist monasteries had been the schools of the Burmese people – the word for 'school' is *kyaung*, which originally meant simply 'monastery', and to this day the same name continues to be applied to both institutions – so that the link between religion and education was very strong. The texts used were often in the form of verse, Burmese and Pali, religious or ethical in content. Many of the children would leave school after acquiring the rudiments of reading and writing, which some might lose in later life through lack of practice. The brighter ones would stay on to acquire further learning, and it was not unusual for some of the brightest to become monks themselves. All

Burmese boys would join the religious order at least once in their lives, usually as a novice in their early teens. In traditional village Burma, it often happened that some would choose to remain in the monkhood for years, if not for life. Little stigma attached to a man who returned to the secular world, and those who had spent long years in a monastery mastering the Pali texts and widening their knowledge of classical literature would be lauded and admired.

Traditional Burmese education did not encourage speculation. This was largely due to the view, so universally accepted that it appears to be part of the racial psyche of the Burmese, that Buddhism represents the perfected philosophy. It therefore follows that there was no need either to try to develop it further or to consider other philosophies. As a result, in spite of the essential tolerance of Buddhist teachings, religion in Burma was monolithic. It had broad but inflexible boundaries. Theological disputes, which were not numerous, centred on the interpretation of the monastic code, the *vinaya*; so the little sectarianism that did exist was confined to the monkhood. The lay people were only affected to the extent that they might prefer to worship at some monasteries rather than at others. Such preferences would in no way lessen the respect given to all monks as the vehicles by which the teachings of the Buddha are disseminated.

In India, besides the presence of a large minority of Muslims, Hinduism presented a far more diversified picture than Buddhism in Burma. The deities are so many, the forms of worship so various and the complex philosophies so compounded by the interpretations of orthodox scholars and the mysticism of saints. One is forced to take refuge behind the excuse that 'Hindu' was originally a geographical term referring to the people who lived in the region of the Indus and could not possibly be defined. The only other alternative would be to resign oneself to at least half a lifetime of intensive research on the subject. Fortunately, for the purpose of this study the latter drastic course is not necessary. It needs only to be pointed out that religious speculation could be nothing alien to a country that has produced the Buddha, Vardharmana Mahavira, Nagarjuna, Kabir and Ramakrishna

Paramhamsa, to name but the best known of the spiritual figures. The Hindu world with all its rigid taboos was strangely flexible. It was in part this heritage of flexibility which enabled the Indian Renaissance thinkers to meet the challenge of British rule in intellectual and philosophical terms.

Nirad C. Chaudhuri, perhaps the only true son of the Bengali Renaissance alive today, in writing of intellectuals in India describes Hindu reaction to the changes brought about by the impact of western governance, ideas and culture as the search for answers to the following questions:

(1) What were the shortcomings of their own institutions and outlooks and how were they to be removed?
(2) How was national self-respect and confidence to be revived?
(3) In what manner were the incoming and irresistible elements of western culture to be absorbed and combined with their own traditions?
(4) What attitude was to be adopted towards British rule and since in the ultimate analysis the only aim could be political independence how was it to be secured?[20]

It would not be far wrong to say that questions (2) and (4) were the only ones which first occurred to the Burmese as they faced the *fait accompli* of foreign domination. Question (1) would have been an absurdity for them. Like Fielding Hall they saw their social system as 'very good', and so it was to a large extent. That the monarchical government could be very bad also they acknowledged. After all, did not the five enemies from whom every Burmese prays he might be protected include the *min* or ruler?[21] That one system had, in fact, produced the other was largely ignored. The shock of the fall of Mandalay had moved some Burmese to rail against their own impotence and foibles, but there was no serious attempt to analyse the causes of the deficiencies.

If question (1) was patently absurd, question (3) was at the least baffling; why should the Burmese people absorb elements of western culture, and what was it all about anyway? Their experience of 'foreign rule' – and that under the Shans several centuries back – had only taught them that it was the conquerors who were eager to acquire the Burmese culture. Therefore, the Burmese felt no particular urge to understand their colonial rulers. This indifference was also encouraged by British attitudes. While the Englishman tended to see the Hindus as 'serious', 'mysterious', 'deep', 'introverted', and so on, he usually saw the Burmese as 'gay', 'open', 'careless', 'childlike', not a people who needed deep philosophical interpretation. The Burmese returned the compliment by assuming that there was not much that they needed to know about the Englishman beyond the necessities of unavoidable intercourse between the ruler and the ruled. How different it was from India, with the earnest, almost obsessive desire for comprehension at the intellectual level that was producing a string of scholars and philosophers in the western mould! It was true that such Indians constituted only a tiny section of the population, but their impact was strong on the upper classes; and they set the tone for those who would be leaders in the independence movements that were to gather momentum in the twentieth century.

II

As colonial rule took on a more settled aspect in Burma, some of the complacency wore off. The Burmese, no less than the other Asian and African peoples of the colonial world, had to recognize that those who wished to get on in the ranks of the British Empire had to learn English and acquire the rudiments of a western-type education. Lower Burma was naturally ahead of Upper Burma in the process of modernization, and many Arakanese numbered among the first people of Burma to be educated under the colonial system. It is interesting to speculate whether the cultural and at times political links which Arakan had forged with Bengal throughout much of her history had created in her people a more receptive attitude to foreign influences. The Mons, who had come under British rule at the same time as the Arakanese, do not seem to have produced as many English-educated people at quite the same speed. Another important ethnic group in Lower Burma, the Karens, were also quick to respond to the missionary activities which proliferated under British rule. With the acquisition of Christianity many of them received missionary education and began to emerge as a modern educated class.

Besides the indigenous peoples, the rapidly increasing immigrant groups were in the forefront of those in the market for modern education. British policy gave active encouragement to large-scale immigration of Chinese and Indians who could undertake those commercial and professional functions which could not be discharged by the predominantly agriculture-oriented people of Burma. Moreover, the increasing acreage of land brought under cultivation gave rise to a need for indentured labour which was supplied by India. Thus it was that Burma found herself not only conquered by the British but also threatened by the overwhelming presence of Indians and Chinese who began to play key roles in the development of the economy. This unchecked influx of foreigners was a major cause of the disintegration of traditional society. Another disruptive factor was the all-pervasive efficiency of an administration that was implementing changes in the time-honoured systems of social custom and usage. The Burmese could no longer afford to be complacent; they had to recognize the need for defensive action. Moreover, they had to decide if the weapons to be used should be traditional or modern.

The Burmese monarchs thought of their capital as the 'centre of the universe'. It was to this centre that men of learning and ambition came if they desired advancement or fame. Thus, the capital was the cultural stronghold as well as the source of possible honours and material rewards. After the only royal couple had been removed from Mandalay a period of cultural hiatus followed. Burmese learning attracted no official patronage, and English became the language which laid the path to new opportunities created by the colonial government. And those opportunities were not within easy grasp of the Burmese, who had to compete with the Indians and the Chinese – peoples so much more experienced in dealing with westerners and their institutions. While Upper Burma remained under Burmese rule, the danger of being outstripped by others in the land where they had always maintained ascendancy did not present itself to the Burmese. Phayre wrote in the Memorandum of 1865 which has already been mentioned: 'The Burmese people must be taught to feel that unless they have their children educated both in sound knowledge, and in a more systematic manner than at present prevails, they will assuredly be surpassed by other races in the country.'[22]

The speed with which Burma changed after the arrival of the British was alarming. Moulmein in Tenessarim and Akyab in Arakan had sprung up as urban centres in a matter of years, bustling with such cosmopolitan and commercial activity as the Burmese could never have imagined. When Rangoon became one of the capital cities of British India, that city, too, rapidly assumed a hybrid character. Already in the nineteenth century, it had begun to be described as a city of Indians rather than Burmese, and by the time of the visit of the Prince and Princess of Wales (later George V and Queen Mary) in 1906, the Special Correspondent of the London *Times* was to write:

> In this modern city where Europeans and Burmese, Hindus and Chinese jostle one another in a kaleidoscopic confusion of types and races, where the Burmese population has in fact been completely outnumbered by immigrants from Southern India and Bengal, where the ubiquitous Chinese asserts his superiority as a trader scarcely less irresistibly than the European his superiority as a ruler of men . . . it is difficult at first sight to tell which is the really preponderating element. But there is one monument essentially Burmese that still dominates Rangoon, that still embodies the soul of a nation . . . the Shaw Dagon pagoda.[23]

The observation of the *Times* correspondent was an astute one which recognized the importance of Buddhism and Buddhist symbols in the lives of the Burmese people. As the twentieth century progressed and the breakdown of traditional society throughout the country accelerated, it was in the realm of religion that the first alarm bells began to be heard. Among those who had led insurrections against the British after the fall of Mandalay, there had been an appreciable number who had exchanged the monastery for the battlefield. Under the Burmese kings a *thathana-baing* (*sangharaja*), usually the abbot of a monastery patronized by the monarch, would be appointed to ensure ecclesiastical discipline throughout the kingdom. When Lower Burma fell to the British, the colonial authorities refused to recognize the authority of the *thathanabaing* in their territories, which was the expression of a narrow and short-sighted policy. The removal of control from above resulted in the deterioration of ecclesiastical discipline, which, combined with fears that Buddhism would wither under rulers of an alien creed, would make the clergy a rallying point for anti-British movements of the early twentieth century. After the annexation of Upper Burma, Burmese appeals to the British for official support to the incumbent *thathanabaing* were rejected, and the office was allowed to lapse with his death in 1895. It was very likely in an effort to respond to an increasingly urgent need for cohesion and a sense of direction that the Buddha Sasana Noggaha Association was founded at Mandalay in 1897 for the preservation and promotion of the Buddhist religion. But the association remained limited in scope, and it was only in the next decade that organizations of national character and compass were to appear in Burma.

It has often been remarked that, while Indian nationalism was essentially a product of British rule, there had always existed a traditional Burmese nationalism arising from Burma's cultural homogeneity. Buddhism obviously played a large part in creating this homogeneity, but it could not be said to have supplied ideas to support nationalism; rather it provided an essential component of the self-concept which enabled the Burmese to see themselves as different from foreigners.[24] And foreigners under the colonial administration were not just the English but also the Indians and the Chinese. Thus, the feeling that grew among the Burmese was not the intense racial antagonism which developed in India but a more diffused xenophobia fed by a well-justified apprehension that their very existence as a distinct people would be jeopardized if the course of colonial rule was allowed to run unchecked. The threat to their racial survival came not so much from the British as from the Indians and Chinese who were the more immediate targets of twentieth-century nationalism. Not only did these immigrants acquire a stranglehold on the Burmese economy, they also set up homes with Burmese women, striking at the very roots of Burmese manhood and racial purity.

As nationalism in Burma was fundamentally a part of the traditional ethos, nationalistic movements also sprang from Burmese sources, even though they were inevitably influenced by western ideas and institutions. The Indian National Congress owed its birth to an Englishman, and English people such as Annie Besant were involved in the political movements of Indian nationalists. Such British involvement in Burmese independence politics did not take place and very likely could not have taken place given the conditions that prevailed. In spite of the open, laughing face that the Burmese presented to the world, the ingrained, if inarticulate, conviction of their own nationhood prevented them from truly admitting those they saw as 'foreign' into their inner sanctums. Alien concepts had to be redefined in Burmese terms before they could be accepted. In a strange way the Burmese seemed to value their cultural integrity almost more than their ethnic identity. They could often feel greater affinity for a foreigner who had adopted Buddhism and Burmese ways of living than for a Burmese who had embraced an alien creed. In one sense, this cultural chauvinism made for a closed mind which adjusted but slowly and painfully to the changing times. In another sense, the attitude was surprisingly modern in its insistence that there had to be an intellectual conviction that new ideas fitted into the basic cultural scheme before they could be assimilated. Because the Burmese had adopted social and religious practices which minimized the need for intellectual activity, this conviction could not come easily.

Language and ideas are intimately connected. The early acceptance of English as the language of the day by the Hindus had given them the edge over their erstwhile Muslim rulers in the race for progress and privilege in British India. The Hindus were able to forge ahead in both the political and the intellectual fields. A crop of lofty personalities sprang up who, reversing Macaulay's conception of the role of the educated Indian, made known to the West the religious and political aspirations of India.[25] Swami Vivekananda, Sri Aurobindo, Tagore, Gandhi, Radhakrishnan, Nehru these men were able to use the English language to make their views known to the world. Because they could handle the western intellectual idiom so masterfully, the world regarded those views as worthy of serious consideration.

The people of India accepted that their leadership came from the ranks of the western educated whom they admired and emulated. *Swadeshi* ideals, which were at least equally based on economic as on cultural considerations, may have put Indian nationalist leaders into homespun, but it was accepted that they would work, write and even dream, as Nehru was popularly believed to do, in English. This was, of course, largely due to the lack of a truly national language in India, but the very acceptance of the necessity of English in their political and intellectual life coloured the outlook of the educated Indian. Nirad C. Chaudhuri puts it cogently:

> The linguistic basis of modern Indian culture, which is made up of a combination of English, a denatured written Vernacular, and a mixed colloquial language, is the first proof of the essentially foreign character of modern Indian culture. The second proof is to be found in the almost exclusively exotic forms of modern Indian literature, art, thought, and moral and spiritual activity. Literary expression in prose is itself a creation of British rule in India.[26]

The same writer gives an idea of the eclectic intellectual tradition inspired by the renaissance in Bengal. In his father's modest house in a small town of East Bengal at the opening decade of the twentieth century, there were such books as the Holy Bible in Bengali, Milton's poetical works, Cunninghams's *History of the*

Sikhs, Burke's speeches on the impeachment of Warren Hastings, some plays of Shakespeare, novels of Bankimchandra Chatterji and volumes of the poems of Michael Madhusudan Dutt.[27] Among the names which belong to Chaudhuri's 'proto-memoric age' were, in addition to those already mentioned, Queen Victoria and Prince Albert (hardly avoidable), Napoleon, Raphael, Wellington, Gladstone, Martin Luther, Julius Caesar and Osman Pasha. These were quickly followed by others which included Fox, Pitt, Mirabeau, Robespierre and Danton. Homer, too, was an early acquaintance alongside the *Ramayana* and the *Mahabharata*.[28]

Bankimchandra Chatterji, whom Nirad C. Chaudhuri regards as one of the most powerful intellects produced by India,[29] has left an interesting picture of the 'Bengali gentleman' – essentially a person of wide erudition in both western and Indian literature, with a cultivated taste in the fine arts.[30] No little wonder it was said that the 'genuine Indo-Anglian synthesis' was to be found in Calcutta before the war.[31]

Bengal was the first British province in India, and Calcutta remained the capital of the Raj for the greater part of colonial rule. It was, therefore, natural that Bengalis should feature in large numbers among modern educated Indians. But there were others from different parts of India who, although they may not have felt as intense a passion for the renaissance ideal as the Bengalis, were remarkably familiar with western learning. Ranade, Gokhale and Tilak came from Maharashtra; Radha-krishnan was a south Indian from the Madras area; Jawaharlal Nehru, scion of a Kashmiri Brahmin family settled in Allahabad, presents the classical picture of a sophisticated, Anglicized Indian. Taught by English tutors at home before going to Harrow and Cambridge, he draws on the words of Euripides, Aeschylus and Yeats to express his thoughts and yearnings.[32] The *Bhagavad Gita* appealed to his questing mind as a 'poem of crisis, of political and social crisis and, even more so, of crisis in the spirit of man'.[33] But he had only read it, as he had read other Sanskrit classics, in the English translation.

Nirad C. Chaudhuri holds that few Indian intellectuals were

perfectly integrated in their mental life, a circumstance which prevented them from achieving a truly intellectual outlook and which returned them to traditionalism and orthodoxy in their later years.[34] Nehru was obviously one of the small minority, a man so thoroughly intellectual in his approach to life that he learnt to accept his own anomalous cultural identity with equanimity. He did not, like Sri Aurobindo, feel the need to balance his western education with a thorough investigation of Hindu thought, although he studied it from a historical perspective in his desire to understand India. He, too, was in the tradition of the renaissance which searched for a synthesis of traditional and western ideas that could help in the struggle to raise India out of the morass of irrational practices and mental inertia into which she had sunk by the end of the Middle Ages. He denounces as a 'kind of art for art's sake'[35] the study of the past which is not linked to the present and which does not derive from it the urge to action. For him the ideal was action which was not divorced from thought but which flowed from it in a continuous sequence.[36]

The link between ideas and action was a theme which featured large in the life of Mahatma Gandhi. It is not easy to decide to what extent, if at all, concepts of the West influenced him in his youth. He came from a traditional family in Gujarat, and had no contacts with westerners in his early years. However, the event which he regarded as a tragedy of his childhood, the secret eating of meat, was caused chiefly by his notion that it was meat-eating which had made the English powerful. Later, as a young man not quite twenty, he persuaded his reluctant and none-too-affluent family to send him to England to train as a barrister. Gandhi, who could be so frank about some matters, was reticent about the sentiments which had spurred him on to this venture. He simply wrote in his autobiography that he jumped at the chance to get away from the difficult studies at his college, when a family friend suggested that he should go to study in England. Reaching England, he became an 'aspirant after being an English gentleman' for about three months, then turned into a serious student and gradually pared his expenses down to the bare necessities.

Gandhi had promised his mother that he would not touch meat in England, an undertaking which caused him some hardship until he discovered a vegetarian restaurant. At the same time he discovered books on vegetarianism. These made him a vegetarian by choice, when previously he had felt bound by his vow and had looked forward to becoming a meat eater 'freely and openly some day'.[37] It was an early personal experience of ideas as an aid to the better working of action. Gandhi was of a practical turn of mind that looked for ideas to suit the needs of situations. In spite of his deeply ingrained Hinduism, Gandhi's intellectual flexibility made him accept those elements of western thought which fitted into the ethical and social scheme he considered desirable.

Synthesis, of East and West, of theory and practice, constituted the vital element in the tradition initiated by the renaissance in India. The lack of a similar tradition in Burma resulted in a gulf between the earlier educated élite and the mainstream of Burmese aspirations. The designation of Rangoon, away from the traditional stronghold of the Burmese, as the capital divorced the political from the cultural centre. At the time King Thibaw and his family were taken away from Mandalay, a large number of Burmese manuscripts from the palace were destroyed in the general looting and vandalism initiated by the British troops. A stop was put to this wanton destruction only when a week had passed. The remaining manuscripts which were then collected made over forty bullock-cart loads. This substantial collection was taken eight years later to Rangoon to be housed in the Government Secretariat. These manuscripts were the source on which a Burmese scholar, U Tin, drew for a history of the Konbaung dynasty.[38] The resulting work was among the first literary stirrings that developed in the early twentieth century after the initial quiescence brought about by the annexation of Upper Burma.

The first Burmese printed books had been produced by the Vatican press in Rome in the last quarter of the eighteenth century. At the beginning of the nineteenth century, the Serampore missionaries acquired a typeface for the Burmese script. Some of these typefaces and a printing press were sent to a Baptist missionary in Burma, Adoniram Judson, in 1816. But the press was not put to much use for some time, and Burmese books continued to be printed in Calcutta until the British annexation of Tenessarim. The first Burmese books printed in Burma were biblical tracts produced by the missionary press in Moulmein, which moved to Rangoon after the second Anglo-Burmese War. The first press in the still independent Burmese kingdom was set up by King Mindon in the north garden of the royal palace in Mandalay (c. 1868). A few years later, the *Mandalay Gazette*, a Burmese newspaper under the proprietorship of the king, began to be issued four times a month. Newspapers had already appeared in British Burma, starting with the *Maulmain Chronicle* of 1836. However, the majority of them were in English, chiefly aimed at the foreign community. The Burmese publications were the *Religious Herald*, a monthly Christian missionary paper, issued from Moulmein in 1841, the *Burmah Herald* of Rangoon which started in 1871 and the *Burmah Gazette*, also started in 1871.

The simultaneous existence of British Burma and the independent Burmese kingdom made the development of the press in Burma somewhat different from what took place in India. The first Indian newspaper was the *Bengal Gazette* or the *Calcutta General Advertiser*, brought out by an Englishman, James Hickey, in 1785. The venture was not welcomed by many Bengal officials, and their fears were confirmed some months later when Hickey's *Gazette* started attacking the government of Warren Hastings, mainly, it appeared, because the latter had given his approbation to another newspaper, the *Indian Gazette*. Thus, the notion of newspapers which either supported or opposed the government was introduced by Englishmen themselves almost at the very inception of the press in India. The freedom of the press was soon to become an issue under the governor-generalship of the Marquess of Wellesley (1798–1805), who established rigid regulations which were to control the activities of the newspapers for many years.

The *Maulmain Chronicle* in Burma had also been started by an

Englishman, but he happened to be the Chief Commissioner of Tenasserim; so it was very much in the nature of a government publication. Other newspapers which followed within the next ten years included the *Maulmain Advertiser*, sponsored by the East India Company, and Christian missionaries' publications. News items in the *Burmah Herald* were written by its English editor, J. A. Haney, and translated with the help of an able Burmese scholar.[39] This newspaper proved to be very popular with the common people as well as with the king in Mandalay, and it set the tone for many Burmese newspapers that were to follow. King Mindon is even said to have invited Haney to come to Mandalay to start a newspaper. The Englishman apparently refused on the grounds that an editor who was in the habit of writing the truth would in Mandalay be like the Persian vizier who had to feel his head every morning to make sure it was still on his shoulders.[40]

When King Mindon set up the *Mandalay Gazette* in 1874, eleven official aims of the newspaper press were recorded. These indicated a desire to make Burma internationally known so that foreigners and foreign trade might be attracted to the kingdom; to refute adverse propaganda about the Burmese kingdom that might be circulated by the European, Indian and Rangoon press; to give incessant information on the affairs of the kingdom to the official class so that they might strive for its progress; to publish foreign works at a low cost with the aim of disseminating knowledge among the people and thus helping them to progress.[41] Such brave hopes read a little sadly in retrospect. Mindon was seen as a good king because he was pious and there was peace during his reign. To some extent he tried to keep up with modern developments; but he had neither the mental equipment, nor perhaps the inclination, to implement political and administrative reforms which would have widened the power base of the kingdom, ensured an ordered succession and perhaps prevented the annexation of Upper Burma. When he died, the weak Thibaw ascended the throne through the machinations of his mother-in-law, although there were several royal princes with stronger claims. There followed seven years of misrule and bloodshed until the third Anglo-Burmese War brought the Burmese monarchy to an end.

The worst period of Thibaw's reign coincided with the golden age of colonial rule. Rapid economic progress and administrative order were the hallmarks of British Burma. But the social system broke down just as rapidly, so the Burmese could still feel that life was better in the land of their monarch. In addition, racial pride and loyalty demanded that they should not compare the administration of the Burmese kingdom unfavourably with that of the foreign government. The press, which might have been a factor in promoting educated criticism, also represented the polarization between king and colonial power. When the former was finally removed, spontaneous rebellions flared up all over Upper Burma. These were in part a demonstration of genuine patriotism and in part a result of the tradition that an empty throne was 'up for grabs'. The turbulent years of the 'pacification of Burma', the series of British military campaigns undertaken to stamp out the insurrections, had an untoward effect on the Burmese psyche, confusing, fissive. The numerous uprisings meant disorder, insecurity and disruption, and gave little promise of a future government that would be any better than those of the past. It was not in the tradition of aspirants after the Burmese throne to see their actions in terms of the betterment of the system; it was simply a question of ensuring that a Burmese sat in the seat of supreme power. And because of their patriotism, the people accepted this essentially irresponsible view of government as part of the traditional order. An early British administrator remarked that

> It is probable that most of the best men of the country were against us. It is certain, I think, that of those who openly joined us and accompanied us in our expedition (against the Burmese insurrections), very, very few were other than men who had some private grudge to avenge or some purpose to gain by opposing their own people.[42]

Burmese patriotism was homogeneously behind the monarchy, unlike the situation which had accrued in India where many Hindus felt no obligation to show loyalty to the Mughal emperor. Once the insurrections in Upper Burma had been stamped out, the people settled down to their age-old habits of living their lives apart from the government. But it gradually dawned upon them that this was no longer possible. The administrative tentacles of the colonial system reached out to the villages, bringing irreversible changes. The need for adjusting their traditional perspectives slowly percolated down to the level of the ordinary man.

It has already been mentioned that, under the Burmese monarchs, opportunities for advancement could only be found in the royal capital. With the British annexation of Lower Burma, Rangoon had developed as a rival centre, but the position of Mandalay as the stronghold of Burmese culture remained unchallenged. However, the deposition of King Thibaw put an end to royal patronage of the arts and literature and shifted the balance of power decisively in favour of Rangoon, which soon began to attract ambitious and able people. The development of the railways together with road and river transport contributed to the crescendo of southward migration.

Rangoon, more than anywhere else in the country, offered opportunities for acquiring an English-based education. But because it was a city of large immigrant communities, because it was removed from the cultural heartland of Burma and because the British government adopted a dismissive attitude towards traditional learning, the climate in which a synthesis of modern education and classical Burmese scholarship could be fostered did not emerge. The culture that had filtered down from Upper Burma was of a popular character. Dramatic performances had become a much loved form of entertainment and many well-known troupes from Upper Burma found it profitable to tour the centres of new affluence in the south. Such was the popularity of drama that the printing presses which were beginning to spring up in Rangoon found the publication of plays a lucrative business. These plays followed loosely in the tradition of the classical playwrights of the Konbaung period, but 'they far outdid their predecessors in the range of character they introduced, and in the elaboration of the comic element and in the verse in which they wrote'.[43] Some of them reflected social conditions, giving vivid pictures of the devastation which new economic practices were

creating in rural Burma.[44] Thus it was that in Burma an awareness of the problems of the times was first voiced through popular
literature and not by the modern educated class. This was to set
the tone for later developments under colonialism.

III

In 1906 the Young Men's Buddhist Association (YMBA), inspired by the Young Men's Christian Association, was founded
by a group of students at Rangoon College. A Buddhist Association had already existed in the college since 1904, but the
YMBA was broader in concept and was to emerge as the first
truly nationalist association of the country.[45] The founder members of the YMBA represented the early generation of Burmese
who had grown up after the fall of Mandalay and received their
education in the English-oriented system of missionary and government schools. The kind of 'new Burman' that this system had
created was described by U May Oung, one of the young
'England-returned ' barristers who joined the YMBA in 1908.
The modern Burman, he said, was

> a Burman to all outward appearance, but entirely out of
> harmony with his surroundings. He laughed at the old
> school of men; they did not understand existence as he did;
> their beliefs and superstitions were childish and silly, their
> way of life was exceedingly uncomfortable – in short, he
> thought there was nothing to be learnt from them ... It
> was one of the greatest curses of their generation that their
> young men were learning to drop Burmese ideals, to forget
> and even to despise the customs and habits of his ancestors,
> and to hanker after much that was bad and very little that
> was good in those alien races. Thus, for instance, he had
> adopted the luxuries but not the steadfastness and high-
> souled integrity of the European, the lavish display of
> wealth but not the business instincts of the Indian, the love
> of sensuous ease but not the frantic perseverance of the
> Chinaman.[46]

Although there is much that is valid in the above description of the modern Burman, it must be pointed out that it is based on the character of the people of Lower Burma. May Oung himself was an Arakanese brought up in Tenasserim and Rangoon. It was widely accepted that the people of Upper Burma had retained their culture and their racial pride. Therefore, when the need for revitalization of the Burmese culture was felt, the modern educated of Rangoon had to look to men of traditional learning from Upper Burma. One such person who became a leading figure in the world of Burmese letters and politics was Hsaya Lun, better known by his later appellation of Thakin Kodaw Hmaing.

Hmaing, born in 1875, was in Mandalay as a young novice at the time of the annexation of Upper Burma. From his monastery he saw Thibaw and the royal family on their melancholy journey to the boat that would take them away to exile. It is said that this experience sowed the seeds of the deep patriotism which would form an essential feature of his literary output. There is little detailed information about Hmaing's early life. The foundation of his classical education was laid in several monasteries in Upper Burma. Later he came down to Moulmein where, as a young monk, he began to write newspaper articles. It is known that at some point he took the government seventh-standard examination, which was in those days a preliminary step towards service either in the civil departments or in the large commercial firms.[47] However, Hmaing seems to have made no practical use of this 'modern' qualification, although he left the monkhood. His writings, which ranged from popular plays, through newspaper articles, history and poetry, were strongly traditional in style. Their content showed a vivid awareness of contemporary economic, social and political developments. In particular, the extended essays, known as digas, provide valuable glimpses of the issues that engaged the attention of the politically awakening public. The Boh Diga, written in 1913, expresses concern over the breakdown of the rural economy in Upper Burma and the increasing instances of Burmese women marrying foreigners which also Hmaing attributed to economic reasons. In 1917 the YMBA passed a resolution condemning such marriages. On the same occasion, the government was urged to prevent land from passing into the hands of aliens, the most damaging consequence of the economic difficulties of the indigenous population. Thus, Hmaing, representing traditional learning, demonstrated an earlier awareness of the ills of colonial society than the modern educated class whose ranks would provide the leaders of the early nationalist movements.

May Oung indicated in his lecture on 'The Modern Burman: His Life and Notions', part of which has already been quoted, that the 'new Burman' had not assimilated and adapted new notions to his own life, he had merely substituted them for his old ones.[48] It was in recognition of this gulf between the old and the new that May Oung, Ba Hpe (with whom the idea of founding the YMBA had originated) and others of the modern educated class sought to understand the Burmese classics through such men as Hmaing, whom they revered greatly. Yet the true synthesis of traditional and modern, Burmese and western, was not achieved by that generation who neither translated new ideas into acceptable traditional terms nor reviewed old notions in the modern context.

Hmaing has been compared to Tagore by the Burmese as a great nationalist poet. Such a comparison is valid only if nationalism is defined in broad cultural terms rather than simply in its political sense. Rabindranath Tagore, though born more than a decade earlier than Hmaing, was undeniably the more modern of the two in experience and in intellectual development. The grandson of the wealthy and unorthodox Dwarkanath Tagore and son of Debendranath who invigorated and reorganized the Brahmo Samaj, Rabindranath inherited much of the renaissance quest for social and spiritual values which would ensure India's integrity in the modern world. He was familiar with English literature from his youth, and the assimilation of foreign elements in Tagore's intellectual apparatus was so complete that they form an integral part of the depth and breadth of his unique talent. A more important influence on his spiritual views were the Hindu Upanisads and the *bhakti* devotional literature with its yearning for union between man and the divine. Tagore's works became known to non-Bengalis in India only after 1912, when English translations of his poems were popularized by the enthusiasm of such literary figures as W. B. Yeats and Ezra Pound. The accepted Indian image of Tagore would seem to be based on the ideas contained in the widely known verse from the *Gitanjali*:

> Where the mind is without fear and the head is held high;
> Where knowledge is free;
> Where the world has not been broken up into fragments by
>   narrow domestic walls;
> Where words come out from the depth of truth;
> Where tireless striving stretches its arms towards perfection;
> Where the clear stream of reason has not lost its way into
>   the dreary desert sand of dead habit;
> Where the mind is led forward by Thee into ever-widening
>   thought and action –
> Into that heaven of freedom, my Father, let my country
>   awake.

Knowledge, freedom, universalism, truth, reason, thought joined with action within a spiritual framework – the aims and ideals of the Indian Renaissance are encapsulated in a few manageable lines. But although Tagore was accepted as a national institution, he was not always viewed as a nationalist. There was his well-publicized rift with Gandhi over the latter's wholesale condemnation of western civilization. This led to a decline in Tagore's popularity even in Bengal, for Gandhi represented the patriotic aspirations of the common people whereas Tagore's internationalist ideals often distanced him from the masses. Nehru, who admired both men, provides a sympathetic comparison of the two:

> Tagore was primarily the man of thought, Gandhi of concentrated and ceaseless activity. Both in their different ways had a world outlook, and both were at the same time wholly Indian. They seemed to represent different but harmonious aspects of India and to complement one with the other.[49]

Hmaing was closer to Tagore in being primarily a man of thought but nearer to Gandhi in his political nationalism. Much of Hmaing's writings were on contemporary events, matters both great and small which had any bearing on nationalist developments in Burma. He lauds May Oung's attendance of an official British function in traditional Burmese costume; he exults over a YMBA delegation going to London to present the views of the Burmese people to the British government; he enthusiastically follows the exploits of a famous dacoit whose success in evading arrest, in spite of the desperate efforts of the police, have turned him into a folk hero. Hmaing was so much a man of the people that the temper of the country could often be judged from his writings. But while he drew public attention to current events and expressed his criticism or approbation, he did not offer a philosophy which could have guided nationalist efforts. The expression of criticism and approbation could be said to have been in the classical tradition: Burmese historical writings sometimes provided critical assessments of monarchs, especially if they were notable failures.[50] There was also in Burmese classical literature the *myittaza* (a communication appealing to *maitri*). This began as epistles from monks requesting favours of the monarch, and later developed into compositions containing appeals, advice and even advertisements. Thus, the didactic role of scholars was an old one which continued to be manifest in the works of the early twentieth century in Burma.

The Burmese language itself was beginning to change under the same influences which had led to the modern forms of many languages in India: the impact of western literature, the growth of printing, the dissemination of newspapers, the creation of a wider reading public. Classical Burmese had become heavily laden with Pali loan words, stereotyped literary expressions and artificial flourishes. The early newspaper articles in Burmese retained many of the old conventions, frequently breaking into verse when reporting such dramatic events as a lovers' suicide pact. However, with the burgeoning of news despatches the style became more factual and terse. Here it is difficult to decide how much of the change was due to the nature of journalistic writings and how much to the influence of English. There is reason to think that the latter might have been more potent: the writings of those Burmese who had learnt English showed earlier and more obvious signs of the modern idiom.

The work which is generally recognized as the first Burmese novel, *Maung Yin Maung Ma Me Ma*, was written by James Hla Gyaw in 1904. The author had been educated in missionary schools and possibly belonged to the Christian faith. His novel, which is an adaptation from the earlier parts of *The Count of Monte Cristo*, does not indicate a great familiarity with Buddhist beliefs and practices. It is written in a simple, straightforward language which entirely dispenses with the ornate classical style. The success of *Maung Yin Maung Ma Me Ma* led to a spate of novels which soon replaced the drama as popular reading. However, many of the early novels were closer in form and language to the old dramas than to the unadorned but effective style adopted by James Hla Gyaw. As to content, the emphasis was on romance; there was little attempt at realism.

Before the 1920s few novels appeared which reflected the contemporary scene. Among the exceptions were the works of U Latt, like James Hla Gyaw a product of the new educational system. But, unlike Hla Gyaw, Latt demonstrated a familiarity with classical Burmese writings as well as with contemporary drama. Born and brought up in Lower Burma, he nevertheless exhibits a strong nostalgia for the days of the Burmese monarchy. The language of Mandalay is shown as graceful, the manners as courtly. In his best-loved novel, *Shwepyiso*, the heroine is the child of a minor royal consort brought up by loyal attendants. She is kept in ignorance of her parentage, although she realizes that she is of noble birth. It was to protect her from the malice of one of the powerful queens that she was so carefully kept incognito. But in the end it is revealed that it has all been a grave misunderstanding; the much feared queen has nothing but goodwill towards the young girl. It would perhaps be going too far to suggest that Latt was trying to counter stories about the atrocities attributed to Thibaw's queen; but it does indicate that already the shortcomings of the monarchy were beginning to be forgiven if not forgotten.

Nostalgia for the past was more likely an indication of the dissatisfaction with the colonial status than a genuine longing for old institutions. No concerted effort was made to reassess the past with a view to formulating a viable philosophy for the future. Many Burmese, in the early twentieth century, felt that their patriotic duty required the preservation of old ways without examining them carefully to see if they were fit for the new times. However, in 1910 there was a development which created a situation in which the heritage of Burma could be examined in the light of modern scholarship. The Burma Research Society was founded at the instance of an Englishman, J. S. Furnivall. He had been inspired by reading a copy of the *Journal of the Siam Society* to create a 'similar society in Burma that should bring together Burmans and Europeans with a common interest in the welfare of the country'.[51] Furnivall also connects the inception of the Research Society with May Oung's lecture on 'The Modern Burman' which he had attended in 1908.[52] There was some official resistance to the founding of the society on the grounds that it might encourage nationalism and subversiveness, but the Governor was in favour of the project. Furnivall, with May Oung and Charles Duroiselle, a French lecturer in Pali at Rangoon College, were the men who organized the Research Society.[53] The *Journal of the Burma Research Society*, which continued until the beginning of the 1980s, remains to this day a most valuable repository of scholarly articles on Burmese history, language, culture and geography. Furnivall, writing in 1916 when the society was passing through a temporary phase in the doldrums, outlines his views of its purpose:

> We were looking for human Burma; that mysterious entity of which each individual Burman, and in a less degree every one living here, is on an infinitesimal scale a manifestation and a representative, which is a norm subsuming all their individual activities, and which represents all that is vital and enduring in this country as we know it; the partnership, as Burke puts it, between the dead, the living and those yet to be born . . .

For the Burma that we hope to assist in building is like some old pagoda recently unearthed and in course of restoration. Much of this restoration is and perforce must be dull work. I remember visiting the Petleik pagoda at Pagan when the excavation was in progress, and seeing a workman with one sweep of his brush remove the earth and plaster from a plaque that had been buried and forgotten for some centuries. But before he could do this it had been necessary to clear away cartloads of rubbish. We have carefully to set in order the foundations and the whole building brick by brick, but I for one firmly believe that if the Burma of the future is to be a lasting fabric, it must be built up on the old foundations.[54]

In such views can be seen the seeds of a renaissance: the urge to create a vital link between the past, the present and the future, the wish to clear away 'cartloads of rubbish' so that old foundations might become fit to hold up a new and lasting fabric. But it was a renaissance that did not really come to full fruition.

The Burma Research Society attracted some of the finest Burmese scholars of the day, including Hmaing, to write for its journal. Yet there remained an indefinable barrier between men of traditional learning and the modern educated. Those who had been grounded in one system somehow seemed incapable of truly mastering the other. There were many highly intelligent men and women in Burma then as at any period; their failure to assimilate two different strains of intellectual tradition must be put down to psychological rather than cerebral factors. Perhaps the most important of these was the reluctance to examine the past with objectivity. There is a Burmese proverb that cautions people from giving up ancient usages. While there is wisdom in refraining from implementing change merely for the sake of change, clinging to old ways solely for the sake of their antiquity is obviously equally futile. May Oung had complained of the modern Burman's failure to assimilate and adapt new notions. He did not point out that old ways, too, should be adapted, pruned, revitalized or in some cases even discarded altogether. Perhaps he and others of a similar educational background felt incompetent to assess traditional values. On one occasion Ba Hpe wrote in the *Thuriya* newspaper, which he had set up in 1911, that the Burmese spent more than 10 million rupees a year on religious institutions and practices when there were other areas where funds were needed. This article created a furore, and the *Thuriya* was attacked for its irreligious tone. In the journalistic battle that followed, Ba Hpe, unable to keep up with some of the learned ripostes of the seasoned Burmese writers, had to recruit the help of Hmaing. Nobody without a mastery of the Burmese language and cultural background could hope to reach out to the people of Burma. Therefore the modern educated felt too diffident to suggest the reassessment and reform of accepted values. The scholars of the old school on the other hand were too close to traditional institutions to be able to judge them objectively.

Fielding Hall was one of those Englishmen who fell in love with Burma and the Burmese, of whom he had a romantic and in some ways simplistic vision. Nevertheless his observations on Burmese society were often shrewd and he noted a phenomenon which must surely lie at the basis of the failure for a true renaissance to take place under colonial rule. He remarked of monarchical Burma that there was no noble or leisured class between the king and the villagers. Consequently, the monarch had to recruit as his ministers men from the villages who, for all their natural capacity, did not have the 'breadth of view, the knowledge of other countries, of other thoughts, that come to those who have wealth and leisure'. The situation had not changed radically under British rule. There were in Burma no Rammohun Roys, no Tagores, no Nehrus, people with the wealth and leisure to pursue knowledge for the sake of knowledge, to travel, to see for themselves how other civilizations worked in their own milieu, to set standards of cultural refinement and intellectual excellence. It is surely no coincidence that men like Vidyasagar, Tilak and Gandhi who came from less privileged homes concentrated more on practical solutions to India's problem's than on intellectual speculation at a universal level. A western scholar, discussing the differences between Tagore and Gandhi, explains them partly in terms of their dissimilar backgrounds:

> India in the eyes of Kathiawad Bania, raised in conservative Jain-Vaishnava religious and Rajput political traditions, appeared a quite different India from that seen by a Bengali Brahman whose unorthodox family had pioneered in assimilating modern Western ideas and synthesizing them with Hindu religious and artistic traditions. Gandhi's image of India and the West also reflected a very different experience with individual Westerners. His treatment in a colonial outpost at the hands of South Africa's white supremacists had been as brutal as Tagore's welcome in literary circles of Western civilization's leading metropolis had been exhilarating.[55]

The men of action in India were imbued with the ideals of the renaissance, but by the twentieth century some of the universal approach had begun to narrow. It is disturbing when a man of Gandhi's vision casually writes of English women as wandering in the streets and slaving away in factories,[56] of western students as recognizing no law 'save that of their fancy'[57] and of those who had received their education through the foreign medium as having lost their intellectual vigour.[58]

Gandhi's ideology was not only the guiding force of Indian nationalist movements in the 1920s, it also provided the themes for many writers of poetry and fiction. Imaginative literature in India as in Burma reflected much of the changing mood of the nation. Hindi poet Maithilisharan Gupt wrote on the occasion of the coronation of George V that there was no nation in the world more loyal than India. He describes Bharat as having two eyes: one filled with tears of love resting on the prosperity which the British regime had given to India and the other filled with tears of sorrow for the degradation which had befallen the Indians.[59] During the period when Indian nationalism had entered a new phase under Gandhi's leadership, the same poet writes eulogistically of the *satyagrahis* of Bardoli, making comparisons with Haldighati and Thermopylae.[60] The most famous of Hindi writers, Premchand, was a staunch follower of Gandhi. Premchand had a strong belief in the didactic role of fiction. He was an admirer of Gokhale while at the same time sympathizing with Tilak's radical politics.[61] In an early book review, he criticized Hakim Barham's *Krishna Kunwar* for its lack of social purpose. Premchand considered it the duty of the novelist to strive for the removal of moral evils. 'The novelist can function sometimes as a friend, sometimes as a guide or philosopher. He can sometimes function as a physician.'[62] In accordance with his views, Premchand used his novels to express social and political ideas. One of his major works, *Sevasadan* (1919), is considered to have been influenced by Gandhi's faith in 'change of heart'.[63] In *Rangabhumi* (1925), the central figure, a blind beggar, becomes the mouthpiece of Gandhian philosophy. His other novels also display the social and political preoccupations of the age: the Hindu–Muslim conflict, *satyagraha*, the peasant movement. Not only Premchand but many other writers of India were deeply influenced by the ideas and actions of their political and intellectual leaders.

Bankimchandra Chatterji's novels in the nineteenth century had also reflected social and political trends; his *Ananda Math* in particular exhibits strong patriotic traits. Yet, in the foreword, Bankim wrote that the book expounded the truths of the suicidal nature of social revolution and the redemption from anarchy which the English had achieved for Bengal.[64] Bankim lived in the period of transition when appreciation of achievements under British governance was giving way to a growing dissatisfaction with the effects of foreign rule. A number of his novels are set against a historical background. Humayun Kabir sees Bankim's predilection for the past as a sign of his inability to achieve a satisfactory synthesis between his Bengali identity and western values. 'Whenever he was faced with a choice, he turned to the past traditions of his own country.'[65] Bankim's attempt to write his first novel in English and his subsequent decision to use only Bengali as the medium of imaginative genius also suggests that there had been a conflict between the western and the Bengali side of his intellectual person.

The song 'Bande Matram' from *Ananda Math* became the 'mantra of nationalism' in the early years of the twentieth century. It is a song of intense patriotism which praises the glory of India and exhibits flashes of militancy:

> Who has said thou art weak in thy lands,
> When the swords flash out in twice seventy million hands
> And seventy million voices roar
> Thy dreadful name from shore to shore
> . . .
> Thou art Durga, Lady and Queen,
> With her hands that strike and her sword of sheen.[66]

The sentiments of 'Bande Matram' do not appear to have appealed to Tagore, who abhorred the extremism which could be perpetrated in the name of patriotism. In his novel, *Home and the World*, Tagore's views are represented by the gentle, moderate Nikhil who feels that 'to tyrannize for the country is to tyrannize over the country'.[67] Sandip, who has no moral values, uses nationalism to satisfy his own ego and laughs at Nikhil's scruples. He is an opportunist, clever and cynical: 'Who says "Truth shall triumph"? Delusion shall win in the end . . . Bengal must now create a new image to enchant and conquer the world. *Bande Matram*.'[68]

Tagore stood fast by the ideals of the renaissance with which he had grown up even when it brought him unpopularity during the years of intense nationalism. It was through such minds that the thoughts of the nineteenth century flowed into the twentieth in India. Ideas put forward by those who had imbibed the tradition of the renaissance influenced the middle intelligentsia, who in turn spread their views at the popular level. In Burma, with its lack of an effective leadership, the people had to fend for themselves in the twentieth century as they had done throughout their history. Traditionally, the Burmese had always had a great respect for education. Unlike India, where ancient learning had been confined to the higher castes, education had always been universally available in Burma. And this education was connected with the teachings of the Buddha who had pointed out the way to *nirvana*. Thus, to be educated meant more than the mere acquisition of book learning; it meant the mastery of the supreme knowledge that would lead to enlightenment. A people with such a view of education could not take easily to the British policy which saw education as practical training for the new jobs and opportunities that had been created under colonialism. And when they did accept the necessity of entering the modern education system the Burmese brought to it a utilitarian, materialistic approach lacking in intellectual curiosity. The age-old conviction that true knowledge resided only in the teachings of the Buddha remained unshaken.

Together with the suspicion of foreign ways, there was also in the Burmese mentality an ingrained resistance to élitism. It was a widely held belief that education of a national character should be made available to as broad a section of the population as possible. And it was this belief which lay behind the boycott against the Rangoon University Act of 1920. The boycott has been described as the result of an 'unfortunate misunderstanding'.[69] The Act was intended to create the University of Rangoon from an amalgamation of the existing Rangoon and Judson colleges. The British authorities proposed that the standard of academic requirements should be raised, and that the university should be of a residential character. The Burmese objected on the grounds that such conditions would have the effect of limiting education to the privileged few. The boycott against the Act is seen by some as a political manoeuvre instigated by elements outside the resident university student body.[70] But the enthusiasm with which it was supported by parents and the country at large denotes that the issues involved had touched a deep chord within the Burmese character. There was certainly a misunderstanding, but it was not just a Burmese misunderstanding of British motives, it was also a British misunderstanding of the Burmese mentality. A people who had derived no real leadership from their rulers (except in the field of battle) could not be expected to understand or welcome a move to create an intellectually privileged class.

The most important outcome of the 1920 boycott was the founding of National Schools, set up with funds raised from the public. Not many of these institutions survived the burst of popular enthusiasm which had provided the initial means for their foundation. Those which managed to keep from shutting down were moved by necessity to accept government subsidies. But the effects of a system of education guided by nationalist principles was far-reaching. A crop of students would grow up whose intellectual foundation was an amalgam of the patriotic spirit and the western tradition of learning based on objective empiricism.

The 1920s were a period of transition for Burma. The associations which had begun as institutions for the preservation of Buddhism and Burmese culture had taken on a political aspect. The newspapers had matured as organs for expressing popular sentiment, in particular the nascent mood of nationalism. Rangoon had become the centre of the hybrid culture produced under colonialism. A nucleus of writers and scholars who combined traditional learning with western methods of scientific analysis was beginning to emerge. The language also was changing to accommodate the needs of the times. Two of the writers who pioneered the modern style were P. Monin and U Po Kya. They favoured short sentences, simple phrasing and few, if any, Pali expressions. The impetus which the Burma Research Society had given towards a scholastic study of Burmese culture and literature had begun to bear fruit. The Burmese language became an important subject in the university curriculum, and the first honours student in Burmese graduated in 1927.

Burmese studies in Rangoon University were fostered and encouraged by U Pe Maung Tin, the first Burmese to be appointed to a professorial post. Under his guidance and with the co-operation of other scholars, Burmese teaching achieved a high standard. Old Burmese, Pyu (the language of the Pyus, a proto-Burman ethnic group), Mon and Pali were also added to the curriculum. Thus, young students, who already had a knowledge of English and the literature of the West, acquired a broad linguistic base and an eclectic intellectual outlook. It was not surprising that some outstanding literary figures should emerge from this pioneer group of modern Burmese scholars.

In the early 1930s there appeared two volumes of *Khitsan Stories* and a volume of *Khitsan Poems*. These were collections of the works of students well known to Professor Pe Maung Tin. *Khitsan* means 'to test the age', and the anthologies were published with the intention of seeing how the public would react to the modern approach. These writings represented the fusion of Burmese and western scholarship achieved by introducing the teaching of Burmese into the westernized higher education system. Some hailed the *Khitsan* publications as an important literary movement; others attacked them as inimical to classical traditions. To the present day, there is controversy over the place of the *Khitsan* writers in the development of Burmese literature.

The *Khitsan* approach was essentially represented by three persons: Theippan Maung Wa, known for his short stories, and two poets who have risen to great eminence, Zawgyi and Min Thu Wun. All three could be described as belonging to the renaissance tradition. They combined knowledge of and respect for the past with a modern spirit of innovation. Their sympathies were broad, covering an ample sweep of cultures and interests. All three of them had opportunities to spend some years pursuing higher studies in the West. Their writings were widely read and admired, yet it cannot be said that they carried the country with them in the spirit of renaissance. There would appear to be three main reasons for this failure. First, the perfect fusion between old and new had not quite taken place: the university students for all their knowledge of classical Burmese works were still looked upon as a breed apart by those who had not been educated in the modern system. Secondly, all three went into government service, Theippan Maung Wa as an administrator and the two poets as university teachers, thus narrowing the scope of their activities. Thirdly, and perhaps most important, they confined the application of their liberal education to the world of arts. It was only very occasionally that their writings touched on social or political matters. Theippan Maung Wa's short stories often reflect conditions in rural Burma, but he did not examine their underlying

causes. It was chiefly for the last reason that the *Khitsan* writers
would be attacked by socialist thinkers of a later era. In a way,
the *Khitsan* movement was an isolated phenomenon contained
within the achievements of a small group of writers. But their
importance goes beyond the immediate boundaries of their literary influence, for they represented a possible goal of East–West,
old–new synthesis at the intellectual level in Burma.

IV

In India, political and intellectual leadership had often coincided.
Moreover, there had been an uninterrupted stream of able leaders
from the last years of the nineteenth century until independence.
This provided a cohesive framework within which social and
political movements could experiment and mature. The course of
Burma's development under colonialism was more fractured.
Actions without ideational content lose their potency as soon as
the situation which called for them ceases to be valid. A series of
pragmatic moves unconnected by a continuity of vision cannot be
expected to sustain a long-term movement. The Burmese who
aspired to positions of leadership under British rule were pragmatic in their approach and prided themselves on it. This lack of
a satisfactory leadership in Burma was recognized by Aung San,
later to emerge as the leader of the independence movement,
while he was still a university student in the 1930s. In an article
on education he remarked that the old did not provide the young
with either example or inspiration:

> We are fully prepared to follow men who are able and
> willing to be leaders like Mahatma Gandhi, C. R. Das,
> Motilal Nehru and Tilak of India; like De Valera of Ireland;
> or Garibaldi and Mazzini of Italy. Let anybody appear
> who can be like such a leader, who *dares* to be like such a
> leader. We are waiting.[71]

Aung San belonged to the generation of students who had
been raised in the patriotic ethos of the National Schools and

whose search for a philosophy to guide their nationalist endeavours would lead them to socialist ideology. The 1920s had been a period of political awakening punctuated by a few significant but largely uncoordinated events. The next decade was an era of change and revolution; it was a time when the younger generation strived to broaden the base of nationalism and to give it an intellectual framework.

The year 1930 was a momentous year for Burma. It was the birth of the Dohbama Asi-ayone, an organization which was to play a major role in the Burmese independence movement. It also witnessed the peasants' uprising led by Hsaya San. One represented the future, a forward-looking movement with revolutionary tendencies based on ideas and tactics imported from the West. The other represented the past, an armed enterprise relying on the call of racial pride and the charisma of the leader. The two were perhaps not entirely separate, but the connection was a somewhat tenuous one. Hsaya San had been a member of the General Council of Buddhist Associations which had been founded in 1920 by amalgamating the YMBA and other minor associations. In that sense, he could be said to have been a part of the contemporary political scene to which the Dohbama Asi-ayone also belonged. The dissatisfaction of peasants with government measures to allay the hardships of the rural economy provided Hsaya San with a following large enough to start a rebellion. But the insurrection collapsed quickly, and by 1931 the leader had been captured, to be tried and executed.

Hsaya San had made an appeal to the atavistic instincts of the Burmese. He had presented himself as a future monarch; his men had fought with a desperate courage, pitting sword and magic amulet against the firearms of government troops. Although there was sympathy for the patriotism of the rebels throughout the country, there was little practical support. The Burmese had quietly decided that they wanted no more of at least one old and outmoded institution. There had not been much cause for the people to love the monarchy in the past – the king in his golden palace had simply been a symbol of the power and glory of their race. Now that the glory was extinguished, the Burmese were too canny to wish the power to go back into autocratic hands if they could help it. But neither did they wish for a continuation of foreign rule. They would find a way to end colonialism on their own terms, not on the terms of men who would be kings.

The Dohbama Asi-ayone was a direct result of the Indo-Burmese riots which had broken out in May 1930. The riots had their origin in the clashes which had taken place between Indian dock workers on strike and Burmese labourers who had been employed as strike-breakers. The Burmese had long resented the role which immigrant groups had come to play in their country. All the passion of their fears for the dignified survival of their own people was poured into the ensuing conflict. Their rallying cry as fighting broke out in the streets was *'Dohbama'* ('We Burmese'). Ba Thaung, a young tutor from Rangoon University, conceived the idea of the Dohbama Asi-ayone (Organization) as he wrote pamphlets on the Burmese who had died during the riots. Its slogan was 'Race, language, religion'. The organization was to become known as the Thakin Party. *Thakin* means 'master', and was the term commonly used in referring to or addressing Englishmen. Ba Thaung and his associates used the word as a suffix to their names to denote that the Burmese, too, were a race of masters, not slaves. It was this simple, effective device for emphasizing their spirited patriotism, combined with the educated approach of Ba Thaung and his association, that attracted young people to the Dohbama Asi-ayone. The Thakins were not satisfied with a mere organization; they began to look around for ideas to give direction to their nationalist aspirations.

Leftist literature became available in Burma around 1931. Books brought back by individuals who had been abroad and those circulated by J. S. Furnivall's Burma Book Club formed the core of socialist and Marxist works introduced into the country. These were eagerly consumed by young Burmese whose eyes had been opened to the exciting political currents which were sweeping across the world. As they were also searching eagerly, perhaps unconsciously, for radical ideas, there was a tendency to swallow much of the whole socialist theory without digesting it properly.

The spread of leftist sympathies among the younger Burmese

nationalists has often been explained in economic and political terms. In fact, Burmese society with its Buddhist values, lack of extreme poverty and freedom from class exploitation was not a natural candidate for Marxist socialist ideology. It was the view that socialism was opposed to imperialism which made the former attractive to young nationalists. The Burmese were caught up in the tide of the times that saw the leftist ideologies as progressive alternatives to capitalism and colonialism. In addition to this, the intellectual climate of Burma was ripe for the broad sweep of ideas which socialism introduced. The young Burmese were very new intellectuals, and their minds longed to grapple with theories, concepts, challenges. They were equipped by their Anglo-vernacular education, not just to absorb new ideas for themselves, but to spread them among the people. Unlike the older generation of politicians who were not at home in the Burmese written idiom, the generation of the 1930s had grown up reading Burmese books, newspapers and magazines. They were as familiar with the anachronistic flavour of Hmaing's language as with the spare elegance of *Khitsan*.

Among the young nationalists who sought for ideas to buttress their actions were Aung San, Soe, Nu, Than Tun and Thein Pe Myint. All of them became politicians; all of them imbibed leftist ideologies, some more deeply than others; all of them wielded the pen with greater or lesser felicity. Soe used Buddhist terminology to interpret communist works, Nu tried to show that communism and Buddhism were, in fact, not incompatible. Leaving aside the question of how far they succeeded in their endeavours, they showed a practical recognition of the Burmese need to translate foreign concepts into their language, literally and metaphorically. Aung San, Than Tun and Thein Hpe Myint, too, searched for ideas to fit the needs of Burmese nationalism. All of them believed in forging strong links between thought and action, particularly Aung San for whom the two followed each on the other in an uninterrupted chain of endeavour.

Thein Hpe possessed outstanding literary gifts. He produced a string of novels and short stories which, while acting as vehicles for his political ideas, were also fine works of art. He, in common with a number of his political colleagues, combined patriotism with a broad-minded approach to the worth of other cultures. The hero of his novel, *Boycott Student*, based on the Rangoon University boycott of 1936, advises a young girl to read translations of good English novels rather than shoddy Burmese fiction. He also states the view that to write Burmese well it was important not only to study the works of traditional scholars such as Hmaing but also to read good English books.

Nu, Aung San and Thein Pe were among the leaders of the boycott of 1936, which was essentially a protest against the heavy-handed attitude of the authorities towards nationalist students. Within the next two years, all three together with Soe and Than Tun joined the Dohbama Asi-ayone. Henceforth, they were to feature among the most widely known Thakin leaders of the independence movement.

Nu, Soe and Than Tun were among the founder members of the Nagani (Red Dragon) Book Club, started in 1937. The aim of this club was to make Burmese translations of works on economics, politics, history and literature available to the public at a low price. The idea behind the venture was that, if Burma wished to be known to the world, Burma herself must first get to know the world. It was a simple, modest, intelligent outlook. A glance at the list of books published by the Nagani Book Club reveals that, among the 101 titles published, there were 38 on war, 36 on nationalism, 32 on revolution and 21 on Michael Collins. Titles on other popular subjects were 19 on Burmese history, 19 on Germany, 18 on government, 18 on economics, 18 on socialism, 15 on communism and 15 on fascism. There was one book on Nehru, two on Gandhi, two on De Valera, three on Stalin, four on Hitler and six on Lenin. The revolutionary, leftist bias of the club was in little doubt.

In the last few years before war came to Burma the Thakins searched indefatigably for ideas and tactics which would help Burma to win her independence. During this time, they came to realize that Burma was a nation not just of the Burmese but also of the Shans, Chins, Kachins, Karens, Mons and other indigenous peoples. There were, in addition, those members of the immigrant communities who had established indissoluble ties of love and loyalty with the country of their adoption. The young nationalists recognized the need to look beyond traditional values, which were simply based on the awareness of the nationhood of the Burmese people. A genuine lack of racial chauvinism, combined with a very real desire to learn from the rest of the world, marked some of the leaders who emerged in the 1930s.

But there was no time to allow political attitudes to mature intellectually before the Second World War came to Burma. With the advance of the Japanese the Burmese had to face a new set of problems. They had to learn to cope with a fellow Asian race whose achievements they had admired and who professed to be their allies but yet treated them with the arrogance and brutality of conquerors. It was against a different background from that which had prevailed under the British that the Burmese had to continue their search for a synthesis of ideas and action which would carry their nation to the required goal as an integrated whole.

A comparison of the intellectual life of Burma and India under colonialism shows two very different societies facing the onslaught of alien forces in their own different ways. In India there was an initial enthusiasm for western ideas and institutions among its leadership. This early admiration was a major factor in the birth of the Indian Renaissance which was to influence intellectual development and political thought in the country right up to the time of independence. The language of the rulers not only helped to spread western ideas but also acted as a unifying factor in the multilingual subcontinent. English became so much a part of Indian intellectual life that Indo-Anglian works acquired their own place in the literature of the nation after independence. Even when Indian attitudes towards the British had changed to resentment and hostility, the intellectual impulse that sought a harmonious fusion of the East and West did not die out completely. And English continued to be accepted as the political language of the nation.

Leftist thought was not without its fascination for the intellectuals of India, where social conditions were such as to make the promises of a communist society seem most attractive. But the majority of the nationalist leaders, who still ascribed to the renaissance view that social, religious and political factors were but different facets of the indivisible life of civilized man, preferred to select critically from the wide range of socialist ideas (in particular those with an economic bearing) rather than to accept whole ideologies in their entirety.

Looking from the Indian situation to that of Burma, there is the almost surreal impression of a time warp. Colonized at a much later date and for a much shorter period, the Burmese experience of British rule is in some ways a concertinaed version of developments in India. But there were also developments which took their own individual course, explainable not so much by the colonial experience common to many Asian and African countries of that era as by the distinct cultural and historical background of Burma.

The Burmese people lacked a leadership which would have helped them to face the challenges posed by their confrontation with alien values. They learnt to adjust to new conditions slowly, almost imperceptibly. Towards the end of British rule some leaders arose who saw the need to adopt a broad assimilative approach and to develop a philosophy which could cope with modern developments. But on the whole, such changes as came about in the traditional values of the Burmese took place because the people themselves willed it and not because they were carried along by the force of dynamic leaders. The leaders that they did follow willingly were those who could communicate with them in their own language. As the founder of the Dohbama Asi-ayone had realized, language, together with race and religion, were the mainsprings of the Burmese sense of their unique identity. Even when the revolutionary young politicians dropped the notions of race and religion from their concept of modern nationhood, the validity of the Burmese language as a unifying factor was tacitly retained.

The aspects of intellectual life on which this study has focused reveal a strong link between nationalism and intellectual developments in Burma and India under colonialism. Indian society, accustomed to the tradition of privileged castes, readily accepted the intellectual élite born of the Indian Renaissance which provided many of its national leaders. This élite led the movement which sought a harmonious union between western thought and Hindu philosophy in the search for nationalist ideals. In Burma, however, traditional attitudes shaped by an essentially egalitarian society militated against the acceptance of an élite. Moreover, the early generation of Burmese who acquired their education under the colonial system were largely ignorant of the classical learning of their own country. As a result they found themselves distanced from the traditional scholars as well as from the people in general. Western education and traditional learning began to merge only in the 1930s when the study of Burmese language and literature became an integral part of the education system. The younger leaders who were the products of this system strived to give to nationalist aspirations an ideological framework which would be acceptable not only to the Burmese but to all the peoples of Burma. There always remained an intellectual, one might almost say a cultural, gap between the old leadership and the young politicians who were to carry on the independence movement after the war.

The situation in neither country could be said to have been wholly satisfactory. In India the élite demonstrated that Indians could reach the topmost ranks of intellectual excellence which combined the best in their own traditions with the best that the West had to offer. But the gap between the élite and the common people was so large that the momentum of the renaissance could not be sustained. The forces which had provided the nationalist movement with ideas and ideals had already begun to dissipate before India became independent.

In Burma, the lack of an élite meant that there was little to guide and spur on the people to reach out for greater achievements. The younger generation of leaders appeared too late to bring about effective changes before the outbreak of the Second World War. Developments in Burma after 1940 took many abrupt twists and turns; and to this day, it still remains a society waiting for its true potential to be realized.

Notes

1 Just as the last Mughal Emperor Bahadur Shah was sent to Rangoon where he died in 1862, Thibaw, the last king of Burma, was exiled to Ratnagiri where he lived until his death in 1914. His queen, Supayalat, was allowed to return to Burma in 1919. She died in Rangoon in 1925.

2 Phillip Woodruff, *The Men Who Ruled India: The Guardians*, London, 1963, p. 122.

3 However, for about a hundred years between 1540 and 1635 the Burmese monarchs of the Taungu dynasty made the port city of Pegu their capital.

4 Woodruff, *The Men Who Ruled India*, p.118.

5 James Morris, *Heaven's Command: An Imperial Progress*, London, 1973, p. 337.

6 Frank Moraes, *Witness to an Era: India 1920 to the Present Day*, Delhi, 1973, pp. 46–7. Nirad C. Chaudhuri presents colour prejudice in India in an original, interesting light in *The Continent of Circe*, London, 1965.

7 Donald Bishop (ed.), *Thinkers of the Indian Renaissance*, New Delhi, 1982, p. 4.

8 Quoted in Arabinda Poddar, *Renaissance in Bengal: Quests and Confrontations 1800–1860*, Simla, 1970, p. 51.

9 Ibid., p. 5. The 'eminent intellectual' to whom he refers is Nirad C. Chaudhuri.

10 U Kaung, 'A Survey of the History of Education in Burma before the British Conquest and After', *Journal of the Burma Research Society* (*JBRS*), vol. xlvi, ii, Rangoon, December 1963, provides appendixes showing the rise of the population, the total areas under cultivation and cultivated area per head for British Burma between 1830 and 1870. He also gives some figures for the export of rice from Pegu, which rose from 457 *maunds* in 1853 to 3,420 *maunds* in 1856–7.

11 Woodruff, *The Men Who Ruled India*, p. 117.

12 H. Fielding Hall, *The Soul of a People*, London, 1902 edn, p. 83.

13 Ram Goppal, *Lokamanya Tilak*, New Delhi, 1956, pp. 220–21.

14 U Kaung, 'A Survey of the History of Education in Burma before the British Conquest and After', Appendix I.

15 *Selections from Educational Records, Part 1 1781–1839*, Calcutta, 1920.

16 The complete letter is reproduced in Wm Theodore de Bary *et al.*, *Sources of Indian Tradition*, New York, 1958, pp. 592–5.

17 Quoted in Bishop (ed.), *Thinkers of the Indian Renaissance*, p. 76.

18 U Kaung, 'A Survey of the History of Education in Burma before the British Conquest and After', Appendix III.

19 See n.3, above.
20 Nirad C. Chaudhuri, *The Intellectual in India*, New Delhi, 1967, p. 16.
21 Dr Than Tun, Burma's foremost historian of today, writing on life in sixteenth-century Burma comments: 'The relationship between the ruler and ruled might well have been of a strained nature since the ordinary common people avoided any dealings with government servants if possible.' See Than Tun, 'Social Life in Burma in the 16th Century', *Southeast Asian Studies*, vol. 21, no. 3, Kyoto, December 1903.
22 U Kaung, 'A Survey of the History of Education in Burma before the British Conquest and After', Appendix III.
23 *The Times*, 15 January 1906.
24 Donald Eugene Smith, *Religion and Politics in Burma*, Princeton, NJ, 1965, p. 86.
25 Arthur Waley has remarked on the 'disquiet caused in some circles at Oxford when Radhakrishnan whose role had been essentially that of an interpreter of the East to the West was succeeded in the Spalding Chair by a scholar who announced his intention of functioning simply as a scholar'. See Arthur Waley, *The Secret Life of the Mongols and Other Pieces*, London, 1963, p. 79.
26 Nirad C. Chaudhuri, *Autobiography of an Unknown Indian*, Bombay, 1951, p. 497.
27 Ibid., p. 25.
28 Ibid., p. 102.
29 Ibid., p. 192. Chaudhuri, *The Intellectual in India*, p. 9.
30 Chaudhuri, *Autobiography of an Unknown Indian*, pp. 191–2, and Poddar, *Renaissance in Bengal: Quests and Confrontations 1800–1860*, pp. 32–3, quote the same passage from *Rajani*.
31 Moraes, *Witness to an Era: India 1920 to the Present Day*, p. 153.
32 Jawaharlal Nehru, *The Discovery of India*, New Delhi, 1947.
33 Ibid., p. 98.
34 Chaudhuri, *The Intellectual in India*, pp. 30–32.
35 Nehru, *The Discovery of India*, p. 5.
36 Ibid., pp. 5–7.
37 Gandhi's experiences in England are recounted in his autobiography, *My Experiments with Truth*, Harmondsworth, 1982.
38 U Tin, *Myanmamin Okchatkwin Sadan*,
39 U Myint Hpe, *Myanma soak thamain-u nhin thamain atweakyon*, Rangoon, 1972, p. 21.
40 Ibid., pp. 23–4.
41 Ibid., pp. 26–30.
42 Fielding Hall, *The Soul of a People*, p. 66.

43 Hla Pe, 'The Rise of Popular Literature in Burma', *JBRS*, vol. li, ii, December 1968, pp. 126–7.

44 Ibid.

45 Maung Maung, *From Sangha to Laity: Nationalist Movements of Burma 1920–1940*, n.p., 1980, p. 2.

46 From the report in the *Rangoon Gazette*, 10 August 1908, reproduced in J. S. Furnivall and U May Oung, 'The Dawn of Nationalism in Burma', *JBRS*, vol xxxi, i, April 1950, pp 1–7.

47 Thireinda Padita, *Thakin Kodaw Hmaing ahtutpati amhadawbon*, Rangoon, 1938.

48 See n. 2.

49 Nehru, *The Discovery of India*, p. 343.

50 Than Tun, 'Historiography of Burma', *Shiryoku*, no. 9, 1976, Kagoshima University.

51 Furnivall and U May Oung, 'The Dawn of Nationalism in Burma', p. 1.

52 Ibid.

53 John F. Cady, *A History of Modern Burma*, New York, 1958, p. 180.

54 Fielding Hall, *The Soul of a People*, p. 80.

55 Stephen Hay, *Asian Ideas of East and West: Tagore and His Critics in Japan, China and India*, Cambridge, MA, 1970, p. 284.

56 M. K. Gandhi, *Hind Swaraj*, Ahmedabad, 1938, p. 37.

57 M. K. Gandhi, *The Problems of Education*, Ahmedabad, 1962, p. 18.

58 Ibid., p. 20.

59 Dharam Paul Saran, *Influence of Political Movements on Hindi Literature, 1906–1947*, Chandigarh, 1967, p. 47.

60 Ibid., pp. 94–5.

61 V. S. Narvane, *Premchand: His Life and Work*, New Delhi, 1980, pp. 30–31.

62 Ibid., p. 33

63 Ibid., p. 102. The author mentions that Premchand once remarked that faith in 'change of heart' was the only important idea stressed by Gandhi with which he fully agreed.

64 Sunil Kumar Banerjee, *Bankim Chandra: A Study of His Craft*, Calcutta, 1940.

65 Humayun Kabir, *The Bengali Novel*, Calcutta, 1968, p. 27.

66 From the translation in Sri Aurobindo, *Bankim-Tilak-Dayananda*, Calcutta, 1940.

67 Surendranath Tagore (trans.), *The Home and the World*, London, 1928, p. 163.

68 Ibid., p. 191.

69 Cady, *A History of Modern Burma*, p. 213.

70 Ibid., p. 217.
71 My translation from Aung San, 'Kyun pyinnya nhin thakin pyinnya', in *Oway e Shweyatu Letyweizin hsaungba mya*, Rangoon, 1972.

4

Literature and Nationalism in Burma

This article first appeared as 'Socio-Political Currents in Burmese Literature, 1910–1940', in Burma and Japan: Basic Studies on their Cultural and Social Structure, *Burma Research Group, Tokyo University of Foreign Studies, Tokyo, 1987, pp. 65–83. The system of Burmese transliteration has here been altered to conform with the one normally favoured by the author. Thanks are due to Patricia Herbert for this.*

The years from 1910 to 1940 witnessed the progressive attempts of the Burmese people to reassert their racial and cultural identity which had been undermined by foreign rule. These attempts took a course set by the social and political conditions which had resulted from the colonial situation imposed on Burma during the nineteenth century.[1] As the twentieth century unfolded, the effects of foreign governance on Burmese culture and society became increasingly evident. In the realm of language and literature, the impact of western influences and ideas gave birth to new approaches and innovative styles which led to marked changes away from classical traditions.

The study of Burmese literature under colonialism is a wide subject which would include among its many components comparisons between classical literary forms and their modern equivalents, an analysis of the effect of new institutions and philosophies on traditional social and religious values, and an investigation into the influence of western intellectual forces. This paper does not aim at covering such broad ground: it is simply intended as an introduction to one aspect of the literature of the period.

The emergence of modern Burmese literature coincided to a large measure with the evolution of those feelings and aspirations which constituted the foundation of the Burmese nationalist movement. Therefore the study of the interrelations between sociopolitical currents and literary trends would serve to enhance the understanding of Burma under colonial rule. In drawing attention to the way in which contemporary writings reflected social conditions and political aspirations, it is hoped that some contribution might be made towards this deeper understanding.

The Colonial Situation

The early years of British rule brought some material prosperity but the *laissez-faire* economic policy adopted by the government and the imposition of administrative and judicial institutions which had originally been formulated for India and which were ill suited to the needs of Burmese society brought about a series of grave problems. The unchecked immigration of Indians and Chinese, the opening up of large tracts of virgin land with its attendant need for capital, the financial activities of Indian money-lenders, land alienation, the monopolies exercised by European commercial firms, the import of foreign goods which diminished the market for indigenous products, the breakdown of the monastic school system, the decline in the discipline and morals of monks removed from ecclesiastical supervision: all these circumstances combined to create forces which led to the disintegration of Burmese society.[2]

This trend first became obvious in Lower Burma, which had fallen earlier to British rule, but by 1910 Upper Burma was also beginning to feel the adverse effects of discordant economic forces and of the corrosion of traditional values.[3] It therefore has to be more than coincidental that movements reflecting the need of the Burmese to reassert their racial and cultural identity began to make themselves manifest around this time. Burmese culture is intimately, one might say indissolubly, connected with Theravada

Buddhism. Thus it was hardly surprising that the early stirrings of nationalism should have been expressed in religious terms. The first association aimed at promoting and preserving Buddhism was started as early as 1897 in Mandalay,[4] but it was only in 1906 that an organization was founded which would acquire a national character. The Young Men's Buddhist Association, inspired by the Young Men's Christian Association, was started by a group of young graduates of Rangoon College and it quickly gained the support of influential, educated Burmese.[5] At the beginning, the activities of the association were of a purely religious, cultural nature and its members could be said to have been loyal subjects of the British Empire.[6] It was only in 1917, at its annual conference in Pyinmana, that the YMBA first passed resolutions of a political character: the institution of 'Europeans only' carriages on trains was condemned; a strong protest was made against Europeans wearing shoes in pagoda precincts contrary to Burmese custom; the government was urged to prevent land from passing into the hands of foreigners; and it was decided that a delegation should be sent to India to present Burmese views to the Montagu Mission which was assessing public opinion on proposed constitutional reforms.[7]

In 1918 the tenor of nationalist politics was given a belligerent tone by the activities of U Ottama, a widely travelled Buddhist monk who had recently returned from India.[8] The attitudes of this unusual cleric were shaped as much by his admiration for the strength and independence of Japan, where he had spent some time, as by the *satyagraha* movement that Gandhi had first launched in India in 1917.[9] Thus, U Ottama was representative of those Burmese who drew inspiration from Japan's achievements but who looked to India for political ideas and tactics.[10]

In 1920 the YMBA and other minor associations united to form the General Council of Buddhist Associations, the GCBA. In 1921 the British government decided that the recommendations of the Montagu Mission, in the form of diarchy, should be extended to Burma. The implementation of these reforms entailed elections to the legislative council and this led to a split in the GCBA over the question of whether or not its members should stand for election. The next decade would find the Burmese divided between the supporters of diarchy and the adherents of the alternative system, Home Rule. The leaders of the GCBA subscribed to a broad spectrum of opinions with regard to the proposed constitutional reforms, and by the end of the 1930s the association had been splintered beyond reconciliation.[11]

It was also in 1920, the year which saw the birth of the GCBA, that the boycott against the Rangoon University Act took place. The Act, which incorporated proposals aimed at creating a residential institution along the lines of Oxford and Cambridge, was generally seen by the Burmese as an attempt to limit higher education to a privileged few.[12] The students registered their protest by going on a strike which was supported by the GCBA as well as by a wide section of the Burmese public. This demonstration of solidarity among the people forced the government to withdraw the proposals which had created so much opposition.[13] An important outcome of the strike was the movement to establish National Schools throughout the country and a National College in Rangoon. Few of the schools survived the first flush of enthusiastic public support, and the National College closed down in 1923. But the establishment of these institutions marked a significant phase in Burmese political development when the need for an educational system based on nationalist ideals became widely recognized.[14]

The 1920s might well be called the *wunthanu* era: *wunthanu* signifies the preservation of one's lineage and as used during the 1920s it denoted patriotism in the form of a preference for traditional values and the eschewal of things foreign.[15] The influence of the *swadeshi* movement of India was clearly discernible.

The 1930s were a decade of unrest. There were serious Indo-Burmese riots towards the middle of 1930 and by the end of the year the peasants' revolt led by Hsaya San had broken out. This rebellion has been variously described as the manifestation of agrarian discontent, the ambitious attempts of a superstitious fanatic to crown himself king (this was the version popular with the colonial administration) and the natural outcome of nationalist aspirations.[16] The insurrection was put down and Hsaya San captured within a year, later to be condemned and executed. Although the rebellion had not received widespread support, it did arouse the patriotic sympathy of the people, who were also repelled by the ruthlessness with which the British dealt with the rebels.[17]

It was also in 1930 that the Dohbama Asi-ayone, later to become popularly known as the Thakin Party, was founded. The word *Thakin*, which means 'master', was the term by which the Burmese were expected to address the British rulers. By adopting it as a prefix to their own names the young nationalists, many of whom would become prominent leaders in the independence movement, made an aggressive proclamation of their birthright to be their own masters. Leftist literature was introduced to Burma around this time and a number of leading 'Thakins' began to look to Marxist theories for guidance in their struggle against British imperialism.[18]

The 1930s saw the old guard of the GCBA generation losing ground to more radical young men whose ultimate goal would be neither diarchy nor dominion status but outright independence. Many of these young men had started their careers in politics as students of Rangoon University and in 1936 they led a strike which created an even greater impact than the one of 1920 and made the student leaders known to the country at large.[19]

The tempo of political agitations continued to increase throughout the second half of the 1930s, and in 1938 there occurred a series of events which came to be known collectively as the 'Revolution of 1300'. (This was the year according to the Burmese calendar, extending from April 1938 to April 1939.) There were Indo-Burmese riots, a march of oil workers from Yenangyaung to demand better conditions, student demonstrations in Rangoon during which a young man died under police *lathi* charges, the march of peasants in sympathy with the oil workers and demonstrations in Mandalay where seventeen people were shot dead by the police.

By the end of the decade which saw the outbreak of the Second World War, the social and political scene in Burma was in some turmoil, representing a situation radically different from that of

1910 when a few religious associations had been working peacefully for the preservation of Burmese Buddhist values.

Burmese Language and Literature under Colonial Rule

The deleterious effect of foreign rule on Burmese language and literature became discernible soon after the annexation of Upper Burma. The decline in the number of monastic schools and the introduction of English as the language of privilege served to belittle the position of Burmese. In contrast to what had happened in India in the late eighteenth century, Burmese classical writings did not attract the interest of western scholars during the early years of colonization. Traditional literature, which had flourished under the monarchs of the last Burmese dynasty, went into eclipse. It was only with the founding of the Burma Research Society in 1910 that an impetus was given towards the systematic study and revival of the Burmese classics. Another decade would then pass before the authorities accepted that the study of Burmese should find a proper place in the curriculum of Rangoon University.

While on the one hand British rule brought about a decline in the quality of Burmese literature, on the other hand the initial improvement in material conditions created a readership for the newspapers, magazines and books whose production had begun after the introduction of the printing press in the nineteenth century.[20] In the early days the greatest number of Burmese books printed were of a religious character, with dramas and novels forming the second biggest category. Reprints of classical works, in particular poetry, were also in demand.[21]

The first Burmese novel, *Maung Yin Maung Ma Me Ma*, published in 1904,[22] was partially adapted from *The Count of Monte Cristo* and triggered off a spate of novels which quickly became popular with the reading public. Many of these showed the influence in form and structure of Burmese drama, but as the twentieth century progressed, western influences became stronger and new literary styles began to emerge.

Only a small selection of those works which reflect social and political trends under colonialism will be discussed here. The choice has been determined partly by the role which such works played in the development of modern Burmese literature and partly, in the case of popular novels, by personal preference.

U Latt

U Latt was born in 1866 in Rangoon, then already under British rule, and educated in one of the earliest missionary schools in the city. He is said to have had a good knowledge of English and to have read many works in that language.[23] His novels, however, are written in a style clearly influenced by the Burmese dramatic performances of which he was said to have been extremely fond. One of the characters in his first book, *Zabebin* (1912), is generally thought to represent the writer himself: a young civil servant (U Latt served for a number of years in the Burma Police) from Lower Burma who has managed to retain much of traditional manners and values and who takes a keen interest in classical literature.[24] Already in U Latt's day it was widely accepted that the people of Lower Burma, which had fallen earlier under British rule, had lost much of their own culture. It was a time when the Burmese were beginning to feel threatened by the presence of large immigrant communities and the *wunthanu* spirit was already in the air. The meaning of this term and the duties that it implies are specifically discussed in U Latt's second novel, *Shwepyiso* (1914).[25]

Both *Zabebin* and *Shwepyiso* are romances in which courtly manners and conservation are depicted with exquisite grace and more than a touch of nostalgia. However, the greatest interest of these works for the purposes of this paper perhaps lies not so much in the charming romances as in the subplots which throw much light on Rangoon society at the turn of the century.

A well-known subplot in *Shwepyiso* introduces the image of a young westernized Burmese, Maung Thaung Hpe, who has just returned from England as a newly qualified barrister. He greets his father with a very British handshake; he refuses to sit on the beautiful new mats especially bought in his honour as he finds a chair better suited to his western clothes; he uses English expressions which impress and confuse his doting father; he speaks Burmese of that peculiar, stilted variety branded as 'missionary Burmese' which might serve well enough for the writing of biblical tracts but is quite out of place in normal conversation.[26] Maung Thaung Hpe's father has incurred large debts with an Indian money-lender to finance his son's education in England, but the young man shows no sense of gratitude. Once established in a good legal practice he does not even see his father without an appointment and later makes no attempt to extricate the old man from the clutches of the money-lender. In the end the father turns to the traditional refuge of the Burmese, valid to this day: religion. He becomes a monk. Maung Thaung Hpe does not, as one might have wished, come to a bad end. He presumably continues to flourish in the manner of most English-trained barristers, for whom worldly success was considered assured in those days.[27] One is led to wonder if this hint of unexpected realism in a romance of morals and manners reflects a situation where the *wunthanu* spirit, which urged the Burmese to preserve their culture from the corrosive effects of westernization, was strongly contested by a keen awareness of the practical advantages to be gained from modern education. This points to the dilemmas which Burma, in common with many Asian colonies, had to face in the process of selecting what should be preserved, what accepted and what rejected.

U Latt's first novel, *Zabebin*, made no specific mention of *wunthanu* ideals (unless the young government officer's attachment to traditional values could be interpreted as such), but it showed an awareness of the increasing role played in Burmese society by the growing immigrant communities. One of the minor characters is a Chinese man who is depicted as lewd and ridiculous and who becomes the butt of an elaborate practical joke in which an Indian policeman who does not understand any Burmese is involved. The incipient feelings of dislike and resentment which were to gather force in the next two decades to burst out in racial riots can already be discerned behind the author's polite humour.

One of the major preoccupations of the times expressed in a subplot of *Zabebin* was the morals of the Buddhist clergy.[28] A monk who is head of a popular Buddhist association lives in the same monastic grounds as a nun who is widely respected for her knowledge of the Pali religious texts. The propriety of their relationship comes under question, and although U Latt does not write with the frankness of a later era, the reader is left with little doubt as to the guilt of the clerical pair. There is no real denouement, nor any overt condemnation, although the episode is said to have been based on the true story of a well-known monk and nun who left the religious life to marry each other in 1910.[29]

An interesting feature of both novels is the almost complete absence of the British. The only English character who makes an appearance does so in a dream sequence in *Zabebin* and takes the form of a woman who comes to the aid of the heroine. The impression is one of distant benevolence – perhaps a reflection of the popular image of the British before the adverse effects of colonial rule began to be felt.

There are many didactic passages in U Latt's novels expounding Burmese Buddhist values in addition to the *wunthanu* awareness already mentioned, but there is no real sign of political consciousness: this became evident only in the 1920s.

Thakin Kodaw Hmaing[30]

Between U Latt and the next writer whose works will be discussed lies a world of difference. Hsaya Lun, Mr Maung Hmaing or Thakin Kodaw Hmaing, as he was successively known, was born nine years later than U Latt. He received a traditional monastic education and spent much of his youth in Upper Burma. As a boy novice in Mandalay, Hmaing witnessed the occasion on which British troops took away King Thibaw and his queen from the royal palace on the first stage of the journey that would take them to exile in India. Despite the known iniquities of Thibaw and his queen, their removal was a traumatic event for the Burmese, whose racial pride was touched to the quick. For the young Hmaing with his strong attachment to the monarchic tradition, it was a great tragedy.[31]

Hmaing, who entered the world of journalism as a young monk in Moulmein, quickly developed into a prolific writer, and it is no simple matter to chart the course of his early literary and political development. However, it would be fairly safe to state that his reputation as an outstanding patriot-writer became firmly established with the publication of the extended essays known as *tikas*, which could be said to provide a record of the milestones along the path of the Burmese nationalist movement.[32]

The *Boh Tika* ('On Europeans'), written in 1913, reflects the early *wunthanu* awareness of the problems created by colonization and the desire to protect traditional Burmese values. One of its best-loved parts is the vivid, evocative verse on a wedding in Upper Burma.[33] Gifts of land, cattle, grain and household implements showered on the bridal couple are described with a relish which conjures up a joyous picture of rural abundance. But in spite of the early promise the couple fall into debt, not through improvidence but through the onslaught of irresistible economic forces. They are reduced to selling their beloved pair of oxen as well as a plot of land. Thus debt, although in this case not to an Indian but to another Burmese, and land alienation are shown as the destroyers of pastoral bliss.

Another theme of the *Boh Tika* is the concern over Burmese women marrying foreigners, which Hmaing again puts down largely to the dictates of economic necessity.[34] This concern was shared by the Burmese in general, and three years after the publication of the *Boh Tika* the YMBA at its conference passed a resolution against Burmese girls marrying foreigners.

The *tikas* published in the 1920s demonstrate the writer's keen interest in nationalist activities. Hmaing evinces joy over such events as the journey of the YMBA delegation to London, the all-Burma conference protesting against the Craddock Scheme and the boycott against the Rangoon University Act, and exults over the patriotic spirit behind the Hsaya San rebellion. On the other hand he expresses anger and indignation over such matters as the arrest of U Ottama and the quarrels among the members of the

GCBA which led to the dissolution of the association. Hmaing's disillusionment with the older politicians steadily increased, and in the *Thakin Tika* of 1935 he proclaims his decision to throw in his lot with the young nationalists of the Dohbama Asi-ayone, mentioning many of them by name in his verse.

Hmaing's language is vigorous and abrasive. His writings show an extraordinary personality which, in spite of its fundamentally traditional character, was able to move with the currents of the times. The issues that engaged Hmaing's attention were legion and the study of his complete works, ranging through dramas, novels, newspaper articles, essays and poetry, would provide a fairly comprehensive picture of Burmese literary and political developments before the Second World War. 'Saya Lun never got into trouble with the Government for any of his writings, but they probably did more to disseminate advanced views in the country in their subtle way than books which brought on their authors the penalties of the law. His was political propaganda at its cleverest.'[35]

It was a paradoxical quality of Hmaing's genius that while he limited himself almost entirely to the traditional Burmese world of letters, he was able to sympathize with the new ideas that younger nationalists acquired from their exposure to western thought and education. In his twilight years Hmaing became a supporter of leftist politics while remaining a devout Buddhist. It is open to question how much he actually absorbed of the Marxist socialist ideologies embraced by many of his young disciples.

Khitsan

An important landmark in the history of Burmese literature was the publication of two anthologies, the *Khitsan Stories* and the *Khitsan Poems* in 1933 and 1934 respectively. The expression *khitsan* means 'to test the age'. The contributors to these volumes were young men who had been students of the first Burmese professor of Rangoon University, U Pe Maung Tin, who was greatly concerned to improve the position of Burmese within the educational system.[36]

A number of the students who contributed to the *Khitsan* stories and poems had studied not only classical Burmese (including the Pagan inscriptions which represented the earliest examples of the written language) and English but also Pali, Pyu and Mon. It has been said of the *Khitsan* writings that

> This literary movement of the thirties retained the best in national legacy from Pagan down to Thakin Kodaw Hmaing and yet, with the aid of foreign influences, suc-ceeded in modernizing Burmese literacy expression, making it compatible with the rapidly rising society ... the advent of *Khitsan* was connected with the revolutionary political awakening of the thirties and this combination promised a sound basis for a national and humanistic literature.[37]

The short, easily comprehensible sentences free from Pali-isms used by the *Khitsan* writers were hailed enthusiastically as modern and appropriate to the times by some, while other criticized them as childish and contrary to classical traditions.[38] The simplifica-tion of written Burmese had been proceeding for some time since the 1920s and the works of such writers as U Hpo Kya and P. Monin might well be regarded as the forerunners of the *Khitsan* prose style.[39] The works which provide the best examples of this style are the short stories of Theippan Maung Wa, one of three writers who are universally accepted as most representative of the *Khitsan* spirit.

Theippan Maung Wa's stories are based on his experiences as a civil administrator in rural Burma. They paint a vivid picture of village life with a distinct touch of humour which has provoked some critics into accusing him of contempt for the peasantry.[40] Such accusations do less than justice to a writer who was not lacking in sympathy for the plight of the rural poor and whose sense of humour was directed as much towards himself as towards others. A further criticism, that he is lacking in a sense of nationalism, is more difficult to refute for he wrote as a civil servant during a period when those who upheld government policy were necessarily antagonistic to the nationalist cause. Theippan Maung Wa was a man with a strong instinct for the

maintenance of law and order, but what might have been an
asset in an independent nation became a questionable virtue
under a foreign government out of step with the aspirations of the
people.[41] Some of Theippan Maung Wa's stories indicated that
his duties as a government official did not always coincide with
his personal inclinations, and his writings on Burmese language,
literature and history reveal a deep love for traditional cultural
values. He was one of those young strikers who served as National
School teachers after the boycott of 1920, and when he went back
to resume his university studies he became the first student to
obtain an honours degree in Burmese.

The two other writers most closely associated with the *Khitsan*
spirit are Zawgyi and Min Thuwun, who have come to be
regarded as Burma's most eminent poets of today. Zawgyi's poem
on the padauk flower, written in 1928, is seen as the first example
of *Khitsan* verse, where a classical theme is viewed from a new
angle. His poetry, which ranges from verses on cats and ducks to
nature poems with an unusual, enigmatic flavour, is considered
to derive its modernity from originality of thought and content
rather than from form and structure, and to reflect his familiarity
with English literature.[42] Zawgyi is also perhaps the *Khitsan*
writer closest to the revolutionary nationalist spirit in those poems
where he prays for the freedom of the Burmese people and
exhorts them to 'rise up' for their country.[43]

Min Thuwun is a gentler poet with an almost magical touch in
his descriptions of traditional life in rural Burma. His choice of
words is exquisite: beautiful, evocative, yet so readily comprehensible that they make a simultaneous appeal to the reader's heart
and mind. Min Thuwun's verse is full of images culled from the
countryside and stresses continuing trends in Burmese society
rather than the disruptive elements that came in with colonial
rule. He paints scenes from village life in idyllic colours which
contrast with the stark, impoverished communities that come to
life under Theippan Maung Wa's pen. Min Thuwun's poems for
children are particularly well known and loved, helping to keep
alive memories of fast-vanishing traditions. His love poems, of
which he wrote a number during the 1930s, combine the Burmese

predilection for pathos with a sensitivity towards inarticulate human emotions that give them a unique appeal.

The *Khitsan* writers together represent a fusion of the realistic, the innovative and the romantic with a broad humanistic approach. Their nationalist spirit was expressed in terms of their efforts to inject new vigour into Burmese language and literature by adapting them to the modern situation rather than through overtly political writings. Thus they might be said to have formed a bridge between the old *wunthanu* spirit and the young revolutionaries who would seek an ideological framework for their political activities in the western intellectual tradition.

A Sense of History

In the course of their endeavours to give coherence to a disjointed present, it was natural that the Burmese should seek reassurance in the past, the study of which was invigorated by the work of archaeologists and historians in the early decades of the twentieth century. Pagan U Tin, Hmawbi Hsaya Thein and Thakin Kodaw Hmaing were among the traditional Burmese scholars who delved into historical records and chronicles and published works which stimulated a growing interest in history among the reading public. In the 1930s there appeared several Burmese books on history aimed at the younger generation written by men who had been educated under the colonial system.[44] The form which many Burmese historical writings took in these years was perhaps dictated more by the need to revitalize a pride in their own race and culture than by a purely scientific spirit of enquiry, and this is particularly evident in the historical novels.[45]

The first one was published in 1919.[46] In its preface the author, Ledi-pandita U Maung Gyi, stated that he had been inspired by the example of western writers to produce a work that would encourage young Burmese to take an interest in their own history. The title of the novel took the name of the hero, Natshinnaung, a poet-king of Taungoo who lived in the sixteenth century. The story is built around his love for the princess Datukalaya, who was eighteen years his senior, a kind of aunt and also, at one

point, married to one of his cousins. However, Natshinnaung
eventually manages to overcome all obstacles and wins the lady
of his heart, although she dies not long after. It has been said that
by concentrating on Natshinnaung's unswerving love and on his
beautiful poetry which is skilfully woven into the narrative, the
novel portrays only the 'bright side' of his life, ignoring the later
period when he joins the Portuguese governor of Syriam to fight
against the Burmese king of Ava, only to be defeated and executed.[47] It should perhaps be said in fairness to U Maung Gyi
that he did intend to bring out another volume of *Natshinnaung*,
which might well have revealed the 'dark side' of the poet's life.
Certainly in a second historical novel published in several volumes
during the 1920s, *Tabinshwehti*, U Maung Gyi shows how a great
king is brought to ruin partly through association with European
adventurers.

During the 1930s two historical novels appeared which depicted
Natshinnaung as a traitor to his race: *Nahkan-daw* (1932) by U So
Myint and *Thabon-gyi* (1936) by Maha Hswe. Both novels are
built around the conflict between the Burmese king at Ava and
the Portuguese governor of Syriam. In *Thabon-gyi* many parallels
are drawn between Syriam under the Portuguese and Burma
under the British: the threat to Buddhism posed by the presence
of unsympathetic foreign rulers of a different creed; the sycophantic manoeuvres of collaborators; the leadership given to the people
by patriotic monks; the nationalist endeavours of a group of
young men whose activities range from a *swadeshi*-type movement
to armed rebellion.

The theme of the Burmese struggle against foreign domination
is once again pursued by Maha Hswe in his novel *Siththwet thu*
(1939). The story is based on the life of the great poet Nawadei
the First and focuses on the hardships which the Burmese suffered
under the oppression of the anti-Buddhist Shan King Tho-
hanbwa. Here also the allegorical allusion to Burma under colonial rule is unmistakable. Particular emphasis is put on the pride,
love and reliance which the Burmese people placed in their
soldiers, thus highlighting the colonial situation where there was
no national Burmese army. In both *Thabon-gyi* and *Siththwet thu*,

patriots are exhorted to sacrifice their loved ones as well as their own lives in the cause of freedom, reflecting the spirit of the 1930s which saw revolution and militant action as the most effective means of achieving independence.

Many of the historical novels touch upon a question which would assume increasing importance in the Burmese independence movement: the relations between the different races of Burma.[48] In the very first historical novel, *Natshinnaung*, the author indicated that a primary reason for the fall of the kingdom of Hanthawaddy was the Burmese monarch's practice of oppressing the Mons of Lower Burma. The theme of unity among the different races of the country is given even greater emphasis in *Thabon-gyi* where the foreign rulers' policy of divide and rule is exposed and the Burmese, Mons and Karens are urged to stand together. *Sithtwet thu* on the other hand underlines hostile relations between the Burmese and the Shans, although it is made clear that only the anti-Buddhist Shans were to be regarded as the enemy.

Novels such as *Myatleshwedaboh*[49] (1921) by Zeya and *Ye Myanma* (1931) by U Thein Maung, which are set in the wars between the Mons and the Burmese, are now seen as inimical to the spirit of unity among the different races of the country. Nationalism in Burma had started as a movement to uphold Burmese religious and cultural values, but as it gathered momentum political leaders began to recognize the necessity for creating unity out of the diversity which characterized the peoples who made up the nation. Parallel to the tendency to look back to past glories for inspiration there thus developed a search for new approaches and ideologies, particularly as the 1930s proceeded and leftist literature began to be disseminated in Burma.

Shwe Sun Nyo (1933) by Dagon Khin Khin Le is a historical novel which might be said to represent the spirit of the new age that preferred to turn its face towards the future. It is the story of a young man who has become the leader of a gang of bandits after the princely family he served has been destroyed by King Thibaw. The heroine is a girl who is fleeing from Mandalay to escape presentation into the royal harem. The cruelties of

Thibaw's queen as well as the inadequacies of the monarch himself are described in no uncertain terms.[50] It is the avowed aim of the hero to take revenge on Thibaw, but when the British annex Upper Burma and take the royal family to exile in India the young bandit leader decides to dedicate his life to fighting the foreign invaders until a Burmese prince can once again be installed on the throne. After the death of the hero Shwe Sun Nyo, his son continues the fight; but by the time of the grandson, the winds of change come sweeping in. The young man lives on the border between Burma and China, and meets an old Russian who introduces him to the ideas of socialist thinkers. Eventually this grandson of Shwe Sun Nyo marries the daughter of the Russian in preference to the child of a fellow bandit chief who still dreams of restoring the Burmese monarchy. The young man rejects the proposal that he should marry both women, implying the conviction that all attachments to the monarchical past should be put aside so that the future might be built firmly on the foundation of modern leftist ideologies.

Thein Pe Myint

A well-known leftist writer without mention of whose works no discussion of modern Burmese literature would be complete is Thein Pe Myint, widely known as *Tet-hpongyi* Thein Pe after the title of a novel he published in 1937. *Tet-hpongyi* translates roughly as 'modern monk', and the book, which is a castigation of the lives of corrupt monks, created a furore on publication. Although he was to become a leading communist politician, Thein Pe was a devout Buddhist at the time he wrote *Tet-hpongyi* and was greatly concerned to purge the Buddhist clergy of the undesirable elements which were damaging its image.[51]

Thein Pe was the political writer *par excellence*. His very first work of fiction wove a nationalist message into a romance partly inspired by *Romeo and Juliet*.[52] *Khin Myo Chit* is the story of a Burmese Muslim girl who is unable to give up her religion to marry the young Buddhist she loves. Nor can she ask the young man to convert to her religion as this would have an adverse effect on his nationalist activities. The couple decide to part and the girl dies of a broken heart, leaving a letter urging the young man to carry on with the struggle for Burma's independence.

Thein Pe's very first piece of fiction gives an insight into the nature of his later works: a highly talented writer with an outstanding gift for both narrative and dialogue, his heavy-handed political messages often detract from the credibility of his stories. Whether he is writing about immoral monks, capitalists, the evils of venereal disease, the privations of the oilfield workers of Yenangyaung or the miseries of children forced to earn their living, Thein Pe readily sacrifices verisimilitude to political and social considerations. The wages of sin have to be paid in full; those who are guilty of social and political misdemeanours must not be allowed to escape unscathed; and it is the duty of writers not only to point out the ills that plague society but also to suggest possible cures.[53] Thein Pe Myint is representative of many young nationalists of that period in believing that such cures could be found within the range of leftist political theories. His writings indicate that the didactic role of literature kept pace with nationalist activities which were gathering force in the 1930s.

Burmese Literature and the Nationalist Movement

The relationship between literature and society is twofold. On the one hand literature is a reflection of current views and values – especially when, as in the case of Burma under colonial rule, writers do not confine themselves to exclusive intellectual circles removed from the public at large. On the other hand literature could serve to shape social and political opinion by spreading new ideas and, more important, by giving concrete verbal form to feelings and aspirations which might otherwise have remained at an inchoate level in the minds of many readers.

The close connection between literature and the nationalist spirit in Burma can be traced back to the time when British rule was first extended over the whole country. Mandalay had hardly fallen when poems lamenting the deportation of Thibaw began to appear, leading to a new genre in Burmese poetry, the *pa-daw-hmu* (roughly 'the taking away of the royal couple') compositions. Together with this nostalgia for a past which although far from perfect was at least their very own, there stirred among the Burmese an insistent longing for a future when the destiny of the country would once again be in their hands. Such aspirations were expressed not only in the form of numerous rebellions (although some of these might well have been prompted by personal ambition rather than true patriotism), which the British stamped out over several years during the course of the so-called 'pacification of Burma'; they also came out in the form of pro-phetic verses, *tabaung*, foretelling the end of British rule. The potency of these verses was such that U Saw Hla, the most popular of these writers, was arrested by the British.[54] The political role of literature was thus recognized by the government during the very early stages of colonialism.

The link between literature and nationalism can be seen not only in Burma but also in other colonial territories such as India and Indonesia where freedom movements gathered momentum before the Second World War. As there are features common to most colonial situations, there are also differences which reflect not only social and cultural factors but also the particular effect of colonialism on each country. Burma, where British rule was established relatively late, was left untouched by the eighteenth-century western liberal tradition which had played an important role in shaping the intellectual processes of the Indian thinkers of the nineteenth and early twentieth centuries. Thus there did not develop to the same extent as in India a body of social and political writings that could be seen as a pointer to the ideas behind the Burmese nationalist movement. In the words of a contemporary English social and intellectual historian, 'for all the defects of imaginative literature as a historical source, there is nothing to surpass it as a guide to the thoughts and feelings of at least the more articulate sections of the population'.[55] Thus in focusing on poetry and fiction rather than on political and philosophical works (of which there are few and none which could be said to have made a major impact on the country at large) it is intended that this article should provide an insight into the impulses and ideas which inspired the people of Burma along the path to independence.

Notes

1 British annexation of Burma took place in three stages consequential to the Anglo-Burmese wars of 1824–6, 1852 and 1885, the last conflict culminating in the termination of the Burmese monarchical system and the incorporation of the whole country into the British Indian Empire.

2 J. S. Furnivall, *Colonial Policy and Practice*, New York, 1956, provides the most comprehensive overall analysis of the adverse effects of colonial administration on traditional Burmese society, a problem to which he had drawn attention as early as 1916 in his article 'On Researching', *Journal of the Burma Research Society*, (*JBRS*) vol. vi, i, April 1916, p. 4. John F. Cady, *A History of Modern Burma*, New York, 1958, chs. 4–5, also discusses the economic and social effects of British administration in Burma. Albert D. Moscotti, *British Policy and the Nationalist Movement in Burma*, Honolulu, HI, 1974, makes effective use of official police reports and statistics to establish a connection between the increase in crime after 1917 and economic and social problems. E. Sarkisyanz, *Buddhist Backgrounds of the Burmese Revolution*, The Hague, 1965, and Donald Eugene Smith, *Religion and Politics in Burma*, Princeton, NJ, 1965, investigates the effects of colonization on Buddhism and the Sangha. For the colonial impact on traditional education, see Maung Kyaw Win, 'Education in the Union of Burma before and after Independence', MA thesis submitted to the American University, Washington, DC, 1959; U Kaung, 'A Survey of the History of Education in Burma before the British Conquest and After', *JBRS*, vol. xlvi, ii, Dec. 1963; Hkin Zaw Win, 'U, Koloni Khit kala (1860–90) ga Myanma pinya-ye dwin Byitisha aso-ya hsaung wet chet mya apaw hsan sit thon thaggin', *JBRS*, vol. lii, ii, Dec. 1969; Michael F. Mendelson, *Sangha and State in Burma*, Ithaca, NY, 1975, pp. 147–61. The effects of introducing the British Indian judicial system to Burma are examined in Okudaira Ryuji, 'Changes in the Burmese Traditional Legal System during the Process of Colonization by the British in the 19th Century', *South-East Asian Studies*, Kyoto University, vol. 23, no. 2, Sept. 1985.

3 Furnivall, *Colonial Policy and Practice*, p. 105.

4 See Cady, *A History of Modern Burma*, pp. 178–9, and Maung Maung, *From Sangha to Laity: Nationalist Movements of Burma 1920–1940*, New Delhi, 1980, ch. 1, for early religious associations.

5 Cady, *A History of Modern Burma*, pp. 179–80; Maung Maung, *From Sangha to Laity*, ch. 1; see also Hla Kun, *Hpe Pu Shein tho-ma-hot Bama naing-ngan-ye-go kaing-hlok-hke-thaw-hto-thon u*, Rangoon, 1976, pp. 76–8.

6 Maung Maung, *Burma's Constitution* The Hague, 1961, pp. 10–12; Maung Maung, *From Sangha to Laity*, ch. 1; Cady, *A History of Modern Burma*, p. 180, and Sarkisyanz, *Buddhist Backgrounds*, pp. 128–9, draw attention to early government suspicions of the YMBA.

7 Maung Maung, *Burma's Constitution*, pp. 11–12.

8 For U Ottama's role in the Burmese nationalist movement, see Cady, *A History of Modern Burma*, pp. 231–4; Maung Maung, *From Sangha to Laity*, chs 2–3; Smith, *Religion and Politics in Burma*, pp. 92–9; Mendelson, *Sangha and State in Burma*, pp. 199–206; U Ba Yin, *U Hsayadaw Ottama*, Rangoon, 1955.

9 In 1912 U Ottama wrote a book on Japan extolling the virtues of its people, but his speeches and activities showed that his political thinking was very much influenced by developments in the Indian nationalist movement. See U Ottama, U Hsayadaw and Thakin Lwin, *U Ottama let ywei zin*, Rangoon (?), 1976.

10 Furnivall, *Colonial Policy and Practice*, p. 143; Cady, *A History of Modern Burma*, pp. 193, 215–16, 218–19; Mendelson, *Sangha and State in Burma*, pp. 201–3. Thinhka, *Azani gaung-zaungyi Didok U Ba Cho*, Rangoon, 1976, pp. 66–9, discusses the differences between the Indian Congress Party and the GCBA.

11 The issues which led to the splits within the GCBA are discussed in detail in Maung Maung, *From Sangha to Laity*, chs 3–5.

12 Maung Maung, *Burma's Constitution*, p. 16; Maung Maung, *From Sangha to Laity*, pp. 21–3. Cady, *A History of Modern Burma*, pp. 213–19, presents the strike as largely a political manoeuvre. Theippan Maung Wa, 'Unibhasiti bwaikot', in *Theippan Maung Wa i khitsan sa pe ahtwe-htwe*, Rangoon, 1966, gives the views of a student who actually took part in the strike. See also *Amyo-tha ne shwe yadu ahtein ahmat sa-zaung 1970*, Rangoon, 1970.

13 Maung Maung, *Burma's Constitution*, p. 16.

14 Cady, *A History of Modern Burma*, pp. 217–21; Maung Maung, *From Sangha to Laity*, pp. 22–3. The views of those young men who were involved in the strike and the National Schools movement can be seen in U Hpo Kya, 'Amyotha ne' and 'Amyotha kyaung mya keitsa', in *U Hpo Kya hsaung-ba-baung gyok*, Rangoon, 1975, and Theip-

1. Wedding photograph of Aung San and Daw Khin Kyi, 1942.

2. Aung San, his wife and children, Aung San Suu Kyi
in the foreground.

3. Aung San Suu Kyi at the age of about six.

4. In her mother's residence in New Delhi, 1965.

5. Alexander delivering the acceptance speech for the Nobel Peace Prize, Oslo, 10 December 1991. (Photo: Odd H. Anthonsen/*Dagbladet*, Oslo)

6. Suu and Michael, Burma, 1973.

7. Mountain trip in Bhutan, 1971.

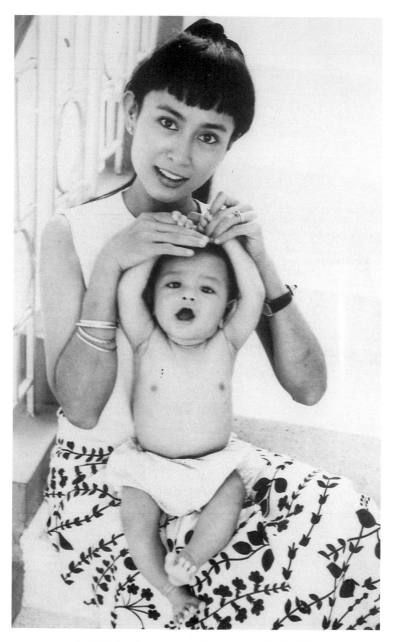

8. With her first-born son, Alexander, in Nepal, 1973.

9. At home in Oxford, 1983.

10. First public address at the Rangoon General Hospital, 24 August 1988, with the author U Thaw Ka.

11. At the first of her mass rallies, Shwedagon Pagoda, 26 August 1988.

12. With former prime minister U Nu and party chairman Tin U,1988.
(Photo: Sandro Tucci, Black Star Inc.)

13. Campaigning up-country in 1989.

14. With supporters at a ceremony in Kachin State, northern Burma,
April 1989.

15. One of the thousand public addresses given in 1988–9.

16. Kim accepting the 1990 Sakharov Prize for Freedom of Thought on his mother's behalf, Strasbourg, 10 July 1991.

pan Maung Wa, 'Amyotha kyaung nhin Myanma Sa pe', in *Theippan Maung Wa Sa Pe Yin kyei Hmu*, Mandalay, 1976.

15 The *'wunthanu* spirit' was an expression commonly used to denote patriotism but there were also *wunthanu athins* (associations), which worked closely with the GCBA. See Cady, *A History of Modern Burma*, ch. 7; Maung Maung, *From Sangha to Laity*, ch. 4.

16 Cady, *A History of Modern Burma*, Moscotti, *British Policy and the Nationalist Movement in Burma*, and Maung Maung, *From Sangha to Laity*, emphasize this aspect.

17 That sympathy for the rebels existed even among Burmese of the official class can be seen in Ba U, *My Burma*, New York, 1959. Mi Mi Khaing in her *Burmese Family*, Bloomington, In., 1962, ch. 8, is careful to point out that Hsaya San's appeal was only to 'a certain section of the population' and to 'some nationalists'; but at the same time, as a student in a missionary school, she seems to have vaguely identified the rebellion with patriotism. That there was considerable sympathy for Hsaya San among the students of Rangoon University is indicated by an article in *The University College Annual*, March 1931, vol. xxi, no. 3, p. 53, where it was said: 'One thing that detaches romantic glamour from the Tharawaddy rebellion is the photograph of Saya San, who ousted the College-beaux from the fluttering hearts of the coy maidens of University College. He was dreamt of as the beau ideal and imagined as something in the way of the dashing dare-devil Don of the "Zorro" type.'

18 The introduction of leftist literature to Burma is studied in Frank Trager (ed.), *Marxism in Southeast Asia*, Stanford, Ca., 1959. A fair idea of the thinking of young leftist nationalists can also be gathered from studying the publications of the Nagani book club during the 1930s.

19 Among the leaders of the strike were Nu, Rashid, Thein Pe, Aung San, Hla Pe, Nyo Mya, Kyaw Nyein and others.

20 Zawgyi discusses the socio-economic forces behind the emergence of the Burmese novel in three articles in his *Ya tha Sa pe ahpwin hnin nidan*, Rangoon, 1976: '20 yazu nhit khit-u Myanma sa pe-i htuchet nhi yat', 'Myanma kalabo wut-htu hpyit po la pon leila chet' and 'Myanma kala-paw wut-htu'. See also Te'katho Win Mun, 'Myanma wut-htu she thamaing', in *Wut-htu She Sa-dan-mya*, Rangoon, 1981.

21 The catalogues of Burmese printed books in the British Library, London, and the India Office Library, London, give a good indication of the kinds of works popular with the Burmese public in the early decades of the twentieth century.

22 The first translated novel, however, was *Robinson Crusoe*, which came

out in 1902. In his '20 Yazu nhit hkitu Myanma sa pe-i htu cha chet', Zawgyi surmises that this book did not capture the imagination of the reading public because it lacked romantic interest.

23 There is as yet no complete biography of U Latt but there is a scattering of articles of which the most comprehensive is Taik So, 'U Latt', in Taik So and Min Yuwe, *Myanma sa meit-hpwe*, Rangoon, 1973.

24 U Latt, *Zabebin*, Rangoon, 1967, p. 24.

25 U Latt, *Shwepyiso*, Rangoon, 1977, pp. 47-8.

26 Ibid., pp. 123-7.

27 Furnivall, *Colonial Policy and Practice*, pp. 127-8, discusses the popularity of the legal profession among the Burmese.

28 See Sarkisyanz, *Buddhist Backgrounds of the Burmese Revolution*; Smith, *Religion and Politics in Burma*.

29 Taik So, 'U Latt'.

30 There are a number of biographies of Hmaing, of which the best known are Thein Pe Myint, *Thakin Kodaw Hmaing U Lun at-htokpatti*, Rangoon, first published in 1937 (countered to some extent by Thireinda Pandita, *Thakin Kodaw Hmaing athtokpatti hma-daw-pon*, Rangoon, 1938); Tin Shwe, *Thakin Kodaw Hmaing*, Rangoon, 1975; Ludu Daw Ama, *Hsayagyi Thakin Kodaw Hmaing athtokpatti*, Mandalay, 1976.

31 This anecdote was first told in Thein Pe Myint, *Thakin Kodaw Hmaing U Lun at-htok-patti*, and repeated in some of the later biographies. Some have levelled the accusation that the monarchist sympathies of Hmaing were so strong that he regarded King George V and Queen Mary with a reverence unbecoming to a nationalist.

32 The links between Hmaing's *tikas* and the Burmese nationalist movement are brought out in Zawgyi, *U Lun: Man and Poet*, Rangoon, 1957' Than Tun, 'Political Thought of Tikas by Hmine', in *Shiroku*, Kagoshima University, no. 10, 1973; Tin Shwe, *Thakin Kodaw Hmaing thu-khit thu bawa thu sa pe*, Rangoon, 1968.

33 'Anya mingala zaung bwe Le-gyo-gyi'. For socio-economic conditions reflected in this work, see Min Thuwun, 'Kyun bawa si-pwa-ye', in Ludu U Hla, Zawgyi, U Ba Hpe and Min Thuwun, *Thakin Kodaw Hmaing nidan*, Rangoon 1971; see also Zawgyi, *U Lun: Man and Poet*, pp. 31-2. Daw Mya Mya Than's article, 'Myanma kabya thamaing (20 yazu)', in *Myanma kabya sa-dan mya*, vol. 1, Rangoon, 1981, points out how Burmese poetry of the early twentieth century reflected social and political conditions in the country.

34 See Than Tun, 'Political Thought of Tikas by Hmine', on the difficulties of gleaning Hmaing's social and political ideas from his *tikas*.

35 Hla Pe, 'The Rise of Popular Literature in Burma', *JBRS*, vol. li, ii, Dec. 1968, pp. 136–7.

36 The ideas behind the publication of the *Khitsan* works are explained by U Pe Maung Tin in his introduction to the first volume of *Khitsan* stories.

37 Min Latt, 'Mainstreams in Burmese Literature: A Dawn That Went Astray', *New Orient: Journal for the Modern and Ancient Cultures of Asia and Africa*, Prague, vol. iii, no. 6, 1962.

38 Some idea of the controversy over the *Khitsan* style can be gathered from Theippan Maung Wa, *Theippan Maung Wa-i khitsan sa pe ahtwe-htwe*.

39 That Theippan Maung Wa himself recognizes this can be gathered from his article on U Hpo Kya in *Theippan Maung Wa Sa Pe Yin kyei Hmu*, p. 45. See also *Theippan Maung Wa-khitsan sa pe ahtwe-htwe*.

40 A leading critic of Theippan Maung Wa was Thein Pe Myint: see his *Tet khit tet lu tet hpongyi Thein Pe*, Rangoon, 1975, pp. 110–13. Yet in his introduction to *Thakin Kodaw Hmaing U Lun at-htokpatti*, while he condemns writers who put themselves above the rest of humanity by purporting to be entirely objective, he makes no mention of Theippan Maung Wa, whose stories had already been published. However, he does protest against works that depict the poor as happy and contented, presaging the criticism that he would later level against Min Thuwun's poems on the delights of village life.

41 The dilemma of writers like Theippan Maung Wa was not unusual under colonialism: for example, Bankimchandra Chattopadhyay, one of the leading figures of the Bengali renaissance, produced his nationalist writings only after retirement from government service. Theippan Maung Wa's early death in 1941 prevents us from knowing how he might have developed as a writer in independent Burma.

42 Min Yuwe, 'Pathama Myanma khitsan kabya', pp. 143–52, and 'Zawgyi-i bawa amyin', pp. 153–68, in Taik So and Min Yuwe, *Myanma sa meit-hpwe*. However, it could be contested that the *Khitsan* poems did introduce new form and structure as the new arrangements of old styles resulted in considerable differences.

43 A collection of five poems by Zawgyi was published under the title 'Zawgyi's Patriotic Poems' in the January 1936 issue of the *Oway Magazine*, vol. 5, no. 1.

44 U Hpo Kya, *Ale-dan Myanma Yazawin*, Rangoon, 1933; U Hpo Kya, *Myanma gon-yi*, Rangoon, 1938: U Ba Than, *Kyaung thon Myanma yazawin*, Rangoon, 1937; U Maung, *Myanma yazawin thit*, Rangoon, 1939.

45 The recourse to history for the bolstering of racial pride and

nationalist ideals can also be seen in the novels of Bankimchandra
Chattopadhyay and other writers of colonial India.

46 It has been speculated that Hmaing's *Dhammazedi wut-htu* may have
appeared earlier, around 1915. See Paragu, 'Thamaing nauk hkan
Myanma wut-htu she mya', in *Wut-htu She Sa-dan-mya*.

47 Ibid., p. 81.

48 It is interesting to note that in his preface to the *Myanma gon-yi
yazawin hpat sa*, U Hpo Kya states specifically that the book was not
only about the Burmese but also about the Mons, Arakanese, Karens
and Shans, while in the earlier published (1924) *Myanma Gonyi* he
simply stated that it was about the people of Burma.

49 Adapted from Baroness Orczy's *Scarlet Pimpernel* (1905).

50 Particular reference is made to the unhappy fate of one of the queen's
ladies-in-waiting, Khin Khin Kyi, with whom Thibaw unwisely fell
in love. Daw Khin Khin Le later develops this story in her magnum
opus, *Sa-hso-daw wut-htu*.

51 Thein Pe Myint explains his reasons for writing *Tet hpongyi* in his *Tet
khit tet lu tet-hpongyi Thein Pe*.

52 Thein Pe Myint, *Kyundaw-i achit-u*, Rangoon, 1974, p. 226.

53 In his introduction to *Thakin Kodaw Hmaing U Lun at-htokpatti*, published in the same year as *Tet-hpongyi*, Thein Pe gives his views on the
duties of writers.

54 See Daw Mya Mya Than, 'Myanma kabya thamaing (20 yazu)';
She haung sa pe thuteithita-u, *Pyi thu sa-hso Maung daung U Kyaw Hla
thu khit-thu bawa thu sa*, Rangoon, 1977. Thein Pe Myint wrote in the
introduction to *Thakin Kodaw Hmaing U Lun at-htokpatti* that 'during
the period between the fall of Burma and the students' boycott of
1920, there have not been known to have been any rebel writers other
than U Kyaw Hla'.

55 Keith Thomas, *Man and the Natural World: Changing Attitudes in
England 1500–1800*, Harmondsworth, 1984, p. 16.

PART TWO

The Struggle

5

In Quest of Democracy

This essay and the two which follow were written by the author for a project she was unable to complete before she was placed under house arrest on 20 July 1989. The project was intended to result in a volume of essays on democracy and human rights which she had been hoping to dedicate to her father as Essays in Honour of Bogyoke Aung San.

I

Opponents of the movement for democracy in Burma have sought to undermine it by on the one hand casting aspersions on the competence of the people to judge what was best for the nation and on the other condemning the basic tenets of democracy as un-Burmese. There is nothing new in Third World governments seeking to justify and perpetuate authoritarian rule by denouncing liberal democratic principles as alien. By implication they claim for themselves the official and sole right to decide what does or does not conform to indigenous cultural norms. Such conventional propaganda aimed at consolidating the powers of the establishment has been studied, analysed and disproved by political scientists, jurists and sociologists. But in Burma, distanced by several decades of isolationism from political and intellectual developments in the outside world, the people have had to draw on their own resources to explode the twin myths of their unfitness for political responsibility and the unsuitability of democracy for their society. As soon as the movement for democracy spread out across Burma there was a surge of intense interest in the meaning of the word 'democracy', in its history and its practical implications. More than a quarter-century of narrow authoritarianism under which they had been fed a pabulum of shallow, negative dogma had not blunted the perceptiveness or political alertness of the Burmese. On the contrary, perhaps not all that surprisingly, their appetite for discussion and debate, for uncensored information and objective analysis, seemed to have been sharpened. Not only was there an eagerness to study and to absorb standard theories on modern politics and political institutions, there was also widespread and intelligent speculation on the nature of democracy as a social system of which they had had little experience but which appealed to their common-sense notions of what was due to a civilized society. There was a spontaneous interpretative response to such basic ideas as representative government, human rights and the rule of law. The privileges and freedoms which would be guaranteed by democratic institutions were contemplated with understandable enthusiasm. But the duties of those who would bear responsibility for the maintenance of a stable democracy also provoked much thoughtful consideration. It is natural that a people who have suffered much from the consequences of bad government should be preoccupied with theories of good government.

Members of the Buddhist *sangha* in their customary role as mentors have led the way in articulating popular expectations by drawing on classical learning to illuminate timeless values. But the conscious effort to make traditional knowledge relevant to contemporary needs was not confined to any particular circle – it went right through Burmese society from urban intellectuals and small shopkeepers to doughty village grandmothers.

Why has Burma with its abundant natural and human resources failed to live up to its early promise as one of the most energetic and fastest-developing nations in South-east Asia? International scholars have provided detailed answers supported by careful analyses of historical, cultural, political and economic factors. The Burmese people, who have had no access to sophisticated academic material, got to the heart of the matter by turning to the words of the Buddha on the four causes of decline and decay: failure to recover that which had been lost, omission to repair that which had been damaged, disregard of the need for reasonable economy, and the elevation to leadership of men without morality or learning. Translated into contemporary terms, when democratic rights had been lost to military dictatorship sufficient efforts had not been made to regain them, moral and political values had been allowed to deteriorate without concerted attempts to save the situation, the economy had been badly managed, and the country had been ruled by men without integrity or wisdom. A thorough study by the cleverest scholar using the best and latest methods of research could hardly have identified more correctly or succinctly the chief causes of Burma's decline since 1962.

Under totalitarian socialism, official policies with little relevance to actual needs had placed Burma in an economic and administrative limbo where government bribery and evasion of regulations were the indispensable lubricant to keep the wheels of everyday life turning. But through the years of moral decay and material decline there has survived a vision of a society in which the people and the leadership could unite in principled efforts to achieve prosperity and security. In 1988 the movement for democracy gave rise to the hope that the vision might become reality. At its most basic and immediate level, liberal democracy would mean in institutional terms a representative government appointed for a constitutionally limited term through free and fair elections. By exercising responsibly their right to choose their own leaders the Burmese hope to make an effective start at reversing the process of decline. They have countered the propagandist doctrine that democracy is unsuited to their cultural norms by examining traditional theories of government.

The Buddhist view of world history tells that when society fell from its original state of purity into moral and social chaos a king was elected to restore peace and justice. The ruler was known by three titles: *Mahasammata*, 'because he is named ruler by the unanimous consent of the people'; *Khattiya*; 'because he has dominion over agricultural land'; and *Raja*, 'because he wins the people to affection through observance of the *dhamma* (virtue, justice, the law)'. The agreement by which their first monarch undertakes to rule righteously in return for a portion of the rice crop represents the Buddhist version of government by social contract. The *Mahasammata* follows the general pattern of Indic kingship in South-east Asia. This has been criticized as antithetical to the idea of the modern state because it promotes a personalized form of monarchy lacking the continuity inherent in the western abstraction of the king as possessed of both a body politic and a body natural. However, because the *Mahasammata* was chosen by popular consent and required to govern in accordance with just laws, the concept of government elective and *sub lege* is not alien to traditional Burmese thought.

The Buddhist view of kingship does not invest the ruler with the divine right to govern the realm as he pleases. He is expected to observe the Ten Duties of Kings, the Seven Safeguards against Decline, the Four Assistances to the People, and to be guided by numerous other codes of conduct such as the Twelve Practices of Rulers, the Six Attributes of Leaders, the Eight Virtues of Kings and the Four Ways to Overcome Peril. There is logic to a tradition which includes the king among the five enemies or perils and which subscribes to many sets of moral instructions for the edification of those in positions of authority. The people of Burma have had much experience of despotic rule and possess a great awareness of the unhappy gap that can exist between the theory and practice of government.

The Ten Duties of Kings are widely known and generally accepted as a yardstick which could be applied just as well to modern government as to the first monarch of the world. The duties are: liberality, morality, self-sacrifice, integrity, kindness, austerity, non-anger, non-violence, forbearance and non-opposition (to the will of the people).

The first duty of liberality (*dana*) which demands that a ruler should contribute generously towards the welfare of the people makes the tacit assumption that a government should have the competence to provide adequately for its citizens. In the context of modern politics, one of the prime duties of a responsible administration would be to ensure the economic security of the state.

Morality (*sila*) in traditional Buddhist terms is based on the observance of the five precepts, which entails refraining from destruction of life, theft, adultery, falsehood and indulgence in intoxicants. The ruler must bear a high moral character to win the respect and trust of the people, to ensure their happiness and prosperity and to provide a proper example. When the king does not observe the *dhamma*, state functionaries become corrupt, and when state functionaries are corrupt the people are caused much suffering. It is further believed that an unrighteous king brings down calamity on the land. The root of a nation's misfortunes has to be sought in the moral failings of the government.

The third duty, *paricagga*, is sometimes translated as generosity and sometimes as self-sacrifice. The former would constitute a duplication of the first duty, *dana*, so self-sacrifice as the ultimate generosity which gives up all for the sake of the people would appear the more satisfactory interpretation. The concept of selfless public service is sometimes illustrated by the story of the hermit Sumedha who took the vow of Buddhahood. In so doing he who could have realized the supreme liberation of *nirvana* in a single lifetime committed himself to countless incarnations that he might help other beings free themselves from suffering. Equally popular is the story of the lord of the monkeys who sacrificed his life to save his subjects, including one who had always wished him harm and who was the eventual cause of his death. The good ruler sublimates his needs as an individual to the service of the nation.

Integrity (*ajjava*) implies incorruptibility in the discharge of public duties as well as honesty and sincerity in personal relations. There is a Burmese saying: 'With rulers, truth, with (ordinary) men, vows'. While a private individual may be bound only by the formal vows that he makes, those who govern should be wholly bound by the truth in thought, word and deed. Truth is the very essence of the teachings of the Buddha, who referred to himself as the *Tathagata* or 'one who has come to the truth'. The Buddhist king must therefore live and rule by truth, which is the perfect uniformity between nomenclature and nature. To deceive or to mislead the people in any way would be an occupational failing as well as a moral offence. 'As an arrow, intrinsically straight, without warp or distortion, when one word is spoken, it does not err into two.'

Kindness (*maddava*) in a ruler is in a sense the courage to feel concern for the people. It is undeniably easier to ignore the hardships of those who are too weak to demand their rights than to respond sensitively to their needs. To care is to accept responsibility, to dare to act in accordance with the dictum that the ruler is the strength of the helpless. In *Wizaya*, a well-known nineteenth-century drama based on the *Mahavamsa* story of Prince Vijaya, a king sends away into exile his own son, whose wild ways had caused the people much distress: 'In the matter of love, to make no distinction between citizen and son, to give equally of loving kindness, that is the righteousness of kings.'

The duty of austerity (*tapa*) enjoins the king to adopt simple habits, to develop self-control and to practise spiritual discipline. The self-indulgent ruler who enjoys an extravagant lifestyle and ignores the spiritual need for austerity was no more acceptable at the time of the *Mahasammata* then he would be in Burma today.

The seventh, eighth and ninth duties – non-anger (*akkodha*), non-violence (*avihamsa*) and forbearance (*khanti*) – could be said to be related. Because the displeasure of the powerful could have unhappy and far-reaching consequences, kings must not allow personal feelings of enmity and ill will to erupt into destructive anger and violence. It is incumbent on a ruler to develop the true forbearance which moves him to deal wisely and generously with the shortcomings and provocations of even those whom he could crush with impunity. Violence is totally contrary to the teachings of Buddhism. The good ruler vanquishes ill will with loving kindness, wickedness with virtue, parsimony with liberality, and falsehood with truth. The Emperor Ashoka who ruled his realm in accordance with the principles of non-violence and compassion is always held up as an ideal Buddhist king. A government should not attempt to enjoin submission through harshness and immoral force but should aim at *dhamma-vijaya*, a conquest by righteousness.

The tenth duty of kings, non-opposition to the will of the people (*avirodha*), tends to be singled out as a Buddhist endorsement of democracy, supported by well-known stories from the *Jakatas*. Pawridasa, a monarch who acquired an unfortunate taste for human flesh, was forced to leave his kingdom because he would not heed the people's demand that he should abandon his cannibalistic habits. A very different kind of ruler was the Buddha's penultimate incarnation on earth, the pious King Vessantara. But he too was sent into exile when in the course of his strivings for the perfection of liberality he gave away the white elephant of the state without the consent of the people. The royal duty of non-opposition is a reminder that the legitimacy of government is founded on the consent of the people, who may withdraw their mandate at any time if they lose confidence in the ability of the ruler to serve their best interests.

By invoking the Ten Duties of Kings the Burmese are not so much indulging in wishful thinking as drawing on time-honoured values to reinforce the validity of the political reforms they consider necessary. It is a strong argument for democracy that governments regulated by principles of accountability, respect for public opinion and the supremacy of just laws are more likely than an all-powerful ruler or ruling class, uninhibited by the need to honour the will of the people, to observe the traditional duties of Buddhist kingship. Traditional values serve both to justify and to decipher popular expectations of democratic government.

II

The people of Burma view democracy not merely as a form of government but as an integrated social and ideological system based on respect for the individual. When asked why they feel so strong a need for democracy, the least political will answer: 'We just want to be able to go about our own business freely and peacefully, not doing anybody any harm, just earning a decent living without anxiety and fear.' In other words they want the basic human rights which would guarantee a tranquil, dignified exist-ence free from want and fear. 'Democracy songs' articulated such longings: 'I am not among the rice-eating robots . . . Everyone but everyone should be entitled to human rights.' 'We are not savage beasts of the jungle, we are all men with reason, it's high time to stop the rule of armed intimidation: if every movement of dissent were settled by the gun, Burma would only be emptied of people.'

It was predictable that as soon as the issue of human rights became an integral part of the movement for democracy the official media should start ridiculing and condemning the whole concept of human rights, dubbing it a western artefact alien to traditional values. It was also ironic – Buddhism, the foundation of traditional Burmese culture, places the greatest value on man, who alone of all beings can achieve the supreme state of Buddhahood. Each man has in him the potential to realize the truth through his own will and endeavour and to help others to realize it. Human life therefore is infinitely precious. 'Easier is it for a needle dropped from the abode of Brahma to meet a needle stuck in the earth than to be born as a human being.'

But despotic governments do not recognize the precious human component of the state, seeing its citizens only as a faceless, mindless – and helpless – mass to be manipulated at will. It is as though people were incidental to a nation rather than its very life-blood. Patriotism, which should be the vital love and care of a people for their land, is debased into a smokescreen of hysteria to hide the injustices of authoritarian rulers who define the interests of the state in terms of their own limited interests. The official creed is required to be accepted with an unquestioning faith more in keeping with orthodox tenets of the biblical religions which have held sway in the West than with the more liberal Buddhist attitude:

> It is proper to doubt, to be uncertain . . . Do not go upon what has been acquired by repeated hearing. Nor upon tradition, nor upon rumours . . . When you know for yourself that certain things are unwholesome and wrong, abandon them . . . When you know for yourself that certain things are wholesome and good, accept them.

It is a puzzlement to the Burmese how concepts which recognize the inherent dignity and the equal and inalienable rights of human beings, which accept that all men are endowed with reason and conscience and which recommend a universal spirit of brotherhood, can be inimical to indigenous values. It is also difficult for them to understand how any of the rights contained in the thirty articles of the Universal Declaration of Human Rights can be seen as anything but wholesome and good. That the declaration was not drawn up in Burma by the Burmese seems an inadequate reason, to say the least, for rejecting it, especially as Burma was one of the nations which voted for its adoption in December 1948. If ideas and beliefs are to be denied validity outside the geographical and cultural bounds of their origin, Buddhism would be confined to north India, Christianity to a narrow tract in the Middle East and Islam to Arabia.

The proposition that the Burmese are not fit to enjoy as many rights and privileges as the citizens of democratic countries is insulting. It also makes questionable the logic of a Burmese government considering itself fit to enjoy more rights and privileges than the governments of those same countries. The inconsistency can be explained – but not justified – only by assuming so wide a gulf between the government and the people that they have to be judged by different norms. Such an assumption in turn casts doubt on the doctrine of government as a comprehensive spirit and medium of national values.

Weak logic, inconsistencies and alienation from the people are common features of authoritarianism. The relentless attempts of totalitarian regimes to prevent free thought and new ideas and the persistent assertion of their own rightness bring on them an intellectual stasis which they project on to the nation at large. Intimidation and propaganda work in a duet of oppression, while the people, lapped in fear and distrust, learn to dissemble and to keep silent. And all the time the desire grows for a system which will lift them from the position of 'rice-eating robots' to the status of human beings who can think and speak freely and hold their heads high in the security of their rights.

From the beginning Burma's struggle for democracy has been

fraught with danger. A movement which seeks the just and equitable distribution of powers and prerogatives that have long been held by a small élite determined to preserve its privileges at all costs is likely to be prolonged and difficult. Hope and optimism are irrepressible but there is a deep underlying premonition that the opposition to change is likely to be vicious. Often the anxious question is asked: will such an oppressive regime *really* give us democracy? And the answer has to be: democracy, like liberty, justice and other social and political rights, is not 'given', it is earned through courage, resolution and sacrifice.

Revolutions generally reflect the irresistible impulse for necessary changes which have been held back by official policies or retarded by social apathy. The institutions and practices of democracy provide ways and means by which such changes could be effected without recourse to violence. But change is anathema to authoritarianism, which will tolerate no deviation from rigid policies. Democracy acknowledges the right to differ as well as the duty to settle differences peacefully. Authoritarian governments see criticism of their actions and doctrines as a challenge to combat. Opposition is equated with 'confrontation', which is interpreted as violent conflict. Regimented minds cannot grasp the concept of confrontation as an open exchange of major differences with a view to settlement through genuine dialogue. The insecurity of power based on coercion translates into a need to crush all dissent. Within the framework of liberal democracy, protest and dissent can exist in healthy counterpart with orthodoxy and conservatism, contained by a general recognition of the need to balance respect for individual rights with respect for law and order.

The words 'law and order' have so frequently been misused as an excuse for oppression that the very phrase has become suspect in countries which have known authoritarian rule. Some years ago a prominent Burmese author wrote an article on the notion of law and order as expressed by the official term *nyein-wut-pi-pyar*. One by one he analysed the words, which literally mean 'silent-crouched-crushed-flattened', and concluded that the whole made for an undesirable state of affairs, one which militated against the emergence of an articulate, energetic, progressive citizenry. There is no intrinsic virtue to law and order unless 'law' is equated with justice and 'order' with the discipline of a people satisfied that justice has been done. Law as an instrument of state oppression is a familiar feature of totalitarianism. Without a popularly elected legislature and an independent judiciary to ensure due process, the authorities can enforce as 'law' arbitrary decrees that are in fact flagrant negations of all acceptable norms of justice. There can be no security for citizens in a state where new 'laws' can be made and old ones changed to suit the convenience of the powers that be. The iniquity of such practices is traditionally recognized by the precept that existing laws should not be set aside at will. The Buddhist concept of law is based on *dhamma*, righteousness or virtue, not on the power to impose harsh and inflexible rules on a defenceless people. The true measure of the justice of a system is the amount of protection it guarantees to the weakest.

Where there is no justice there can be no secure peace. The Universal Declaration of Human Rights recognizes that 'if man is not to be compelled to have recourse, as a last resort, to rebellion against tyranny and oppression', human rights should be protected by the rule of law. That just laws which uphold human rights are the necessary foundation of peace and security would be denied only by closed minds which interpret peace as the silence of all opposition and security as the assurance of their own power. The Burmese associate peace and security with coolness and shade:

> The shade of a tree is cool indeed
> The shade of parents is cooler
> The shade of teachers is cooler still
> The shade of the ruler is yet more cool
> But coolest of all is the shade of the Buddha's teachings.

Thus to provide the people with the protective coolness of peace and security, rulers must observe the teachings of the Buddha. Central to these teachings are the concepts of truth, righteousness and loving kindness. It is government based on these very qualities that the people of Burma are seeking in their struggle for democracy.

In a revolutionary movement there is always the danger that political exigencies might obscure, or even nullify, essential spiritual aims. A firm insistence on the inviolability and primacy of such aims is not mere idealism but a necessary safeguard against an Animal Farm syndrome where the new order after its first flush of enthusiastic reforms takes on the murky colours of the very system it has replaced. The people of Burma want not just a change of government but a change in political values. The unhappy legacies of authoritarianism can be removed only if the concept of absolute power as the basis of government is replaced by the concept of confidence as the mainspring of political authority: the confidence of the people in their right and ability to decide the destiny of their nation, mutual confidence between the people and their leaders and, most important of all, confidence in the principles of justice, liberty and human rights. Of the four Buddhist virtues conducive to the happiness of laymen, *saddha*, confidence in moral, spiritual and intellectual values, is the first. To instil such confidence, not by an appeal to the passions but through intellectual conviction, into a society which has long been wracked by distrust and uncertainty is the essence of the Burmese revolution for democracy. It is a revolution which moves for changes endorsed by universal norms of ethics.

In their quest for democracy the people of Burma explore not only the political theories and practices of the world outside their country but also the spiritual and intellectual values that have given shape to their own environment.

There is an instinctive understanding that the cultural, social and political development of a nation is a dynamic process which has to be given purpose and direction by drawing on tradition as well as by experiment, innovation and a willingness to evaluate both old and new ideas objectively. This is not to claim that all those who desire democracy in Burma are guided by an awareness of the need to balance a dispassionate, sensitive assessment of the past with an intelligent appreciation of the present. But threading through the movement is a rich vein of the liberal, integrated spirit which meets intellectual challenges with wisdom and courage. There is also a capacity for the sustained mental strife and physical endurance necessary to withstand the forces of negativism, bigotry and hate. Most encouraging of all, the main impetus for struggle is not an appetite for power, revenge and destruction but a genuine respect for freedom, peace and justice.

The quest for democracy in Burma is the struggle of a people to live whole, meaningful lives as free and equal members of the world community. It is part of the unceasing human endeavour to prove that the spirit of man can transcend the flaws of his own nature.

6

Freedom from Fear

The following was first released for publication by the editor to commemorate the European Parliament's award to Aung San Suu Kyi of the 1990 Sakharov Prize for Freedom of Thought. The award ceremony took place in her absence at Strasbourg on 10 July 1991. In the same week the essay appeared in full or in part in The Times Literary Supplement, *the* New York Times, *the* Far Eastern Economic Review, *the* Bangkok Post, *the* Times of India *and in the German, Norwegian and Icelandic press.*

It is not power that corrupts but fear. Fear of losing power corrupts those who wield it and fear of the scourge of power corrupts those who are subject to it. Most Burmese are familiar with the four *a-gati*, the four kinds of corruption. *Chanda-gati*, corruption induced by desire, is deviation from the right path in pursuit of bribes or for the sake of those one loves. *Dosa-gati* is taking the wrong path to spite those against whom one bears ill will, and *moha-gati* is aberration due to ignorance. But perhaps the worst of the four is *bhaya-gati*, for not only does *bhaya*, fear, stifle and slowly destroy all sense of right and wrong, it so often lies at the root of the other three kinds of corruption.

Just as *chanda-gati*, when not the result of sheer avarice, can be caused by fear of want or fear of losing the goodwill of those one loves, so fear of being surpassed, humiliated or injured in some way can provide the impetus for ill will. And it would be difficult to dispel ignorance unless there is freedom to pursue the truth unfettered by fear. With so close a relationship between fear and corruption it is little wonder that in any society where fear is rife corruption in all forms becomes deeply entrenched.

Public dissatisfaction with economic hardships has been seen as the chief cause of the movement for democracy in Burma, sparked off by the student demonstrations of 1988. It is true that years of incoherent policies, inept official measures, burgeoning inflation and falling real income had turned the country into an economic shambles. But it was more than the difficulties of eking out a barely acceptable standard of living that had eroded the patience of a traditionally good-natured, quiescent people – it was also the humiliation of a way of life disfigured by corruption and fear. The students were protesting not just against the death of their comrades but against the denial of their right to life by a totalitarian regime which deprived the present of meaningfulness and held out no hope for the future. And because the students' protests articulated the frustrations of the people at large, the demonstrations quickly grew into a nationwide movement. Some of its keenest supporters were businessmen who had developed the skills and the contacts necessary not only to survive but to prosper within the system. But their affluence offered them no genuine sense of security or fulfilment, and they could not but see that if they and their fellow citizens, regardless of economic status, were to achieve a worthwhile existence, an accountable administration was at least a necessary if not a sufficient condition. The people of Burma had wearied of a precarious state of passive apprehension where they were 'as water in the cupped hands' of the powers that be.

> Emerald cool we may be
> As water in cupped hands
> But oh that we might be
> As splinters of glass
> In cupped hands.

Glass splinters, the smallest with its sharp, glinting power to defend itself against hands that try to crush, could be seen as a vivid symbol of the spark of courage that is an essential attribute of those who would free themselves from the grip of oppression. Bogyoke Aung San regarded himself as a revolutionary and searched tirelessly for answers to the problems that beset Burma during her times of trial. He exhorted the people to develop courage: 'Don't just depend on the courage and intrepidity of others. Each and every one of you must make sacrifices to become a hero possessed of courage and intrepidity. Then only shall we all be able to enjoy true freedom.'

The effort necessary to remain uncorrupted in an environment where fear is an integral part of everyday existence is not immediately apparent to those fortunate enough to live in states governed by the rule of law. Just laws do not merely prevent corruption by meting out impartial punishment to offenders. They also help to create a society in which people can fulfil the basic requirements necessary for the preservation of human dignity without recourse to corrupt practices. Where there are no such laws, the burden of upholding the principles of justice and common decency falls on the ordinary people. It is the cumulative effect of their sustained effort and steady endurance which will change a nation where reason and conscience are warped by fear into one where legal rules exist to promote man's desire for harmony and justice while restraining the less desirable destructive traits in his nature.

In an age when immense technological advances have created lethal weapons which could be, and are, used by the powerful and the unprincipled to dominate the weak and the helpless, there is a compelling need for a closer relationship between politics and ethics at both the national and international levels. The Universal Declaration of Human Rights of the United Nations proclaims that 'every individual and every organ of society' should strive to promote the basic rights and freedoms to which all human beings regardless of race, nationality or religion are entitled. But as long as there are governments whose authority is founded on coercion rather than on the mandate of the people, and interest groups which place short-term profits above long-term peace and prosperity, concerted international action to protect and promote human rights will remain at best a partially realized ideal. There will continue to be arenas of struggle where victims of oppression have to draw on their own inner resources to defend their inalienable rights as members of the human family.

The quintessential revolution is that of the spirit, born of an intellectual conviction of the need for change in those mental attitudes and values which shape the course of a nation's development. A revolution which aims merely at changing official policies and institutions with a view to an improvement in material conditions has little chance of genuine success. Without a revolution of the spirit, the forces which produced the iniquities of the old order would continue to be operative, posing a constant threat to the process of reform and regeneration. It is not enough merely to call for freedom, democracy and human rights. There has to be a united determination to persevere in the struggle, to make sacrifices in the name of enduring truths, to resist the corrupting influences of desire, ill will, ignorance and fear.

Saints, it has been said, are the sinners who go on trying. So free men are the oppressed who go on trying and who in the process make themselves fit to bear the responsibilities and to uphold the disciplines which will maintain a free society. Among the basic freedoms to which men aspire that their lives might be full and uncramped, freedom from fear stands out as both a means and an end. A people who would build a nation in which strong, democratic institutions are firmly established as a guarantee against state-induced power must first learn to liberate their own minds from apathy and fear.

Always one to practise what he preached, Aung San himself constantly demonstrated courage – not just the physical sort but the kind that enabled him to speak the truth, to stand by his word, to accept criticism, to admit his faults, to correct his mistakes, to respect the opposition, to parley with the enemy and to let people be the judge of his worthiness as a leader. It is for such moral courage that he will always be loved and respected in Burma – not merely as a warrior hero but as the inspiration and conscience of the nation. The words used by Jawaharlal Nehru to describe Mahatma Gandhi could well be applied to Aung San: 'The essence of his teaching was fearlessness and truth, and action allied to these, always keeping the welfare of the masses in view.'

Gandhi, that great apostle of non-violence, and Aung San, the founder of a national army, were very different personalities, but as there is an inevitable sameness about the challenges of authoritarian rule anywhere at any time, so there is a similarity in the intrinsic qualities of those who rise up to meet the challenge. Nehru, who considered the instillation of courage in the people of India one of Gandhi's greatest achievements, was a political modernist, but as he assessed the needs for a twentieth-century movement for independence, he found himself looking back to the philosophy of ancient India: 'The greatest gift for an individual or a nation . . . was *abhaya*, fearlessness, not merely bodily courage but absence of fear from the mind.'

Fearlessness may be a gift but perhaps more precious is the courage acquired through endeavour, courage that comes from cultivating the habit of refusing to let fear dictate one's actions, courage that could be described as 'grace under pressure' – grace which is renewed repeatedly in the face of harsh, unremitting pressure.

Within a system which denies the existence of basic human rights, fear tends to be the order of the day. Fear of imprisonment, fear of torture, fear of death, fear of losing friends, family, property or means of livelihood, fear of poverty, fear of isolation, fear of failure. A most insidious form of fear is that which masquerades as common sense or even wisdom, condemning as foolish, reckless, insignificant or futile the small, daily acts of courage which help to preserve man's self-respect and inherent human dignity. It is not easy for a people conditioned by the iron rule of the principle that might is right to free themselves from the enervating miasma of fear. Yet even under the most crushing state machinery courage rises up again and again, for fear is not the natural state of civilized man.

The wellspring of courage and endurance in the face of unbridled power is generally a firm belief in the sanctity of ethical principles combined with a historical sense that despite all setbacks the condition of man is set on an ultimate course for both spiritual and material advancement. It is his capacity for self-improvement and self-redemption which most distinguishes man from the mere brute. At the root of human responsibility is the concept of perfection, the urge to achieve it, the intelligence to find a path towards it, and the will to follow that path if not to the end at least the distance needed to rise above individual limitations and environmental impediments. It is man's vision of a world fit for rational, civilized humanity which leads him to dare and to suffer to build societies free from want and fear. Concepts such as truth, justice and compassion cannot be dismissed as trite when these are often the only bulwarks which stand against ruthless power.

7

The True Meaning of *Boh*

Reprinted from Asian Survey, *vol. 31, no. 9 (pp. 793–7), by permission of the Regents of the University of California. An editorial note explained how it had been submitted in draft to the journal some years earlier and that it was decided to publish it as it stood, even though the author had intended to make further revisions. In her accompanying letter to* Asian Survey *the author explained her wish to reprint the essay eventually in a volume dedicated to her father: 'The more I learn about modern Burmese politics the more I realize how essential is my father's role in keeping alive the spirit of truth and justice during all these years under a corrupt regime. When I honour my father I honour all those who stand for political integrity in Burma.'*

Boh is the official Burmese term for an army lieutenant. But in common parlance a *boh* is any military officer, a commander, a leader. It was in that sense that the word was applied to officers of the fledgling Burma Independence Army when it first made its appearance on Burmese soil in 1942, vibrant with the hopes of a country poised to realize its dream of freedom. In the febrile, hazardous atmosphere of wartime, heroes were at a premium and every *boh* was seen through a haze of glamour and romance. Foremost among them was Aung San, barely twenty-seven, intense, upright, the very image of the patriotic young commander-in-chief, inspiring poetry and song.

Parents of Burma
You must give birth to heroes
Like *Boh* Aung San . . .
He will make history
His deeds will be recorded in annals
The noble *Boh* Aung San.

Such adulation would have intoxicated men of greater age and experience, but Aung San remained steady and clear-sighted, kept stone-sober by the extremely high standards he set himself. On a not untypical occasion when a panegyric was read out hailing him as one who would be renowned in world history, he remarked crisply that, let alone the history of the world, he had not yet earned himself a place even in the history of Burma. After he had led his army through the resistance movement against the Japanese and when negotiations with the re-established British administration had reached the stage where he had been appointed the Deputy Chairman of the Governor's Executive Council, he was still saying: 'I have not even started, I have not yet done anything, so if there is to be praise I do not want it yet.' By that time he was already a national hero, the acknowledged leader of the people of Burma, known throughout the country simply as 'our *Bogyoke*'.

Bogyoke indicates the rank of major-general, but as applied to Aung San the title acquired a unique significance in Burma. It stood for the father of the army, for strong, selfless leadership, for a 'ruler of *Bohs*' in the best sense of its literal meaning. *Boh* is derived from *bala*, the Pali word for strength. But the dividing line between praiseworthy strength and undesirable force is very thin. For when *kara*, action, is joined to *bala*, it becomes *balakara*, violence. In other words, strength turns destructive when acted out beyond acceptable limits. The menace which might, uncontrolled by principle, poses is predictably greatest in times made turbulent by sweeping social or political changes, and it was at such a time that Aung San found himself at the helm of the Burmese struggle for independence. The product of a Buddhist monastery school, he would have acquired early the concept of strength as a mental and spiritual force, learning that the five *bala* (synonymous with the five *indriya* or controlling faculties) were confidence, energy, mindfulness, mental discipline and wisdom. The five strengths which were desirable from a wordly point of view – those of conduct, body, wealth, knowledge and friendship – would be considered relatively inferior, capable of reaching honourable fruition only when regulated by a proper cultivation of the mind and spirit. But Aung San was not influenced simply by an intellectual understanding of the positive and negative aspects of strength. As the commander-in-chief of a young army which had to be welded into a responsible military organization and as the leader of a national movement which comprised many volatile elements, he was well acquainted with the practical dangers of undisciplined force.

Aung San visualized the army he had founded as an austere and honourable institution carved out of such rock-solid virtues as incorruptibility, self-sacrifice and self-discipline, its strength wholly dedicated to the service of the nation without thought of personal gain. He exhorted his soldiers to refrain from adopting a stance which would make their strength of arms seem an instrument of oppression. Pointing out the human tendency of the strong to bully the weak, he urged the fearless opposition of immoral strength and the practice of scrupulous justice towards the weak. He warned that if the army came to be detested by the people, the reason for which it had been founded would be vitiated. 'This army must be such that . . . the people can revere it, take refuge in it, depend on it.' And to deserve the respect and affection of the country there must be a continuous striving for excellence. But it had to be excellence without élitism. Aung San stated in unambiguous terms that the Burmese army had not been founded for one man or one party, it was for the whole country. He rejected the blinkered view of those military personnel who harboured the opinion that only they were capable of patriotism. 'There are others who are not soldiers who have suffered and made all kinds of sacrifices for their country . . . You must change this notion that only the soldiers matter.'

Aung-San would admonish his soldiers sternly not because, he explained, he wished to undermine the army but because he wanted to make it quite clear that 'although we bear arms, we do not commit injustices, we are not the nation's enemies, we are the nation's friends'. For him the honour of the nation meant the honour of the people, and the honour of the people was inextricably linked with his own honour and that of his soldiers. His ideal of the armed forces was one in which the conduct of every single member would have been instinctive with the sentiment expressed in the lines of an eighteenth-century courtier-poet, Let-We Thondara (*c.* 1723–99):

> How superior
> The tactics of war
> How potent
> The weapons!
> Without gathering in
> The hearts of the people,
> Without relying on
> The strength of the people,
> The sword edge
> Will shatter,
> The spear
> Will bend.

That *Bogyoke* Aung San himself gathered in the hearts of his countrymen and that he relied on their strength became increasingly manifest as the independence movement approached its climax. He asked the people to stand firm and resolute behind him in the struggle, for he held that no man however able could successfully conclude any national enterprise of historic significance without the support and active co-operation of the public. He knew that genuine support could not be coerced and he would not stoop to court it with flattery or false promises. He saw plain honesty as the only foundation for the mutual trust and respect which would have to be established between him and the people of Burma if they were to carry out unitedly the task of creating an independent, self-reliant nation out of a land devastated by war. To indulge in political guile and deceit would be to insult the people and to violate his own self-respect.

Aung San simply worked on the assumption that the majority of the people of Burma were wise, that they preferred the true to the false and that they were capable of distinguishing between the two. The assumption could not have been false, for the people reciprocated by giving him their full understanding and placing their united strength behind his endeavours, returning in the elections of April 1947 an overwhelming majority of candidates from his Anti-Fascist People's Freedom League.

Aung San did not much care for the trappings of governmental power, but his standing as the chosen leader of the people he frankly cherished. He took the responsibilities of leadership very seriously, seeing it as a trust which had been earned through his courage to do what he believed to be right without fear of calumny or death, and which would have to be forfeited if he failed in his duties towards the nation. When he said that the day he and his government lost the respect of the country they would resign, the people knew that it was not mere rhetoric, that it was a promise which would not be broken. To rule without honour held no attractions for a soldier-statesman for whom strength had value only when it served a just cause.

The heroes of a people represent their aspirations, while their actual leaders reflect the degree to which these aspirations are capable of being realized. In those rare moments of history when the two coincide there is an inner harmony and a climactic release of spiritual and physical vigour, the memory of which constitutes a reservoir of strength and pride which can be drawn upon when the times are impoverished of dignity and achievement. During the brief years of Aung San's leadership, the people of Burma were filled with the hope and purposeful energy of those who had been given confidence in their own worth. Even when their *Bogyoke* rebuked them with characteristic bluntness for their lack of diligence, perseverance and discipline, they were undismayed, encouraged to further exertions by the sure knowledge that he considered them desirous of correcting their shortcomings as he desired to correct his own.

Aung San saw life as a 'pilgrimage in quest of truth and perfection' and he sought to carry his country with him in the quest. That he succeeded to an astonishing degree in what might seem as an almost quixotic undertaking was a tribute to the people of Burma as well as to Aung San's ability to put his words into action, to demonstrate that integrity and honesty could be an effective basis for practical politics. He was a soldier who could fight – and fight well – when he had to fight, but who when the fighting was over could lay aside his sword without fear and pursue the path of peace. When political power came into his hands he could say with absolute sincerity and a complete lack of self-consciousness that he would govern 'on the basis of loving kindness and truth'. Those who followed him could feel secure in the certainty that he would not be prodigal with their lives, their happiness or their trust. He was not, as he put it, a political stunt man who would put his country into an unnecessary turmoil. He boldly guaranteed that if the people would place their confidence in his leadership, independence would be achieved within a year, as peaceably as possible: 'You know that I have never broken my promises.' These words were spoken exactly eleven months before the Union of Burma was declared an independent republic on 4 January 1948.

Aung San was no longer alive when independence came to his country. The basic tendency to regard his fellow men as intelligent beings amenable to reason and responsive to genuine goodwill made him vulnerable to the treachery of opponents who were less concerned with principles than with the drive to gain power. It has been said that if he had given as much thought to his personal safety as he had to the realization of his dreams for Burma, he would not have fallen victim to the bullets of assassins. But then he would not have been the Aung San whom the people of Burma regard as their *Bogyoke*, the supreme *boh* who brought to life the tradition of the leader who is the strength of the nation.

8

Speech to a Mass Rally at the Shwedagon Pagoda

The following is the English translation prepared by the author of the speech she delivered in Burmese to a mass rally on the open ground west of the great Shwedagon Pagoda in Rangoon on 26 August 1988 (see Plate 11). Of the approximately one thousand public addresses she calculated she had given throughout the length and breadth of Burma between August 1988 and July 1989, this was the first and the only one for which she had prepared text to hand. Two days earlier she had made a brief appearance in front of the Rangoon General Hospital, the main focus of popular demonstrations at the time, in order to announce her intention to address the rally and to call for discipline and unity (see Plate 10).

Reverend monks and people! This public rally is aimed at informing the whole world of the will of the people. Therefore at this mass rally the people should be disciplined and united to demonstrate the very fact that they are a people who can be disciplined and united. Our purpose is to show that the entire people entertain the keenest desire for a multi-party democratic system of government.

It is the students who have paved the way to the present situation where it is possible to hold such a rally. The occasion has been made possible because the recent demonstrations have been spearheaded by the students and even more because they have shown their willingness to sacrifice their lives. I therefore request you all to observe a minute's silence in order to show our deepest respect for those students who have lost their lives and, even more, in order to share the merit of their deeds among all of us. So while doing this please keep perfect silence for the duration of one minute.

I believe that all the people who have assembled here have without exception come with the unshakeable desire to strive for and win a multi-party democratic system. In order to arrive at this objective, all the people should march unitedly in a disciplined manner towards the goal of democracy.

In this connection I would like to explain the part I have played in this movement. This is needed because a fair number of people are not very well acquainted with my personal history. It is only natural and right that those who do not know me would like to know some facts.

A number of people are saying that since I have spent most of my time abroad and am married to a foreigner I could not be familiar with the ramifications of this country's politics. I wish to speak from this platform very frankly and openly to the people. It is true that I have lived abroad. It is also true that I am married to a foreigner. These facts have never interfered and will never interfere with or lessen my love and devotion for my country by any measure or degree.

Another thing which some people have been saying is that I know nothing of Burmese politics. The trouble is that I know too much. My family knows best how complicated and tricky Burmese politics can be and how much my father had to suffer on this account. He expended much mental and physical effort in the cause of Burma's politics without personal gain. That is why my father said that once Burma's independence was gained he would not want to take part in the kind of power politics that would follow.

Since my father had no such desire I too have always wanted to place myself at a distance from this kind of politics. Because of that I have kept away from politics. Some might then ask why, if I wished to stay out of politics, should I now be involved in this movement. The answer is that the present crisis is the concern of the entire nation. I could not as my father's daughter remain indifferent to all that was going on. This national crisis could in fact be called the second struggle for national independence.

This great struggle has arisen from the intense and deep desire of the people for a fully democratic parliamentary system of government. I would like to read to you something my father said about democracy:

> We must make democracy the popular creed. We must try to build up a free Burma in accordance with such a creed. If we should fail to do this, our people are bound to suffer. If democracy should fail the world cannot stand back and just look on, and therefore Burma would one day, like Japan and Germany, be despised. Democracy is the only ideology which is consistent with freedom. It is also an ideology that promotes and strengthens peace. It is therefore the only ideology we should aim for.

That is what my father said. It is the reason why I am participating in this struggle for freedom and democracy in the footsteps and traditions of my father. To achieve democracy the people should be united. That is very clear. It is a very plain fact. If there is no unity of purpose we shall be unable to achieve anything at all. If the people are disunited, no ideology or form of government can bring much benefit to the country. This must be firmly fixed in the minds of the people. If there is no discipline, no system can succeed. Therefore our people should always be united and disciplined.

While I am talking about the need for unity I would like to say one thing. Some may not like what I am going to say. But I believe that my duty is to tell the people what I believe to be true. Therefore I shall speak my mind. If my words meet with your approval, please support me. If they are not acceptable, it cannot be helped. I am only doing what I believe to be right. What I wish to say is that at this time there is a certain amount of dissension between the people and the army. This rift can lead to future dangers. The present armed forces of Burma were created and nurtured by my father. It is not simply a matter of words to say that my father built up the armed forces. It is a fact. There are papers written in my father's own hand where he lays out in detail how the army should be organized and built up. So what objectives did my father have for the armed forces? Let me read to you one of them:

> The armed forces are meant for this nation and this people, and it should be such a force having the honour and respect of the people. If instead the armed forces should come to be hated by the people, then the aims with which this army has been built up would have been in vain.

Let me speak frankly. I feel strong attachment for the armed forces. Not only were they built up by my father, as a child I was cared for by his soldiers. At the same time I am also aware of the great love and affection which the people have for my father. I am grateful for this love and affection. I would therefore not wish to see any splits and struggles between the army which my father built up and the people who love my father so much. May I also from this platform ask the personnel of the armed forces to reciprocate this kind of understanding and sympathy? May I appeal to the armed forces to become a force in which the people can place their trust and reliance. May the armed forces become one which will uphold the honour and dignity of our country.

For their part the people should try to forget what has already taken place, and I would like to appeal to them not to lose their affection for the army. We shall reach our goal of a strong and lasting Union only if we are all able to go forward in unity. We have not yet achieved this goal. Let us not be disunited. Therefore let us resolve to march forward in unity towards our cherished goal. In doing so please use peaceful means. If a people or a nation can reach their objectives by disciplined and peaceful means, it would be a most honourable and admirable achievement.

I have a few things to say about the students who have been at the forefront of this nationwide movement. The students are most able. They have already demonstrated their physical courage. I believe that they will now go on to demonstrate their moral and mental ability. May I appeal to the students to continue to march forward with the same kind of unity and resolve? At this moment there are a number of student groups. I would like these groups to come together as a unified body. I understand that they are soon going to call a conference for this purpose. Should this occasion arise may I pray that it will result in an entire cohesion and unity of the students.

Some students have asked me which politicians are standing behind me. They are apprehensive that such politicians might manipulate me and then take over the students. I am happy that the students have been so open and honest with me. Young people are frank and free from deviousness. I answered them truthfully. There are no politicans behind me. What I am trying to do is to help achieve the democratic system of government which the people want. For the achievement of this system, there are some veteran politicians who wish to help me in various ways. I have told such politicians that if their object is to obtain positions of political power for themselves, I would not support them in any way. Should these politicians try to obtain positions of political power I promise in front of this assembly of people that I myself will not hesitate to denounce them.

There is a sort of gulf between the older and younger generations. This gulf will have to be bridged. There is the feeling that the older and younger generations are quite apart from each other. This is something that should not happen. Whether young or old the entire people should be united.

The strength of the people is growing day by day. Such growing strength has to be controlled by discipline. Undisciplined strength or strength which is not in keeping with right principles can never lead to a beneficial fruition. It could lead to danger for many. Therefore please continue to use our strength in accordance with rightful principles. At this juncture when the people's strength is almost at is peak we should take extreme care not to oppress the weaker side. That is the kind of evil practice which would cause the people to lose their dignity and honour. The people should demonstrate clearly and distinctly their capacity to forgive.

If we are to examine what it is that we all desire, that is what the people really want at this time, the answer is multi-party democracy. We want to get rid of the one-party system. The President, Dr Maung Maung, has said that he is calling an emergency party congress to decide whether there should be a national referendum. So far as I am concerned I do not think it is necessary to have this referendum. The entire nation's desires and aspirations are very clear. There can be no doubt that everybody wants a multi-party democratic system of government. It is the duty of the present government to bring about such a system as soon as possible.

For the people's part they should continue to demonstrate for this through peaceful and disciplined means. May I emphasize again that we have not yet arrived at our cherished goal. Please think in advance of what should be done to bring about a firmly established Union. Please think of the country's future. Unless we consider the future of our country, the changes that are coming into being may not be able to achieve much benefit for the country. My father said there is a great need for the people to be disciplined and this cannot be repeated too often.

We do not need to have a referendum. What we do need is a multi-party system. It should be introduced as quickly as possible by means of free and fair elections. Conditions necessary for the holding of free and fair elections should be created throughout the country. The people have lost their confidence in the government of the day. If the holding of free and fair elections requires an interim government, such a forerunner should be created.

The main objective is not to have either the present form of government, nor an interim government, nor to have some other new government, but to have a government that can bring about a strong and prosperous Union of Burma. Please do not lose sight of the main objectives, nor forget the future welfare of the country. Should we lose sight of these, present victories will change to future failures.

What stage have we reached now? Well, our cherished aim is clearly within sight. Let us march forward together towards that goal. Let no divisions creep in. It is important that divisions of opinion should not arise among the students. There should be a complete restraint on creating such divisions. Therefore should

198 Freedom from Fear

differences arise between them now the country's future unity will be jeopardized.

While I am on the subject of unity may I speak for a while on the union of states of which Burma is composed. The different peoples of Burma should also remain united. The majority people of course remain the Burmese. They must strive with ever-increasing efforts to live in this accord and amity. Because the Burmese people form the biggest majority, they should make the greatest efforts to live in this accord and amity and to achieve that much needed unity and friendship among national racial groups.

Those who have the greater strength should show restraint and tolerance towards those who have less strength. Here I wish to say one thing regarding those people who are supporting the one-party system. The fact is many members of the Lanzin Party (Burma Socialist Programme Party) have themselves lost faith and confidence in their party. Such party members should resign from the Lanzin Party. They should hand in their party cards.

However, those who continue as members of the Lanzin Party out of conviction should not be molested. Democracy is an ideology that allows everyone to stand up according to his beliefs. They should not be threatened or endangered. Each one should go forward towards his own goal. Do not because of your greater strength be vengeful towards those who are of weaker strength.

We have gone far beyond the intended time, so I must cut this short. The final remark I wish to make is for our rally to maintain unity and discipline. Our strength should be used for the cause of what is right. Only by observing these requirements shall we be able to find our goal.

May the entire people be united and disciplined. May our people always do what is in complete accord with rightful principles. May the people be free from all harm.

To conclude I would like to reiterate our emphatic demands and protests, namely that we have no desire at all for a referendum, that the one-party system should be dismantled, that a multi-party system of government should be established, and we call for free and fair elections to be arranged as quickly as possible. These are our demands.

9

The Objectives

In The Times *of 29 August 1988 there appeared the following interview with Aung San Suu Kyi by Karan Thapar under the title 'People's Heroine Spells Out Objectives'.*

Q: There is considerable confusion about the present state of affairs in Rangoon and Burma. How would you describe the atmosphere and the state of the country?

A: The atmosphere is understandably very tense. The machinery of the government has almost come to a complete standstill in many parts of the country. But the people are rising to the occasion. Demonstrations are being conducted in a systematic manner. Vigilante groups have taken charge of local security. The people are spearheading a movement for discipline and order.

Q: You have emerged in recent days as perhaps the principal leader of the present people's movement. What are you fighting for? How would you describe your aims?

A: I am one of a large majority of people in Burma struggling for democracy. It is my aim to help the people attain democracy without further violence or loss of life.

Q: You have recently spoken of the need for a 'second struggle for Burmese independence'. What exactly did you mean by that?

A: A political system that denies the full enjoyment of human rights to the people militates against the ideal of full independence. That is why I say that the present demands of the people of Burma for democracy constitutes their second struggle for independence.

Q: How do you respond to President Maung Maung's offer of a special party congress on 12 September [1988] to decide whether a referendum should be held on the issue of multi-party politics?

A: If the ruling party had agreed to a referendum last month when it was first suggested, the people would have accepted it with thanks. But now it is the old story: too little too late. The people have demonstrated beyond a shadow of a doubt that they want multi-party democracy. A referendum would be totally redundant.

Q: Do you then want the Burmese people to continue with their demands until they actually topple the present government?

A: It is not a question of toppling the government, or a question of what I want. The people will continue with their demands until they get the sort of political system they want.

Q: Are you not worried that, given the generally spontaneous and unorganized nature of the people's movement, Burma could end up in a state of anarchy, with no authority in control and no law and order?

A: It is true that the movement started out as a spontaneous demonstration of the people's frustration, but it is becoming better organized with every passing day. The public are now making arrangements for local security and planning more systematic demonstrations and strikes. So one can make too much of that fear.

Q: What sort of assistance are you looking for from the army?

A: I am not looking for any assistance from the army. What I said on 25 August was that there should be no dissension between the army and the people. The army should be a force which people should honour and trust. I strongly believe that the army should keep away from politics to preserve its own integrity, as well as for the good of the nation.

Q: If the regime does fall, what will take its place? What sort of transitional arrangement could there be?

A: An interim government in which people have confidence would be able to put the country back on an even keel and see that conditions are created for free and fair elections.

Q: Do you see a role for yourself in that transition and, if so, what?

A: There is no particular role in which I see myself. I shall wait on events to see how I can be of most use in bringing about a peaceful transition.

Q: Let's turn to the future, which in fact may not be all that far away. If multi-party democracy does come about, Burma, of course, does not have any parties. What sort of parties would you like to see formed?

A: Ideally one would like to see parties headed by able and honest people dedicated to the preservation of a democratic system of government.

Q: Will you try to form one yourself?

A: Not if it is at all avoidable.

Q: Are you committed to a life of politics and if you are how would you analyse your talents and gifts as a politician?

A: A life in politics holds no attraction for me. At the moment I serve as a kind of unifying force because of my father's name and because I am not interested in jostling for any kind of position.

Q: Who would you therefore support as a future leader, perhaps in a transitional capacity?

A: To answer this question would mean getting involved in the kind of politics I want to avoid as far as possible.

Q: What can you or any future government say or do to attract home educated Burmese?

A: A democratic government which gives people enough scope to exercise their talents will surely attract home many Burmese. However, it would not be right to underestimate the pool of skill and talent which already exists inside the country. The removal of an oppressive political and economic system will reveal many able people who so far have had no chance to show their abilities.

Q: What sort of relations with the outside world should a democratic Burma pursue?

A: Burma has always pursued a policy of non-alignment and should continue to do so. However, it could adopt a more open attitude towards contacts with the outside world.

Q: One of the traditional concerns important to the Burmese people has been their desire to preserve the purity of their culture and religion. Is that important to you too?

A: I think it is important for every people to work for the preservation of their culture and religion. At the same time it must be remembered that a progressive nation should move with the times and avoid bigoted and narrow-minded attitudes.

Q: Given your father's historical association with the Burmese army, what sort of role would you like to see it play in any future democratic Burma? Do you feel that a country like Burma requires an institutionalized role for the army in politics?

A: My father said that the army should keep out of politics, and I support that view totally.

10

In the Eye of the Revolution

Excerpts from this essay appeared in The Independent *on 12 September 1988 under the title 'Belief in Burma's Future'. Published here in full for the first time, it was written in the crucial period between the outbreak of spontaneous demonstrations throughout Burma on 8 August and the imposition of direct military rule on 18 September.*

There are moments of tragedy, horror, anger and sheer disbelief. Surpassing all is the conviction that a movement which has risen so spontaneously from the people's irresistible desire for the full enjoyment of human rights must surely prevail. For twenty-six years the talents of the people of Burma have been suppressed by a regime which allowed no freedom of thought or initiative of any kind. Yet the last few weeks have revealed that the people can respond to a situation which requires quick thinking as well as decisive action. Since the wheels of government have stopped turning and the police can no longer guarantee security, local vigilante groups chiefly composed of Buddhist monks and students have sprung up throughout the country. Myriad unions and groups, all resolved upon democracy, have established links to enable them to work together with a unity of purpose amazing in a nation where freedom of association, albeit illegal, has only become possible within the last month. With the breakdown of government administration, difficulties in transport and communications have led to high prices and scarcity of foodstuffs. In this matter as well as in matters of medical supplies the people are taking matters into their own hands to organize relief. The latest manifestation of the growing discipline and solidarity of the people is the way in which the mass demonstrations of today (8 September), comprising perhaps a million or more participants, were successfully concluded without mishap.

Much publicity has been given to looting, arson and other acts of vandalism. It has been evident that the worst incidents have been and are still being instigated by a faction of the government. It is a strange and horrifying situation where the people are trying to preserve order and unity while a faction of the government tries its utmost to promote anarchy. It is very much to the credit of the popular movement for democracy that things are no worse than they are. Some members of the present regime are obviously determined, for reasons beyond the understanding of any responsible person, to resist the manifest will of the people. Their actions seem to be directed solely towards creating chaos and maximum suffering for the people who have rejected them with a unanimity seldom seen in the course of a nation's history. It is obvious that not all members of the government are involved in the crude and often barbaric plots directed against the people's movement for democracy. Such plots are almost without exception aborted at an early stage and one is forced to the conclusion that a few desperate and inept hardliners are making a last-ditch attempt to save their positions at all costs.

It might be asked who indeed are 'the people' working for democracy. They are the vast majority of the Burmese public who have suffered civil, political and economic privations under the rule of the Burma Socialist Programme Party (BSPP). It could be said that the party by its wanton oppression and lack of sensible economic policies has become the unwitting instrument for unification. It is almost beyond doubt that the only remaining adherents of the BSPP are those who fear that not only their positions but perhaps their safety is at stake. This illustrates yet again the large gap between the BSPP leadership and the people. For while it is undeniable that there are those who might wish to take full revenge on the regime, the majority of the people are more likely to pursue a line of justice tempered by mercy.

The role of the army in Burma is crucial. It was created by my father, General Aung San, who gave many warnings against the army turning into a tyrannical force of oppression. It is the belief of the majority of the people of Burma that the army is being manipulated and misused by a handful of corrupt fanatics whose powers and privileges are dependent on the survival of the present system. It is also becoming increasingly obvious that many members of the armed forces themselves strongly object to the way in which their honour has been tainted by the role forced upon them by the policies of the present regime. All right-thinking citizens of Burma fear that the army might split into irreconcilable factions, and they desire an early and peaceful transition to the kind of political system acceptable to the people wherein the army can return to their barracks with grace and honour.

Many people ask me how I came to be involved in this nationwide movement for democracy. As the daughter of the man regarded as the father of modern Burma it was inevitable that I should have been closely attuned to political currents in the country. From childhood I was deeply interested in the history of the independence movement and in the social and political development of the Union of Burma. Since my father died when I was only two years old it cannot really be said that I knew him. I was taught to think of him as a loving and indulgent father, and as an upright and honourable man who put the welfare of his country above his own interests. It was only when I grew older and started collecting material on his life and achievements that I began to learn what he had really been like and how much he had managed to achieve in his thirty-two years. Not only did I then conceive an admiration for him as a patriot and statesman but I developed a strong sense of empathy as I discovered many similarities in our attitudes. It is perhaps because of this strong bond that I came to feel such a deep sense of responsibility for the welfare of my country.

The present regime came into power in 1962 while I was a student in India, where my mother was serving as the Burmese ambassador. My relationship with this regime has been an uneasy one. There have always been individual members of the government who entertained such strong sentiments of love and loyalty towards my father that they regard his family with warm affection and respect. On the other hand there are those who, while using my father's name for their own purposes, have never practised the principles that he laid down as essential for the good of the nation. Among such people are a number who harbour strong feelings of jealousy towards our family and who see us as a threat. In 1974 during one of my visits home it was put to me informally that the authorities were anxious to know if I intended to get involved in anti-government activities. I replied that I would never do anything from abroad and that if I were to engage in any political movement I would do so from within the country.

My years abroad provided me with the opportunity to assess Burma's problems from the broad perspective of the international scene, while my frequent visits home kept me in touch with developments within the country. It was not difficult to recognize that the nation was inexorably deteriorating under the governance of the BSPP. But I could not see any signs of a popular opposition movement which I could support whole-heartedly until I came to Burma last April. Then I found that the mood of the people had changed and that the time for a popular anti-government movement was fast approaching. The massacre of peaceful demonstrators last August precipitated such a movement and decided me to come out in support of the people's aspirations. This decision was prompted partly by the belief that as my father's daughter I have a responsibility towards my country.

There have been speculations that some politicians might be influencing my actions. Those who wish to discredit me and a few who entertain genuine fears have also implied that I am surrounded by communists. While it is true that a number of veteran politicians of varying political colour are giving me practical assistance, I have only accepted their help on the clear understanding that they are working for the democratic cause without expectation of future political advantage or personal gain. I myself am strongly opposed to those who put their political creed, party or ideology before the welfare of the nation. Every country and people must search for a political and economic system tailored to their unique situation. At the moment I am working in close association with non-political groups including many students whose only aim is to achieve the kind of democratic system under which the people of Burma can enjoy human rights to the full. This is a time to strive for national unity, not a time in which to build up power bases for future party politics. When asked if I intend to form a political party my reply is that it is not a prospect which I find at all attractive. However, I am prepared to engage in the very kind of party politics I wish to avoid if I am convinced that it would be necessary to uphold the democratic system for which we are all striving at this moment.

Another question I am frequently asked is how long I intend to stay in Burma. It has always been my intention to come back and live in my country some day in order to set up a chain of public libraries and to organize scholarship schemes for students. Whether or not I continue to engage in political activities after a transition to a democratic system of government I would hope to fulfil these aims.

A third question that is often put to me is whether I believe that the people's movement for democracy will succeed. The answer is an unequivocable YES. Contrary to the predictions of those who are totally out of touch with the mood of Burma today, I believe that not only will the people achieve democracy but that once it is achieved they will be able to make it work for the greater good of the nation.

At this point I cannot resist mentioning the inspiring role played by students in this national movement. I have found the great majority of them not only brave and resourceful but also broad-minded and receptive to new ideas. Their organization and dedication have been amazing and moving. It is most heartening to think that these are the young people who will in the course of time come to shoulder the responsibilities of our country. I cannot help but feel that the future of Burma is assured.

11

Two Letters to Amnesty International

Copies of the following letters to the Secretary-General of Amnesty International came into the hands of the military authorities and were printed by them in the official publication The Conspiracy of Treasonous Minions within the Myanmar Naing-ngan and Traitorous Cohorts Abroad, *Rangoon, 1989, pp. 220–23.*

I

24 September 1988

On 1 September Mr Heder of your organization spoke to my office here requesting firstly that Amnesty should be informed as soon as conditions in Burma have changed sufficiently to permit Amnesty staff to enter the country and secondly that Amnesty be kept informed of all new violations of human rights. As you are doubtless aware, the country has in recent weeks been subjected to such turmoil and suffering at the hands of the military regime that conditions have not so far allowed me to pursue contact with Amnesty.

I am writing now to suggest that there is a very practical way in which your organization can be of service to the cause of human rights in Burma. From next Tuesday the foreign ministers of the world will begin to address the General Debate of the United Nations Assembly. I and my associates who are struggling for the restoration of peace and democracy in Burma believe it is vital that as many ministers as possible should in their speeches express their gravest concern for the continued violation of basic human rights in Burma and in particular their unqualified condemnation of the way in which unarmed demonstrators, including school children and Buddhist monks, have been massacred in large numbers by the armed forces. We appeal to you to bring these matters to the urgent attention of the foreign ministers who are addressing the Debate under Item 4 of the Agenda and to urge them to make substantive reference in their speeches to the prevailing situation. For my part I shall today be raising this matter with the ambassadors of those nations represented in Burma. I would further urge you to communicate the substance of this letter to any other international organization with which you are in contact, such as the International Commission of Jurists, who might be in a position to influence the course of the General Debate.

Your assistance in this matter will earn your organization the gratitude of millions of people in Burma.

II

16 October 1988

On the subject of the continued violation of human rights in Burma we wish to submit to you the following facts which have been confirmed by numerous eyewitness reports.

On 15 October over six hundred men, mostly young students, were seized by the armed forces as they sat in teashops and eating stalls in Rangoon. Buses were stopped at checkpoints set up at frequent intervals in the streets, and young men who could not produce evidence of their employment as civil servants were taken away in military trucks. Furthermore, low-income housing areas were entered by troops, even during the hours of curfew, and men taken away.

All are believed to be taken to the front lines where the Burmese army is engaged in action against insurgent forces. Those seized in Rangoon in recent days are very likely being forced to act as so-called 'porters' to carry the rations and arms of the government troops. It is also widely believed that they are driven ahead of the troops in order to detonate the mines laid by the insurgent forces. A high percentage of government casualties are caused by such land mines. The Burmese army lacks mine detectors.

All this appears to be connected to reports we received about five days ago that on 6 October over five hundred people, mostly students in their early teens, were seen at the town of Pa-an, tied together in groups of two and three and guarded by the armed forces. When the people of the town attempted to give them food and water they were cursed by the soldiers, who told them not to bother feeding 'those who are about to die'. They were kept overnight in the town hall and were taken off early the following morning in the direction of the continuing conflict.

The forced conscription of young men for service as 'porters' by the Burmese army is known to have taken place several times in recent years. However, this appears to be the first time it has actually taken place on the streets of Rangoon for all to see.

We request you to bring this news to the attention of all those concerned with the violation of human rights in Burma.

Letter to the Ambassadors

Source: The Conspiracy of Treasonous Minions, *p. 222 (see italic note on p. 214).*

26 September 1988

I wish to make a personal appeal to the foreign ministers of all countries accredited to Burma to address the issue of human rights in this country in the most unqualified terms under Item 4 of the Agenda of the General Debate during the current session of the United Nations Assembly. The Debate is scheduled to begin in New York on 27 September 1988, so you will appreciate there is a great urgency. I would be most grateful if you would therefore kindly forward this appeal to your Foreign Minister on my behalf. I have made similar appeals to Amnesty International and the International Commission of Jurists to urge them to raise this issue with the foreign ministers attending the Debate. I feel sure it will be agreed that the indiscriminate killing in recent weeks of unarmed demonstrators including school children, students and Buddhist monks is a legitimate subject for international condemnation.

13

The Role of the Citizen in the Struggle for Democracy

The speech from which only excerpts are given here was delivered by Aung San Suu Kyi on the National Day of Burma, 3 December 1988. These excerpts were translated by Thant Myint-U and Lewis Woodworth.

Even though we don't know what will happen, we need to carry on as best we can, without wavering, along the correct path. Even though we don't know what will happen, it is right that we take part in this struggle. Because we believe that it is proper, we have all joined in. If you ask whether we shall achieve democracy, whether there will be general elections, here is what I shall say: Don't think about whether or not these things will happen. Just continue to do what you believe is right. Later on the fruits of what you do will become apparent on their own. One's responsibility is to do the right thing.

We have all entered this struggle for democracy because we believe that we can win. For example, a person enters a race or buys a lottery ticket because he believes it's possible to win. So also if someone were to ask me whether I believe we can win in our fight for democracy, I should reply honestly, 'Yes, we can', and because I believe we can, I have chosen to take part. I should like the students and young people to continue their work while keeping in mind that we can win. We still have great struggles ahead of us; we still have work yet to do, and not merely for months. We are going to have to work and struggle for years. Even if there are elections and the forces of democracy win, the movement is not yet finished with its work; we still have to continue. Today the students and young people are around twenty years old. Life expectancy in Burma is about sixty, and maybe under democracy and improved living conditions it will become seventy. That means that the youth of today will have possibly fifty years of struggle ahead of them. Democracy is something one must nourish all one's life, if it is to remain alive and strong. Like the health of a person: even if his parents have raised him to healthy adulthood, if he fails to take care of himself, his health will deteriorate. If each of you keeps in mind all your life that you have a responsibility for the welfare of your country, then we shall have no reason to worry that our country's health will deteriorate. We want to work hand in hand with everyone working for democracy. I don't mean working together half-heartedly – we want to work together heart and soul.

This is National Day. I should like everyone to decide, beginning today, that you will work for the nation's interest, meaning your fellow countrymen, for the stability of the Union and the good of all the people. When working for the national interest, we must not have loyalties to particular people or to short-term objectives. Don't keep these personal loyalties. I should like us to continue our journey with genuine sympathy and a clear mind. I always tell people to have high aspirations – have the highest aspirations.

14

Open Letter to the United Nations Commission on Human Rights

Although this letter is undated, it is clear that it was submitted to the Commission by Aung San Suu Kyi while official harassment of her party was mounting and before she was placed under house arrest on 20 July 1989. In 1990 the Commission took steps to investigate the human rights situation in Burma under the confidential 1503 procedure, a process which continues today.

I   The chief aim of the National League for Democracy (NLD) and other organizations working for the establishment of a democratic government in Burma is to bring about social and political changes which will guarantee a peaceful, stable and progressive society where human rights, as outlined in the Universal Declaration of Human Rights, are protected by the rule of law.

II   Those working for democracy in Burma would wish to differentiate between the 'rule of law' which would mean the fair and impartial administration of legal rules – i.e. measures passed by a legally elected assembly after free and open discussion and debate – and the process of law and order which merely involves the enforcement of arbitrary edicts decreed by a regime which does not enjoy the mandate of the people.

III   Those who believe in the sanctity of human rights do not reject the concept of law and order as such but they would wish to ensure that the law is not just 'the will of the dominant faction' and that order is not simply 'the reflex of an all-pervading fear'. The majority of the people in Burma desire a state which preserves *dhamma* and *abhaya* – righteousness and absence of fear.

IV   The claim that human rights considerations have to be balanced against respect for the law would be valid only if the law ensures that justice is done and seen to be done. Decrees designed to expedite repressive measures against those who resist the erosion of rights recognized by the United Nations as essential for the foundation of freedom, justice and peace cannot be said to have either the moral force or the legal sanction necessary to elevate mere edicts to the status of just laws.

V   It has been the consistent policy of the NLD to respect and uphold all just laws. At the same time the NLD in common with the majority of the people of Burma recognizes that those who wish to build a strong and peaceful nation have a duty to resist measures which attack the very foundations of human dignity and truth.

VI   The large numbers of political prisoners held in Burma today have been charged with so-called criminal offences because of their efforts to uphold Articles 19, 20 and 21 of the Universal Declaration of Human Rights. Further they have been subjected to the kind of treatment which runs contrary to Articles 5, 6, 7, 8, 9, 10, 11 and 12.

VII   Neither the NLD nor the people who demonstrate their support for the NLD desire the kind of conflict and confrontation which can only bring more suffering on a populace already troubled by much political and economic hardship. Seeking understanding through dialogue and negotiations is an accepted principle of the democratic tradition to which the NLD has been unswervingly committed since its inception in 1988.

VIII Those who wish for an early and peaceful transition to democratic government acknowledge the validity of the statement that 'to deny human beings their rights is to set the stage for political and social unrest'. Their efforts are thus directed towards bringing about conditions which will avoid social and political unrest. However, their efforts have been hampered by the refusal of the authorities to respect the will of the majority.

IX It is hoped that it will be possible for the UN Commission on Human Rights to obtain such conditions as would enable those with an interest in promoting human rights in Burma (in particular political prisoners) to express their views frankly without fear of reprisals on themselves, their families or their associates.

X While realizing that they must depend on their own powers of courage, perseverance and fortitude to bring their struggle for a political system which will guarantee their human rights to a successful conclusion, the people of Burma look to the UN Commission to support the justice of their cause.

15

Dust and Sweat

The following is taken from a letter to the editor dated Rangoon, 14 April 1989. The reference to the Danubyu trip alludes to an incident when soldiers were ordered to shoot Aung San Suu Kyi as she walked calmly towards them. They were countermanded by a senior officer just as the countdown was ending.

The last trip (after the Danubyu one) was rather gruelling, travelling by bullock cart and small boats in the blazing sun – alas, your Suu is getting weather-beaten, none of that pampered elegance left as she tramps the countryside spattered with mud, straggly-haired, breathing in dust and pouring with sweat! I need a few months in grey, damp Oxford to restore my complexion! But in spite of all the difficulties I feel that what I am doing is worthwhile – the people of Burma deserve better than this mess of inefficiency, corruption and misuse of power.

16

The Need for Solidarity among Ethnic Groups

The following speech, translated from Burmese by Thant Myint-U and Lewis Woodworth, was delivered by Aung San Suu Kyi to a meeting held at a pagoda in Myitkyina, Kachin State, on 27 April 1989. Two days later she wrote a letter to the editor from Mokaung in which she spoke of 'all those crowds who come to support us with such hope and trust. I think this is going to be the biggest cross I have to bear – the feeling that I can never do enough to deserve all that trust and affection.'

We should like to thank you very much for coming and supporting us. We of the National League for Democracy believe very strongly that it is important in our movement for democracy that all ethnic groups in the country work together. It is in trying to help bring together all ethnic groups, all peoples, that we go on these organizational tours and try to visit as many places as possible. In the Kachin State there are many different peoples. Because of this ethnic variety, I think that you already know what problems there are in creating a unified country, what problems must be overcome.

We must all work together if we are all to live together in unity and harmony. I don't think I need to tell the people of the Kachin State how important it is for us all to be broad-minded and observe good political values. We must have as our goal the building of a real and lasting Union. Only after building this Union can we really work towards peace and prosperity for all. We must all sacrifice our own needs for the needs of others.

Without this, it will be impossible to build the kind of Union that we need.

I have heard many times on this trip that people are afraid to become involved in politics, but this has been nowhere true in all of the Kachin State. In some areas people are joining the movement with great courage. In these areas I have seen that the local people are enjoying more political rights. What we have seen on our organizational tours is that in those areas where people are daring to be politically active, they enjoy more rights. Where people are fearful, however, they suffer more oppression. Because of this, if we want democracy, we need to show courage. By this I don't mean the courage to cause trouble. I must often remind people of this. By courage I mean the courage to do what one knows is right, even if one is afraid. We should do what we believe is right, even if we are afraid. Of course, we cannot help being afraid; we just have to work to control our fear.

In Burma we have a tendency to use threats in raising our children. I should like to ask you kindly not to do this. In our country we threaten children in teaching them to do or not do something, rather than explaining to them so that they understand themselves. This kind of teaching by intimidation is now so prevalent that the rulers who govern us don't try to explain things to ordinary people, but, instead, use threats to control them. This is part of our culture, one that we should change. Let us teach our children by explaining to them. This is our responsibility; we have a duty to teach the children a sense of justice and compassion. Our young people are very important to me. We need to do more to look after them.

Children's minds are like a clean slate. That's why we have a great responsibility in raising them. We must not teach them things that will divide them because of linguistic or ethnic differences; we must teach them so that they understand the idea of the Union. In the Kachin State, for instance, we have Jingpaw, Lisu, Shan, Burmans and other peoples. For all of them to live together in harmony we must teach our children from earliest childhood the concept of national unity, of nationhood.

From my earliest childhood my mother taught me this idea of

national unity; not by merely talking about it but by including it in everyday work. For example, we always had people from various ethnic groups living with us. At that time my mother was working with nurses. Nurses from all over the country would come to Rangoon to attend classes on child care. She would invite those from ethnic minorities to stay at our home. Since my youth, then, I was taught to live closely with people from other ethnic groups.

In this way we need to give thought to ethnic groups other than our own. We need to show sympathy and understanding. Without this, progress for the country will be impossible.

Not thinking only of our own interests can also be applied to economic issues. Not just in the Kachin State, but all over the country, there are people who value their own businesses more than politics. Actually, though, only if there is a good political system will it be possible to reach economic goals. Even if business is doing well, if the political system is unjust, the nation will not prosper. For example, during the era of the BSPP (Burma Socialist Programme Party) there were some people who were very successful in business, but what could they do with their money? In a country like Burma, where the situation was constantly worsening, how could they find prosperity with their money? Quite a few of them sent their children abroad with the money. Just think of how much money the country lost with these young people! What is important is using this money for the good of the whole country, not just for one's own interest or the interests of one's family. Please, then, don't place economics above politics, for it is a fact that all nations that prosper economically are those that also have an equitable political system.

During the Second World War, Germany and Japan practised fascism. At that time, too, the Germans and Japanese were very disciplined people, they were brave and they valued education. Yet however disciplined, however brave, however educated they were, because of their political philosophy and their political systems their countries were really not able to develop. Despite initial victories in the war, they eventually lost.

Fascism is not an ideology that benefits the majority. With this kind of ideology a country can never truly develop over the long run.

After the war, both Germany and Japan adopted democratic institutions. By introducing democracy, these countries have also gone on to become two of the most prosperous nations in the world. This shows clearly that only with an effective government and equitable political system can a country really progress. We as citizens still need to be more self-disciplined; we still need to be more courageous, but in addition, we also need a proper form of government. So far we haven't even reached the zero level. If we want democracy, we need to reach that zero level. Only by so doing can we begin our work. Now, though, however hard we try, we cannot really work for our country freely.

There are those who say they would rather not be involved in the movement for democracy, but when the elections come, they will vote on the side of democracy. This is not enough. We still need to work towards free and fair elections. We have to work hard if we want our basic freedoms. Only if we have these freedoms can we continue to progress after achieving democracy. Will people who are not involved now become involved after we gain democracy? If people are still unwilling to take part in public life after we achieve a democratic government, that government will not be a stable one.

But let me ask about the real meaning of democracy. Those who want popular government should also become involved in politics. They should have individual political ideas. They should have positive attitudes and a willingness to sacrifice. Without this there is no way we can win. It has been more than forty years since Burma gained independence. If we ask what progress has been made in these more than forty years, only depressing answers appear. When I visited Myitkyina over thirty years ago, there was no problem of electricity – it was always available. Now there is not even enough electricity and we find power in short supply. So we see that in these past thirty years and more there has been not only no progress but actual decline. We must ask ourselves, then: Why has this decline occurred? Most will answer that it is because the BSPP was bad. I won't argue with that, but we must ask again: Why was the BSPP able to last so long, then? I think the answer to this has to do with the people at large. Because we, the citizens, simply stood by and watched, the system was able to last as long as it did. When the time came to take up independence, I think that the BSPP gained control of the government because the citizens failed to carry out the duties of citizenship. If we want a stable democracy in the future, every single one of us must bear this responsibility conscientiously. We must be willing to sacrifice. We must all understand that there is great merit in sacrificing for others and that by so doing we live the full life.

It's not by living to the age of ninety or one hundred that one lives the full life. Some people live well until they are ninety or one hundred without ever having done anything for anyone. They come into the world, live, then die without doing something for the world. I don't think that this is living a full life. To live the full life one must have the courage to bear the responsibility of the needs of others – one must want to bear this responsibility. Each and every one of us must have this attitude and we must instill it in our youth. We must bring up our children to understand that only doing what is meritorious is right.

Early in the Second World War, Germany and Japan were still victorious, but only because the people at home worked self-sacrificingly. When they no longer sacrificed their own self-interest, they were unable to win the war. As an example, during that war the people of Great Britain made great sacrifices and, because of that, from a position of weakness Britain was able to grow stronger and defeat the enemy. That's why, if we walk along the right path, we are sure to gain the victory over whatever enemy. Therefore, people of the Kachin State, act with courage; don't give too much thought to economics. Now is not the time to be concentrating on economics, but rather on politics. One must always act according to the season and the situation. At this time we have the historic responsibility to rebuild our nation. In this country we must work for the establishment of a just form of government. It is not our historic responsibility at this time to go into business. After establishing democracy, we may have new responsibilities in the economic sphere, but at this time work towards democracy. It is not part of our work to fight anyone. Nowadays many charges are laid against political parties; often charges are made that political parties are trying to split the army from the people. That is not true at all. Actually, it was to bring together the army and the people that the movement towards democracy was initiated. When my father founded the armed forces, he founded them as the armed forces of the people. At that time the people cherished strong feelings of love and sympathy towards the armed forces. It was with these feelings that the people were able to rise in revolt against the Japanese army of occupation. I should like to see again such a close relationship between the army and the people – the army as an organization standing behind the people with love and sympathy.

We are working so that there may be this kind of organization, so we need to be careful about these charges, which are being made only to hinder our movement and cause division between the people and the army. We need to be extremely careful that our attitudes are proper and just. The people must also develop courage, but this courage they must strive to keep controlled by ideas of good and right. If we can't control our courage with such ideas, then there may be danger for others and for ourselves.

At this time there is very great need for all our ethnic groups to be joined together. We cannot have the attitude of 'I'm Kachin', 'I'm Burman', 'I'm Shan.' We must have the attitude that we are all comrades in the struggle for democratic rights. We must all work closely together like brothers and sisters. Only then will we succeed. If we divide ourselves ethnically, we shall not achieve democracy for a long time.

We won our independence [in 1948] through the unity of the various nationalities. So because of that this independence can be one that lasts and is of benefit to the people at large. I conclude by asking all the ethnic groups to remain united and to continue to work together.

17

The People Want Freedom

Aung San Suu Kyi gave the following interview to Dominic Faulder of Asiaweek *on 1 July 1989, nineteen days before she was placed under house arrest.*

Q: How would you describe the present situation?

A: Obviously, I am the main target – and I have been for some time. But now it's come out into the open. It's the same with the National League for Democracy. The attacks have been aimed at us because we have the greatest support among the people. Some people think that if we just sit tight and wait until the elections, we're bound to be elected. But it's not as simple as that. Day by day we're losing more and more of our basic political rights – whatever political rights we had. The SLORC (State Law and Order Restoration Council) is totally ignoring all the complaints we've made about injustice and unfairness – totally ignoring them. Which is why we've got to say what's really happening.

Q: Have you studied the new election rules?

A: Yes, I went through them quite carefully. They haven't paid any attention to all the suggestions that must have poured in. We made a large number which were totally ignored. We have also asked for special provisions to do with the transfer of power, and they haven't touched on that at all.

Q: Assuming there are elections, what do you think will happen afterwards?

A: We don't know; this is the problem. Whoever is elected will first have to draw up a constitution that will have to be adopted before the transfer of power. They haven't said how the constitution will be adopted. It could be through a referendum, but that could mean months and months, if not years. That's why provisions for the transfer of power are so important. Unless we know how it will take place, we can't really trust the SLORC to set up a democratically elected government.

Q: But the opposition itself hasn't reached agreement on a draft constitution.

A: With more than two hundred parties it's not easy to draw up a constitution acceptable to everybody . . . Why can't the SLORC begin a dialogue instead? It's the political way to solve political problems. I suspect they can't because U Ne Win hasn't given them the green light. He won't hear of the SLORC starting a dialogue with anybody. So they say they can't talk to those parties that attack them, only to those that don't. Why didn't they say that before? It's just an excuse. And we say, 'SLORC is not doing this or that. Will they please try to do it?' – when poor SLORC doesn't have the authority to do anything at all.

Q: Poor SLORC?

A: Yes, poor SLORC. Any organization totally under the thumb of a dictator can be described as poor. They have to act under his orders. I don't think there will be free and fair elections so long as U Ne Win is at the helm of power.

Q: Do you think the authorities will move against you?

A: I suppose they'll try. They've been trying that all the time with false propaganda about me – all sorts of nonsense. Things like I have four husbands, three husbands, two husbands. That I am a communist – although in some circles they say I am CIA. They have been trying to get prominent monks to say I have been insulting the Buddha. They can say I'm married to a foreigner – but I've always admitted that freely – I'm not trying to hide that.

Q: Is it difficult to get the people to listen to you?

A: No, the people want freedom. The only thing is that they have become used to being frightened. On 19 June [1989] a foreign photographer was taking pictures of me and he was harassed. Some of the people with me were astonished that he spoke back. I said: 'But that's normal for people who've come from a free society.' Fear, like so many things, is a habit. If you live with fear for a long time, you become fearful. This is why I think when people say I'm so brave, perhaps it's just that I'm not used to being frightened.

Q: You have put political reform before economic development. But material well-being is one of the SLORC's pre-conditions for holding elections.

A: What I am saying is that people shouldn't be sidetracked by all these so-called economic reforms from the fight for democracy. If we don't change the political system, we're not going to progress economically either. A government that cannot guarantee basic human rights certainly won't be able to guarantee any economic rights.

Q: What will you do if the League is elected to power?

A: I suppose I'll play a role in the government. It's something I would have to do. I can tell you the next government is not going to have an easy time. After twenty-six, twenty-seven years of having to suffer silently, the people are going to speak out. No government will be able to bring about reforms fast enough to please everybody. People are going to give the next government a very uncomfortable time.

The Agreement to Stand for Election

While under house arrest the authorities delivered to Aung San Suu Kyi the papers prepared by her party to gain her agreement to stand in the forthcoming elections of May 1990. Her agreement was signed on 22 December 1989 and contained the following statement, her own translation from the original in Burmese. Although the military authorities eventually contrived to block her candidacy, her party went on to win more than 80 per cent of the seats contested.

I have been detained since 20 July 1989 because of my political endeavours. In spite of my continuing detention I am submitting my application as a prospective candidate for the forthcoming elections in obedience to the decision made in December 1989 by the Bahan Township Committee of the National League for Democracy for the selection of the Pyithu Hlutaw delegates. I am submitting my application out of respect for the decision taken by my party in accordance with democratic practices; to honour the courage and perseverance of the people who are striving for democracy; and from a desire to help fulfil the just aspirations of the people to the best of my ability.

The 1991 Nobel Prize for Peace

Speech by Professor Francis Sejersted, Chairman of the Norwegian Nobel Committee, on the occasion of the award to Aung San Suu Kyi of the Nobel Prize for 1991, Oslo, December 10, 1991. Translation from the Norwegian text.

Your Majesties, Your Excellencies, Ladies and Gentlemen,

We are assembled here today to honour Aung San Suu Kyi for her outstanding work for democracy and human rights and to present to her the Nobel Peace Prize for 1991. The occasion gives rise to many and partly conflicting emotions. The Peace Prize Laureate is unable to be here herself. The great work we are acknowledging has yet to be concluded. She is still fighting the good fight. Her courage and commitment find her a prisoner of conscience in her own country, Burma. Her absence fills us with fear and anxiety, which can nevertheless only be a faint shadow of the fear and anxiety felt by her family. We welcome this opportunity of expressing our deepest sympathy with them, with her husband, Michael Aris, and with her sons, Alexander and Kim. We feel with you and we are very grateful to you for coming to Oslo to receive the Nobel Prize on behalf of your wife and mother.

Our fear and anxiety are mixed with a sense of confidence and hope. In the good fight for peace and reconciliation we are dependent on persons who set examples, persons who can symbolize what we are seeking and mobilize the best in us. Aung San

Suu Kyi is just such a person. She unites deep commitment and tenacity with a vision in which the end and the means form a single unit. Its most important elements are: democracy, respect for human rights, reconciliation between groups, non-violence and personal and collective discipline.

She has herself clearly indicated the sources of her inspiration: principally Mahatma Gandhi and her father, Aung San, the leader in Burma's struggle for liberation. The philosopher of non-violence and the General differ in many respects but also show fundamental similarities. In both one can see genuine independence, true modesty and 'a profound simplicity', to use Aung San Suu Kyi's own words about her father. To Aung San, leadership was a duty and could only be carried out on the basis of humility in face of the task before him and the confidence and respect of the people to be led.

While no doubt deriving a great deal of inspiration from Gandhi and her father, Aung San Suu Kyi has also added her own independent reflections to what has become her political platform. The keynote is the same profound simplicity as she sees in her father. The central position given to human rights in her thinking appears to reflect a real sense of the need to protect human dignity. Man is not only entitled to live in a free society; he also has a right to respect. On this platform she has built a policy marked by an extraordinary combination of sober realism and visionary idealism. And in her case this is more than just a theory: she has gone a long way towards showing how such a doctrine can be translated into practical politics.

For a doctrine of peace and reconciliation to be translated into practice, one absolute condition is fearlessness. Aung San Suu Kyi knows this. One of her essays opens with the statement that it is not power that corrupts, but fear. The comment was aimed at the totalitarian regime in her own country. They have allowed themselves to be corrupted because they fear the people they are supposed to lead. This has led them into a vicious circle. In her thinking, however, the demand for fearlessness is first and foremost a general demand, a demand on all of us. She has herself shown fearlessness in practice. She opposed herself alone to the rifle barrels. Can anything withstand such courage? What was in that major's mind when at the last moment he gave the order not to fire? Perhaps he was impressed by her bravery, perhaps he realized that nothing can be achieved by brute force.

Violence is its own worst enemy, and fearlessness is the sharpest weapon against it. It is not least Aung San Suu Kyi's impressive courage which makes her such a potent symbol, like Gandhi and her father Aung San. Aung San was shot in the midst of his struggle. But if those who arranged the assassination thought it would remove him from Burmese politics, they were wrong. He became the unifying symbol of a free Burma and an inspiration to those who are now fighting for a free society. In addition to his example and inspiration his position among his people, over forty years after his death, gave Aung San Suu Kyi the political point of departure she needed. She has indeed taken up her inheritance and is now in her own right the symbol of the revolt against violence and the struggle for a free society, not only in Burma, but also in the rest of Asia and in many other parts of the world.

We ordinary people, I believe, feel that with her courage and her high ideals Aung San Suu Kyi brings out something of the best in us. We feel we need precisely her sort of person in order to retain our faith in the future. That is what gives her such power as a symbol, and that is why any ill-treatment of her feels like a violation of what we have most at heart. The little woman under house arrest stands for a positive hope. Knowing she is there gives us confidence and faith in the power of good.

Aung San Suu Kyi was born in 1945. Her father was killed when she was two. She has no personal memories of him. Her mother was a diplomat, and Aung San Suu Kyi was to spend many of her early years and much of her later life abroad. In 1967 she took a degree in Politics, Philosophy and Economics at St Hugh's College, Oxford. From 1969 on she worked for two years for the United Nations in New York. In 1972 she married Michael Aris, a British specialist on Tibet. For a time the family lived in Bhutan, but in the mid-seventies they moved back to Oxford. In addition to being a housewife with two small children Aung San Suu Kyi kept up her academic work, gradually concentrating on modern Burmese history and literature. She was a visiting scholar at Kyoto University in Japan and at the Indian Institute of Advanced Studies in New Delhi. On her return to Burma in 1988 she broke off her studies at the London School of Oriental and African Studies. There is little in these outward events to suggest the role she was to embark on in 1988. But she was well prepared.

There is a great deal of evidence that the fate of her own people had constantly weighed on her mind. Her husband has told us how she often reminded him that one day she would have to return to Burma and that she would count on his support. Her studies, too, as we have seen, became increasingly concentrated on Burma's modern history. The study of her father and the part he played in Burmese history no doubt increased her political commitment and her sense that his mantle had fallen on her.

In moving to Japan she was virtually following in her father's footsteps. During the Second World War, it was from a base in Japan that Aung San built up Burma's independent national army. When Japan invaded Burma, Aung San and his men went too. Before long they switched from fighting the British colonial power to resisting the occupying Japanese and supporting the retaking of Burma by the Allies. After the war he led the negotiations with the British which were to lead to final independence. Aung San Suu Kyi appears to have felt an urgent need to study the process which led to Burma's independent statehood and to understand the ideals governing the politics. In a beautiful essay comparing the Indian and Burmese experiences of colonization she also brings out the special features of Burma's cultural heritage.

History is important. You choose who you are by choosing which tradition you belong to. Aung San Suu Kyi seeks to call attention to what she sees as the best aspects of the national and cultural heritage and to identify herself with them. Such profound knowledge and such a deep sense of identity are an irresistible force in the political struggle.

The occasion of Aung San Suu Kyi's return to Burma in 1988 was, characteristically enough, not the political situation but her old mother's illness. The political turbulence had just begun, however. There had been demonstrations and confrontations with the police, with some 200 killed. The unrest continued while she was nursing her dying mother. That was the situation in which she resolved to take an active part in what she herself called 'the second struggle for national independence'.

The military regime had seized power in Burma in 1962. The disturbances which broke out in 1988 were a reaction to growing repression. In the summer of that year, at a time when the situation was very uncertain, Aung San Suu Kyi intervened with an open letter to the government, proposing the appointment of a consultative committee of respected independent persons to lead the country into multi-party elections. In the letter she emphasized the need for discipline and for refraining from the use of force on either side and demanded the release of political prisoners.

A couple of days later she addressed several hundred thousand people in front of the large Shwedagon pagoda in Rangoon, presenting a political programme based on human rights, democracy and non-violence. On 18 September, after hesitating for a few weeks, the armed forces reacted by tightening the restrictions. The so-called 'State Law and Order Restoration Council' (SLORC) was established, and martial law was introduced, under which meetings were banned and persons could be sentenced without trial.

Political parties were not prohibited (perhaps with meetings banned it was thought unnecessary). A week after the establishment of the SLORC Aung San Suu Kyi and a few other members of the opposition founded the National League for Democracy (NLD). She went on to engage in vigorous political activity, defying the ban on meetings and military provocations and holding heavily attended political meetings all over the country. One remarkable feature of her political campaign was the appeal she held for the country's various ethnic groups, traditionally at odds with each other.

It must have been her personal prestige which caused the regime to hesitate so long, but in July 1989 she was placed under house arrest. In May 1990 elections were held in which the NLD won an overwhelming victory and over 80 per cent of the seats in the National Assembly. There is general agreement that this was, principally, a triumph for Aung San Suu Kyi.

Why did the SLORC allow free elections? Probably because it expected a very different result, a result which would somehow have provided the legitimacy it needed to retain power. The dilemma of such regimes was demonstrated – trapped in their own lies. At any rate, they refused to accept the election result. The election was, in effect, annulled. The SLORC continued, but with reduced legitimacy. Lack of legitimacy is often made up for by increased brutality. Amnesty International has reported continuing serious violations of human rights. Today the Burmese regime appears to have developed into one of the most repressive in the world.

In recent decades the Norwegian Nobel Committee has awarded a number of Prizes for Peace in recognition of work for human rights. It has done so in the conviction that a fundamental prerequisite for peace is the recognition of the right of all people to life and to respect. Another motivation lies in the knowledge that in its most basic form the concept of human rights is not just a Western idea, but one common to all major cultures. Permit me in this connection to quote a paragraph of Aung San Suu Kyi's essay, *In Quest of Democracy*:

Where there is no justice there can be no secure peace. . . . That just laws which uphold human rights are the necessary foundation of peace and security would be denied only by closed minds which interpret peace as the silence of all opposition and security as the assurance of their own power. The Burmese associate peace and security with coolness and shade:

The shade of a tree is cool indeed
The shade of parents is cooler
The shade of teachers is cooler still
The shade of the ruler is yet more cool
But coolest of all is the shade of the Buddha's teachings.

Thus, to provide the people with the protective coolness of peace and security rulers must observe the teachings of the Buddha. Central to these teachings are the concepts of truth, righteousness and loving kindness. It is government based on these very qualities that the people of Burma are seeking in their struggle for democracy.

This is not the first time that political persecution at home has prevented a Peace Prize Laureate from receiving the prize in person. It happened to Carl von Ossietzky in 1936, ill in one of Hitler's concentration camps. It happened to Andrei Sakharov and to Lech Walesa. Ossietzky died before the regime fell, but both Sakharov and Walesa saw their struggles succeed. It is our hope that Aung San Suu Kyi will see her struggle crowned with success.

However, we must also face up to the likelihood that this will not be the last occasion on which a Peace Prize Laureate is unable to attend. Let that remind us that in a world such as ours, peace and reconciliation cannot be achieved once and for all. We will never be able to lower our standards. On the contrary, a better world demands even greater vigilance of us, still greater fearlessness and the ability to develop in ourselves the 'profound simplicity' of which this year's Laureate has spoken. This applies to all of us as individuals but must apply especially to those in positions of power and authority. Show humility and show fearlessness – like Aung San Suu Kyi. The result may be a better world to live in.

20

The Nobel Prize Acceptance Speech

Delivered on behalf of Aung San Suu Kyi, by her son Alexander Aris, on the occasion of the award to her in absentia *of the 1991 Nobel Prize for Peace.*

Your Majesties, Your Excellencies, Ladies and Gentlemen,

I stand before you here today to accept on behalf of my mother, Aung San Suu Kyi, this greatest of prizes, the Nobel Prize for Peace. Because circumstances do not permit my mother to be here in person, I will do my best to convey the sentiments I believe she would express.

Firstly, I know that she would begin by saying that she accepts the Nobel Prize for Peace not in her own name, but in the name of all the people of Burma. She would say that this prize belongs not to her but to all those men, women and children who, even as I speak, continue to sacrifice their well-being, their freedom and their lives in pursuit of a democratic Burma. Theirs is the prize and theirs will be the eventual victory in Burma's long struggle for peace, freedom and democracy.

Speaking as her son, however, I would add that I personally believe that by her own dedication and personal sacrifice she has come to be a worthy symbol, through whom the plight of all the people of Burma may be recognized.

And no one must underestimate that plight. The plight of those in the countryside and the towns, living in poverty and destitution; those in prison, battered and tortured; the plight of

236 Freedom from Fear

the young people, the hope of Burma, dying of malaria in the jungles to which they have fled; that of the Buddhist monks, beaten and dishonoured. Nor should we forget the many senior and highly respected leaders besides my mother, who are all incarcerated.

It is on their behalf that I thank you, from my heart, for this supreme honour. The Burmese people can today hold their heads a little higher in the knowledge that in this far-distant land their suffering has been heard and heeded.

We must also remember that the lonely struggle taking place in a heavily guarded compound in Rangoon is part of the much larger struggle, worldwide, for the emancipation of the human spirit from political tyranny and psychological subjection. The prize, I feel sure, is also intended to honour all those engaged in this struggle, wherever they may be. It is not without reason that today's events in Oslo fall on International Human Rights Day, celebrated throughout the world.

Mr Chairman, the whole international community has applauded the choice of your committee. Just a few days ago the United Nations passed a unanimous and historic resolution welcoming Secretary-General Javier Pérez de Cuéllar's statement on the significance of this award and endorsing his repeated appeals for my mother's early release from detention. Universal concern at the grave human rights situation in Burma was clearly expressed. Alone and isolated among the entire nations of the world, a single dissenting voice was heard from the military junta in Rangoon, too late and too weak.

This regime has through almost thirty years of misrule reduced the once-prosperous 'Golden Land' of Burma to one of the world's most economically destitute nations. In their heart of hearts even those in power now in Rangoon must know that their eventual fate will be that of all totalitarian regimes which seek to impose their authority through fear, repression and hatred. When the present Burmese struggle for democracy erupted on to the streets in 1988, it was the first of what became an international tidal wave of such movements throughout Eastern Europe, Asia and Africa. Today, in 1991, Burma stands conspicuous in its continued suffering at the hands of a repressive, intransigent junta, the State Law and Order Restoration Council. However, the example of those nations that have successfully achieved democracy holds out an important message to the Burmese people: in the last resort, through the sheer economic unworkability of totalitarianism, this present regime will be swept away. And today, in the face of rising inflation, a mismanaged economy and near-worthless Kyat, the Burmese government is undoubtedly reaping as it has sown.

However, it is my deepest hope that it will not be in the face of complete economic collapse that the regime will fall, but that the ruling junta may yet heed such appeals to basic humanity as that which the Nobel Committee has expressed in its award of this year's prize. I know that within the military government there *are* those to whom the present policies of fear and repression are abhorrent, violating as they do the most sacred principles of Burma's Buddhist heritage. This is no empty wishful thinking, but a conviction my mother reached in the course of her dealings with those in positions of authority, illustrated by the election victories of her party in constituencies composed almost exclusively of military personnel and their families. It is my profoundest wish that these elements for moderation and reconciliation among those now in authority may make their sentiments felt in Burma's hour of deepest need.

I know that if she were free today, my mother would, in thanking you, also ask you to pray that the oppressors and the oppressed should throw down their weapons and join together to build a nation founded on humanity in the spirit of peace.

Although my mother is often described as a political dissident who strives by peaceful means for democratic change, we should remember that her quest is basically spiritual. As she has said, 'the quintessential revolution is that of the spirit', and she has written of the 'essential spiritual aims' of the struggle. The realization of this depends solely on human responsibility. At the root of that responsibility lie, and I quote, 'the concept of perfection, the urge to achieve it, the intelligence to find a path towards it and the will to follow that path if not to the end, at least the distance needed to rise above individual limitation . . .' 'To live the full life', she says, 'one must have the courage to bear the responsibility of the needs of others . . . one must *want* to bear this responsibility.' And she links this firmly to her faith when she writes '. . . Buddhism, the foundation of traditional Burmese culture, places the greatest value on man, who alone of all beings can achieve the supreme state of Buddhahood. Each man has in him the potential to realize the truth through his own will and endeavour and to help others to realize it.' Finally, she says, 'The quest for democracy in Burma is the struggle of a people to live whole, meaningful lives as free and equal members of the world community. It is part of the unceasing human endeavour to prove that the spirit of man can transcend the flaws of his nature.'

This is the second time that my younger brother and I have accepted a great prize for my mother in Norway. Last year we travelled to Bergen to receive for her the Thorolf Rafto Prize for Human Rights, a wonderful prelude to this year's event. By now we have a very special feeling for the people of Norway. It is my hope that soon my mother will be able to share this feeling and to speak directly for herself instead of through me. Meanwhile, this tremendous support for her and the people of Burma has served to bring together two peoples from opposite ends of the earth. I believe much will follow from the links now forged.

It only remains for me to thank you all from the bottom of my heart. Let us hope and pray that from today the wounds start to heal and that in the years to come the 1991 Nobel Prize for Peace will be seen as a historic step towards the achievement of true peace in Burma. The lessons of the past will not be forgotten, but it is our hope for the future that we celebrate today.

21

Towards a True Refuge

The following is the text of the Eighth Joyce Pearce Memorial Lecture, composed by Aung San Suu Kyi in the fourth year of her house arrest, and delivered on her behalf by her husband Dr Michael Aris on 19 May 1993 at Oxford University. The lecture was introduced by Sir Claus Moser, Pro-Vice-Chancellor and Warden of Wadham College, and a response was given by Dr Peter Carey, Fellow of Trinity College. The Joyce Pearce Lecture, delivered annually on a theme of human rights, is organized by the Refugee Studies Programme, Oxford, and the Ockenden Venture. The text of this lecture was first published in pamphlet form in Oxford, 1993.

When I was told that I had been invited to deliver the Joyce Pearce Memorial Lecture for 1993, I felt very honoured. I also felt warmed by all that I had heard about Miss Pearce's Ockenden Venture, especially from Patricia Gore-Booth and her late husband Paul, dearly loved friends who taught me much about kindness and caring. The thought that the lecture would be held under the auspices of Queen Elizabeth House gave me particular pleasure. It is a place where I have spent many fruitful hours attending seminars and lectures and meeting people from different parts of the world. Those hours now appear to me suffused in Oxford tranquillity, reason and good fellowship. So I would like to thank the Refugee Studies Programme and the Committee of the Annual Joyce Pearce Memorial Lecture for more than just the invitation. I would also like to thank them for the delightful recollections conjured up by their invitation.

As Joyce Pearce put so much of her life and talents into her work for refugees, I wondered whether the lecture should not be related to refugee issues. But I felt very reluctant to take up a topic with which the audience is probably well acquainted, while I am not.

Then it occurred to me that the Burmese expression for refugee is *dukkha-the*, 'one who has to bear *dukkha*, suffering'. In that sense, none of us can avoid knowing what it is to be a refugee. The refuge we all seek is protection from forces which wrench us away from the security and comfort, physical and mental, which give dignity and meaning to human existence.

The answer to how such protection might be provided can be found only when the destructive forces have been identified. Well-publicized catastrophes which rock the sensibilities of the world have small beginnings, barely discernible from the private and contained forms of distress which make up the normal quota of everyday suffering. No man-made disaster suddenly bursts forth from the earth like warring armies sprung from dragon's teeth. After all, even in the myth the dragon's teeth were procured and sown by a man for reasons quite unrelated to innocent zoological or agricultural pursuits.[1] Calamities that are not the result of purely natural phenomena usually have their origins, distant and obscure though they may be, in common human failings.

But how common need those failings be? In a world which no longer accepts that 'common' germs and diseases should be left unchecked to take their toll on the weak and defenceless, it would not be inappropriate to ask if more attention should be paid to correcting 'common' attitudes and values which pose a far more lethal threat to humankind. It is my thoughts on some of these attitudes and values, which seem to be regarded as inevitable in an increasingly materialistic world, that I would like to communicate to you on this occasion.

The end of the Cold War has been represented as a signal for shifting the emphasis of national and international concern from ideology and politics to economics and trade. But it is open to debate whether policies heavily if not wholly influenced by economic considerations will make of the much bruited 'New World Order' an era of progress and harmony such as is longed for by peoples and nations weary of conflict and suffering.

As the twentieth century draws to a close it has become obvious that material yardsticks alone cannot serve as an adequate measure of human well-being. Even as basic an issue as poverty has to be re-examined to take into account the psychological sense of deprivation that makes people *feel* poor. Such a 'modern' concept of poverty is nothing new to the Burmese, who have always used the word *hsinye* to indicate not only an insufficiency of material goods but also physical discomfort and distress of mind: to be poor is to suffer from a paucity of those mental and spiritual, as well as material, resources which make a human being feel fulfilled and give life a meaning beyond mere existence. It follows as a matter of course that *chantha*, the converse of *hsinye*, denotes not only material prosperity but also bodily ease and general felicity. One speaks of *chantha* of the mind and of the body and one would wish to be possessed of both.

It is widely accepted, if not too often articulated, that governments and international agencies should limit their efforts to the elimination of the more obvious forms of suffering, rather than take on a task so uncertain, so abstruse and so susceptible to varying interpretations as the promotion of happiness. Many believe that policies and legislations aimed at establishing minimum standards with regard to wages, health care, working conditions, housing and education (in the formal, very limited sense of the word) are the most that can reasonably be expected from institutions as a contribution towards human well-being. There seems to be an underlying assumption that an amelioration in material conditions would eventually bring in its wake an improvement in social attitudes, philosophical values and ethical standards. The Burmese saying 'Morality (*sila*) can be upheld only when the stomach is full' is our version of a widely held sentiment which cuts across cultural boundaries. Brecht's '*Erst kommt das Fressen, dann kommt die Moral*' (first comes fodder, then come morals) also springs to mind.

But such axioms are hardly a faithful reflection of what actually goes on in human society. While it is undeniable that many have been driven to immorality and crime by the need to survive, it is equally evident that the possession of a significant surplus of material goods has never been a guarantee against covetousness, rapacity and the infinite variety of vice and pain which spring from such passions. Indeed, it could be argued that the unrelenting compulsion of those who already have much to acquire even more has generated greater injustice, immorality and wretchedness than the cumulative effect of the struggles of the severely underprivileged to better their lot. Given that man's greed can be a pit as bottomless as his stomach and that a psychological sense of deprivation can persist beyond the point at which basic needs have been adequately met, it can hardly be expected that an increase in material prosperity alone would ensure even a decline in economic strife, let alone a mitigation of those myriad other forces that spawn earthly misery.

The teachings of Buddhism which delve into the various causes of suffering identify greed or lust – the passion for indulging an intemperate appetite – as the first of the Ten Impurities[2] which stand in the way of a tranquil, wholesome state of mind. On the other hand, much value is attached to liberality or generosity, which heads such lists as the Ten Perfections of the Buddha,[3] the Ten Virtues[4] which should be practised and the Ten Duties of Kings.[5] This emphasis on liberality should not be regarded as a facile endorsement of alms-giving based on canny calculation of possible benefits in the way of worldly prestige or other-worldly rewards. It is a recognition of the crucial importance of the liberal, generous spirit as an effective antidote to greed as well as a fount of virtues which engender happiness and harmony. The late Sayadaw Ashin Janaka Bivamsa of the famous Mahagandharun monastery at Amarapura taught that liberality without morality cannot really be pure. An act of charity committed for the sake of earning praise or prestige or a place in a heavenly abode, he held to be tantamount to an act of greed.

Loving kindness, compassion, sympathetic joy and equanimity, Buddhists see as 'divine' states of mind which help to alleviate suffering and to spread happiness among all beings. The greatest obstacle to these noble emotions is not so much hatred, anger or ill will as the rigid mental state that comes of a prolonged and unwavering concentration on narrow self-interest. Hatred, anger or ill will that arises from wrongs suffered, from misunderstanding or from fear and envy may yet be appeased if there is sufficient generosity of spirit to permit forbearance, forgiveness and reconciliation. But it would be impossible to maintain or restore harmony when contention is rooted in the visceral inability of protagonists to concede that the other party has an equal claim to justice, sympathy and consideration. Hardness, selfishness and narrowness belong with greed, just as kindness, understanding and vision belong with true generosity.

The act of willingly subtracting from one's own limited store of the good and the agreeable for the sake of adding to that of others reflects the understanding that individual happiness needs a base broader than the mere satisfaction of selfish passions. From there, it is not such a large step to the realization that respecting the susceptibilities and rights of others is as important as defending one's own susceptibilities and rights if civilized society is to be safeguarded. But the desirability of redressing imbalances which spoil the harmony of human relationships – the ultimate foundation for global peace and security – is not always appreciated. Buddhism and other religious and ethical systems, however, have long recognized and sought to correct this prejudice in favour of the self. A scholar of Judaism, commenting on the Torah, wrote: 'In morals, holiness *negatively* demanded resistance to every urge of nature which made self-serving the essence of human life; and *positively*, submission to an ethic which placed service to others at the centre of its system.'[6]

It would be naive to expect that all men could be persuaded to place service to others before service to self. But with sufficient resolve on the part of governments and institutions that influence public opinion and set international standards of behaviour, a greater proportion of the world's population could be made to realize that self-interest (whether as an individual, a community or a nation) cannot be divorced entirely from the interests of others. Instead of assuming that material progress will bring an improvement in social, political and ethical standards, should it not be considered that an active promotion of appropriate social, political and ethical values might not only aid material progress but also help ensure that its results are wisely and happily distributed? 'Wealth enough to keep misery away and a heart wise enough to use it'[7] was described as the 'greatest good' by Aeschylus, who lived in an age when, after decades of war, revolution and tyrannies, Athenian democracy in its morning freshness was beginning to prove itself as a system wonderfully suited to free, thinking men.

A narrowly focused materialism that seeks to block out all considerations apparently irrelevant to one's own well-being tends finally to block out what is in fact most relevant. Discussing the 'culture of contentment' that poses a challenge to the social and economic future of the United States of America, Professor John Kenneth Galbraith has pointed out that the fortunate and the favoured are so preoccupied with immediate comfort and contentment they have ceased to contemplate or respond to their own longer term well-being: 'And this is not only in the capitalist world, as it is still called; a deeper and more general human instinct is here involved,' he wrote.[8] If the instinct to opt for narrow short-term benefits can present a significant threat to the continued prosperity and stability of a rich, industrialized state shored up by strongly established democratic institutions, how much more of a threat might it be to nations that have but recently embarked, rather unsteadily, on the grand adventure of free market economics and democratic politics? And it would surely be of the utmost danger to those societies still hovering on the edge of liberty and justice, still dominated by a minority well content with its monopoly on economic and political power.

In newly emergent democracies many who have been disappointed in their expectations of immediate material betterment have sought to work out their frustrations by subscribing to outmoded and obscure conspiracy theories which foster prejudice, paranoia and violence. The search for scapegoats is essentially an abnegation of responsibility: it indicates an inability to assess honestly and intelligently the true nature of the problems which lie at the root of social and economic difficulties and a lack of resolve in grappling with them. The valuation of achievement in predominantly material terms implies a limited and limiting view of human society, denying it many of the qualities that make it more than a conglomerate of egoistic consumer-gatherers who have advanced little beyond the prehistoric instinct for survival.

It is perfectly natural that all people should wish for a secure refuge. It is unfortunate that in spite of strong evidence to the contrary, so many still act as though security would be guaranteed if they fortified themselves with an abundance of material possessions. The greatest threats to global security today come not from the economic deficiencies of the poorest nations but from religious, racial (or tribal) and political dissensions raging in those regions where principles and practices which could reconcile the diverse instincts and aspirations of mankind have been ignored, repressed or distorted. Man-made disasters are made by dominant individuals and cliques which refuse to move beyond the autistic confines of partisan interest. An eminent development economist has observed that the best defence against famine is an accountable government. It makes little political or economic sense to give aid without trying to address the circumstances that render aid ineffectual. No amount of material goods and technological know-how will compensate for human irresponsibility and viciousness.

Developed and developing nations alike suffer as a result of policies removed from a framework of values which uphold minimum standards of justice and tolerance. The rapidity with which the old Soviet Union splintered into new states, many of them stamped with a fierce racial assertiveness, illustrates that decades of authoritarian rule may have achieved uniformity and obedience but could not achieve long-term harmony or stability. Nor did the material benefits enjoyed under the relatively successful post-totalitarian state[9] of Yugoslavia succeed in dissipating the psychological impress of brooding historical experience that has now led to some of the worst religious and ethnic violence the Balkans have ever witnessed. Peace, stability and unity cannot be bought or coerced; they have to be nurtured by promoting a sensitivity to human needs and respect for the rights and opinions of others. Diversity and dissent need not inhibit the emergence of strong, stable societies, but inflexibility, narrowness and unadulterated materialism can prevent healthy growth. And when attitudes have been allowed to harden to the point that otherness becomes a sufficient reason for nullifying a person's claim to be treated as a fellow human being, the trappings of modern civilization crumble with frightening speed.

In the most troubled areas of the world reserves of tolerance and compassion disappear, security becomes non-existent and creature comforts are reduced to a minimum – but stockpiles of weapons abound. As a system of values this is totally mad. By the time it is accepted that the only way out of an impasse of hate, bloodshed and social and economic chaos created by men is for those men to get together to find a peaceful solution through dialogue and compromise, it is usually no longer easy to restore sanity. Those who have been conditioned by systems which make a mockery of the law by legalizing injustices and which attack the very foundations of harmony by perpetuating social, political and economic imbalances cannot adjust quickly – if at all – to the concept of a fair settlement which places general well-being and justice above partisan advantage.

During the Cold War the iniquities of ruthless governments and armed groups were condoned for ideological reasons. The results have been far from happy. Although there is greater emphasis on justice and human rights today, there are still ardent advocates in favour of giving priority to political and economic expediency – increasingly the latter. It is the old argument: achieve economic success and all else will follow. But even long-affluent societies are plagued by formidable social ills which have provoked deep anxieties about the future. And newly rich nations appear to be spending a significant portion of their wealth on arms and armies. Clearly there is no inherent link between greater prosperity and greater security and peace – or even the expectation of greater peace. Both prosperity and peace are necessary for the happiness of mankind, the one to alleviate suffering, the other to promote tranquillity. Only policies that place equal importance on both will make a truly richer world, one in which men can enjoy *chantha* of the body and of the mind. The drive for economic progress needs to be tempered with an awareness of the dangers of greed and selfishness which so easily lead to narrowness and inhumanity. If peoples and nations cultivate a generous spirit which welcomes the happiness of others as an enhancement of the happiness of the self, many seemingly insoluble problems would prove less intractable.

Those who have worked with refugees are in the best position to know that when people have been stripped of all their material supports, there only remain to sustain them the values of their cultural and spiritual inheritance. A tradition of sharing instilled by age-old beliefs in the joy of giving and the sanctity of compassion will move a homeless destitute to press a portion of his meagre ration on strangers with all the grace and delight of one who has ample riches to dispense. On the other hand, predatory traits honed by a long-established habit of yielding to 'every urge of nature which made self-serving the essence of human life' will lead men to plunder fellow sufferers of their last pathetic possessions. And of course the great majority of the world's refugees are seeking sanctuary from situations rendered untenable by a dearth of humanity and wisdom.

The dream of a society ruled by loving kindness, reason and justice is a dream as old as civilized man. Does it have to be an impossible dream? Karl Popper, explaining his abiding optimism in so troubled a world as ours, said that the darkness had always been there but the light was new. Because it is new it has to be tended with care and diligence. It is true that even the smallest light cannot be extinguished by all the darkness in the world because darkness is wholly negative. It is merely an absence of light. But a small light cannot dispel acres of encircling gloom. It needs to grow stronger, to shed its brightness further and further. And people need to accustom their eyes to the light to see it as a benediction rather than a pain, to learn to love it. We are so much in need of a brighter world which will offer adequate refuge to all its inhabitants.

Notes

1 A harvest of armed men sprang from the dragon's teeth sown by Cadmus. He killed the men by setting them to fight one another.

2 The Ten Impurities (*dasa-kilesa*) consist of greed (*lobha*), anger (*dosa*), ignorance (*moha*), pride (*mana*), wrong view (*ditthi*), doubt (*vicikiccha*), obduracy (*thina*), disquietude (*uddhacca*), shamelessness (*ahirika*) and recklessness (*anottappa*).

3 The Ten Perfections of the Buddha (*dasa-paramita*) consist of generosity (*dana*), morality (*sila*), renunciation (*nekkhamma*), wisdom (*pañña*), diligence (*viriya*), patience (*khanti*), truth (*sacca*), determination (*adhitthana*), loving kindness (*metta*) and equanimity (*upekha*).

4 The Ten Virtues (*dasa-kusala-kamma*) consist of generosity (*dana*), morality (*sila*), meditation (*bhavana*), being respectful to teachers and elders (*apacayana*), undertaking meritorious actions great and small (*veyyavacca*), sharing out merit acquired by oneself (*pattidana*), praising meritorious acts by others (*pattanumodana*), listening to the teachings of the Buddha and others (*dhammasavana*), preaching the teachings of the Buddha and others (*dhammadesana*) and having a firm belief that the preceding nine activities bring peace of mind (*ditthijukamma*).

5 The Ten Duties of Kings (*dasa-raja-dhamma*) consist of generosity (*dana*), morality (*sila*), liberality (*pariccaga*), rectitude (*ajjava*), gentleness (*maddava*), self-control (*tapo*), non-anger (*akkodha*), non-violence (*avihimsa*), patience (*khanti*) and non-opposition to the will of the people (*avirodhana*).

6 Isidore Epstein, *Judaism: A Historical Presentation* (Harmondsworth, 1959), p. 23.

7 The quotation is from *Agamemnon*, 378–9, translated in Edith Hamilton, *The Greek Way* (New York, 3rd edn, 1964), p.51.

8 John Kenneth Galbraith, *The Culture of Contentment* (London, 1992), pp. 6–7.

9 I use 'post-totalitarian state' in the sense given to it by Václav Havel in his essay on 'The Power of the Powerless' (1979), when he applies the term to the neo-totalitarianism of the now-dissolved Soviet bloc and the forms of state repression found there, which are markedly different from those obtaining in classical dictatorships. See Václav Havel *et al.*, *The Power of the Powerless: Citizens Against the State in Central-Eastern Europe*, ed. John Keane (New York, 1985), esp. pp. 8, 24–7.

22

The Need for Dialogue

On 14 February 1994 Aung San Suu Kyi received her first visitors outside her immediate family during all the years of her incarceration. The following are excerpts from the conversation she held with Bill Richardson, Democrat Congressman from New Mexico, Jehan Raheem, Resident Representative of the UNDP in Rangoon, and Philip Shenon of the New York Times. To date, the only other meetings allowed her since then have been with U Rewata Dhamma, a Burmese Buddhist abbot resident in the United Kingdom, and two well-publicized meetings with leaders of the SLORC in September and October 1994.

RICHARDSON: What do you see as the prospects for a national reconciliation?

ASSK: This is precisely why I've always asked for dialogue. You have to work out the terms and conditions under which national reconciliation can be brought about. If the SLORC refuses to talk, how can they bring about national reconciliation?

RICHARDSON: My view is that General Khin Nyunt should talk to you.

ASSK: I've always said he should talk to me . . .

RICHARDSON: I think the key . . . to democratic change in Burma is a dialogue between you and Khin Nyunt . . .

ASSK: I think I would rather put it as between the SLORC and the NLD, or the democratic forces, because I'm not in favour of promoting any kind of personality cult or personality politics. This is something we've got to avoid from the very beginning.

When we set up a democracy we want to see a democracy which is based on solid principles, not on any personalities. You will say, 'but this is what happens all over Asia,' but [there's] no reason why we can't change that, why we shouldn't *try* to change that . . . I'm only human and of *course* I like it when people care for me. But it's also rather worrying. I would like people to think of the democracy movement as a whole, not just as me. Just releasing me tomorrow is not going to do any good if the attitude of SLORC does not change . . . Whatever they do to me, that's between them and me. I can take it. What is more important is what they are doing to the country. And national reconciliation doesn't just mean reconciliation between two people – I don't accept that at all. It's a reconciliation between different ideas . . . What we need is a spiritual *and* intellectual reconciliation . . . I've always said that the only answer to Burma's problems is dialogue . . . I'm ready at any time, but they [SLORC] seem not terribly keen. And I wonder why.

RICHARDSON: The SLORC did say that during the period 1992–93 you rebuffed them on a dialogue.

ASSK: I must make it quite clear that they made *no moves* to have a dialogue of any kind. There were indications that they would quite like to negotiate with me on the terms under which I would leave Burma. That's not what I would call dialogue. And that's not what I would call negotiation . . .

RICHARDSON: They told me when I was here in August . . .

ASSK: I believe they told a Japanese delegation about it as well . . . [the] 92–93 period was when they allowed my family to come and when they were quite nice to me. And there were indications that they would be prepared to negotiate with me . . . on the terms under which I would leave Burma. That is the impression I got. There was never a mention of dialogue. I mentioned dialogue. I said that the only real answer was negotiation and dialogue – it was no use letting some political prisoners free and it was no use letting my family come to see me. In fact I was not keen on the idea of my family coming to see me at all because I felt that I did not want [them to come] until other prisoners had been released. In the end I did let Michael come, basically to show that I would compromise and I would be flexible. But the SLORC has to understand that flexibility is not the same as weakness. And rigidity doesn't mean strength . . . 'give and take' means 'I give a little, I take a little; you give a little, you take a little.' It doesn't mean 'you give and I take' . . . Also, they should not think that by making my personal circumstances easier for me this would in any way induce me to give up my political convictions. I don't care if they deprive me of all my privileges . . . I was brought a renewal of the detention order in January – for another year . . . The explanation they gave says that under the law under which I was detained, the Central Committee (which I'd never heard of before and which, according to the BBC, nobody else had heard of before either) is the one which decides I'm put away . . . under house arrest without trial for one year. At the end of the year [a] Council of Ministers . . . [is] allowed to extend this for three years. Then they changed the law to make it a total of five years. And then they said it means a total of five years from the time that the Council of Ministers extends my period of detention . . . I explained to [them] that, under all existing norms of international justice, when you say . . . a *maximum* of five years, you do count it from the day on which you're put under arrest . . . I said that [they] had better not go on pushing this because it's very exhausting for [them] to go on lying to me all the time.

RICHARDSON: What message would you want me to take back to President Clinton?

ASSK: We would like a clear-cut policy on Burma. If you want to support a movement which has been attacked on all sides within the country . . . you have to be very strong and clear.

RICHARDSON: Do you think it's [US policy on Burma] been strong enough?

ASSK: I think the United States has not been very clear-cut – I think it's an expression which the Senate used? . . . I think in the resolution they asked for a more clear-cut policy on Burma and I think I endorse that. A more clear-cut policy on Burma, in favour of the movement

for democracy if you please – just to make it quite clear what I mean!
RICHARDSON: Is there any message for the international community . . . that you would like to convey?
ASSK: If I had to give one single message to the international community it would be to remind them that the success of any economic or political system is confidence. And without confidence, nothing will work. That means confidence in the government and in the people, confidence between the business sector and the government and the public sector . . . It's no use setting up a National Convention if nobody has any confidence in it. It's not going to solve any problems. No economic measure which cannot win the confidence of the people [is] going to work in the long term . . . I don't think that trade and other economic measures will lead to any real progress if there's no confidence. Confidence is the most important item for the success of any policy, whether it's economic or whether it's political. And of course, when you come down to it, there is a need for confidence between those who want democracy and those who don't. We've got to learn that people have different ideas, but that doesn't mean that we can't coexist. We've just got to agree to differ, for the sake of the country.

SHENON: On [the] questions of economic assistance and trade . . . how should the world treat Burma? At this point?
ASSK: Of course, you are probably thinking of sanctions, aren't you? . . . Well, there have always been two schools of thought about sanctions. Some would say they only harm the people; they don't harm the government against which they are directed. I don't think this controversy has ever been fully resolved and certainly I would not like anything that *harms* the people. But then . . . is whatever trade [that is] going on really helping the people or is it simply helping the government to dig its heels in? This is the question that has to be asked. Of course people say, 'first, economic progress; then democratization', and I have to ask, 'which examples are you giving?' . . . If you're thinking of the ASEAN countries, the pattern of the development is very, very different from that of Burma. And . . . the *crucial* thing is

confidence. For example, Indonesia, which is currently the country with which people are comparing Burma: the conditions under which Suharto came into power are very, very different from the conditions under which the SLORC came into power. One of the reasons why confidence is at such a low level in Burma is precisely because of the way in which the elections have been treated. Elections were promised, elections were held, but they [led] nowhere at all. And I think the people feel cheated. A lot of people's confidence is very much shaken ... I don't think this sort of thing happened in all those other countries. There was sufficient confidence in the governments of those ASEAN countries that have made progress. Even from the economic point of view, one of the things which always struck me about Indonesia after 1965 – after Suharto took over – one of the first things he did was to cut down public expenditure and defence expenditure. Total opposite of what's happening in Burma ...

RICHARDSON: [Japan and Singapore] told me, basically, that they felt United States policy towards Burma is too rough, that the way to get SLORC to do more in the area of human rights is to engage them, trade with them more and give them assistance ... There are some in the United States who would like to see a carrot-and-stick policy. There's a perception ... in the United States that our policy on Burma is isolation ...

ASSK: I'm not sure that those who are advocating constructive engagement have made themselves quite clear ... What's the stick supposed to be? ... The carrot is, I suppose, the economic help. What's the stick?

RICHARDSON: The stick right now is aid. And there is no aid. Burma gets no World Bank, no Asian Development Bank aid. It gets limited UN aid. It wants foreign investment – there's hardly any. It wants infrastructure. It wants more economic movement here ... This is traditionally Japan's position on everything: the way you improve relationships anywhere is economically. You give them more aid, you give them more assistance ... The view is that United States policy is just stick ...

ASSK: I just want to know what the Japanese think is the stick.

SHENON: They could argue the stick is the fact that there is now no aid, there is now very little trade with Japan. The stick is in place now, would be their argument, I suppose.

ASSK: They seem to be actually advocating the removal of the stick rather than a carrot-and-stick approach. But this is why I'm not quite clear – what do they *mean* by a carrot-and-stick approach? . . . I'm just saying that you can stuff a mule to death with carrots.

RAHEEM: I think it's reform with support. Speaking for others, there is a policy that says reform needs support. There is a price to reform . . . Any time you urge a reform you support it with technical knowledge, training programmes, open opportunities for debate and discussion.

ASSK: In that case, are they talking merely of economic reform?

RAHEEM: No, a system of reform.

ASSK: Then it's very simple. There have to be conditions. If they need conditional help I'm not arguing about it . . . But it's got to be conditions which are meaningful.

RICHARDSON: What conditions do you think are meaningful?

ASSK: Dialogue . . . Dialogue can lead to a lot of things . . . I want to confront them [the SLORC] across a table, and I think that's what they mean when they say I'm confrontational, because I've never asked for any other sort of confrontation at all. It seems to me very strange that they're prepared to talk to armed insurgents but not to legal political parties . . .

RICHARDSON: You would set no preconditions on talking with the SLORC?

ASSK: I don't think anyone should set conditions on talking . . . I would meet with the SLORC at any time . . . People say, 'don't be in such a hurry' . . . but time makes a difference. Look at South Africa . . . This polarization between the Inkatha and the ANC came about in the 1970s, and there have been allegations that the government forces incited a lot of the violence that took place between [them] . . . If those talks between the government and the ANC had taken place ten years earlier, things might not have been so bad . . . Look at Yugoslavia . . . There was no confidence between the various groups in Yugoslavia . . . So, you see, as long as you cannot foster confidence, time is *not* going to heal all wounds.

RICHARDSON: What would be your vision for Burma, if you were in power?

ASSK: It's not *my* vision . . . We must *not* emphasize this personality business. I'm quite happy to be a figurehead . . . [But] I'm not Burma . . . There are a lot of very, very able people in the NLD and in the country . . . I am sure there are still some very able people in the NLD . . . You say, what is my vision of Burma? Well, my vision of Burma is of a country where we can all sort out our problems by trying to understand each other and by talking to each other and by working together. Democracy is not going to solve all our problems. If people think that democracy comes today and everything's fine tomorrow, they're very much mistaken. I've always told them so: democracy is just a beginning. I subscribe to the view that democracy is not perfect but it does happen to be better than other systems. One of the best things about democracy is that practising liberal democracies always think of talking first and fighting as the last resort. Whereas in a lot of cases talking is the last resort, when they've fought themselves to exhaustion and there's nothing else they can do, then they talk. By that time, quite often it's done *so* much harm . . . 'Parliament' comes from the word [in French] 'talk', doesn't it? You *talk*, you talk about your problems, you talk about your differences. It's better to shout at each other than to kill each other. It's not that I like shouting, but it's certainly much better than shooting each other . . . All this thing about democracy the Asian way, democracy the Burmese way – really you don't need to say this, because whatever system you establish in any country it will become unique to that country. American democracy is different from British democracy. It is different from French democracy, and so on. There will always be differences, but that doesn't mean that there are not certain fundamental principles which you *have* to accept. Without these fundamental principles it's not a democracy . . . I dread to think what the 'Burmese way to democracy', which is more or less the same as the 'Burmese way to socialism' [might be like]. One doesn't want just a difference in name. One wants a difference in attitude. And *that* is my vision, of a country where people are *not* afraid to work out their differences. You don't have to hold back from dialogue because you *think* you're going to lose face in some way, or because you *think* you're not going to be able to come to an agreement. When you go to sit down to discuss something you always go ... with the idea that some kind of agreement is possible. It may take time, it may have to be a compromise, but agreement is always possible as long as the will is there. Sincerity and goodwill are the foundations of confidence, and confidence is the foundation of *any* system that can succeed ...

SHENON: You do see the opportunity for the NLD and the SLORC to reach a peaceful agreement that would lead to a democratic Burma?

ASSK: There is nothing on the side of the NLD that prevents this. It's the *SLORC* which is not taking this up. The NLD has always been prepared to talk to them ...

SHENON: Well, assuming the dialogue begins [and] some confidence is developed in each others' words, do you see the possibility that there *could* be a democratically oriented government in Burma which could include a substantial component of the army? A political prospect?

ASSK: I'm not prepared to discuss it, because that's not for me to say. What I *do* want to make clear is that it's got to be a serious democracy, not a sham. That I would insist on. But of course, everybody in Burma has a role to play in the country and we've never ruled it out ... We've just got to agree on who plays what role and how. But one group should not impose that on the country.

SHENON: But you can see a situation in which authority – influence – could be shared?

ASSK: I don't think I'm going to talk about shared influence. I want the government of Burma, the political system of Burma, to be based on confidence, and any arrangement that can win the confidence of the people will be acceptable. You could have a nominally and tokenly democratic government, but if the practical fact is such that the people have no confidence in it as a democracy, it's no use at all. You can have a country where there's no constitution at all, such as Britain, but nevertheless it is a democracy and nobody doubts that it's a democracy, least of all its own people. They have confidence in the fact that the government's a democracy. But in fact there is no document which says, 'these groups have this sort of influence.' And you must accept that it is very difficult for me to make pronouncements on important matters on my own. It's not what I want to do. Whatever is agreed on must be agreed on through discussion and through consensus among ourselves and perhaps, eventually, compromise with other groups . . . I do know that a lot of us in the NLD were very anxious about giving the opposition a proper role, honouring it, respecting it, giving it an effective role. We didn't want a democracy in name only, because that's very bad for a democracy. I think it will keep the NLD on their toes if they have a good opposition . . . Even if there were very few of them [in opposition], we would have made sure that their voice was heard and that their views were listened to and that they were not persecuted . . . All of us in the EC of the NLD are completely agreed on this – the importance of a loyal opposition, loyal to the nation. It is a great pity that the SLORC didn't take the opportunity in 1990 to speak to the NLD and establish a system which could have been acceptable to everybody. I don't know what's happened to the NUP now, but certainly, if the NLD had been allowed to form a government at that time [after the elections] I'm sure that we would have heard a lot more of the NUP's voice than we do. We would have allowed them a very loud voice in government. ([The USDA is a different party.] This is the sort of pseudo-Golkar party, the USDA.)

SHENON: You're uncomfortable with this question of personality. The fact is, you did win the Nobel Prize –
ASSK: Well, that is only because so many Burmese suffered.
SHENON: You have become a symbol for many people, and many people around the world know your name where they might not know the names of other Burmese.
ASSK: Well, that's very understandable. It's very much easier to give the Nobel Prize to one person . . . [Others] must have had a

terrible time. Certainly, I wasn't beaten up . . . I can read. I've got books here. I may be alone, but I can read, I can listen to the radio.

SHENON: How did you find out you'd won the Nobel Prize?

ASSK: On the radio. I heard it on the BBC.

SHENON: Did you have a response when you heard that?

ASSK: Well, I'd heard about it for some time. I think I heard about it first at the time when Václav Havel put up my name. Then, the weekend before the announcement of the prize the BBC and VOA [Voice of America] said that I was one of the front runners. So it was not altogether a surprise when the news finally came . . .

RICHARDSON: I saw your award . . .

ASSK: I've seen a photograph.

SHENON: When you heard it, was there a sense of satisfaction about it, or pleasure?

ASSK: [*Hesitant*] No. I actually wrote to the Nobel Committee very frankly about how I felt, and I felt tremendous humility and tremendous gratitude . . . I was very grateful because the prize meant that the movement for democracy would get a lot more recognition. Of course [I felt] humility because I know that other people have suffered a lot more . . . other people have died . . .

RICHARDSON: What's your main message for me?

ASSK: Well, my main message is that since [you say] that [the SLORC] is refusing nothing, please keep asking . . .

RICHARDSON: We [the US Government] have been very strongly for democracy [in Burma] . . . The United States feels very strongly about you . . . The Secretary of State last week asked Boutros-Gali to appoint a Special Envoy for dealing with the Burma issue. We're very strongly committed. I want to make it clear to you that I have asked the SLORC for your unconditional release . . .

ASSK: When I joined the democracy movement I made hardly any promises . . . because I don't want to make promises which I'm not able to keep. But one of the things that I did promise was that I would work for the movement for democracy until we

achieved our goal. And I *can't* go back on that promise . . . But
I'm prepared to discuss ways and means of bringing about
national reconciliation. One of the things that does not bother me
is the question of not getting public office. I'm not hungry for
public office. That is not a goal of my political work. But I
suppose there are certain values which I must continue to uphold.
If there's anything they [SLORC] are afraid of . . . if they're
really *serious* about thinking that I have some sort of neo-colonial-
ist bogey behind me – they've got to talk to me about that. I
don't think they believe that anyway. That's just pure nonsense
and I think they know it. . . . My loyalties are to Burma, but I
recognize the importance of the international community. I'm
not going to abuse other countries, I'm not going to abuse the
international community in order to prove my patriotism. It
doesn't mean that just because I love my country I hate other
people. That doesn't follow at all . . . I'm not at all surprised by
[the qualifications for President proposed under the new constitu-
tion]. One does not like to think that it's personal vindictiveness
but, if it isn't, then what it reflects is a misunderstanding of the
notion of democracy and an underestimation of the Burmese
people. If they truly believe that somebody who is married to a
foreigner . . . would put Burma under the foreign yoke, (i) they
don't understand . . . that democracy means you're in office only
so long as the people agree that you should be; and (ii) they think
that the Burmese people will keep in the position of leadership
somebody who doesn't have their interests at heart . . . They [the
Burmese people] will only support me as long as they are confident
that I have their interests at heart. And if they lose that confidence
they won't support me any more. It's very simple . . .

23

Empowerment for a Culture of Peace and Development

An address presented on behalf of Aung San Suu Kyi, and at her request, by Mrs Corazon Aquino, former President of the Philippines, to a meeting of UNESCO's World Commission on Culture and Development, Manila, 21 November 1994, and also at the forum for Democratic Leaders in the Asia-Pacific in Seoul, Korea, 1 December 1994. The address was composed at the invitation of the World Commission's chairman, Mr Javier Pérez de Cuéllar, former Secretary-General of the United Nations. Aung San Suu Kyi has been an honorary member of the Commission since it was founded in 1992. In June 1992 the Commission issued a public appeal to the Burmese military authorities to free Aung San Suu Kyi, pointing out that her fundamental freedoms under the Universal Declaration of Human Rights, adopted by Burma in 1948, had been constantly denied. In 1992 she was awarded UNESCO's Simon Bolívar Prize jointly with Julius K. Nyerere of Tanzania.

At its third meeting, held at San José, Costa Rica, 22–6 February 1994, the World Commission on Culture and Development set itself three goals, the third of which was 'to promote a new cultural dynamic: the culture of peace and culture of development'. The Commission undertook to 'endeavour to recommend the concrete measures that could promote, on a national and international scale, a culture of peace' and went on to state that 'a culture of peace, culture of democracy and culture of human rights are indivisible. Their effective implementation must result in a democratic management and ... the prevention of inter-cultural conflicts'.[1]

Peace as a goal is an ideal which will not be contested by any government or nation, not even the most belligerent. And the close interdependence of the culture of peace and the culture of development also finds ready acceptance. But it remains a matter of uncertainty how far governments are prepared to concede that democracy and human rights are indivisible from the culture of peace and therefore essential to sustained development. There is ample evidence that culture and development can actually be made to serve as pretexts for resisting calls for democracy and human rights. It is widely known that some governments argue that democracy is a Western concept alien to indigenous values; it has also been asserted that economic development often conflicts with political (i.e. democratic) rights, and that the second should necessarily give way to the first. In the light of such arguments culture and development need to be carefully examined and defined that they may not be used, or rather, misused, to block the aspirations of peoples for democratic institutions and human rights.

The unsatisfactory record of development in many parts of the world and the ensuing need for a definition of development which means more than mere economic growth became a matter of vital concern to economists and international agencies more than a decade ago.[2] In *A New Concept of Development* published in 1983, François Perroux stated that 'development has not taken place: it represents a dramatic growth of awareness, a promise, a matter of survival indeed; intellectually, however, it is still only dimly perceived.'[3] Later in the same book he asserted that 'personal development, the freedom of persons fulfilling their potential in the context of the values to which they subscribe and which they experience in their actions, is one of the mainsprings of all forms of development.'[4]

His concept of development therefore gives a firm place to human and cultural values within any scheme for progress, economic or otherwise. The United Nations Development Programme too

262 Freedom from Fear

began to spell out the difference between growth and development in the 1980s.[5] With the beginning of the 1990s the primacy of the human aspect of development was acknowledged by the UNDP with the publication of its first *Human Development Report*. And the special focus of the 1993 report was people's participation, seen as 'the central issue of our time'.[6]

While the concept of human development is beginning to assume a dominant position in the thinking of international economists and administrators, the Market Economy, not merely adorned with capital letters but seen in an almost mystic haze, is increasingly regarded by many governments as the quick and certain way to material prosperity. It is assumed that economic measures can resolve all the problems facing their countries. Economics is described as the '*deus ex machina*, the most important key to every lock of every door to the new Asia we wish to see'; and 'healthy economic development' is seen as 'essential to successfully meeting the challenge of peace and security, the challenge of human rights and responsibilities, the challenge of democracy and the rule of law, the challenge of social justice and reform and the challenge of cultural renaissance and pluralism.'[7]

The view that economic development is essential to peace, human rights, democracy and cultural pluralism, and the view that a culture of peace, democracy and human rights is essential to sustained human development, may seem on the surface to differ only in the matter of approach. But a closer investigation reveals that the difference in approach itself implies differences of a more fundamental order. When economics is regarded as 'the most important key to every lock of every door,' it is only natural that the worth of man should come to be decided largely, even wholly, by his effectiveness as an economic tool.[8] This is at variance with the vision of a world where economic, political and social institutions work to serve man, instead of the other way round; where culture and development coalesce to create an environment in which human potential can be realized to the full. The differing views ultimately reflect differences in how the valuation of the various components of the social and national entity are made; how such basic concepts as poverty, progress, culture, freedom, democracy and human rights are defined and, of crucial importance, who has the power to determine such values and definitions.

The value systems of those with access to power and of those far removed from such access cannot be the same. The viewpoint of the privileged is unlike that of the underprivileged. In the matter of power and privilege the difference between the haves and the have-nots is not merely quantitative, for it has far-reaching psychological and ideological implications. And many 'economic' concerns are seldom just that, since they are tied up with questions of power and privilege. The problem of poverty provides an example of the inadequacy of a purely economic approach to a human situation. Even those who take a down-to-earth view of basic human needs agree that 'whatever doctors, nutritionists and other scientists may say about the objective conditions of deprivation, how the poor themselves perceive their deprivation is also relevant.'[9] The alleviation of poverty thus entails setting in motion processes which can change the perceptions of all those concerned. Here power and privilege come into play:

> The poor are powerless and have no voice. Power is the possibility of expressing and imposing one's will in a given social relationship, in the face of any resistance. The poor are incapable of either imposing, coercing or, in many cases, having any influence at all.[10]

It is not enough merely to provide the poor with material assistance. They have to be sufficiently empowered to change their perception of themselves as helpless and ineffectual in an uncaring world.

The question of empowerment is central to both culture and development. It decides who has the means of imposing on a nation or society their view of what constitutes culture and development and who determines what practical measures can be taken in the name of culture and development. The more totalitarian a system, the more power will be concentrated in the hands of the ruling élite and the more culture and development will be used to serve narrow interests. Culture has been defined as 'the most recent, the most highly developed means of promoting the security and continuity of life'.[11] Culture thus defined is dynamic and broad, the emphasis is on its flexible, non-compelling qualities. But when it is bent to serve narrow interests it becomes static and rigid, its exclusive aspects come to the fore and it assumes coercive overtones. The 'national culture' can become a bizarre graft of carefully selected historical incidents and distorted social values intended to justify the policies and actions of those in power.[12] At the same time, development is likely to be seen in the now outmoded sense of economic growth. Statistics, often unverifiable, are reeled off to prove the success of official measures.

Many authoritarian governments wish to appear in the forefront of modern progress but are reluctant to institute genuine change. Such governments tend to claim that they are taking a uniquely national or indigenous path towards a political system in keeping with the times. In the decades immediately after the Second World War socialism was the popular option. But since the 1980s democracy has increasingly gained ground. The focus on a national or indigenous way to socialism or democracy has:

> the effect of stressing cultural continuity as both process and goal; this in turn obviates the necessity of defining either democracy or socialism in institutionally or procedurally specific terms; and finally, it elevates the existing political élite to the indispensable position of final arbiter and interpreter of what does or does not contribute to the preservation of cultural integrity.[13]

It is often in the name of cultural integrity, as well as social stability and national security, that democratic reforms based on human rights are resisted by authoritarian governments. It is insinuated that some of the worst ills of Western society are the result of democracy, which is seen as the progenitor of unbridled freedom and selfish individualism. It is claimed, usually without adequate evidence, that democratic values and human rights run counter to the national culture and therefore, to be beneficial, they need to be modified – perhaps to the extent that they are barely recognizable. The people are said to be as yet unfit for democracy; therefore an indefinite length of time has to pass before democratic reforms can be instituted.

The first form of attack is often based on the premise, so universally accepted that it is seldom challenged or even noticed, that the United States of America is the supreme example of democratic culture. What tends to be overlooked is that although the USA is certainly the most important representative of democratic culture, it also represents many other cultures, often intricately enmeshed. Among these are the 'I-want-it-all' consumer culture, the megacity culture, the superpower culture, the frontier culture, immigrant culture. There is also a strong media culture, which constantly exposes the myriad problems of American society, from large issues such as street violence and drug abuse to the matrimonial difficulties of minor celebrities. Many of the worst ills of American society, increasingly to be found in varying degrees in other developed countries, can be traced not to the democratic legacy but to the demands of modern materialism. Gross individualism and cut-throat morality arise when political and intellectual freedoms are curbed on the one hand while on the other fierce economic competitiveness is encouraged by making material success the measure of prestige and progress. The result is a society where cultural and human values are set aside and money value reigns supreme. No political or social system is perfect. But could such a powerful and powerfully diverse nation as the United States have been prevented from disintegrating if it had not been sustained by democratic institutions guaranteed by a constitution based on the assumption that man's capacity for reason and justice makes free government possible and that his capacity for passion and injustice makes it necessary?[14]

It is precisely because of the cultural diversity of the world that it is necessary for different nations and peoples to agree on those basic human values which will act as a unifying factor. When democracy and human rights are said to run counter to non-Western culture, such culture is usually defined narrowly and presented as monolithic. In fact, the values that democracy and human rights seek to promote can be found in many cultures. Human beings the world over need freedom and security in order to be able to realize their full potential. The longing for a form of governance that provides security without destroying freedom goes back a long way.[15] Support for the desirability of strong government and dictatorship can also be found in all cultures, both Eastern and Western: the desire to dominate and the tendency to adulate the powerful are also common human traits arising out of a desire for security. A nation may choose a system that leaves the protection of the freedom and security of the many dependent on the inclinations of the em- powered few; or it may choose institutions and practices that will sufficiently empower individuals and organizations to pro- tect their own freedom and security. The choice will decide how far a nation will progress along the road to peace and human development.[16]

Many of the countries in the Third World now striving for meaningful development are multiracial societies where there is one dominant racial group and a number – sometimes a large number – of smaller groups: foreign, religious or ethnic minorities. As poverty can no longer be defined satisfactorily in terms of basic economic needs, 'minority' can no longer be defined merely in terms of numbers. For example, it has been noted in a study of minorities in Burmese history that:

> In the process of nation-building . . . the notion of minority in Burma changed, as one group defines itself as a nation those outside the group become minorities . . . There were, of course, minorities in traditional Burma – people close to the power élite who considered themselves superior and people estranged from the power élite who were considered inferior. These criteria for establishing majorities (who might in fact be a small portion of the population as, say, white people in South Africa today) were not based on race or even ethnic group, but on access to power. Minorities, thus, are those people with poor access to power.[17]

Once again, as in the case of poverty, it is ultimately a question of empowerment. The provision of basic material needs is not sufficient to make minority groups and indigenous peoples feel they are truly part of the greater national entity. For that they have to be confident that they too have an active role to play in shaping the destiny of the state that demands their allegiance. Poverty degrades a whole society and threatens its stability while ethnic conflict and minority discontent are two of the greatest threats to both internal and regional peace. And when the dispossessed 'minority' is in fact an overwhelming majority, as happens in countries where power is concentrated in the hands of the few, the threat to peace and stability is ever present even if unperceived.

The Commission for a New Asia notes that:

> the most rapid economic transformation is most likely to succeed within the context of international peace and internal political stability, in the presence of social tranquillity, public order and an enlightened and strong government; and in the absence of societal turbulence and disorder.[18]

This comment highlights the link between economic, political and social concerns. But there is a danger that it could be interpreted to imply that peace, stability and public order are desirable only as conditions for facilitating economic transformation rather than as ends in themselves. Such an interpretation would distort the very meaning of peace and security. It could also be used to justify strong, even if unenlightened, government and any authoritarian measures that such a government may take in the name of public order.[19]

If material betterment, which is but a means to human happiness, is sought in ways that wound the human spirit, it can in the long run only lead to greater human suffering. The vast possibilities that a market economy can open up to developing countries can be realized only if economic reforms are undertaken within a framework that recognizes human needs. The *Human Development Report* makes the point that markets should serve people instead of people serving markets. Further, 'both state and market should be guided by the people. The two should work in tandem, and people should be sufficiently empowered to exert effective control over both.'[20] Again we come back to empowerment. It decides how widespread will be the benefit of actions taken in the name of culture and development. And this in turn will decide the extent of the contribution such actions can make to genuine peace and stability. Democracy as a political system which aims at empowering the people is essential if sustained human development, which is 'development of the people for the people by the people', is to be achieved. Thus it has been rightly said that:

> National governments must find new ways of enabling their people to participate more in government and to allow them much greater influence on the decisions that affect their lives. Unless this is done, and done in time, the irresistible tide of people's rising aspirations will inevitably clash with inflexible systems, leading to anarchy and chaos. A rapid democratic transition and a strengthening of the institutions of civil society are the only appropriate responses.[21]

The argument that it took long years for the first democratic governments to develop in the west is not a valid excuse for African and Asian countries to drag their feet over democratic reform. The history of the world shows that peoples and societies do not have to pass through a fixed series of stages in the course of development. Moreover, latecomers should be able to capitalize on the experiences of the pioneers and avoid the mistakes and obstacles that impeded early progress. The idea of 'making haste slowly' is sometimes used to give backwardness the appearance of measured progress. But in a fast-developing world too much emphasis on 'slowly' can be a recipe for disaster.

There will be as many kinds of democracies as there are nations which accept it [democracy] as a form of government. No single type of 'Western democracy' exists; nor is democracy limited to a mere handful of forms such as the American, British,

French or Swiss. Each democratic country will have its own individual characteristics. With the spread of democracy to Eastern Europe the variety in the democratic style of government will increase. Similarly there cannot be one form of Asian democracy; in each country the democratic system will develop a character that accords with its social, cultural and economic needs. But the basic requirement of a genuine democracy is that the people should be sufficiently empowered to be able to participate significantly in the governance of their country. The thirty articles of the Universal Declaration of Human Rights are aimed at such empowerment. Without these rights democratic institutions will be but empty shells incapable of reflecting the aspirations of the people and unable to withstand the encroachment of authoritarianism.

The democratic process provides for political and social change without violence. The democratic tradition of free discussion and debate allows for the settlement of differences without resort to armed conflict. The culture of democracy and human rights promotes diversity and dynamism without disintegration; it is indivisible from the culture of development and the culture of peace. It is only by giving firm support to movements that seek to empower the people through democratic means that the United Nations and its agencies will truly be able to promote the culture of peace and the culture of development.

Let me, in conclusion, summarize my argument. The true development of human beings involves much more than mere economic growth. At its heart there must be a sense of empowerment and inner fulfilment. This alone will ensure that human and cultural values remain paramount in a world where political leadership is often synonymous with tyranny and the rule of a narrow élite. People's participation in social and political transformation is the central issue of our time. This can only be achieved through the establishment of societies which place human worth above power and liberation above control. In this paradigm development requires democracy, the genuine empowerment of the people. When this is achieved, culture and development will naturally coalesce to create an environment in which all are valued and every kind of human potential can be realized. The alleviation of poverty involves processes which change the way in which the poor perceive themselves and their world. Mere material assistance is not enough; the poor must have the sense that they themselves can shape their own future. Most totalitarian regimes fear change but the longer they put off genuine democratic reform the more likely it is that even their positive contributions will be vitiated: the success of national policies depends on the willing participation of the people. Democratic values and human rights, it is sometimes claimed, run counter to 'national' culture, and all too often the people at large are seen as 'unfit' for government. Nothing can be further from the truth. The challenge we now face is for the different nations and peoples of the world to agree on a basic set of human values, which will serve as a unifying force in the development of a genuine global community. True economic transformation can then take place in the context of international peace and internal political stability. A rapid democratic transition and strengthening of the institutions of civil society are the *sine qua non* for this development. Only then will we be able to look to a future where human beings are valued for what they are rather than for what they produce. If the UN and its agencies wish to assist this development they must support these movements which seek to empower the people, movements which are founded on democracy and which will one day ensure a culture of peace and of development.

Notes

1 'Draft Preliminary Outline of the World Report on Culture and Development', UNESCO, CCD-III/94/Doc. 2, Paris, 7 Feb. 1994, p. 16.

2 It has been pointed out that the idea of growth not as an end in itself but as a performance test of development was put forward by economists as early as the 1950s: Paul Streeten *et al.*, *First Things First: Meeting Basic Human Needs in the Developing Countries*, Oxford, 1982 edn.

3 François Perroux, *A New Concept of Development*, UNESCO, Paris, 1983, p. 2.

4 *Ibid.*, p. 180.

5 'Growth normally means quantifiable measure of a society's overall level of production or incomes such as GNP or GDP per capita, while development involves qualitative aspects of a society's advancement such as under- and unemployment, income distribution pattern, housing situation, nutritional level, sanitary condition, etc.': *UNDP Selected Sectoral Reviews: Burma, December 1988*, p. 333.

6 *Human Development Report 1993*, UNDP, Oxford, 1993, p. 1.

7 *Towards a New Asia*, a Report of the Commission for a New Asia, 1994, p. 39.

8 'The logic of an economy governed by solvency and by profit, subject to the increasing value attached to capital and to the power of those who command it is to reject as "non-economic" everything which cannot be immediately translated into quantities and prices in market terms': Paul Marc Henry (ed.), *Poverty, Progress and Development*, London, 1991, p.36.

9 Streeten *et al.*, *First Things First*, p. 19.

10 Henry (ed.), *Poverty, Progress and Development*, p. 34.

11 *The New Encyclopaedia Britannica*, Chicago, 1993 edn, vol. 16, p. 874.

12 Edward Said comments that governments in general use culture as a means of promoting nationalism: 'To launder the cultural past and repaint it in garish nationalist colors that irradiate the whole society is now so much a fact of contemporary life as to be considered natural'. See Edward Said, 'Nationalism, Human Rights and Interpretation' in Barbara Johnson (ed.), *Freedom and Interpretation: The Oxford Amnesty Lectures, 1992*, New York, 1993, p. 191.

13 Harry M. Scoble and Laurie S. Wiseberg (eds.), *Access to Justice: Human Rights Struggles in South East Asia*, London, 1985, p. 57.

14 See Clinton Rossiter's introduction to Hamilton, Madison and Jay, *The Federalist Papers*, Chicago, 1961. I owe thanks to Lady Patricia Gore-Booth for the original quotation on which Rossiter presumably based his words: 'Man's capacity for justice makes democracy possible; but man's inclination to injustice makes democracy necessary,' from Reinhold Niebuhr's foreword to his *Children of Light and Children of Darkness: A Vindication of Democracy and a Critique of its Traditional Defence*, London, 1945.

15 'The best government is that which governs least' are the words of a westerner, John L. O'Sullivan, but more than a thousand years before O'Sullivan was born it was already written in the *Lao Tzu*, a Chinese classic, that 'the best of all rulers is but a shadowy presence

to his subjects.' The notion that 'in a nation the people are the most important, the State is next and the rulers the least important' is to be found not in the works of a modern Western political theorist but in that of Mencius.

16 Ehran Naraghi has shown in his memoirs, *From Palace to Prison: Inside the Iranian Revolution*, London, 1994, that a critical attitude towards the monarch, decentralization of power and division of responsibilities were part of oriental tradition. His fascinating conversations with Shah Mohammed Reza Pahlavi throw into relief the dangers of cultural and development policies divorced from the aspirations of the people.

17 Ronald D. Renard, 'Minorities in Burmese History', in K. M. de Silva *et al.* (eds.), *Ethnic Conflict in Buddhist Societies: Sri Lanka, Thailand and Burma*, London, 1988, p. 79.

18 *Towards a New Asia*, p. 40.

19 'Practically any human behaviour can be, and historically has been, rationalized as threatening to damage the security of the nation': Scoble and Wiseberg (eds.), *Access to Justice*, p. 58.

20 *Human Development Report 1993*, p. 53.

21 *Ibid.*, p. 5. In *Access to Justice*, Scoble and Wiseberg (eds.) point out the difference between fundamental reform that 'involves a redistribution of power, a broadening of participation and influence in the making of authoritative decisions' and contingent reform that 'involves a sharing of the benefits of power holding, or the uses of power, in order to avoid the sharing of power itself'.

PART THREE

Appreciations

24

A Flowering of the Spirit: Memories of Suu and Her Family by *Ma Than E*

A solemn and special session of the European Parliament of twelve countries meeting at Strasbourg on 19 July 1991 awarded Aung San Suu Kyi of Burma the 1990 Sakharov Prize for Freedom of Thought. In previous years Nelson Mandela of South Africa, Anatoli Marchenko of the USSR and Alexander Dubček of Czechoslovakia had been so honoured. The President of the Parliament, Baron Crespo, spoke in sonorous Spanish and on our earphones we heard the interpreter say, 'We are awarding this prize to a brave Asian, a woman whose name has been synonymous with the non-violent struggle for freedom and democracy.'

At the end of his speech the President handed a scroll to thirteen-year-old Kim, Aung San Suu Kyi's younger son, who was on the rostrum with his father Michael Aris, and the brief but emotionally charged ceremony came to a close. Suu, as her friends know her, had not been able to accept the award in person. She was beginning her third year of detention, a captive of Burma's military regime and under house arrest in Rangoon.

Reflecting on the course of Suu's life which has brought her this imprisonment and now this honour, I asked myself: How had it come about? What was the source, the wellspring of the spirit upholding her, enabling her to endure this adversity, this oppression? How does she view the prospect of further detention for who knows how long, and the deliberate erosion by the military regime of all she has achieved in the arena of Burmese politics? She entered that arena in 1988 when she established a political party, and it was her party which won an overwhelming victory in the elections of 1990, in spite of her arrest ten months earlier.

To my mind, the firm roots of Suu's indomitable spirit and unusual personality lie in the ineffaceable memory of her father General Aung San and in her upbringing by her remarkable mother Daw Khin Kyi. The story of General Aung San's life is part of Burma's history, well known and often recorded, most recently by his daughter. The early days of his military training in Japan as leader of the legendary 'Thirty Comrades' who spearheaded the Japanese advance into British Burma, his turning to support the re-invading Allies after the years of phoney independence under the Japanese, and finally his intense activities after peace was gained, leading to British acceptance of his demand for complete independence – all this has been described in detail by many writers. Daw Khin Kyi's life, however, is not so well recorded.

Some of my recollections of the general are particularly nostalgic. England was locked in the grip of one of the fiercest winters when he arrived there in January 1947 leading a delegation to discuss the terms for Burma's independence with the Attlee government. Snow lay deep and uncleared in the heart of London, almost blocking the approach to the Dorchester Hotel where the delegation was housed. Post-war austerity affected all, and the Burmese suffered with other Londoners from the daily cuts in electricity which lasted for hours at a time. There were no open fires, only small electric heaters in the hotel rooms. It was an uncomfortable time, but it was also a time of great hope and enthusiasm.

The general made it a point to meet all the Burmese who were in London – students, those living and working in London, people passing through and long-term visitors like myself. We had a reception for him in a small Burmese restaurant in Soho where he addressed the rather crowded assembly and later talked to each of us informally. 'The fragrance of his good name', as we Burmese say, had reached us long before. His impressive reputation, his shining honesty, his adroitness in dealing with opponents, the respect he evoked among his confrères and the highest authorities with whom he had dealt, including the Japanese during the occupation and the British in the last phases of the war and its aftermath, his activities which had brought Burma to this point of discussion for an independence of his fashioning – all this was common knowledge. Each one of us already held this national hero in the highest respect and regard, but his unassuming friendliness won our hearts.

On many evenings when the general had no other engagements I was invited to dine with him and the delegation in their suite at the Dorchester. After the meal, crowding in front of a rather feebly glowing electric fire, there would be talk of pre-war times, the days of their military training in Japan and now the days of hope to come. There was less talk about the actual war years in Burma or the later manoeuvrings and struggles to make the British accept his proposals. It was a time of relaxation for the whole company. For the duration of the war I had been in India working for All India Radio in New Delhi, which had an extensive service in many languages, broadcasting to Japanese-occupied territories throughout Asia. Later I went to San Francisco on the same broadcasting assignment for the US Office of War Information, now the Voice of America. I had not seen these friends for ages, and there was not enough time for us to tell each other all we had seen and done in the intervening years.

In that company, round that faintly glowing fire, there would be the general, his aide, various members of the delegation, a Burmese working at the BBC and sometimes visitors like myself. There was Bo Set Kya, who had been one of the Thirty Comrades in Japan, and who later served in Tokyo as military attaché of the nominally independent Burma of the Japanese occupation. When talk slackened, Bo Set Kya would sing plaintive love songs he had learned there, and we would sing our own Burmese songs. The general would talk about his family, his wife and his three children, the youngest a girl, and would I buy some presents he could take to them? So it was that when, their mission accomplished, the delegation left London, the general took home the gifts I had bought for each member of his family. For Suu there was a large doll. Years later I was surprised and pleased to see she still had it, well preserved.

Some days before their departure, the general prepared a script for broadcasting on the BBC's Burmese service in which he described what his mission had accomplished. We were to meet him and his aide at a lunch in the BBC restaurant. The lunch was not a success. There was a silence at the table and a thundercloud on the general's face. The head of the BBC Burmese service, an Englishman, had made cuts and alterations in the English translation of the Burmese text, insisting that these should be made in the original Burmese script. There were certain BBC rules and regulations about the political content of such talks which must be observed, he said. The general was in two minds as to whether he should agree to these cuts or whether he should make his broadcast at all. I had arrived a little late, bringing the presents he had asked me to buy for his family, and gradually the tension and the gloom lifted and the lunch proceeded. The general went to make his report to the Burmese people though he made it clear how much he resented what he regarded as this uncalled-for editing of his script, about which he had not been forewarned. This was the other face of the general.

The work of the mission ended and soon it would be time to leave. At his reception for his English hosts and those who had worked with him, there was a large gathering of guests, members of Parliament of both parties, all the high officials detailed to see to the smooth running of the mission's work, editors of newspapers, journalists and writers and those interested in Burma and its future, and of course all the Burmese who could come. The general had said the previous night that I must sing at this reception and I had demurred saying I thought it was rather unusual. On the day, I had gone to see an Englishman who had been an administrator in Burma until the Japanese had invaded, a very old friend. Getting back to London from his home in Kent was nightmarishly slow. I and the friend accompanying me were on tenterhooks because we would be late for the reception, our last chance to see the general and our other friends, as we thought. But when we arrived after hastily getting into better clothes the general was waiting. After some refreshments to warm us up he led me to a piano on a small platform and announced to the company, 'A Burmese girl will sing for you.' So I sang. Of the three songs I sang, one in English, one in French and the last in Burmese, I now think that I should have sung only the last. But it was only the Burmese there who would have appreciated that song known to all of us. There was no piano accompaniment for this; it needed Burmese musical instruments. It was a song set to a classical mode of music, whose lyrics were a poem written by the Burmese queen Hlaing Hteik Khaung Tin. Wakeful all night with thoughts of the king who has for too long denied her his presence, she hears the palace gong strike the hour of dawn. The gathering applauded politely, and the general came and led me down, telling me my singing had given him great pleasure.

When the delegation left by special plane from a military airport in north London, the country was still snowbound. There was a large group of senior English government officials there to say goodbye. Some of us Burmese also went along and joined the members of the delegation and the others in a large waiting room heated by a roaring fire in an open grate. We sat around and spoke to our friends. After a while the general got up from among the English and came over to talk to us. To me he said with a smile, 'Why don't you come back with us?' Later my companions and I stood in the snow, watching and waving as the delegation walked to the plane and feeling the sadness of a winter's day and of parting from our friends, especially the general. How were we to know what a short span of life was left for him?

That very year, after the general's return, with hopes high for a new era in Burma and the rehabilitation of a country devastated by war and Japanese occupation, a political rival destroyed the dream. Assassins stormed into a meeting of the Executive Council, aiming their sten guns first at the general in the centre, and then sweeping to each side, killing eight others. It was 19 July 1947, a day of yearly national remembrance since then, Martyrs' Day.

General Aung San's widow, Daw Khin Kyi, took up life again after this disastrous personal and national bereavement. She was appointed Director of Social Welfare in Burma's now independent government. Immersed in the busy routine of her work she was yet to suffer another blow of fate. The younger of her two sons, Suu's favourite and much loved brother, was drowned while playing on the bank of a large ornamental lake in the grounds of their house in Rangoon. The trauma of this tragedy for Suu took a long time to dissipate. She has never forgotten this brother as she has never forgotten her father, the study of whose life, writings and exhortations to his people, and the amazing achievements of his thirty-two-year life, has been a continuing obsession. It is her way of getting to know a father whom fate deprived her of knowing in life.

Daw Khin Kyi made her children, from their earliest years, aware of their father's heritage. His comrades and the members of the army he had founded kept up their ties of friendship with the family. Suu could say with literal truth that she was cradled in the arms of her father's soldiers. There were others, Burmese of ability, great experience and high standing, whose close association with Daw Khin Kyi strongly influenced the growing children. U Myint Thein, who ended a long and distinguished career as Chief Justice, was her close and lifelong friend. There were the relatives coming and going, her sisters and their families, the general's brothers and their families, many old friends and many new. An aura of respect, admiration and affection surrounded her and her family.

In keeping with this, Daw Khin Kyi impressed upon the children their obligations to Burmese social and moral values and brought them up in the Buddhist faith. Suu, in my view, is an exemplar of what we Burmese regard as seemly, in matters of dress, comportment, conduct and bearing, in public and in private. To take a small example, the courtesy and deference shown to those older than oneself even by a few years, a slight inclination of the body when passing before them, an economy and refinement of gesture, a tone of voice and a choice of language implying respect. Such traits are ingrained in Suu's nature, giving her behaviour an unmistakably Burmese complexion, an emphatic and (to the Burmese) an endearing Burmese identity which has never been blurred and which is so apparent, in spite

of long years abroad. This has been a major factor in drawing her
people to her and in their giving her their most enthusiastic, one
could almost say delirious, support.

In 1961 U Nu's government appointed Daw Khin Kyi as
Burma's ambassador to India, a post she was to keep even after
Ne Win's military coup of 1962, a measure of the respect and
esteem in which she was held. At the end of her assignment in
1967 she retired to her home, now on the Inya Lake, a great
spread of interlocking natural lakes on whose shores lived many
of those prominent in the world of Burmese politics and com-
merce. This is where Suu is now interned.

Suu was a young girl of fifteen with long thick plaits of hair
when she arrived with her mother in New Delhi. Her schooling
continued at Lady Sri Ram College, a large, well-run institution.
Her circle of Indian friends widened. This was a wonderful
opportunity to explore and understand the country of Mahatma
Gandhi and Jawaharlal Nehru. Her father had been here before
and had met and consulted Nehru, with whom he came to a close
understanding. It was to Nehru's government that her mother
was appointed ambassador.

Among some of the activities arranged for Suu by her mother
were Japanese flower arrangement classes and riding lessons at
the exercise grounds of the President's bodyguard. At the riding
school she met the children of Indian officials, diplomatic personnel and also Pandit Nehru's grandsons, Indira Gandhi's sons
Rajiv and Sanjay. There were piano lessons at home at 24 Akbar
Road, a large house in extensive grounds with a magnificent
garden, housing meant for the most senior Indian officials and, as
a special mark of esteem, offered to Daw Khin Kyi and maintained by the government as beautifully as in British days. But
Suu's favourite occupation and passion was reading. For encouraging her great love of books she always remembers with affection
U Ohn, who had known her father. He had been a journalist and
had represented Aung San's political party in London, and he
was later Burma's ambassador to Moscow. He among others gave
her books, and long lists of books, to read in Burmese and in
English. Her passion had started long before she arrived in India.

In Mehrauli, then on the far outskirts of New Delhi, there was a Buddhist centre in a rather dilapidated state from long neglect. For its revival Daw Khin Kyi sought the co-operation of all Buddhists in Delhi including, and especially, the ambassadors of the countries whose professed religion was Buddhism. Those of the faith in Delhi, and some from other parts of India, were able to celebrate the major Buddhist festivals yearly at this centre now restored to life, or just visit it for contemplation, retreat and prayer.

There were a great many other occasions, national and personal, formal and informal, at which Suu assisted. Buddhist monks of Burmese, Thai or Cambodian nationality were regular guests. Her brother, home on holidays from England, would share in these occasions. The respect and affection felt by all Burmese for mother and daughter were mirrored in the feelings of Daw Khin Kyi's ambassadorial colleagues and members of the Indian government from Pandit Jawaharlal Nehru down. India for Suu was a throbbing, vital experience. Her bonds of remembrance and love for this country have remained strong to this day.

The British High Commissioner in Delhi at this time was Sir Paul (later Lord) Gore-Booth. During his previous posting as ambassador to Burma, he and his wife Patricia had come to know Daw Khin Kyi and her family well. Now the friendship was renewed, and when it was time for Suu to go for further studies to Oxford University they offered to look after her, standing in as parents so to speak. She became part of the family, a sister to their two sons and two daughters. At their house she got to know many of their personal friends and to meet the politicians and officials of the government who enjoyed their hospitality. She took a great interest in their appearance, behaviour, talk and idiosyncrasies, these members of a wider adult world she was about to enter.

Suu usually went to her mother in New Delhi for the summer holidays, but one year she came to stay with me in Algiers. I had been transferred from New Delhi's United Nations Information Centre to establish such a centre in Algeria, newly independent since the signing of the Treaty of Evian with Charles de Gaulle's government in 1962. The country was very slowly recovering from its eight-year struggle for independence from the French. Not surprisingly, in the city of Algiers there was great scarcity of accommodation, many devastated areas, few hotels in good shape and drastically curtailed services of all kinds. Newly opening embassies, United Nations offices and incoming commercial concerns, as well as Algerians themselves, were desperate for housing and working quarters. French settlers of long standing had left in great numbers but others were arriving, young men on various jobs in lieu of military service, men and women teachers and workers on aid projects, and just visitors.

Suu arrived a few days after Houari Boumedienne had ousted Ahmed Ben Bella in an exemplary, bloodless coup. She was much more interested in getting to meet Algerians and in what was happening in the country than in the many parties to which she was invited. She had a suitcase full of books for study. We got in touch with an Algerian organization which ran several projects to help those affected by their long struggle. The young man in charge of one came to explain his project. Algerians and young men and women of every nationality were welcome, he said, to help in the building of houses for the widows of freedom fighters. Suu went to live and work in that large camp for a number of weeks. There was a Russian instructor, and her co-workers were young people from Algeria, France, Lebanon, Holland and Germany. There were meals and accommodation but no pay. Her Algerian friends took her to a wedding in the Kabyle mountains. We went for a long trip to the edge of the Sahara but no further since in summer the heat was too great. Another trip was to a city of Roman ruins where on the flagstones of the arena of the open-air theatre loyalists had inscribed in large letters 'Vive Ben Bella'. Suu was taken on a trip to Morocco and touched the southern shore of Spain. She came back to her reading and later returned to Oxford well content.

After gaining her degree, followed by a short spell of teaching and another of research with the historian Hugh Tinker, Suu came to me in New York. I had returned to the UN headquarters there after four years' duty in Algiers. Frank Trager, a family friend, was Professor of International Affairs at New York University where Suu planned to do her postgraduate studies. He had spent some years in Burma on a programme of American aid and had a wide-ranging interest in the countries of South-east Asia and the Far East where he had done much travelling. His book *Burma: From Kingdom to Republic* had just been published. He took a keen interest in Suu's progress. Getting to and from New York University meant a long bus ride there and back from our apartment in mid-town Manhattan, and it was a trial for Suu, who was given to giddiness on bus rides. There were also the hazards from toughs who frequented her route from the bus-stop across the park to Washington Square and the classes she had to attend. The UN was about six minutes' walk from where we lived. Why shouldn't she try for a job there and do her studies later? After applications, recommendations, interviews and the usual delays and difficulties, Suu was in. She worked there for three years, the last two as part of a small, select staff group supporting the deliberations and activities of the Advisory Committee on Administrative and Budgetary Questions. The members of this small, compact committee were appointed not as representatives of their countries but as experts on financial matters. The programmes and budgets of the United Nations and all its branches as well as all the Specialized Agencies, such as the WHO and the FAO, were submitted to this committee for appraisal, comment, modification and final approval. It was extremely hard work, but most interesting for its close examination of the financial implications of all UN activities, and for its members, people with quite exceptional minds. Suu came to know them well.

Staff members of the UN often devoted their evenings and weekends to voluntary aid activities. Belleview is part of a large New York hospital, a short ten-minute bus ride from where we lived in Manhattan. It is mainly concerned with the city's poorest incurables and derelicts, who are brought in when life becomes too much for them, a temporary refuge for those on the verge of physical and mental collapse. Men and women are always needed to help with programmes of reading and companionship. Suu chose to volunteer many hours of her time every week for this. It was in the same tradition of service as her mother's.

U Thant of Burma was the UN Secretary-General at this time. Some of our most enjoyable times were the Sunday lunches at his large house overlooking the Hudson River in the suburb of Riverdale, about an hour's ride from where we lived in Manhattan. Other Burmese and friends would be there, a convivial company, and Burmese food much to our taste would be served. On special occasions such as the birthday of one of his grandchildren, the grounds of the house would be decked out to receive the Burmese, and also the heads of many of the permanent delegations to the UN. The food as always was superbly Burmese. U Thant and his family would be warmly welcoming. But we often observed how much more we liked the smaller gatherings, though even there we could never get into animated discussions on people and politics, the state of the world and the problems U Thant was handling. His duties as host seemed to preclude this.

Invitations from U Soe Tin, the permanent delegate of Burma to the UN at that time, were a little different. He too lived in Riverdale, in a house less imposing than U Thant's. During sessions of the General Assembly lasting from the second week of September to mid-December, he would be occupied with work, and meals and receptions for the Burmese and other delegations. At other times of the year he would ask the New York Burmese to his house for Buddhist festivals. We liked him and his wife and children. He was a liberal type who did not divide us into sheep and goats. The goats were those suspected of being critical of what was happening in Burma under the Ne Win regime and usually were left severely alone. At his house it was possible to discuss, debate and argue, sometimes heatedly but in the main with much good nature.

During one UN General Assembly, Suu and I received an invitation to lunch at his house. Some members of the delegation had said they would like to meet us. Pleasant and polite as U Soe Tin always was, I felt there was more to this invitation than met the eye. We arrived at his house in Riverdale about midday. The large rectangular living room filled with plants and flowers and

an excess of black-and-gold Burmese lacquer had been rearranged
so that sofas and chairs were placed against the wall with large
coffee tables in front of them. And on those sofas and chairs was
ranged a whole battery of Burmese ambassadors attending the
current General Assembly. We were introduced to those we had
not met before, and Suu was led to one end of the room to a seat
between two of these men. I was given a place between two
others not far from where the head of the delegation, Colonel
Lwin, had taken his seat. U Soe Tin's wife passed glasses of fruit
juice, set large bowls of crisps and other small eats on the coffee
tables, then retreated to the room next door to put the finishing
touches to a meal bound to be worthy of such distinguished
guests. We made some slight, inconsequential remarks and so did
the others. U Soe Tin was smiling politely but looked uneasy. It
became clear to me that the company was preparing to sit in
judgement on Suu. But for what? I didn't quite know. The chief
delegate led the attack. How was it that Suu was working for the
UN? What passport was she using? Since her mother was no
longer ambassador, Suu should have given up her diplomatic
passport. Was it true that she had not done so? She must be
aware that she was holding her diplomatic passport unlawfully.
It was most irregular and should be put right as soon as possible.

The whole company listened to this tirade with a sort of
sycophantic deference, turning their eyes on Suu and murmuring
agreement. Suu's calm and composure were for me very reassur-
ing. She replied with great dignity and in very quiet tones. She
had long ago applied for a new passport to the embassy in
London but had not received a reply up to now. She could not
say what could be the reason for this most extraordinary delay.
She had come to New York to study and therefore had used her
old passport. In order to live she had to find work, and she had
been fortunate to find a job at the United Nations where her
passport had been necessary to prove she was Burmese. She was
still waiting for the embassy in London to send her the passport
she had applied for months before. She would be most happy to
surrender the one she was now holding when the new one
arrived. She was sure all the uncles in the room would understand

that one must have a passport, of whatever kind, to live and work in a foreign country. She spoke in the politest of tones and in exquisite Burmese.

The ambassador from London then stood up to confirm that Suu had indeed applied months ago for a new passport but as usual the application had been sent on to Rangoon. He did not know why there had been this delay of months in receiving a response. All of us in that room knew, of course, of the bureaucratic confusion and incompetence in Burma which had created similar delays. The ambassadors now joined in to agree that Suu had no other choice of action. The chief delegate's demeanour became non-committal. Making an apologetic noise he remarked that he had not quite understood the situation, but he would now personally see to it on his return that things were speeded up at the passport office in Rangoon. These were Suu's elders, but not necessarily her betters, I thought. Now it was my turn to say with a smile, 'The day will come, soon we hope, when passports will no longer be necessary', and we went in to lunch. Another friend, an official in the permanent delegation, with whom we felt free to talk about the situation in Burma, would say teasingly when he felt that Suu's remarks were too boldly critical, 'You not only have the courage of your convictions, Suu, you have the courage of your connections.' He meant that being the daughter of General Aung San and Daw Khin Kyi she could not be taken down. I felt that she was their daughter in the flesh but more truly in the spirit.

At the end of her third year of service in the UN Secretariat Suu made a choice. She decided that a husband and children would be greatly preferable to a career in the UN, however brilliant it was promising to be. And so began a different life. The story from now on is well known. She spent a year in the eastern Himalayan kingdom of Bhutan where her husband Michael Aris had long been working as tutor to the royal family and translator to the government. Bhutan had become a member of the UN while Suu was in New York, and she immediately found work advising Bhutan's Foreign Minister on UN matters. She and Michael then returned to England for the birth of their first son,

Alexander. Michael started his doctorate at London University and soon after took up his academic career at Oxford. A second son, Kim, came in 1977. Life went on placidly with raising the family and regular visits with the children to her mother in Rangoon.

Along with caring for her family Suu began to do some writing. With her passion for reading she had collected a large number of books in English and French, a language which interested her. Michael too had his expanding library of books concerned with his Tibetan studies and research, and so their house in Oxford overflowed with books. The children too were growing into readers. Now Suu began to think about writing a biography of her father. She began an intensive study of Japanese. A large library of books in English and Burmese about Burma, and books in Japanese and English about Japan, began to accumulate. She began research for a book about her father's life. She also started to make plans for a doctoral thesis at the School of Oriental and African Studies in London. A determined diligence is how I would describe her activities during this time.

In 1985 she accepted the offer of a scholarship from the University of Kyoto in order to pursue research on the Japanese part of her father's career. She met members of the Japan–Burma Association who in turn put her in contact with those still alive who had known her father. Everyone she met could tell her something of those days. Her knowledge of Japanese grew and her contacts widened. Michael at this time was on a fellowship at the Indian Institute of Advanced Studies in Simla in northern India. Their older son was with him while Suu had their younger son with her. She invited me in 1986 to stay with her and Kim at the International House of Kyoto University for a period of three months. Her relations with the Japanese and the scholars of many nationalities, on Japanese fellowships for a great variety of studies, were close and most cordial. She felt she was accomplishing much. The next year she joined her husband in Simla and the family was together again. There Suu was also appointed to a fellowship at the institute where Michael was working. I happened to be in India early in 1987 and had the pleasure of a month with them in their apartment at the institute, the great building which in pre-independence days was the residence and summer retreat of the British viceroys and their staff.

That year her mother Daw Khin Kyi arrived in London for the removal of cataracts in both eyes. These operations were successful and it was a happy time for her in spite of the strain of the treatment. Suu interrupted her work in Simla and came to care for her mother. Her brother, now living and working in America, came for ten days. I was in London and was able to see her almost every day. Other friends, old and new, came to call, and there was much cheerful conversation and laughter and reminiscing over old times. Her flat was filled with fruits and flowers and cards wishing her well and a quick recovery. Suu had visited her mother regularly in Burma before and after her marriage. Daw Khin Kyi had seen her grandsons grow up to the age when they could be initiated as novices into the Buddhist monkhood. This traditional ceremony which wins much merit for those arranging it had been held the previous year at her house in Rangoon. She returned after two months to Burma in good spirits, her eyesight much improved, writing to her many friends to say how much she had enjoyed their visits and her time in London. But in late March of the next year, 1988, barely ten months after her return, she suffered a severe stroke. Suu, Michael and their two sons were in Oxford then, back from their Indian sojourn in September of 1987, settling back to their old academic life when the news came. Suu took the next flight to Rangoon to care for her mother again, this time in her last illness.

The events of 1988 in Burma are well known. Trouble had been brewing since the early months of the year when student demonstrators had been shot, and greater demonstrations and violence were to come. August 8 was the day when great numbers marched, demanding democracy. The shooting and killing in the government's suppression of these protest marches claimed many more victims than the slaughter in Tienanmen Square in Peking a year later. Suu could not stand aside. Her father was not there to lead his people against this new tyranny. As her father's daughter she must now act and be involved.

When Suu started on her round of campaign tours all over Burma as the general secretary of her newly founded political party, the National League for Democracy, it was not only to set up centres for the party but to arouse the Burmese from the habit of fear into which they had fallen over the years of Ne Win's repressive military rule, which in the latter years had worn a deceptive civilian cloak. She has a perfect command of the English language more than matched by her brilliant and inspired use of Burmese. With Burmese she reaches the hearts and minds of her people, like her father before her. With English she interprets her ideas and actions to the world. The first is of more immediate importance in her effort to awake a people sunk in the apathy of years and only recently roused to protest. This has involved the most strenuous physical and mental exertion attended by obvious as well as hidden and incalculable risks and dangers, more especially since the military government's decree that an assembly of more than four people was illegal and could be dispersed by force.

On one occasion, presumably in accordance with this ruling, an army captain stopped Suu and a party of her campaigners at gunpoint, threatening to open fire should they advance. With great calm Suu told her companions to step aside and wait while she took the road alone. It was her instant decision that only one life must be put at risk, and that life must be hers alone. It was a bold move and it was successful, for at the very last moment a major on the sidelines intervened and prevented the shooting. But it was like walking on a knife's edge. Talking at times about her upbringing, Suu would say that it had been very strict, perhaps too much so, but that it had often stood her in good stead in many of life's unpleasant and unpredictable surprises. This was certainly one of them, and not the last.

Hearing and reading about this encounter again put me in mind of Daw Khin Kyi. Many a time she had needed physical courage, quick wits and decision, ingenuity, persuasive powers and diplomatic tact to save a situation or avert disaster. Many were the stories she told us of such occasions and Suu knew them all. Even in her life after retirement she had needed the utmost discretion and fine judgement. General Aung San's life had of course been a long exercise in physical courage and mental agility.

In exploring the sources of Suu's character and strength of personality I have not troubled myself with looking for weaknesses and blemishes. She surely has some. Who is there in this world who has none? There are, however, those whose virtues so far outweigh their faults that the latter mean little in the sum of the whole, and for me Suu is one of those. Let others point out her faults, such as they are, if they wish. I am not at all concerned with what is called a balanced assessment of character. My aim has been to trace the lines leading from the parents to the child, the soil, so to speak, that nurtured this unusual and outstanding growth and flowering.

Suu has an integrity, a steadfastness of purpose, an unswerving determination and single-minded persistence in attaining a goal, a seriousness going hand in hand with a strong sense of humour, a dignity and resolve in the face of persecution and adversity. Her years of study in Oxford, her married life and the upbringing of her children, her care and concern for the weak and the elderly, her wide-ranging and far-flung friendships, cultivated and continuing though smothered at the moment under the heavy hand of her gaolers, her increasing new interests, her pursuit of academic excellence inspired, she says, by her husband's example, and the weathering, shall we say, of her later years of life – all these have brought about a maturity, an adaptability, an ability and a willingness to take on challenges of more than parochial significance. In a word, she has become the hope and inspiration of an oppressed people. Though time seems to stand still for her at this moment, the further growth and flowering of her spirit cannot be stifled. Perhaps even her oppressors have more than a sneaking admiration for her. In her efforts to dispel what she calls 'the miasma of fear' overshadowing her people, she is wrestling, as the Bible puts it, 'against spiritual wickedness in high places'. She has indeed been given a great cause and with it the mental and physical, moral and spiritual vigour to do battle for it. May hers be the victory.

25

Suu Burmese *by Ann Pasternak Slater*

When I first met Aung San Suu Kyi I had other friends called
Sue. For myself, and later my family, she was quickly distinguished from them by a private nickname. 'Who did you see
yesterday?' 'Suu.' 'Which Suu?' 'Suu Burmese.' It was a surname,
a title, not a mere subordinate adjective. Not Burmese Suu, like
Chicago Pete, but Suu Burmese, like Caius Martius Coriolanus,
the title won from Corioli, the town he conquered. It was not a
name I ever used to her face, but it has come to epitomize
everything she represents. We got to know each other in Oxford,
as freshwomen at St Hugh's College in 1964. I have to admit that
I first approached her simply because she was so beautiful and
exotic. She was everything I was not. I came from an Oxford
home and Oxford schooling. I was neither a hippy nor an active
member of the Campaign for Nuclear Disarmament. But I had
spent the long summer between school and university in statutory
fashion – hitching round Greece, picking grapes and maize in
Israel, travelling deck-class across the Mediterranean with *Anna
Karenina* for a pillow. Suu's tight, trim *lungi* (the Burmese version
of the sarong) and upright carriage, her firm moral convictions
and inherited social grace contrasted sharply with the tatty dress
and careless manners, vague liberalism and uncertain sexual
morality of my English contemporaries.

St Hugh's was one of Oxford's five single-sex women's colleges.
It was popularly dismissed as 'too far out' – a full three minutes'
bike ride from Balliol or St John's – with a demeaningly high
reputation for hockey. As freshers we were housed in the heavy

main building. Dark brown doors; long, dim corridors; bleak sculleries where the homelier students simmered hankies and bedtime cocoa. When we first arrived there was an active myth that news of the rare male visitor used to be tapped out on the central-heating pipes running from room to room. Only a decade or two previously, another rumour ran, when men came visiting, the women's beds had to be moved out into the corridor until their guests had left. We certainly had to be in by 10 p.m., or sign a late pass releasing us until midnight at the latest. A warren of nervous adolescent virgins and a few sexually liberated sophisticates made for an atmosphere airless and prickly as a hot railway compartment. In this setting Suu was delightfully antithetical, an original who was at once laughably naïve, and genuinely innocent. All my memories of her at that time have certain recurring elements: cleanliness, determination, curiosity, a fierce purity. How do I see her? Eyebrows furrowed under a heavy fringe, shocked incredulity and disapproval: 'But *Ann!*. . .' We are in the basement laundry room, starching piles of *lungis* and little sleeveless blouses. She is teaching me to iron. She is teaching me to eat rice neatly by hand (like making shortcrust pastry, you roll it between your fingers, dibbling no deeper than the first joint). She is showing me how to carry off long dresses plausibly. Those were the days of ruffled gypsy skirts, swirls of Indian cottons, woven sweat bands, low, wide hems and flowing bits and bobs. Suu taught me to twist and tie a *lungi* round my inappropriately broad, unoriental waist; to sit on the floor, legs tucked away so that not even an ankle showed; to walk upstairs with only a slight furl of skirt twitched aside, not a great heaved armful in the English manner. Even with familiarity, much remained exotic – her proud parentage, above all. But no less evocative now is the tiny tuft of silky hair under her chin, the block of sandalwood she ground for face powder, the abundant scraps of sample silk collected for dress trimmings, the fresh flower worn daily in her high pony-tail. Others added to this collection of alien lore. Suu's friends were mainly Indian and African. Together we chose tiny flowers from St Hugh's wide rock garden, in those days still the college's pride, and learned to push their tiny stiff stems through our pierced ears (a Ghanaian custom).

There were tea parties of interminable oriental decorum, whose wit and finesse were imperceptible to my coarse western ear. And then the long night gossip in other students' rooms, where Suu's assumptions seemed merely absurd. Everyone was on the hunt for boyfriends, many wanted affairs, sex being still a half-forbidden, half-won desideratum. Being laid back about being laid was *de rigueur* – except that most of us were neither laid back nor laid. There was excitement and anxiety about the unknown, an atmosphere of tense inexperience dominated and dragooned by the few vocal and confident sexual sophisticates. It was extremely difficult to preserve any kind of innocence in such a setting. To most of our English contemporaries, Suu's startled disapproval seemed a comic aberration. One bold girl asked her, 'But don't you want to sleep with someone?' Back came the indignant reply – 'No! I'll never go to bed with anyone except my husband. Now? I just go to bed hugging my pillow.' It raised a storm of mostly derisive laughter.

By the popular morality of the time Suu was a pure oriental traditionalist. Even the way she held herself was instinctively strait-laced. At the same time she was curious to experience the European and the alien, pursuing knowledge with endearing, single-minded practicality. Climbing in, for instance. Social kudos came with climbing into college after a late date. One actress friend was a precociously blasé habitué of late-night scramblings: by her second year she spent full nights and days away from college; by the third she was breaking college rules by renting a pad shared by a variety of boyfriends. After two demure years in Oxford, Suu wanted to climb in too, and requested a respectable Indian friend to take her out to dinner, and then – as any gentleman should – hand her over the crumbling college garden wall. No infringement of university regulations could have been perpetrated with greater propriety.

Then there was cycling. Most students have bikes – it is a practical way of getting about, but tricky in a *lungi*. In the first summer term Suu bought a pair of white jeans and the latest smart white Moulton bike with minute wheels. One sunny evening spent on the sandy cycle-track running alongside the

University Parks and that was mastered. Then there was punting – another essential qualification for an Oxford summer. A punt is a flat-bottomed, low-sided tray of a boat. Its weight, inertia and ungainliness defy description. It is like sailing a sideboard. It really is difficult learning to punt, especially on your own. The boat swings in dull circles that modulate to a maddening headstrong zigzag from bank to bank, until you learn to steer, like a gondolier, by hugging the pole tight against the punt as you push, and letting it swing like a rudder. Suu set out, a determined solitary figure in the early-morning haze, to return at dusk dripping and triumphant. She did learn to do that in her *lungi*, no western concessions required. And finally there was alcohol, alien and taboo to boot. Suu consistently refused it on social and religious grounds. But she was curious to know what it was like. At the very end of her final year, in great secrecy, she bought a miniature bottle – of what? sherry? wine? – and, with two rather more worldly Indians as accoucheuses and handmaids at this rite of passage, retired to the ladies' lavatory in the Bodleian Library. There, among the sinks and the cubicles, in a setting deliberately chosen to mirror the distastefulness of the experience, she tried and rejected alcohol for ever.

With degrees safely behind us we went different ways, Suu to the United Nations in New York and then three years later to Bhutan, where she joined the man she married, an old friend from student days. Fragmentary memories of that period lie like fanned-out photographs – some of them, indeed, real snaps from her letters. Suu in London, head high in a green armchair, serious, sad, uncertain where to go, all determination and an unknown void to cross. Suu laughing by the side of a Mini Moke, with Michael and Puppy, their Himalayan terrier, the mountains of Bhutan behind them – the well-wishing adventurers setting forth, man, wife, dog and jeep bright and tiny in that vast landscape. Suu and Michael later in their nursery-white London flat, their new-born son Alexander propped up on a sofa, with astonishing upright back and steady head, his mother's deportment at three weeks. Happy memories that now seem infinitely vulnerable.

By the mid-1970s we were all back in Oxford again. Michael had a junior fellowship at St John's College. I had also married and was doing research. After a short spell in a pretty but impractical house outside Oxford, Suu, Michael and Alexander moved to a college flat near the centre of Oxford, which happened to be just round the corner from mine.

In retrospect, memories of that time are still sunlit but with a sense of strain. The flat provided by St John's was on the ground floor of a pleasant North Oxford house, with high ceilings and tall windows. But its apparent spaciousness was deceptive. Apart from the large, south-facing living room, where all the family life took place, on the gloomier northern side was a tiny kitchen, one bedroom and a box-room doubling as a nursery and frequently occupied spare room. There were always guests – not only Suu's much loved aunt, who regularly spent a portion of the year with them, but Burmese relatives, Bhutanese visitors and numerous acquaintances welcomed and uncomplainingly entertained for punishing periods. On my way to the library I often saw Suu laboriously pedalling back from town, laden with sagging plastic bags and panniers heavy with cheap fruit and vegetables. When I called in the afternoons with my own baby daughter, I would find her busy in the kitchen preparing economical Japanese fish dishes, or at her sewing machine, in an undulating savanna of yellow cotton, making curtains for the big bay windows, or quickly running up elegant, cut-price clothes for herself. Michael was working hard at his doctorate. Alexander had to be cared for without disturbing him. There were endless guests to be housed and fed. Still Suu maintained a house that was elegant and calm, the living room warm with sunny hangings of rich, dark Bhutanese rugs and Tibetan scroll paintings. But battened down at the back, hidden away among the kitchen's stacked pots and pans, was anxiety, cramp and strain.

Life became even harder when their second son, Kim, was born, and to her intense distress Suu found she could not feed him. I doubt whether the anguish felt by her at this time can be understood by anyone who has not had the same experience. Characteristically, too, it was a suffering Suu instinctively imposed on herself, her pain the inevitable result of her rooted reluctance to accept defeat, or to allow herself the indulgence of a second-best way. Kim was kept happy, bottle-fed and healthy, but with dimmed lamp she nightly tried to nurse him, in vain.

That pertinacity persisted. Perhaps in unconscious recompense for what she had not been able to give the baby, she learned to massage him, back bent over him as he lay naked on the towelled floor on winter evenings, gently kneading him with warm oil. That, too, has come to rest as a soft image of the utter commitment none of her friends could emulate. A few years later it was Suu, of course, who gave the copy-book children's parties with all the traditional party games – except that the rules were enforced with unyielding exactitude, and my astonished children, bending them ever so slightly, once found themselves forbidden the prize. To them Suu was kindly but grave, an uncomfortably absolute figure of justice in their malleable world.

Yet it is Suu's kindness that is most sharply present to me now. She is kind by conviction as well as by nature. In her years at Oxford she acquired many friends who were written off as lame ducks by others, less genuinely charitable than herself. At college she took under her wing an elderly German artist, a friend of my mother's, for whom we put on an exhibition in our last year. Miss Plachte had suffered from meningitis as an adolescent; in her late sixties there was something ineradicably childish about her still. She became increasingly difficult. In her latter years my husband, Suu and I went to one of her somewhat painful tea-parties. No one else turned up. Finally she offered us a plate of cucumber sandwiches, and completely lost her temper when my husband took two. (They were very small.) Of course we felt sorry for her. But it was Suu who maintained the friendship over two decades, inviting her to meals and visiting her with unwavering sweetness. She was one of the few, together with my mother, still caring for Miss Plachte in her mild last senility.

Suu is that rare thing, a true egalitarian. The college matron, her guardians' housekeeper – all were cherished as warmly as her intimate friends and with greater generosity. It is not social rank but moral fibre that evokes her affection or reserve. She kept her powerful disapprobation for her closest family and friends. (She would have cut the above paragraph as uncharitable.) I often aroused her frank disapproval, but it was what made friendship with her so interesting. She was incapable of glossing over moral shortcomings: she could not help but be the moral litmus-paper for our wishy-washy ethics. At the same time she was neither pious nor self-important, simply instinctively expostulatory, wryly down-to-earth, humorously common-sensical.

As circumstances grew easier Suu's interests widened. The family moved to a beautiful house in Park Town, a then shabby-genteel nineteenth-century crescent curving elaborately round a quiet central garden, and ringed by unfrequented overgrown back lanes. The house was tall and narrow, the top three of its five floors initially occupied by sitting tenants, and extensive work needed in the basement and ground floor. The extra space Suu and Michael gained was soon lost to a further succession of needy guests. Finances remained hard with expenditure on the house and school fees to be met. With greater time at her disposal, though, Suu was impatient for new challenges. As an undergraduate she had tried to change courses from Philosophy, Politics and Economics, to English Literature, or Forestry, and was twice refused. With her intellectual curiosity still unsatisfied, she re-applied to St Hugh's to take a second undergraduate degree, in English. I can still remember two sample essays on *Othello* − her sharp, unsentimental response, the Austenesque irony with which she drily analysed the tragedy, even the characteristically firm, clear hand in which the essays were written. It was the college's loss, more than hers, when they rejected Suu's application. She taught herself Japanese instead and wrote a biography of her father. Suu took Kim with her for a year at Kyoto University, and spent a further year with all the family in India, where she and Michael held academic posts at Simla.

Life at this time speeded up impossibly. I had four children and a university job. Suu was busy writing, yet dissatisfied with a life that failed fully to engage her energies, her relentless determi-

nation, the inherited diplomatic and political skills she had just
begun to feel burgeoning during her years at the United Nations.
Occasionally, in the rush of our individual responsibilities, we
would meet when I visited my mother, a neighbour of Suu's.
Walking meditatively round and round the crescent, Suu confided
some of her anxieties and heard out my own with sympathetic
firmness. Her moral standards and ethical convictions remained
unshakable as ever.

But everything was getting older and life was no longer simple.
My mother was ageing and ill. A brief period of delusion had left
her painfully gaunt, her fragile skull bony to my hand when I
stroked her hair. Like Lear, she seemed set on guard at the
extremest verge of life – poor perdu, with this thin helm – watching
with haunted clarity as death approached. Among the many
friends who visited her, Suu was one of the few she welcomed, a
serene presence at her side.

One early morning I came to see my mother, as I did every
morning, and found Suu with her. She had discovered my mother
wandering, half-dressed and confused, and brought her home. I
will not forget the serious gentleness with which Suu talked to
her, the grave concern with which she turned to me as she left.
Within a week she was called to Burma, to her own mother's
bedside. The rest of her story is well known.

My mother died at the same time as Suu's. I moved into our
house in Park Town. In the mornings I might see Alexander, a
tall sixteen-year old, cycling to school, or Kim in the dusty blue
of his prep-school uniform, scuffing past with his skateboard
under his arm. On early summer mornings and dusky autumnal
evenings I met Michael walking an honourably aged, stiff-limbed
Puppy down the grassy lane behind our houses.

In the fullness of time Puppy died. Michael is at Harvard,
Alexander in London, Kim at boarding school. Suu is under
house arrest. Every evening, as I put away my car in the garage
behind her house, I think of her, and one line of Yeats comes
repeatedly to mind. In an early poem addressed to Maud Gonne,
a political reformer like Suu, but, unlike her, a militant advocate
of armed rebellion, Yeats recalls

How many loved your moments of glad grace,
And loved your beauty with love false and true.
But one man loved the pilgrim soul in you.

Many, like myself, must first have been drawn to Suu by her beauty. Our perdurable love and admiration are for her pilgrim soul – for her courage, determination and abiding moral strength – gifts already glowing in her chrysalis period as a student and young mother.

26

Aung San Suu Kyi: Is She Burma's Woman of Destiny?   *by Josef Silverstein*

Until 26 August 1988, when she first entered the struggle, few among the people in the midst of the peaceful revolt against a military-backed dictatorship knew or had any idea who Aung San Suu Kyi was or for what she stood. Seth Mydans, writing in the *New York Times*, said, 'She has not previously been involved in politics, but her name was described by one diplomat as "magic" among the public.'[1] The 'magic' stems from the fact that she is the daughter of Aung San, the leader of the post-Second World War nationalist movement who was assassinated on the eve of Burma's independence. His name is the most revered in the nation and his memory is still alive. From the moment his daughter stepped into the political arena, she has been at the centre of Burma's political struggle.

Today, her voice is stilled because she is under house arrest; she was denied the right to participate in the May 1990 election or to communicate with her supporters. But there is no doubt that she continues to cast a long shadow over the military rulers who have prevented the elected representatives from taking their seats in a reconstituted Pyithu Hlutaw (national assembly), to which they were elected, and forming a legal government. If the election was intended to be an example of a Burmese version of Indonesian *wayang* (shadow play) with the soldiers-in-power acting as the *dalang* (puppeteer) moving the puppets (the parties and leaders) behind the lighted cloth and controlling their speech, it proved to be a revolt of the audience who voted against the military and for the party of Aung San Suu Kyi. Although she was not a candidate – despite appeals by foreign governments and international human rights groups to lift the ban against her participation – she is the leader of the National League for Democracy (NLD) and, as such, the people wait impatiently for her to be released from imprisonment, assume the leadership of the nation and fulfil their belief that she is Burma's woman of destiny.

Who is Aung San Suu Kyi and how does one account for her meteoric rise and continued popularity in a country where the military has dominated all aspects of life for the past twenty-nine years and where no woman in modern times has ever been seriously considered for national leadership? Is she destined to wear the mantle of leadership that her assassinated father dropped more than forty years ago or is she a fleeting phenomenon?

There are no real cultural impediments to a woman as a leader in Burma. Throughout its history, women have enjoyed equality with men in the household and the economy. Marriage was and is a civil act; women retain their own names during marriage, and divorce is a simple procedure with no stigma attached to either party. More important, women have always had the right of inheritance. Only in Buddhist religious terms were they considered inferior. In commenting on the relationship of the sexes in Burma, a modern Burmese woman – who played a leading role in the nation's history – wrote:

> We like to give precedence to our men in our own homes
> because we acknowledge them, until their death, as head of
> household. Possibly we can afford to offer this courtesy
> because we are secure in our rights and status. But part of
> the deference we offer them stems from the influence of
> Buddhism . . . We believe when a new Buddha comes to the
> world it will be as a man (though, to be sure, one of us who
> is now a woman may, in later life, be born as a man and
> eventually progress to Buddhahood). We feel that this gives
> men an inherent superiority: mentally, they can reach higher
> than women.[2]

In Burmese history, there are instances where women attained positions of power and influence. For example, in the Pegu kingdom, during the fifteenth century, Shin Saw Bu succeeded to the throne and, upon retirement, devoted herself to religion and merit-making. In the Konbaung dynasty, during the nineteenth century, Supayalat, the queen of Burma's last king, exercised great power over her husband and was reported to have worked closely with royal councillors in deciding matters of state.

During the colonial period, Burmese women held important positions in the professions and even in politics. In the 1920s women held offices in the Rangoon City Corporation, and in the last year of that decade a woman was elected to the Legislative Council. The Students' Union at Rangoon University – the incubator of Burmese nationalist leaders – included women in its leadership from the outset, and women students participated alongside men in the 1936 strike.[3] Following the introduction of the new constitution in 1937, a woman was elected to the legislature. An outstanding woman of the period was Daw Mya Sein, a scholar, author, teacher, wife and mother. The daughter of a distinguished jurist and scholar, she was chosen to represent Burmese women at a special Burma Round Table Conference in London 1931, and, later, on the eve of the Second World War, to lead a delegation to China.

After the Second World War, a few women were active in politics, administration and diplomacy, but none achieved national prominence by holding high government or party positions. In the election to the 1947 Constituent Assembly three women won seats, while four others were added as replacements for their assassinated husbands.[4] Following independence, two were elected in 1952 in the first national election; four years later, five won seats; and in 1960 three were elected. None achieved cabinet rank or leadership in the parliament. Because of the unique federal constitution of Burma in that period, the Prime Minister was responsible for selecting the representatives of the states in his cabinet. Those whom he chose also served as heads of their states. In 1953 Prime Minister U Nu named Mrs Ba Maung Chein to represent the Karen State, making her the first and only woman to reach cabinet rank. Later, she broke with the Prime Minister and led the opposition in her state.

From the colonial period onwards, women's organizations were attached to political parties. The post-Second World War dominant party, the Anti-Fascist People's Freedom League (AFPFL), included the Women's Freedom League. While its leaders were given administrative posts, they never became a major factor in party politics. Until 1960 no woman served as head of a diplomatic mission. In that year Aung San Suu Kyi's mother, Daw Khin Kyi, was named ambassador to India and held the post until 1967.

Countless women participated in the nationalist struggle of the colonial period and many worked closely with the men who were the leaders. But they never achieved leadership in their own right. Under the military dictatorship, which began in 1962, women played a much smaller political role. Nine were elected in 1974 to the first Pyithu Hlutaw under the new constitution, and thirteen won seats four years later. During this period, the military dominated all aspects of government and the political party it created. Women were and continue to be in the armed forces, but none has attained command or senior levels.

Although Aung San Suu Kyi has instant name recognition and acceptance as the daughter of a national hero, she has a number of qualities of her own which prepared her well to sustain her in the political arena in her own right. First, she is intelligent and well educated. During the first fifteen years of her life, she was schooled in Burma, where she developed her knowledge and use of Burmese as any other child of her day. Later, in India and Great Britain, she continued her education and in 1967 earned a degree at St Hugh's College, Oxford, where she studied Politics, Philosophy and Economics. She later learned the Japanese language, and during 1985–6 Aung San Suu Kyi was a visiting scholar at Kyoto University. In 1987 she was a fellow at the Indian Institute of Advanced Studies in New Delhi. At the time of her return to Burma in 1988, she was enrolled in the London School of Oriental and African Studies, where she was working for an advanced degree.

During this period, she found time to publish two scholarly works and several popular books. Her scholarly publications demonstrate a deep interest in and knowledge of modern Burmese history. In 1982 she published a long essay on her father, which appeared as a book; in 1987 she published a scholarly article on modern Burmese literature.[5] Her most important literary achievement to date is her recent pioneering intellectual history essay in which she compares the Indian and Burmese reactions to colonial rule.[6]

Second, she was widely travelled. In 1969, two years after leaving Oxford, she went to New York where she was employed at the United Nations Secretariat. In 1972 she married a British scholar, a Tibetan specialist, Michael Aris, and while they lived in Bhutan where he was first tutor to the royal family and then government translator, she worked for the Bhutan Foreign Ministry as a research officer on United Nations affairs. Two years later the family moved to England, where her husband assumed an appointment at Oxford in Tibetan and Himalayan studies. During the 1970s and 1980s she made frequent trips to Burma to visit her ageing mother; while there, she had many opportunities to observe conditions at first hand – the decline in the economy, the hardships of the people and the corrupt authoritarian rule of the military. On the basis of her education and writing, her experience at the United Nations, in Japan, in India and in the Himalayan states, and her observations in Burma, she was better prepared than most to comment on and criticize the rule of the military and to argue for an alternative system – a return to the democratic ideas of her father.

Small and thin in stature, she resembled her father in many ways – a warm smile, strong facial features and piercing eyes, direct speech and a commanding presence. If she had no political skills and experience when she stepped into the peaceful revolution in 1988, she quickly acquired them. Dressed always in traditional Burmese clothing and speaking idiomatic and perfect Burmese, she quickly won the hearts and backing of the people who came to hear her speak and stayed to support her movement. 'She speaks directly and with modesty,' a Burmese shopkeeper in

Mandalay told a reporter. 'When we listen to the government leader, and then listen to her, I think every Burmese can agree about who is the better person.'[7] From the outset, she sensed that the people in the streets, who were calling for change, wanted something new and different. Therefore, she refused to join either U Nu or any other older politicians who sought to head the leaderless revolution. Instead, she initially joined former Brigadier Aung Gyi and later they, together with former General Tin U, formed the National League for Democracy.

Aung San Suu Kyi never doubted that her immediate acceptance by the people stemmed from the fact that she was identified with her father. But she was not the only child of a revolutionary or independence leader to come forward to lead. Cho Cho Kyaw Nyein, the daughter of a co-worker of Aung San and a leader of the former Socialist Party and the original AFPFL, and a senior cabinet member during the administration of U Nu, also stepped forward; but while she attracted a few to her banner, neither she nor any other was a match for Aung San's daughter.

It is important to remember who Aung San was and why he holds such a special place in the memory of the Burmese people. He vaulted to national attention in the university student strike of 1936, and later secretly negotiated with the Japanese to aid the Burmese revolutionary struggle. When the Pacific War began he formed the Burma Independence Army and led it into Burma, where units fought against the British. During the war, when Japan gave Burma independence, he became Minister of Defence, but when he and others around him became disillusioned with the Japanese, he organized a revolt of the Burma army and joined with the Allies in recovering his country from the Japanese. In the post-war period, he led the nationalist coalition, the AFPFL, and won Burma's independence through peaceful negotiations with the British. He was assassinated while leading the Constituent Assembly in writing a constitution for independent Burma. His death robbed the nation of the one man whom Burmans and non-Burmans alike trusted. No leader after him had the political support he engendered nor the ability to translate his vision of a united, peaceful and prosperous Burma into reality.[8] In the midst of the peaceful revolution of the summer of 1988, demonstrators carried his picture 'as their standard'.[9]

Aung San Suu Kyi shares her father's belief in democracy and its achievement through peaceful means. Initially, she called for the creation of an impartial interim government to oversee a national election in which the people were free to form parties, choose leaders and contest for power. She saw no role for herself in this process or future government. 'A life of politics,' she said at the end of August 1988, 'holds no attraction for me. At the moment, I serve as a kind of unifying force because of my father's name and because I am not interested in jostling for any kind of position.'[10]

As a pragmatist, she responded to changing conditions, in both her role and speech. In response to the military's seizure of power on 18 September 1988, she joined in the founding of the NLD and became its general secretary. She spoke out sharply against the murder in the streets of non-violent demonstrators by the soldiers as they consolidated their power. She spoke out strongly as the military increased its violations of human rights, intimidation and repression. She continued to call for peaceful change through free and fair elections, but this became more difficult as the military rulers began to arrest her followers and harass her. As she travelled about the country her attacks became more focused upon the behaviour of the military, which she eventually described as fascist, and an obstruction to peaceful change. By June 1989 she publicly accused Ne Win of being the real leader of the military government, the source of the people's hardships and the man who destroyed everything her father stood for and tried to achieve.

In making the attacks upon the men in power and Ne Win as the force behind them, it was not her intention to weaken the military or split the army.

> I know a split army is against the interests of the nation . . . We just want what my father wanted: a professional army that understands that a really honourable army doesn't engage in politics.[11]

> My father didn't build up the Burmese army in order to
> oppress the people . . . He made many speeches where he
> specifically said, don't start oppressing the people just be-
> cause you have weapons. You are to serve the country. You
> are for the country, the country is not for you. [12]

She recognized, very early, that the military had no real
intention of allowing free and open politics to flower. Registration
as a political party meant the right to display a signboard, hold
gatherings of less than five and obtain extra petrol so that it was
theoretically possible to move around and build support. But, in
reality, the decrees made it impossible to hold meetings, print
and distribute party literature and say anything which might be
construed as criticism of the military, present and past. Several
times she said, 'The law on gatherings is totally ridiculous – they
allow people to register as political parties but then they don't
allow them to move . . . There is no freedom of the press. The
government newspapers are attacking us all the time, but there is
no way to retaliate.'[13] By the time of her arrest she was a
seasoned politician who became second to none in her forthright
speech and her ability to debate with her opponents.

Like her father, Aung San Suu Kyi showed courage in the face
of adversity. The military feared her popularity with the people
and did not know how to respond to it. Even before the army-led
coup, the military intelligence and police launched the idea that
she was manipulated by the communists. They arrested Thakin
Tin Mya, a former member of the Burma Communist Party
(BCP) politburo and, later, central committee member of the
army's own Burma Socialist Programme Party (BSPP), who
they said was advising her. She responded by saying that while
he was assisting with office work, she did not solicit and he did
not give any political advice.[14]

In November, her co-party leader, Aung Gyi, made similar
charges, saying that she was surrounded by BCP members and
demanded that she remove them. Again, she denied any BCP
influence on either her thinking or her actions and, backed by the
other NLD leaders, expelled Aung Gyi from the party. But the

charge would not go away; during the next few months the
military spokesmen picked up and repeated the accusations. In
June 1989 a government spokesman equated her party with the
banned BCP, the first time that either Aung San Suu Kyi or her
party was directly attacked.[15] On 5 August 1989 Brigadier Khin
Nyunt, head of the Directorate of Defence Services Intelligence,
held a press conference and launched a major campaign against
her as a dupe of the BCP.[16] Despite her earlier refutation of the
charges, the military rulers persisted in this line of attack.

Initially, they overlooked her violation of their order on public
gatherings. But as she travelled around the country and drew
crowds in the thousands and dominated the political scene, they
responded. First, they warned people away from her rallies and,
when she departed after an appearance, arrested local members
of her party. Second, they began to attack her personally with
vulgar posters suggesting abnormal sexual behaviour; they attacked her as working for foreign nations, ready to sell out the
country if she gained power; and they attacked her for being
anti-Buddhist.[17] She ignored the first, but responded vigorously
to the second and third charges. During the spring of 1989 a
political crisis began to build up as Aung San Suu Kyi spoke out
more forcefully; the crowds at her rallies increased and foreign
journalists sought her out for interviews and published her ideas
and comments worldwide. On 5 April while campaigning in
Danubyu, an army captain ordered six soldiers to load and aim
their rifles at her; before the countdown ended an army major
stepped forward, countermanded the order and prevented her
assassination. Although local military authorities later told her
supporters that they regretted the incident, it marked an escalation
in the military's effort to intimidate her.[18]

As anniversaries came due marking specific past attacks upon
students, Aung San Suu Kyi and her party planned memorial
celebrations. At the 21 June memorial, she and several students
were in the process of paying homage when the military opened
fire and killed one person. As tensions built, she called off a
memorial service on 7 July, but planned to honour her father on
19 July, the date of his assassination. The military sought to

control the ceremonies and invited her to join their leaders in marking the event; she refused, saying that she would honour her father in her own way. In the face of the tensions caused by this train of events, Aung San Suu Kyi called off her memorial visit in order to prevent bloodshed as it was known that a large delegation of students intended to accompany her. The next day, the military struck; they put her under house arrest and cut off all her communications with her followers and the outside world. They also arrested Tin U, the Chairman of the NLD.

In December 1989 Aung San Suu Kyi allowed her name to be put forward as a candidate for a seat in the forthcoming election. Although the Election Commission initially approved her candidacy, it was challenged by one of her opponents from the National Unity Party (NUP) – the new name for the army's former party, the BSPP – who charged that she was in contact with dissident groups fighting against government forces. The challenge was allowed and an appeal was made directly to the Election Commission to return her to the list of candidates. However, on 17 February her name was not among those officially designated as candidates, thus indicating that her appeal had been denied.[19]

It is assumed by all who have followed events in Burma that if Aung San Suu Kyi had been allowed to stand for election, she would have won. But she was not allowed to run, and her leading supporters were either gaoled or forced into hiding for fear of arrest. In addition, the NLD had no leader with the prominence and support given to Aung San Suu Kyi and Brigadier Tin U; therefore, it had to rely upon local party organization and the bravery of the ordinary people to achieve victory in the face of harassment from, and intimidation by, the military.

Despite the obstacles created by the military to intimidate the people, the outcome of the election proved to be one of the real surprises to emerge under military rule. Although 234 parties actually registered, only 93 fielded candidates. Long before all the vote was counted, it was clear that the NLD was the overwhelming choice of the people. It won 392 seats in the 485 constituencies where elections were held. Twenty-six other parties won seats, with the NUP winning a mere ten. One leading Asian journal concluded that the election was not really between several parties competing, but a 'referendum in which the NLD represented democratic aspirations while the NUP stood for the old system'.[20] Even though Aung San Suu Kyi was not a contestant, it was clear to all that the people had voted for her and against the military and its proxy.

The victory of the NLD did not bring political change in Burma. From the outset, the military did not indicate whether it really planned to transfer power immediately after the election or at some unknown future date. However, while its spokesmen said both, they generally argued that the election would only produce a constituent assembly with a mandate to write a new constitution. After the new constitution was written and approved by the people and became the law of the land, a second election probably would be held to fill the offices created by the new basic law. As they embellished the theme, they argued that the new constitution had to produce a strong government, had to guarantee the unity of the state and would have to have the approval of all 135 minorities resident in the land. Only then would power be transferred. In the meantime, the military continues to rule under its decrees, and democracy will have to wait before it is reintroduced.

But all the elected members of the national assembly were not content to wait. With Aung San Suu Kyi still silenced and under house arrest and the successor head of the party, U Kyi Maung, and others also arrested, tried and given prison sentences, the military systematically sought to destroy its popular political rival. In the face of intimidation and arrest of leaders and supporters of other opposition parties, as well as those of the NLD, elected members to the national assembly who were still free held a secret meeting in Mandalay in November and decided some should try and make their way to the border area, where the minorities in revolt held control, and form a provisional government. On 18 December 1990 seven who got to their destination, Manerplaw, the headquarters of the Karens, proclaimed a rival government to the military. The National Coalition Government of the Union of Burma (NCGUB) was led by Dr Sein Lwin, a cousin of Aung San Suu Kyi, and it was given the backing of the Democratic Alliance of Burma (DAB), a broad coalition of ethnic parties and religious groups who seek a peaceful end to the civil war and a return to civilian democratic rule in Burma. The NCGUB argued that since its members had been elected by the people and given a mandate to participate in governing as well as in writing a new constitution, they took the only course open to them in the face of the endless reign of terror inflicted on party leaders and the people by the military. With legal and moral force, and the backing of the DAB, they seek to fill the void in political leadership and to unite Burmans and minorities in a truly national coalition against military rule.

All these events took place while Aung San Suu Kyi was and remains under house arrest and it is unknown whether or not she was consulted secretly and involved in shaping them.

If Aung San Suu Kyi had been permitted to run and win, what sort of leader would she be? Given her intellect and her emergence as a vigorous campaigner and excellent speaker there is no reason to doubt that, as leader of an elected parliament that was free to govern the nation, she probably would have no hesitation in accepting the responsibility and challenges imposed by leadership. Her power to inspire devotion and enthusiasm would be a major asset in getting support for the difficult and possibly unpopular choices she no doubt would be called upon to make.

It is not known if she was consulted either openly or secretly by her party either before or after the election. As a student of her father's career, she knows well that he would not play by the 'rules of the game' as dictated by the British. If she were to model her leadership after his and was faced with a decree that the people who were elected on 27 May 1990 had but one duty – to write a new constitution – she would challenge the soldiers in power immediately and demand that those elected be given power to govern, as they constituted the Pyithu Hlutaw as defined in the election law. She knows that under the 1974 constitution, which is still in force, the Pyithu Hlutaw is the highest body in the nation and it alone has the power to choose the nation's leaders from among its members and make laws. She would have sought to emulate her father in the period between 1946 and 1947 when he headed the Executive Council under British authority and later also led the Constituent Assembly in writing a constitution. She probably would demand the same dual responsibility from the current military rulers.

If Burma is to get beyond rule by self-chosen leaders and groups taking power at will, there has to be an early confrontation with the soldiers in power on this issue. Based on Aung San Suu Kyi's short career in politics, she may be the only person presently on the political scene to lead such a fight. But, accepting that scenario and postulating her becoming the leader of the legislature and constituent assembly, what is known of her ideas, other than those expressed in her campaigns before her arrest?

Thus far, it has not been demonstrated that she is a systematic thinker with a well-thought-out set of goals and a plan for achieving them. Before her arrest, she had no time for quiet reflection as she sought to make herself known and to be identified with the creation of a democratic political system. What is known is that most of her remarks centred on a political process which any democratic system demanded if it was to function as intended. Thus, it is known that she stands for the protection of social and political rights which flow from the idea of a political system based on the will of the people. But what sort of system would she support? Clearly, from her campaign speeches, she did not call for a return to the system authored by her father.

A clue to her thinking may be found in the manifesto the National League for Democracy adopted on 6 November 1989. While it is not clear as to her exact input, it must be assumed that she was forced to consider the future when she might be called upon to lead the nation; and since the manifesto was made public and not repudiated, either directly or indirectly, it must be assumed that no document of this kind could have been made public without her knowledge and approval. Also, it must be recognized that this is a campaign statement and not necessarily a finished document which the author or authors offer as their blue-print for Burma's future.

The manifesto is broad and seemingly all inclusive. It contains contradictions and ambiguities suggesting that it was either a compromise between conflicting points of view or hastily prepared and not carefully thought out. It begins with a strong statement in support of the principle of human rights and democratic procedures as found in the UN Charter and rests on popular sovereignty. The parliament, it says, 'must have the right to exercise the sovereign power of the State without exception'.[21] But it then goes on to contradict this by saying that the three traditional branches of government 'must stand separate without mutual interference'. If the parliament is supreme, is the executive responsible to it; and, if not, in a clash between branches of government, how would the issue be resolved and in whose favour?

A second and more important issue, in the light of Burma's civil war, is the future relationship between the minorities and the Burman majority. When Aung San Suu Kyi was able to speak out and was asked about this question, she always replied that once civil government was established it would not be difficult to resolve this question. In short, the peoples of the Burma heartland would first form a government and then would take up the issue of majority/minority relations as two separate and identifiable groups with separate interests. In the manifesto, the same idea is set forth with a little more detail. Only after the parliament is established, and prior to the drafting of the constitution, 'the parliament will enact a law to form regional administrative bodies in the states.' When the constitution is drafted it will incorporate the principle that 'every minority will have the right to promulgate laws for its own region in the spheres of administration, politics and economics'. Does this imply a federal form of government or some sort of unitary state with autonomous regions with limited power? Only after 'a democratic system is successfully adopted in the country' would there be a conference between the Pyithu Hlutaw leaders and the minorities, on the model of the 1947 Panglong Conference, 'to lay down the foundation of a democratic society'. Does that mean that the temporary system initially suggested might be altered towards a full federal or unitary state; and if so, can those minorities who disagree have

the right to opt out? In short, it still is the same idea posed
by Aung San Suu Kyi earlier – the organization of a Burman-
dominated polity first, then, after the constitution is written, to
begin negotiating with the minorities. With no say or participation in the parliament at the outset, the minorities will not be
equal partners in the future state of Burma.

If the above interpretation is correct and it reflects the thinking
of Aung San Suu Kyi, then she has departed as far as possible
from the thinking of her father when this issue seized the nation
at its birth. His goal was a federal state in which the minorities
were full partners from the outset, sharing in governing the
country before independence, in writing the constitution and in
the nation's future, whatever it might be. The issue of national
unity has been the central issue in Burma since the end of the
Second World War and it seems no closer to an acceptable
solution now than it was at the time of Aung San's death.

Is Aung San Suu Kyi Burma's woman of destiny? It would
appear so at this time. There is no other person who has achieved
her status, love and respect from the people of Burma and the
support from foreign governments who have appealed on her
behalf. She is her father's daughter – intelligent, honest, tough and
fearless. Most of all, she has no past connection with the failures
of the democratic government of U Nu or the corrupt, incompetent and brutal dictatorship of Ne Win and his military successors.
By not allowing her to run in the first free election since 1960, the
military may have inadvertently helped to raise her stature with
the people. The coup leaders' inability to give her freedom after she
completed the initial year-long sentence, or expel her from the
country, or take any action other than the continuation of her
house arrest, can be seen only as a further example of arbitrary
rule. In the face of three international awards for her fight for
human rights and democracy in Burma and a growing call from
world leaders to free her, the military rulers responded in the
spring of 1991 saying that she can go into voluntary exile whenever she wants even though she could be charged with high
treason and sentenced either to life imprisonment or to death.[22]
But no one is fooled by this act of 'generosity', especially since the

military let it be known that her term of house arrest has been extended to three more years.[23] Her strength and fortitude in the face of a corrupt and brutal military regime are an inspiring example for the people of Burma, who know of her personal sacrifices, and it gives them a model to emulate. It strengthens her ties with the people, who overwhelmingly chose her party to represent them in the future democratic government of Burma.

Silenced and unable to act while under house arrest, she is playing no part in the future constituent assembly that the military is slowly shaping and directing. Whatever its outcome, the people are likely to look to her for its approval or rejection, as she remains the people's leader who was denied the right to fulfil that role. For many in Burma she appears to be the reincarnation of her father and destined to carry out his unfinished job of leading Burma into the modern world.

But if she is Burma's woman of destiny, she stands to inherit more problems than her father imagined; and although she is intelligent and informed about Burma, she has given no clear answers to the questions of how democracy can be institutionalized, how national unity can be achieved, how the economy can be improved or how the violations of human and political rights by the military in the past and present will be rectified. The Burmese people have been in search of leadership since the death of Aung San and many believe that they have found it in his daughter. So long as she remains untried in a responsible position and isolated from the people, they will continue to believe that she is the one who can set them on a new course. But until she is given the chance to use her new-found skills of democratic politics in the crucible of parliamentary politics and bears the responsibility for her decisions, no one will know if she is destined to lead Burma towards a new and better life than its peoples have had or if she will be forced to compromise and accept the realities of Burma that developed over the past forty-three years.

Notes

1 *New York Times,* 26 August 1988.
2 Daw Mya Sein, 'The Women of Burma', in 'Perspective on Burma', *Atlantic Monthly,* 201 (February 1958), p.24.

3 Aye Kyaw, *The Voice of Young Burma*, a forthcoming publication on the student and nationalist movement in the 1920s and 1930s, to be published by the Cornell University Southeast Asia Program, Ithaca, NY.

4 Government of Burma, *Burma's Fight for Freedom: Independence Commemoration*, Rangoon, 1948, pp. 86–8. Mi Mi Khaing, *The World of Burmese Women*, London, 1984, reported that four women were elected to the Constituent Assembly but this is contradicted in the official record of that body.

5 See this volume, pp. 140–64.

6 See this volume, pp. 82–139.

7 Tom Nagorski, 'In Burma, a Season of Anniversaries', *The Nation* (Bangkok), 19 July 1989.

8 Studies of Aung San, in addition to that of Aung San Suu Kyi, are found in Josef Silverstein (ed. and contrib.), *The Political Legacy of Aung San*, Cornell University Southeast Asia Program, Data Paper 86, Ithaca, NY, 1972; and Maung Maung (comp. and ed.), *Aung San of Burma*, The Hague, 1962.

9 *New York Times*, 14 August 1988.

10 *The Times*, London, 29 August 1988.

11 *New York Times*, 22 January 1990.

12 *Christian Science Monitor*, 15 June 1989.

13 *The Nation* (Bangkok), 23 February 1989.

14 *Working People's Daily* (Rangoon), 18 September 1988.

15 *New York Times*, 24 June 1989.

16 Ministry of Information, *Communist Party's Conspiracy to Take Over State Power*, Rangoon, 1989.

17 There were many reports by responsible foreign journalists. See *New York Times*, 9 January 1989; *The Nation* (Bangkok), 6 April 1989; *New York Times*, 24 June 1989; also see '50th State SLORC Press Conference, 21 July 1989', *Working People's Daily* (Rangoon), 22 July 1989, for a list of infractions – from the military's point of view – by Aung San Suu Kyi that led up to her house arrest.

18 *Bangkok Post*, 16 April 1989.

19 Ibid., 18 February 1990.

20 Far Eastern Economic Review, *Asia 1991 Yearbook*, Hong Kong, p. 86.

21 Manifesto of the National League for Democracy (typescript photocopy). All successive quotations are from this document.

22 Interview with Burma's ambassador to Thailand, U Nyunt Swe, *The Nation* (Bangkok), 27 July 1991.

23 *Bangkok Post*, 27 August 1991.

27

Aung San Suu Kyi and the Peaceful Struggle for Human Rights in Burma
by Philip Kreager

From a state of profound isolation, Burma has moved rapidly and conspicuously on to the world stage, especially in the assertion by its people of the need for basic human rights. Spontaneous mass demonstrations began in August 1988. At first an instinctive reaction to a quarter-century of official repression and gratuitous military violence, the demonstrations formed part of a truly widespread popular movement, as tens and sometimes hundreds of thousands of people met and marched, with the manifest support of the general population, which greeted, cheered and joined them. Events in Burma have tended, inevitably, to be overshadowed by those in its large neighbour to the north, where similar demonstrations occurred a year later. And the immediate outcome, both in Burma and China, seems to have been the same: their governments swiftly adopted methods of exceptional brutality in order to silence opposition.

The Burmese situation, however, is different, and unusual, in at least one fundamental respect. Out of the inherently disorderly phenomenon of spontaneous mass uprising, further disturbed and disrupted by violent military suppression, there has emerged a clear leader, advocating non-violent methods, who commands widespread admiration and support: Aung San Suu Kyi. Her position is at once formidable and extremely vulnerable: she is physically at the mercy of a military regime which retains power by use of force; yet the military has not so far dared to apply physical violence to her.

The emergence of Aung San Suu Kyi at the very centre of the

Burmese struggle for human rights, and the unique role she has been able to play, are the consequence of three facts which have bound her life inextricably to the modern history of her country. Two of these are now widely recognized, but it is the third factor which has given them moment.

The first is that she is the daughter of the unquestioned architect of independent Burma in the modern period, Aung San. His role, as attested in many sources,[1] was that of a unifying figure of unblemished character with a strong vision of a free, democratic Burma. His assassination, on the eve of independence, along with the cabinet of the transitional government he headed, had tragic implications for the stability of the new country. Not surprisingly, Aung San has become a powerful symbol and martyr of Burmese freedom. His legacy has made Aung San Suu Kyi an appropriate symbol of the people's legitimate rights and aspirations.

Second, the identification of daughter and father carries with it the terrifying prospect of history repeating itself. The current military dictatorship came to power twenty-eight years ago, overthrowing the elected government formed by Aung San's surviving associates in the aftermath of his assassination. Having established without free and fair elections a system based on a single socialist party, the military dealt with strikes, demonstrations and other popular expressions – for example, in 1962, 1974 and 1976 – with gunfire.[2] When the period of mass demonstrations began in 1988, the government adopted a policy of intimidation and severe restrictions on freedom of information, making exact counts of persons killed or imprisoned impossible. On at least three separate occasions in the twelve-month period from August 1988 to July 1989 troops were instructed to break up mass demonstrations by firing directly and repeatedly into crowds, with intent to kill: government statements subsequently admitted several hundred deaths and over one thousand arrests; independent estimates have been much higher.[3] The military naturally focused its attention on the leadership of the opposition. Most reports stress lack of information on the whereabouts and condition of many persons arrested; use of torture has been attested by reliable sources and many eyewitness accounts.[4]

Aung San Suu Kyi was placed under a very strict form of house arrest in her own home on 20 July 1989. All contact with her followers and access to the media to express her views were stopped. Her immediate demand that she should be subject to the same conditions of imprisonment as her followers was ignored. However, following a hunger strike of twelve days, in which she accepted only water, the military government agreed not to torture or maltreat her imprisoned followers. Reports now suggest that, once Aung San Suu Kyi had been effectively cut off from her supporters, the military government ceased to honour this promise.[5]

The historical legacy which Aung San Suu Kyi represents is undoubtedly very awkward for the military government; a second martyrdom would hardly be to its advantage, whether in the short or the long term. But these facts are not sufficient to explain the role which she has come to play, or the different treatment the government has, thus far, felt necessary in her case. We need, in short, to consider the words and actions which have been her specific contribution to a rapidly developing situation, a contribution which not only reveals her profound and wider reflection on the nature of human responsibility, but which enabled her to exercise a moderating influence both on her followers and, at least for a time, on the military government. At present her contribution remains the one locus of opposition and hope which the otherwise brutally effective techniques employed by the military have not been able to break.

In a few short months – from mid-August 1988 to mid-July 1989 – Aung San Suu Kyi, although not previously part of any opposition movement and, indeed, present in Burma for personal reasons unconnected with the popular uprising, began to make her distinctive position known. First by open letter to the government, then in speeches to public meetings and demonstrations, in the formation and leadership of the National League for Democracy (NLD), and in her own tours of the country – conducted, when necessary, at gunpoint – she stuck consistently to a small number of fundamental themes, which made her the moral and spiritual focus of the popular movement to restore human rights. These themes may be briefly summarized:

1   Priority must be given to the restoration of human rights – freedom of speech, of assembly, of political organization, of information, free elections, freedom from fear – which are currently denied in Burma, and which are the only true basis for national unity and social evolution. Political and economic reform, she maintains, will only be possible after these rights have been constituted in Burmese society.

2   The only legitimate and effective means to this end are non-violent ones.

3   The conduct of states and their governments requires principles which must always be distinguished from personalities, factions and merely tactical issues. This means, in the Burmese case, that it is not the military as such which is the enemy of human rights; the military remains, at base, a friend, and has its own legitimate sphere in government (for example, to maintain secure borders). The problem of human rights has arisen in Burma because the military, under the dictatorship of Ne Win, usurped the exercise of government. It should return to its normal, honourable role.

4   Personal and collective discipline is crucial. Short-term objectives – such as mass demonstrations, the formation of political parties and elections – are worthless if human rights are not consistently observed. Members of the NLD, and all other opponents of the military dictatorship, must not actively provoke the military to do anything more than lay down its ill-chosen methods.

These principles reflect the inspiration which Aung San Suu Kyi derived from her study and reflection on Gandhi's philosophy and practice of non-violent civil disobedience. They were demonstrated repeatedly in the conduct of her campaign of public meetings and demonstrations, and they remain no less evident in her cool response to the intimidation and slander which the military government has continued to direct against her. Long-term observers of the Burmese scene stress that it was Aung San Suu Kyi who first introduced the issue of human rights into Burmese political discussion. These matters will be discussed in more detail below.

Popular passions naturally mounted during the year of mass demonstrations, as government acts of violence increased. Many student leaders who played an important role in the early stages of the uprising, and who were themselves willing to consider violent means, were imprisoned, killed or driven into hiding.[6] Under such severe pressures, and against tremendous odds, Aung San Suu Kyi's reasoned insistence on the sole legitimacy of non-violent means and the priority of human rights has proven the only enduring answer: by her example, and her prevention of bloodshed, she was able to establish a real alternative for the people, who otherwise face only submission. As student representatives told a foreign correspondent, 'Aung San Suu Kyi is our only leader. She's the only one left. There is no one else.'[7]

The third and crucial fact about Aung San Suu Kyi's unique place in Burma today thus stands out very clearly. Facts of parentage may have provided her with immediate and special public recognition; her heartfelt and determined insistence on higher principles is certainly appropriate to the deep reverence in which the memory of her father is generally held. But it is the guidance she has brought to a highly unstable situation, sustained by the personal force, courage and sound judgement manifest in her words and actions, that continues to provide the main hope for Burma.

The arrest and long isolation of Aung San Suu Kyi – now of more than two years' duration – place the strongest possible importance on the response of the international community. Without her active presence, and the principled approach she has taken, prospects for stability and peaceful development are far from clear. The military government has indicated the road it proposes to follow. The elections which were held in May 1990 resulted in a landslide victory for Aung San Suu Kyi's party: it gained some 392 of the 485 legislative seats at stake in the National Assembly, representing 72 per cent of the 13 million votes cast.[8] The military government's own party meanwhile captured a mere ten seats.[9] The results were interpreted both in

Burma and internationally as a referendum on Aung San Suu Kyi's proposed leadership of a free and democratic Burma, and, more specifically, as her personal triumph.[10] The military, however, has simply refused to hand over power, keeping her and other opposition leaders under lock and key, and using its superior force and intimidation to maintain control. International observers having declared the election free of corruption, the military have not dared to declare it void. Instead, it has indicated that it will consider the transfer of power only when a new constitution is written, and more particularly one of which it approves.[11] As the National Assembly can scarcely convene with less than a fifth of its members, the situation remains at a standstill.

Such a cruel parody of the democratic process points the way to continued violence. The military's determination to retain power despite widespread opposition is paralleled also in the presence of armed separatist movements among the main non-Burma ethnic groups – the Karen, Shan, Mon, Kachin and others. Many young Burmans have been compelled by circumstances to join these groups, some to be trained in arms by them.[12] Civil war, which has already torn apart Cambodia, has become a definite possibility in Burma.[13] The three facts which have led to Aung San Suu Kyi's unique role in the Burmese struggle for human rights have also made her the natural and primary focus of international attention. In 1990 she was awarded in Norway the Thorolf Rafto Memorial Prize for Human Rights and the European Parliament awarded her the Sakharov Prize for Freedom of Thought. The aim here is to bring together for a wider audience a summary of the main elements in the development of Aung San Suu Kyi's thought and action in defence of human rights in Burma. In the following two sections her position is set out – in her own words, as far as possible – against the chronology of recent Burmese history. This is followed by a brief recitation of the international response to date.

Aung San Suu Kyi, Non-Violence and Democracy

To understand the present situation in Burma, it is necessary to consider more closely Aung San Suu Kyi's own life and practice of non-violence. Her insistence that violent and non-violent means belong to strictly separable domains of human action reflects her personal experience of the sad consequences of their mixture in Burmese history. Perhaps more important, it reflects careful study – over many years – of the ideas, problems and constraints which shaped her father's short life. While Aung San Suu Kyi has been directly inspired by his example, the problems of continued militarism and factionalism which he foresaw – and which over-took him at his assassination – led her very early to seek general principles of moral, social and political action which not only incorporate the lessons of his life but would also help to re-establish and sustain the framework of Burmese democracy which remained tentative and fragile at his death.

Aung San is remembered by the Burmese today not only as father of the nation but also as founder of its army. The term by which he was widely known – *Bogyoke* – was an expression of admiration for what he had achieved for Burma and of respect for his selfless attitude to power.[14] His army was built up for the sole and express purpose of asserting Burmese nationhood against British and Japanese colonial control; its existence was a major factor prompting the peaceful transition to an independent Burma which he successfully negotiated. Under his influence the Burma Independence Army was not a weapon used against other ethnic groups; Aung San was sufficiently able to restrain factions within its ranks that it became possible to integrate a battalion of Karen troops, and for a Karen general to assume command of the army during the first years of independence. Nor did the army become involved in countering the potentially divisive activities of socialist and communist groups, most of which Aung San was able to persuade to participate in elections.

The potential dangers, however, of a strong military in the context of a new democracy were something of which Aung San was well aware, and cautioned against: a military which engages in politics dishonours itself and earns the hatred of the people.[15] For his own part, he resigned his military position at the point when the political phase of independence negotiations began. But the circumstances of his assassination provide telling evidence of his prophecy of problems to come: he was killed, without provocation, by a small number of soldiers loyal to a jealous political rival.[16]

Aung San Suu Kyi was two years old when her father was assassinated. The army as a whole remained loyal to her father's precepts of non-intervention in politics during the early years of the democratically elected government of U Nu. Aung San Suu Kyi has attested its positive role at this time, making clear her own identification with her father's military legacy: 'as a child I was cared for by his soldiers'; 'I have a rapport with the army. I was brought up to regard them as friends.'[17] However, when the army leadership passed to Ne Win in the mid-1950s, a quiet consolidation of power began. When the military seized control of the government in 1962, Aung San Suu Kyi was with her mother, who was then Burmese Ambassador to India.

Aung San Suu Kyi was seventeen when the *coup d'état* took place. Her schooling in India, and then a two-year course in political science at Delhi University, thus came at a time and age when she needed to come to terms with events in Burma for herself. It was during this period that she acquired her lasting admiration for the principles of non-violence embodied in the life and philosophy of Mahatma Gandhi. Her campaign of civil disobedience in Burma was directly inspired by that example. She cited both Gandhi and Martin Luther King as models.[18]

She continued her education at Oxford University, where she studied Modern Greats (Politics, Philosophy and Economics), 'because economics seemed to be of most use for a developing country'.[19] Following a period of employment at the United Nations Secretariat in New York, she married the British Tibetologist, Michael Aris. While living in England and raising a family of two sons (born in 1973 and 1977), she continued to visit Burma regularly, and engaged in research and teaching in Burmese studies at Oxford. This happy and comparatively peaceful period of her life gave her time to write, and it led to a visiting scholarship at Kyoto University in Japan and a fellowship at the Indian Institute of Advanced Study in Simla.

Her enduring concerns are apparent in her main works, a short

biography of her father[20] and studies of Burmese social and
political thought in the period leading up to independence.[21] 'In
my thoughts,' she remarked in a BBC interview, 'I have never
been away from my country and my people.'[22]

> From childhood I have been deeply interested in the history
> of the independence movement and in the social and polit-
> ical development of Burma. My father died when I was only
> two years old, and it was only when I grew older and
> started collecting material on his life that I began to learn
> how much he achieved in his thirty-two years. I developed
> an admiration for him as a patriot and statesman. Because
> of this strong bond I feel a deep responsibility for the
> welfare of my country.[23]

Aung San Suu Kyi's writings, although interrupted and, consequently, left incomplete by her return to Burma and involvement
in recent events, deserve our attention. The biography of Aung
San, for example, is no partisan statement, but a clear narrative
in neutral language of the development of his thinking and the
main events in his life; her candid treatment of his strengths and
weaknesses helps us to understand the substance underlying the
observation, made by several foreign correspondents, of the 'mys-
tical awe' in which Aung San Suu Kyi, as Aung San's daughter, is
regarded by the common people. Her first public appearance, on
26 August 1988, has been described by Aung Lwin, a well-known
actor and subsequently a member of the National League for
Democracy, now imprisoned by the government: 'We were all
surprised. Not only did she look like her father, she spoke like him
also: short, concise and to the point.'[24] Her message emphasized
widely acknowledged themes of her father's: her democracy rests
on deep personal commitment; that national unity only comes
through discipline; that strictly fair treatment of opponents must
be maintained, whatever legitimate grievances the people may
hold against them; that a leader's view must be subject to wider
debate; that violent means are the legitimate function of the
military, belonging to a separate sphere outside politics; and that

basic human rights must be established first – meaning, in particular, open and free elections in a multi-party system. Like Aung San, she expressed a deep distaste for power politics and political manoeuvring behind the scenes. Her entry on to the political stage, like Aung San's, was because the obstruction of democracy by the government of the day left no other alternative: 'I could not as my father's daughter remain indifferent to all that was going on.'[29]

Similarly, her monograph comparing intellectual life in Burma and India under colonialism is something more than an academic account of why the independence movements in the two countries developed differently. Her research, not surprisingly, is bound up with her own intellectual development: the comparison of India and Burma gives rise to those aspects of Burmese history which make Gandhi's philosophy the appropriate basis for a moral and practical response to Burma's troubled modern history. It is Aung San Suu Kyi's recognition of the relevance and singular importance of Gandhi's teachings to Burma that distinguishes her contribution, and which represents a major step beyond the position of her father.

Her starting point in the essay is well known in the history of national movements in South Asia (and elsewhere). In both countries an admiration for European culture ran up against the brute facts of British political and military domination, leading to an attempt by local thinkers to formulate fundamentally Burmese and Indian national identities and ideologies which would none the less be able to draw selectively on the best aspects of European experience. Aung San Suu Kyi lays particular stress on (i) the village basis of Burmese democracy, (ii) the Burmese attitude to education as a moral activity embracing all aspects of person and nation and (iii) the relatively short period in which Burmese leadership has had to mature. Her treatment of these themes helps us to understand how she came to see a non-violent Gandhian approach to democracy as the historically legitimate – and realistic – course of action in Burma:

(i) The history of Burmese society is notable for the relative absence of hierarchical structures. Monarchy existed without a noble or leisure class between the king and the people, and ministers of state were consequently drawn from the villages. Daily life in the villages was self-governing. British abolition of the Burmese monarchy left a society not only lacking rigid castes or an emerging bourgeoisie, but without a politically aware intellectual élite. The tradition of local village government, however, remained, and did not disappear with British rule. Aung San Suu Kyi notes that it was precisely from such humble village contexts that Gandhi drew inspiration;[26] and that, just as Gandhi's thinking inspired a wider Indian literature espousing the wisdom and strength of village government, so in Burma national consciousness was rooted in a literature espousing the moral and economic autonomy of the traditional village.[27]

(ii) The emergence of the national movement in Burma owes directly to this fundamental egalitarian tendency. The traditional bases of this movement, although resting in Buddhism rather than explicitly in Gandhian philosophy, none the less found non-violent, mass expression:

> In Burma, with its lack of an effective leadership, the people had to fend for themselves in the twentieth century as they had done throughout their history. Traditionally, the Burmese had always had a great respect for education. Unlike India, where ancient learning had been confined to the higher castes, education had always been universally available in Burma. And this education was connected with the teachings of the Buddha who had pointed out the way to *nirvana*. Thus, to be educated meant more than the mere acquisition of book learning; it meant the mastery of the supreme knowledge that would lead to enlightenment. A people with such a view of education could not take easily to the British policy which saw education as a practical training for the new jobs and opportunities that had been created under colonialism . . . there was also in the Burmese mentality an ingrained resistance to élitism. It was a widely held belief that education of a national character should be made available to as broad a section of the population as

> possible. And it was this belief which lay behind the boycott against the Rangoon University Act of 1920 ... on the grounds that such [a university as the British were planning] would have the effect of limiting education to the privileged few.[28]

Aung San Suu Kyi goes on to point out how the boycott resulted in the creation of National Schools, financed by public subscription and based on 'an amalgam of the patriotic spirit and the western tradition of learning'; and that the first generation of Burmese leaders – which included Aung San and his associates – was the direct product of this system.[29]

(iii) The young men who emerged from the National Schools in the 1930s consciously 'strived to broaden the base of nationalism and to give it an intellectual framework'.[30] But like Gandhi in his youth, they were sometimes susceptible to foreign doctrines which they had not properly digested; most of them, caught up in the tide of the times, embraced socialist ideologies because the opposition of such doctrines to colonialism and capitalism gave them a progressive character – even though the relative absence of class exploitation made Burma an unlikely candidate for such models.[31] The central problem of the new generation was, consequently, to forge a link between ideas and action; here Aung San Suu Kyi singles out Aung San, not only because he cited Gandhi amongst the world figures to whom Burmans looked for guidance, but because Aung San (possibly echoing Gandhi's ultimate scepticism of European morals, and his idea of the need for unceasing action) was led by his own practical efforts to set aside the stock European 'isms' of the period; for him ideas and actions 'followed each on the other in an uninterrupted chain of endeavour'.[32]

The concluding note to her study emphasizes the unfinished nature of the independence movement. In implicit reference to her father's death, she writes: 'The younger generation of leaders appeared too late to bring about effective changes before the outbreak of the Second World War. Developments in Burma after 1940 took many abrupt twists and turns; and to this day, it still remains a society waiting for its true potential to be realized.'[33]

Later history has confirmed that the fusion of ideas and actions which the first generation of national leaders had sought was not attained. The national movement led, after a brief period of democracy, to a quarter-century of military dictatorship, under a programme of 'Burmese socialism' which has been criticized both within Burma and without for having neither intellectual coherence nor economic good sense.[34] As Aung San Suu Kyi has written, 'Actions without ideational content lose their potency as soon as the situation which called for them ceases to be valid. A series of pragmatic moves unconnected by a continuity of vision cannot be expected to sustain a long-term movement.'[35]

> A revolution which aims merely at changing official policies and institutions with a view to an improvement in material conditions has little chance of genuine success. Without a revolution of the spirit, the forces which produced the iniquities of the old order would continue to be operative, posing a constant threat to the process of reform and regeneration.[36]

Aung San Suu Kyi's writings and speeches in the course of the year of mass demonstration returned again and again to the theme of a 'revolution of the spirit' and its meaning in the context of Burmese and wider South Asian history. It is clear from her analysis of past Burmese experience, outlined in the preceding paragraphs, that the popular uprising of 1988 could in her view never hope to succeed unless its demands were anchored in a 'continuity of vision' such as her father had for a time achieved – but which none the less must go beyond his vision. The immediate need for action – the transformation of her ideas into some kind of practical programme – arose from the rapidly escalating conflict between demonstrators and the military in August and September 1988. Reading her essay 'Freedom from Fear',[37] which belongs to the tense period of confrontation between the people and the military regime, we can begin to discern how the connection between her thought and action took shape. Starting from the thesis that 'It is not power that corrupts but fear', she proceeds directly to explaining the effects of military repression in terms of moral categories (*a-gati*, or corruption; *abhaya*, or fearlessness) familiar to a Burmese audience. Where just rule has become corrupted, 'the burden of upholding the principles of justice and common decency falls on the ordinary people'. The means available to them in this struggle may seem unbalanced by the advantages of modern weaponry held by the army. But the courage of an Aung San or a Gandhi are alike models for ordinary people; and where Aung San provided an example with which Burmese can and do identify, it was Gandhi, in his doctrine and practice of non-violence, who showed how the principle of *abhaya* could be instilled in the people. Aung San Suu Kyi underlined this parallel to the immediate post-war era by calling the current Burmese situation 'the second struggle for national independence'.[38] It is to her role in the opening phase of this struggle that we now turn.

The Second Struggle for National Independence

On 13 March 1988 riot police were sent to deal with a small student protest. The students threw stones and, in response, the police opened fire. One student was killed. The event became the focus of much wider discontent, not only with such senseless violence, but against repressive government policies, both social and economic. During the next five days, demonstrations spread; the universities were closed, and townspeople joined the students. One writer, on the basis of twenty hours of interviews with participants in this and later opposition activities, has reported that these demonstrations involved 12,000 to 15,000 persons: over 200 were killed (including 41 officially admitted to have suffocated in a police van), and those arrested were subjected to beatings and torture; some women were raped repeatedly.[39] When the government enquiry reported on 9 May that only three students had been killed, and ignored the treatment of detainees, the whole process of spontaneous protest, often with violent outcomes, began again, now spreading beyond Rangoon, and continuing on into July and August.

The same writer has also provided evidence detailing other aspects of the military government's policy in this period, including the incitement of communal violence[40] and the extraordinary session of the Burmese Socialist Programme Party (the party Ne Win established as the basis of the one-party state following the military take-over in 1962). At that meeting Ne Win formally resigned as head of government, in a speech which both encouraged multi-party elections and supported the violent conduct of the riot police. Any impression that the government might in fact be changing was rapidly quashed by the appointment of Sein Lwin, a close associate of Ne Win, who was responsible for the first use of riot police to suppress popular protests in 1962.[41]

In retrospect it is clear that the government was hardening its position; according to the London *Times* (8 August 1989) and *Guardian* (18 August 1988), two to three thousand persons were killed by riot police during the period from 8 to 13 August; *The New York Times* (11 January 1989) cited a further thousand deaths on 18 September 1988. As Lintner details, although protests started peacefully, the participants, when confronted by police or troops, turned to violence: stones, poison darts, even beheadings. The violence spread to more than forty places all over the country, and in most of them the numbers killed have never been reported. Troops fired on staff at the Rangoon General Hospital; the secret police began a series of night raids, arresting any possible demonstration leaders in their homes; the escalation of violence, in short, proceeded on terms in which the government, with its superior arms, retained the advantage.

Despite the growing scale of the demonstrations, there remained no single, clear agenda of demands: some focused on release of detainees and compensation for the victims' families; others began to attack the accumulated wealth of the Ne Win family, and to call for elections. It was clear at least that some admission of wrongdoing on the part of government was needed if demonstrations were not to continue to grow. On 12 August, Sein Lwin resigned after a violent reign of eighteen days, and it was clear that the military was once again considering its position.

Aung San Suu Kyi's intervention begins at this crucial moment, with her open letter to the government of 15 August 1988, proposing that a consultative committee be formed, composed of respected independent persons, who would steer the country towards multi-party elections. The letter (a copy of which is included in this volume) stresses the need for restraint from violence on the part of the government and demonstrators, and the release of persons arrested. It gained the support of U Nu, the last elected Prime Minister, and other pre 1962 leaders.

Only a few days later on 26 August, the occasion of a general strike, Aung San Suu Kyi addressed a crowd of several hundred thousand people outside the Shwedagon pagoda. At the very beginning of what was to be a sustained campaign, she set out, to mass acclaim, the principles of personal commitment, discipline, unity, non-violence and the restoration of basic human rights – and especially multi-party democracy – which form her creed and the legacy of Aung San and Gandhi discussed above. Aung San Suu Kyi's emergence was duty noted in the international press:[42] the government was at this time reported as uncertain of what course to take; here, surely, in the unexpected entry of the daughter of a national hero, who expressed due regard for the military traditions of Burma, was someone to whom the military could turn?

It was not to be. For a few weeks the military experimented with a more lenient policy, but demonstrations continued to swell, and on 18 September a military council was established (the State Law and Order Restoration Council, or SLORC) to rule the country. All existing judicial institutions were abolished, meetings of more than four persons were banned, and arrangements for arrest and sentencing without trial were reaffirmed. Paradoxically, political parties were now allowed to form – provided, apparently, that they did not meet! The government policy set out in Ne Win's speech of 'resignation' was thus being carried out; and the extent to which Ne Win had really retired from the scene, or was in fact directing government policy in private, naturally became a matter of increasing popular conviction. Against this background, the Gandhian tradition of non-violent civil disobedience and unremitting action advocated by Aung San Suu Kyi acquired renewed relevance.

Aung San Suu Kyi's own role and activities increased steadily as the government tightened its grip – that is, until her house arrest on 20 July 1989. Amnesty International has noted that an estimated 3,000 political prisoners were detained between 18 September 1988 and 1 July 1989, although it has only been able to compile minimal data on 107 of them.[43] The sequence of events during this period is perhaps most easily summarized by a chronological outline summarizing the main developments.

It is important to recall, in considering this chronology, that every speech and public statement made by Aung San Suu Kyi represented an active violation of the government ban on opposition meetings and activities; and that, aside from the interviews given to the foreign press, many events in which she was involved took place in the presence of armed troops. Each event thus provided a pointed opportunity to spread her message of non-violence and human rights to an ever wider audience. The chronology shows, in addition, her remarkable ability to check the occurrence of violent confrontations, to control the less disciplined passions of her followers and to gain the endorsement of non-violent approaches from other groups. The meetings and interviews listed represent a tiny fraction of her activities or, indeed, of what was going on in the country at large. Burma remains a secretive place: it will probably be many years before we have access to the whole story.

The events included in the following chronology took place against a background of mounting arrests, official harassment, and summary executions. Much of this background is detailed in the Amnesty International report cited above, as well as in the reports of foreign correspondents and embassy officials of western governments. As the military government confiscated Aung San Suu Kyi's papers at the time of her house arrest, and have made external contact with her impossible, the chronology has been compiled on the basis of printed sources, chiefly newspapers and journals. Its main purpose is to provide a cohesive account of what would otherwise be a disparate and uneven public record.

24 September 1988: The National League for Democracy (NLD) was formed by Aung San Suu Kyi, together with Tin U and Aung Gyi, senior military officers who had previously broken with Ne Win and were for a time imprisoned by him. Its founding statement emphasized the principles enunciated by Aung San Suu Kyi in her address of 26 August. The NLD rapidly came to be regarded as the largest opposition party, with a formal membership estimated between one and three million persons.[44]

Aung San Suu Kyi appealed to the international community to condemn recent military violence against unarmed Burmese civilians, including children, Buddhist monks and students; the appeal was addressed to foreign ambassadors in Burma, and the Secretary-General of Amnesty International, suggesting that the strongest possible concern be raised in the United Nations General Assembly Debate on 27 September.[45]

16 October 1988: Aung San Suu Kyi called the attention of Amnesty International to the military government's policy of forced conscription: young men are seized, bound and transported to areas where the army is fighting insurgent forces; there the young men are used as 'porters' of military supplies, and are driven ahead of troops in order to detonate mines laid by the insurgents.

28 October 1988: An interview in *Asiaweek* magazine with prominent leaders of the second largest party, the Democratic Party for a New Society (DPNS), which is closely associated with the main student group, the All-Burma Federation of Student Unions (ABFSU), signalled their abandonment of armed struggle as their current strategy, in favour of co-operation with parties advocating non-violent means.[46]

30 October–10 November 1988: Aung San Suu Kyi toured more than fifty towns in Pegu, Magwe, Mandalay and Sagaing districts, and Shan State. 'Even in relatively small towns . . . tens of thousands of people turned out in the streets, in effect defying the ban on outdoor gatherings of more than four persons. The army, surprisingly, did not interfere; there were even reports of soldiers presenting flowers to the entourage.'[47]

3 December 1988: Aung Gyi left the NLD to establish his own party, alleging communist infiltration of the NLD. Although he was unable to substantiate his claim, it was immediately taken up by the military government. Commentators such as S. Sesser, a friend of the U Thant family and observer of the Burmese situation for many years, subsequently remarked that, in light of Aung Gyi's intimate association with Ne Win, 'there is some merit to the view that Aung Gyi might have been planted by Ne Win to discredit the opposition'.[48]

8–18 December 1988: Aung San Suu Kyi toured Moulmein and south-east Burma; she was preceded by army vehicles with loudspeakers, warning people not to receive her. Thousands of people defied that order, and the welcome she received in Moulmein was as enthusiastic as the one in the north. After her trip, thirteen local NLD workers were arrested – and on 19 December the SLORC warned the political parties 'to behave; this is not the time to incite the people . . . if [politicians] want democracy, it is necessary for them to abide by rules, orders, laws and regulations'.[49]

In this period, foreign correspondents remarked on several forms of harassment to which Aung San Suu Kyi was subjected: authorities banned NLD campaign signs; soldiers distributed crudely drawn cartoons alleging that she indulged in abnormal sexual practices and had had several husbands, etc.; repeated statements were made in the media that she was surrounded by communist advisers; and so forth.[50]

27 December 1988: Daw Khin Kyi – Aung San's widow and Aung San Suu Kyi's mother – died in Rangoon, at the age of seventy-six. In the ensuing days 20,000 people visited the family home to pay respects to Daw Khin Kyi and Aung San Suu Kyi.[51]

2 January 1989: Thousands joined in the funeral procession of Daw Khin Kyi. Before the funeral Aung San Suu Kyi appealed to her supporters to be 'calm and disciplined in sending my mother on her last journey'. No violent incidents occurred as the procession moved towards a site close to the Shwedagon Pagoda, Burma's most sacred shrine, where the body was entombed. 'What the events surrounding the funeral tell us,' said a western diplomat,

> is that Aung San Suu Kyi is bringing unity and order to her National Democracy League, which is the biggest opposition party. She has shown the army very clearly that she is no flash in the pan but a political force to be reckoned with. The size of the funeral procession and its discipline was a significant gesture of support for her. To be able to restrain the hotheads among her followers as she is doing augurs well for the future.[52]

23 January 1989: At the end of Aung San Suu Kyi's tour of the Irrawady district during mid-January, NLD spokesmen reported that thirty-two of its supporters and two supporters of the Democratic Party for a New Society were arrested in connection with non-violent gatherings to which Aung San Suu Kyi spoke. Amnesty International reported that 'most of them were reportedly later released on bail, but their current status is unknown'; Amnesty also reported that a further fifteen to twenty-five NLD members were arrested in this period.[53]

14 February 1989: After a campaign trip to the Shan State in the north-east, Aung San Suu Kyi said in an interview broadcast by the BBC that NLD activists there had been threatened that they would be arrested once she left the area. She again called for the lifting of Order Number 2/00 (banning public meetings), saying that it was a 'great obstacle' to the organizational efforts of political parties. This call was repeated in several interviews published during the remainder of the month.[54]

13 March 1989: The anniversary of the first student death was declared 'Burma Human Rights Day' by the NLD and other political parties; in addition to an NLD rally at its Rangoon office, a rally was held at Rangoon University, attended by Aung San Suu Kyi. Both rallies passed without violence, despite the presence of troops and interruptions by police loudspeakers.

25 March 1989: In an interview broadcast by All India Radio, Aung San Suu Kyi further clarified the NLD position, in response to the demands of student organizations on the formation of an interim government. She returned the discussion once again to first principles: she declared that her party was 'aiming neither for an interim government nor for the election, but [was] seeking the attainment of basic human rights as soon as possible'. She said that her party's position was that 'if these basic human rights are achieved, one of the rights – free and fair elections – will materialize'.[55]

At this time government radio reported using troops to break up an NLD supported demonstration; according to Amnesty International, the march in question was organized by high-school students, and

> both Aung San Suu Kyi and senior ABFSU figures ... counselled against staging marches because of the danger of clashes with the security forces, but had been successful ... The sources agree that fleeing students took refuge in Aung San Suu Kyi's house, as well as other private residences in the area where they hoped they would not be arrested.[56]

26 March 1989: In a further interview she expressed sympathy for students who had fled to border areas and joined armed insurgent groups. But she reiterated, 'I don't believe in the armed struggle.' She said:

> In order to have free and fair elections, we must create the kind of condition in which elections can be free and fair, which means that first of all the people must be entitled to

basic human rights and democratic freedom. We must have these basic human rights so that people are allowed to believe what they want to without fear of arrest or intervention or unfair treatment. And we must have freedom of speech, publication and assembly.[57]

At a press conference on the same day,

Aung San Suu Kyi denied the authorities' suggestions that the NLD was inciting demonstrations. At the same time she called for the release of those arrested in connection with them. She reportedly said that although some NLD supporters had been involved in the gatherings and speech-making, the party leadership had actively tried to prevent demonstrations, and emphasized that the party continued to maintain a policy of achieving democracy through peaceful means. Aung San Suu Kyi said she had consistently told young dissidents not to make defamatory statements against the armed forces, 'because there is a difference between the armed forces and those who abuse the power of the armed forces . . .' She said the NLD had often said it welcomed investigations, questions, or consultations related to any incidents raising dissatisfaction within the SLORC, but that these offers were never accepted.[58]

31 March 1989: In an interview

Aung San Suu Kyi alleged that more than 160 people had been arrested in connection with anti-military gatherings and speech-making since 14 March . . . The NLD leader estimated that more than a thousand people had been detained for political activities since September 1988, and said she believed many were held without charge and had no access to legal representation . . . March arrests 'indicate we are still a long way from the basic freedoms to take us to free and fair elections'.[59]

5 April 1989: In a further tour of Irrawaddy District the following attempt was made on Aung San Suu Kyi's life:

As she was walking down the street with some followers during a campaign visit, six soldiers under the command of an Army captain jumped down from a jeep, assumed a kneeling position, and took aim at her. She motioned her followers to wait on the sidewalk, and she herself walked down the centre of the road towards the soldiers. 'It seemed so much simpler to provide them with a single target than to bring everyone else in,' she said. 'It was at this point that a major ordered the captain to revoke the shooting orders.' [60]

18–19 April 1989: In a press conference to mark the Burmese New Year, Aung San Suu Kyi 'called for a dialogue between the military government and the opposition parties, a request that has so far been refused by the army'. She also 'criticized foreign businessmen for dealing with the government and "coming to do business when it is a matter of life and death for all of us"'.[61]

24 April 1989: In a BBC interview,

Aung San Suu Kyi reiterated that it was not the intention of the NLD 'to cause a rift between the Defence Forces and the people, and we do not want the Defence Forces to break up', but complained that 'one traditional chorus group after another is being arrested, probably because they criticized the government'.[62]

(During the traditional New Year celebrations, NLD members staged political satires depicting the lack of democracy, in front of party headquarters in Rangoon.)

21 May 1989: In an interview, Aung San Suu Kyi expressed support for the reopening of schools (closed since August 1988), provided that the authorities created a peaceful atmosphere.

While reiterating her long-standing call for an end to restrictions on freedom of assembly and opinion, Aung San Suu Kyi also continued to counsel students and others against

organizing possibly unruly mass gatherings or attacking the
military and government unfairly . . . She said her speeches
explained 'that democracy doesn't just mean demonstrations' and that 'freedom of speech doesn't mean freedom to
abuse anyone you feel like abusing'. She said that while
'working for basic human rights', she also used her speeches
to emphasize the need for 'discipline', and that she was
committed to working within the guidelines laid down by
the military authorities, as long as she was convinced it was
ready to hold free and fair elections.[63]

2 June 1989: Military spokesmen announced that the martial law
regime would remain even after the elections scheduled for May
1990; it would not relinquish its right to rule until parliament
had decided on a new constitution and form of government under
that constitution. Aung San Suu Kyi responded to this by saying
that the NLD could not participate in elections 'until the question of
power transfer is resolved'; and that the 'NLD had always said and
accepted the fact that there are officers within the Defence Forces
who are good, who prefer freedom of movement for democracy in
accordance with the people's desire, and who wish the Defence
Forces would remain neutral with dignity'. She declared that the
NLD had 'no desire whatever to confront the Defence Forces'.[64]

5 June 1989: In response to the military government's announcement of restrictions on printing and distributing opposition statements, Aung San Suu Kyi 'said she believed that the NLD and
other legally registered political parties had the right to publish
documents, and that her party would continue to do so since this
was its main form of communication with the public'. The NLD
position was that the 'law should be interpreted as giving political
parties the right to print and publish freely, and that it would
therefore ignore the authorities' efforts to require it to obtain
their approval before publishing party materials'.[65]

21 June 1989: A memorial service was held at the NLD headquarters in Rangoon, after which wreaths were laid at Myenigon

Circle, where protestors in past months had been killed. Aung San Suu Kyi was briefly detained by security forces, during which time a conflict broke out between demonstrators and police; shots were fired, killing one person (as it turned out, a member of the government party). Aung San Suu Kyi later condemned the military for breaking up what had been a peaceful ceremony; 'if the military resort(s) to arms every time anniversaries are held for those who died during pro-democracy movements, the shedding of blood will never end'. She claimed that the authorities were 'trying to imply that we were trying to incite unrest, but it's nothing like that . . . We are not interested in that.' 'Unless there are human rights and democratic freedoms, I don't think these elections are going to be the kind of elections we want.'[66]

22 June 1989: The military government published an eight-page special press supplement, 'devoted mainly to denouncing the NLD as communist-inspired and accusing Aung San Suu Kyi of everything from blasphemy to trying to split the army'.[67] At this time government radio cited her as saying:

> There are two sides within the Defence Forces; one side represents the Defence Force personnel who honourably stand on the side of the people, while the dishonourable ones only strive to prolong their hold on power. We shall have to do a lot to influence them. Some stand openly on the side of people while others do so in a reserved way, and there are also others who oppose the people.

Official radio further cited Aung San Suu Kyi as saying:

> The issue of reopening the schools should be reconsidered as it could give rise to renewed disturbances . . . when the schools reopened she would not like to tell the students either to attend or not to attend . . . but those who attend as well as those who do not attend schools are to wage a struggle for democracy.

Referring to a meeting on 17 June in Sanchaung township, the broadcast described Aung San Suu Kyi as saying that 'the people should observe laws that are just but should not obey laws that are unjust . . . the NLD would stand on the side of the people and defy authority'. According to the broadcast, all of the above remarks constituted evidence of 'fomenting disturbances and [encouraging] the people and children to defy authority'. In reply, Aung San Suu Kyi told journalists 'that she and her party were anti-communist'; she reportedly admitted that some NLD figures had previously been communists or had communist connections, but said that all of them had already rejected this ideology and were no longer party members.[68]

26 June 1989: Aung San Suu Kyi further responded, in a press conference,

> by charging that General Ne Win, [who is] still widely believed to control Burma behind the scenes, was responsible for alienating the army from the people, fashioning the military into a body responsive solely to him . . . She also denied she was a communist or sacrilegious, and reminded the country's military leaders of two Buddhist precepts, against lying and killing. She said the National League would continue to print uncensored political pamphlets, defying recent military government restrictions, because such printing rights were guaranteed under a 1962 law. In addition she announced plans to commemorate other important dates in Burmese history: July 7, when, in 1962, the government blew up the building housing the Rangoon Students Union; July 19, Martyrs' Day, when, in 1947, her father was assassinated . . . August 8, when, last year, the army opened fire on unarmed demonstrators, and unleashed a week of military slaughter; September 18, when, last year, the military officially assumed power amid a wave of shootings. And she invited the Burmese military leaders to join hands with her, in an effort to prevent further disturbances.[69]

344 Freedom from Fear

Amnesty International added that Aung San Suu Kyi 'reportedly said that basic human and democratic rights were currently "being eroded bit by bit" and that "repressive acts [were] getting worse", so it was the duty of everyone to "defy unlawful commands in the present struggle for democracy"'. She also reportedly vowed that she and the NLD would be 'disciplined and systematic', specifying that 'We shall not resort to unjust or secretive measures or instigate violence.' She denied that she was trying to split the military, but reiterated her belief that 'some elements in the military and SLORC were against all forces of democracy' because they hoped to enable Ne Win to retain power. 'The opinion of all our people,' she continued, was 'that U Ne Win is still creating all the problems in this country.'[70]

30 June 1989: SLORC spokesmen reiterated that Aung San Suu Kyi's tours, meetings and speeches constituted violation of the ban on public gatherings, and hence constituted attempts to create disturbances. They cited speeches made at Myenigon (21 June), various places in Rangoon (22 and 23 June), Bago (23–24 June), Insein (25 June) and Tamwe (29 June), and warned that 'effective action' would be taken to stop such activities.[71]

At about this time, Aung Lwin and Tin Win, members of NLD Executive Committee, were arrested; Amnesty International has cited both as prisoners of conscience who have not been released.

In an interview at about this time Aung San Suu Kyi

> continued her criticisms of Ne Win and again denied allegations of communist influence over the NLD . . . She said allegations about communist influence were part of an effort by some military leaders to create suspicions about her and the NLD among other elements in the army, explaining that 'having fought the communist insurgents for years and years and years, the army has very strong feelings about communism'.[72]

2 July 1989:

> Aung San Suu Kyi reportedly spoke to a peaceful gathering of some three thousand people. About one hundred NLD members are said to have urged the crowd to refrain from causing any disturbances and to have directed traffic. Student activists were apparently absent from the gathering, and there was no shouting of slogans or any expression of anti-government sentiment. In her speech, Aung San Suu Kyi reportedly made no direct criticism of the military government, but objected to the authorities' restrictions on the publication of printed material.[73]

3 July 1989:

> Aung San Suu Kyi reportedly spoke to a peaceful gathering of some 10,000 people who assembled near Sule Pagoda Road in [Rangoon's] Pabedan Township. Hundreds more people are said to have crowded the balconies of buildings along the street as Aung San Suu Kyi spoke from the NLD township office. She is said to have urged military authorities to meet political parties to 'thrash out existing misunderstandings' and 'to use political means to solve political problems rather than the force of authority'. She is said to have pointed to the peaceful crowd as proof people did not want violence, declaring: 'If there is no provocation, people can gather peacefully without any disruption.' She exhorted the crowd to support the movement for democracy 'with discipline and courage', and neither to expect to 'get democracy overnight' nor to settle for 'pseudo-democracy'.

Aung San Suu Kyi's 3 July call for a dialogue between political parties and the military authorities came on the same day that she was reportedly designated by a group of opposition parties as their representative for such talks. In a statement issued that day, the parties declared their belief that the chances for elections in May 1990 were 'in danger of fading away' because of what they described as the 'repressive actions of the SLORC'. The statement reportedly said a 'timely and suitable political solution' needed to be found to 'prevent further deterioration of the situation' and called for a dialogue 'as a first step' towards this.[74]

5 July 1989: 'Aung San Suu Kyi spoke to a crowd estimated at more than 10,000 people who gathered in [Rangoon's] Chinatown district. She reportedly reiterated demands for democratic change and protested against harassment and arrest of NLD members.'[75]

5 July 1989:

> Aung San Suu Kyi gave speeches in [Rangoon's] Pazundaung and Bothathaung Townships, which she estimated attracted audiences of 10,000 and 20,000 ... she reportedly asked NLD followers to continue to adhere to a 'peaceful, non-confrontational' struggle for democracy. Declaring that the party was planning to go ahead with memorial activities on 7 July, she said they would be peaceful and that their purpose was not 'to make confrontation'. Instead, she said 'the spirit to hold the commemoration is just so we can take lessons from the past'.[76]

At this time SLORC Chairman General Saw Maung appealed specifically to Aung San Suu Kyi not to infringe on the ban against public meetings.

7 July 1989: Aung San Suu Kyi and Tin U addressed a meeting at the NLD headquarters, to mark the anniversary.

> About two hundred people attended the meeting, including representatives of about seventy other political parties many of whom are allied with the NLD ... Foreign news media reports said 'several thousand' people gathered as she spoke. According to an NLD spokeswoman, Aung San Suu Kyi spoke of the hopelessness of the authorities' efforts to solve problems by force, as several truckloads of armed troops stood by in the vicinity.[77]

8 July 1989: In an interview

Aung San Suu Kyi explained that the NLD had decided not to participate in the student demonstrations on 7 July because it believed demonstrations were 'not the only way to carry out the struggle' or for people to show how they felt about the authorities. She reiterated that the NLD did 'not want violence', but refused to rule out the possibility of its participation in street demonstrations, saying that its commitment to non-violence did 'not mean we are going to sit back weakly and do nothing'. She also said that the party would not use 'communist methods', but would employ civil disobedience. She said that this type of political activity had 'a great history' and pointed out that she had recently begun putting forward Mahatma Gandhi and Martin Luther King as models in her speeches. She reiterated her belief that U Ne Win was behind the SLORC's refusal to hold a dialogue with the opposition. She declared that the NLD wanted 'the army to realize that they have been made to play the role of thugs, to make sure that a few old men can remain in power'. She said: 'We want the army to remain neutral. That is what a professional army ought to do.'[78]

10 July 1989: In an interview

Aung San Suu Kyi confirmed that the NLD was still planning to hold gatherings to mark such dates as her father's assassination, the resignation of U Ne Win . . . the demonstrations and killings of 8 August 1988, and the military coup of 18 September. She reportedly again stressed that these gatherings would be based on the NLD's principle of non-violence, and that the party was not seeking any confrontation with the security forces. She said the NLD wanted a democracy movement that was 'strong, but in a peaceful and disciplined way', adding: 'We don't want violence.'

On the same day Aung San Suu Kyi spoke to a crowd near Rangoon's Sule Pagoda which she estimated at 30,000, vowing that her party was going to continue its campaign of civil disobedience against what she described as 'unjust laws'. She declared: 'What I mean by defying authority is non-acceptance of unlawful orders meant to suppress the people.' However, she also said that 'at the moment our civil disobedience consists in putting out as many pamphlets as possible in defiance of the SLORC'. She added, 'There's nothing violent about it. It's no more violent than is necessary in banging the keys of a typewriter.' In this speech she continued to criticize U Ne Win and alleged that he remained politically powerful. She said her party was 'convinced that U Ne Win is still pulling the strings from behind Saw Maung'.[79]

16 July 1989: Aung San Suu Kyi said that her own and other opposition parties would go ahead with plans for their own Martyrs' Day ceremonies on 19 July and other anniversary gatherings despite the repeated warnings from the government. According to foreign news media interviews, she declared: 'We don't have any intention to seek a confrontation . . . We do not want any trouble . . . We intend to carry on peacefully with our rallies . . . We will continue to hold anniversaries . . . to protest the use of arms to solve political problems.' She added she expected that political arrests would continue on a daily basis up to 19 July and increase thereafter. According to foreign news media reports, she and other top NLD figures expected that those likely to be arrested soon included herself and other members of the party's original Executive Committee. This body was therefore expanded from nine to thirteen members in the hope that the authorities would not be able to detain the entire party leadership.[80]

The SLORC at this time announced further regulations 'allowing military officers, even those of junior rank, to arrest political protesters and administer one of three sentences on the spot: three years at hard labour, life imprisonment, or execution'.[81]

17 July 1989: Aung San Suu Kyi said in an interview that the new regulations allowing summary trials by military tribunals were 'part of a series of repressive measures which have been taken against the people'. She said NLD members, students and young people were still 'going to go to the Martyrs' Mausoleum and lay wreaths' in a 'very quiet and peaceful' way. She added that in her view 'people are fed up with all these restrictions and of course all the arrests'. She promised that NLD members would not create problems on Martyrs' Day, but warned, 'there's always the possibility of problems if armed troops are running around'.[82]

18 July 1989: Aung San Suu Kyi responded to the authorities' allegations about NLD involvement in bombing incidents. She reportedly said that acts of terrorism were 'entirely against the principles of our party'. She added that the NLD accepted 'the possibility' that those detained 'could well be NLD members who have taken to such acts', but that the party condemned the bombings 'very, very strongly', and that if they were indeed guilty they would be expelled from the party.[83]

19 July 1989: In anticipation of NLD and other opposition ceremonies on Martyrs' Day, the SLORC deployed several thousand additional troops in Rangoon, bringing in an estimated twelve light infantry battalions. A 6 a.m. to 6 p.m. curfew was also ordered. The NLD decided to cancel its march; in so doing,

> it believed it was acting to save lives, because it 'had no intention of leading our people straight into a killing field'. The NLD had issued a warning that people should stay indoors to 'let the world know that under this military administration we are prisoners in our own country' . . . Aung San Suu Kyi said the army 'could easily have found an excuse to open fire' on marchers. She expressed her belief that the authorities had shown that 'the only way they know how to handle the situation is by bringing out force and more force' . . . She added that the NLD considered the main aim of its recent activities was to oblige the

authorities to observe the rule of law by organizing people to 'ask for basic human rights [and] democratic freedom'.[84]

Amnesty International has noted that

despite the official curfew and the NLD's call for people to stay off the streets, some 3,000 mostly young people reportedly attempted to march to a statue of Aung San near [Rangoon's] Kandawgyi Lake to lay wreaths. The NLD reportedly denied they were party members. They are said to have dropped wreaths in the road when soldiers armed with automatic rifles, grenade launchers and truncheons chased them away with a baton charge and beat some of them. According to one account, an eyewitness said he saw 'about twenty-five or so soldiers advance . . . in line' with 'bayonets levelled' at one group, which they 'pursued down a side street'. He said that soldiers dragged some of them out and beat them, and that he 'saw about fifteen or twenty picked up and put in a truck'.[85]

20 July 1989: According to Amnesty International, in the military build-up for Martyrs' Day, eleven truckloads of troops were stationed outside Aung San Suu Kyi's home. When she tried to leave to pay a private visit to the Martyrs' Mausoleum, she was prevented from doing so, and forced back inside. The military government announced that she and NLD Chairman, Tin U, were being placed under house arrest for a period of up to twelve months, during which they would have access only to immediate family members. Their telephones and all other means of communication were cut. Meanwhile the authorities began arresting other members of the NLD Executive Committee. After this new wave of arrests, the London *Times* estimated that as many as two thousand NLD supporters were in prison. Amnesty International was able to identify six members of the Executive Committee as imprisoned, as well as Aung San Suu Kyi's immediate staff.[86] *The New York Times* cited US Embassy statements of 'credible, first-hand reports of routine and sometimes fatal mistreatment of pro-democracy figures in custody. The abuses reportedly include beatings and torture.'[87]

Aung San Suu Kyi, in response to her house arrest, 'demanded a transfer to Insein jail in Rangoon and asked to be kept under the same conditions as supporters who were arrested as part of the crackdown on her party'.[88] She immediately began a hunger strike when her request was ignored. The strike, during which she accepted water only, lasted twelve days. The military government explicitly denied that her hunger strike was taking place, although it was widely reported in the international media. Her strike stopped only upon her 'receiving solemn assurances from the [Burmese] authorities that her supporters were not being subjected to inhuman interrogation and that their cases would be dealt with by due process of law'.[89]

The Popular Mandate Denied

Aung San Suu Kyi's hunger strike was described at the time as 'the most serious challenge the Burmese military government has faced'.[90] Forty of her supporters similarly marked the anniversary of the 8 August massacre with a fast at the NLD office in Rangoon. They demanded the release of Aung San Suu Kyi and reiterated NLD appeals for political freedom.[91] Buddhist monks on the same day took advantage of a feature of their monastic routine which the military could scarcely obstruct: they turned out in a show of large numbers on the streets, ostensibly as part of their daily round of receiving food from the faithful – staging what was seen as a silent march in protest at the government clampdown.[92]

However, as these examples show, once the compelling force of Aung San Suu Kyi's imaginative leadership was removed, the opposition was reduced to isolated and for the most part symbolic gestures. The government thenceforward concentrated on tightening its grip. Tin U, Aung San Suu Kyi's associate and NLD Chairman, was sentenced to three years hard labour. U Nu and the leaders of his small party were rounded up and also put under house arrest. The ban on political meetings and the censorship of election pamphlets could now be effectively enforced. Western journalists were banned. The campaign of vilification against Aung San Suu Kyi continued, without her being given opportunity of reply. Her name was struck off the list of eligible candidates for the election.[93] When her husband, Dr Michael Aris, arrived in Burma to visit her, he was apprehended by the military at the airport; all information as to his whereabouts and condition was refused, despite repeated protests by British and other western embassies. The world only learned that Aung San Suu Kyi had survived her hunger strike when he was at last allowed to meet with embassy officials in the presence of military personnel. In fact, the government did not mistreat Dr Aris, only confining him to house arrest together with Aung San Suu Kyi. However, after January 1990 they have refused to allow him or any other family members to visit her. Their teenage sons have been deprived of their Burmese citizenship. Since July 1990 even postal contact with her has been broken off.

By its own heavy-handed tactics, the military appears to have convinced itself that it was actually succeeding in stifling the desire for human rights, and that, in the apparent absence of Aung San Suu Kyi and her senior associates, the people would have no option but to vote for the military's own National Unity Party (NUP). Foreign journalists (although not Burmese specialists) were allowed into the country to observe the election and, in the event, were able to confirm that the military, despite its conduct to that point, made no attempt to intimidate voters on election day. Nor was tampering with voting boxes reported.[94]

The result was an overwhelming victory for the NLD, which took more than 80 per cent of the seats; parties allied to the NLD, notably the United Nationalities League for Democracy (the UNLD, representing non-Burman ethnic minorities), took nearly 14 per cent. The NUP failed to win any seats in Rangoon, even losing those in which military voters vastly outnumbered civilians, and in which its party leader was the candidate. The situation was summed up by a western diplomat who remarked: 'Burmese throughout the country were often unaware of the NLD

candidate they were actually voting for. But they had all heard of
Aung San Suu Kyi. It was yes to her and no to Ne Win . . .'[95]
Aung San Suu Kyi's influence was unmistakable in one of the
most important features of the poll: 'There was not a single
reported incident of violence or misbehaviour on the part of the
public on election day. The Burmese went to the polls with unity
and dignity.'[96]

The election, however, did nothing to stop the military government's monopoly of force. It waited until just before the first
anniversary of Aung San Suu Kyi's arrest to announce formally
that all opposition to its policies remained forbidden, and that, as
far as it was concerned, the election did not alter its monopoly of
legal as well as military power. Small popular demonstrations
none the less marked the anniversary of Aung San Suu Kyi's
arrest and the second anniversary of the 8 August massacre. In
Mandalay, troops opened fire on a small 8 August rally, killing at
least two students and two monks, and leading to a major
nationwide boycott by monks, who refused to administer religious
services to the military, the police and their families. On 29
August the NLD and UNLD jointly called on the government
to convene parliament, to lift restrictions on human rights and to
release Aung San Suu Kyi and Tin U.

The military government responded characteristically to these
several developments. Claiming that the monks' boycott was
communist inspired, monasteries were raided, some religious organizations banned, and many monks imprisoned under threat of
the death sentence. According to Amnesty International,[97] between October 1990 and January 1991 'more than 25 members
of parliament representing the NLD were reported to have been
sentenced to terms of imprisonment ranging from 10 to 25 years
. . . Throughout 1990 reports of torture and ill-treatment of
prisoners were received from prisons in urban centres and in
ethnic minority areas.' Civilians continued to be forcibly con-
scripted as porters by government forces, and used by troops as
'human minesweepers'. At the end of October 1990 only four of
the members of the Central Executive Committee of the NLD
remained at liberty.

There has been widespread international condemnation of the military's continuing policy of repression, and of its attempt to deny the popular mandate given to Aung San Suu Kyi and the NLD in the elections of May 1990. While member countries of the European Community, Japan and the United States have withdrawn all programmes of bilateral aid to Burma, and called repeatedly for the transfer of power to the elected parliament,[98] Amnesty International and the media have, as noted, continued to document the pattern of arrest, torture and denial of human rights for which the military government is responsible. In September 1990 the European Community led an eighteen-nation protest (with Australia, Canada, Japan, New Zealand, Sweden and the United States) against human rights violations in Burma. All arms sales to Burma from these countries have been placed under strict embargo. The British government has condemned in particular the treatment of Aung San Suu Kyi, especially the refusal of visits from her husband and children. In May 1991 the British Foreign Secretary, Douglas Hurd, speaking at a meeting between the European Community and ASEAN (Association of South East Asian Nations) reiterated the Community's concern at the abuse of human rights in Burma, and sought active support from ASEAN in observing the arms embargo.[99]

There can be little question that international awareness of the situation in Burma was changed dramatically by the emergence of the cohesive movement for human rights led by Aung San Suu Kyi. Her presence has, more than anything else, concentrated the world's attention on the problems there, and has continued to do so, as the award of the Sakharov Prize and the Rafto Prize, and the Nobel Peace Prize for 1991, clearly indicate. The military government, very conscious of her continuing power to influence events, has offered to release her on condition that she agrees to forsake her campaign for human rights, and leave Burma. This offer she has not deemed worthy even of consideration, despite the very real personal danger in which she remains.

In the course of the last three years, Aung San Suu Kyi has had to lead not only her people but the western world as well through a considerable learning process. In the early days of her campaign, the media found themselves casting about, often wildly and superficially, for some category in which to put her. The English press proposed that she was like Benazir Bhutto or Corazon Aquino – but at the same time had to admit that, unlike these women leaders, she inherited no party organization, and that the Burmese military government (unlike those of General Zia and President Marcos) was still very much in control. More important, the appeal of such leaders was not based on non-violent struggle. In the American press, Aung San Suu Kyi was compared both to George Washington and Jane Fonda. The French press suggested that Burma was an 'Asian Poland', and that Aung San Suu Kyi was like La Pasionara, the Spanish Republican leader. Such bizarre comparisons seem now to have been replaced by a recognition of Aung San Suu Kyi as a different kind of figure, a person whose international stature has to be defined in primarily moral terms, and that it is by the conviction and application of her vision of human rights in Burma that a sea change in the situation there has become possible. Perhaps Aung San Suu Kyi's hunger strike is the crucial reminder in all of this that the model, in her case, is a very different one. At the time of her hunger strike, the London *Times* referred to Aung San Suu Kyi simply as 'Burma's Gandhi'.[100]

Notes

1 J. F. Cady, *A History of Modern Burma*, Ithaca, NY, 1958, pp. 536–59; M. Collis, *Last and First in Burma, 1941–1948*, London, 1956, pp. 261–91; J. Silverstein, *Burmese Politics: The Dilemma of National Unity*, New Brunswick, NJ, 1980, pp. 93–144; F. N. Trager, *Burma: From Kingdom to Republic*, London, 1966, pp. 43–68.

2 B. Lintner, *Outrage: Burma's Struggle for Democracy*, Hong Kong, 1989 (2nd edn, London and Bangkok, 1990), pp. 56–8, 74–8. Pages cited here and below are from the first edition.

3 Estimates vary, albeit within a consistent range. French newspapers (e.g. *Le Monde*, 9 September 1989; *Télégramme*, 27 August 1989) cited 1,000 to 3,000 deaths; *The New York Times* having initially cited 1,000 deaths on 11 January 1989 revised its estimate to 3,000 on 22 July 1989, a figure which agrees with reports in the *Wall Street Journal*, 9

September 1989, the *Financial Times*, 9 August 1989, *The Times*, 8 August 1989, and the *Guardian*, 18 August 1988. J. Silverstein, *The New York Times*, 15 September 1989, noted that more students were killed by the military in Burma between 8 August and 18 September 1988 than in Peking during the student unrest there. Extensive eyewitness accounts have been published in the *New Yorker*, 9 October 1989, and in Lintner, *Outrage*, passim. *Time* magazine, 14 August 1989, and the London *Times* puts arrests in the month of July 1989 alone at 2,000 – a figure which refers only to members of the National League for Democracy, and not to the population as a whole. It seems very likely that these figures significantly underestimate the true number of deaths, since they refer only to figures for riot police and army activity on a few separate occasions; they take account neither of events in cities other than Rangoon, nor of deaths of persons in detention (see n. 4 below).

4 E.g. 'US Embassy Reports Torture in Burmese Jails', *The New York Times*, 24 August 1989.

5 Amnesty International, 'Myanmar' (Report of the European Community Representative, Brussels), July 1991.

6 *The Times*, 6 August 1989; Amnesty International, *Myanmar (Burma): Prisoners of Conscience. A Chronicle of Developments since September 1988*, November 1989, p. 13 (hereafter AI 1989).

7 *New Yorker*, 9 October 1989, p. 90.

8 *Time International*, 11 June 1990.

9 B. Lintner, *Aung San Suu Kyi and Burma's Unfinished Renaissance*, Bangkok, 1990, p. 28.

10 Ibid., p. 29; J. Silverstein, 'Aung San Suu Kyi', this volume, pp. 276–7; *Time International*, 11 June 1990.

11 Silverstein, this volume, p. 277; Statement of the State Law and Order Restoration Council (SLORC) on 2 June 1989, reported in AI 1989.

12 Lintner, *Aung San Suu*, pp. 196–215.

13 *Far Eastern Economic Review*, 11 May 1989.

14 On the meaning of *bogyoke*, see Aung San Suu Kyi, 'The True Meaning of *Boh*', this volume, pp. 186–91.

15 J. Silverstein (ed. and contrib.), *The Political Legacy of Aung San*, Cornell University Southeast Asia Program, Data Paper 86, Ithaca, NY, 1972.

16 N. Tarling, *The Fourth Anglo-Burmese War*, Gaya, 1987, p. 325.

17 *The New York Times*, 11 January 1989; English translation of the speech delivered in Burmese by Aung San Suu Kyi to a mass rally, 26 August 1988, this volume, pp. 198–204.

18 AI 1989, p. 59.
19 *Financial Times*, 24 October 1988.
20 See this volume, pp. 3–38.
21 See this volume, pp. 82–139, 140–64.
22 *Independent*, 31 August 1988.
23 Ibid., 12 September 1988.
24 Lintner, *Aung San Suu*, p. 158.
25 *Spectator*, 12 August 1989.
26 Aung San Suu Kyi, 'Intellectual Life in Burma and India', this volume, pp. 107–8.
27 Ibid., pp. 108ff.
28 Ibid., pp. 124–5.
29 Ibid., p. 126; Aung San Suu Kyi, 'My Father', this volume, p. 5.
30 Aung San Suu Kyi, 'Intellectual Life in Burma and India', this volume, p. 129.
31 Ibid., pp. 130–31.
32 Ibid., p. 131.
33 Ibid., p. 135.
34 *Le Monde*, 26 August 1988; *Time* magazine, 14 August 1989; *Far Eastern Economic Review*, 11 May 1989. The United Nations General Assembly approved Least Developed Country status for Burma on 11 December 1987.
35 Aung San Suu Kyi, 'Intellectual Life in Burma and India', this volume, p. 128.
36 Aung San Suu Kyi, 'Freedom from Fear', this volume, p. 183.
37 Ibid., pp. 180–85.
38 Aung San Suu Kyi, speech of 26 August 1989, this volume, p. 199.
39 Lintner, *Aung San Suu*, pp. 9–23, 100–101, 116–17.
40 Ibid., pp. 112–15.
41 Ibid., pp. 116–21.
42 E.g. *Independent*, 31 August 1988; *Financial Times*, 24 October 1988; *Le Monde*, 9 September 1988; *Indian Express*, 31 August 1988; *Télégramme*, 27 August 1988.
43 AI 1989, pp. 8–9.
44 *Wall Street Journal*, 9 August 1989; *Financial Times*, 9 September 1989; AI 1989, pp. 14–15.
45 See this volume, p. 214–17.
46 *Asiaweek*, 28 October 1988; AI 1989, p. 12.
47 Lintner, *Aung San Suu*, p. 224.
48 *New Yorker*, 9 October 1989, p. 91.

49 Lintner, *Aung San Suu*, p. 224.
50 E.g. *New Yorker*, 9 October 1989, p. 91; *Independent*, 2 May 1989.
51 *The New York Times*, 11 January 1989.
52 *The Times*, 3 January 1989.
53 AI 1989, pp. 22–3.
54 Ibid., p. 23.
55 Ibid., pp. 25–6.
56 Ibid., p. 36.
57 *Bangkok Post*, 26 March 1989; AI 1989, p. 26.
58 AI 1989, pp. 35–6.
59 Ibid., p. 38.
60 *New Yorker*, 9 October 1989, p. 92; *Independent*, 13 April 1989; *Far Eastern Economic Review*, 11 May 1989.
61 *Guardian*, 11 April 1989.
62 AI 1989, p. 40.
63 Ibid., pp. 42–3.
64 Ibid., pp. 46–7.
65 Ibid., p. 45.
66 Ibid., pp. 48–9.
67 *Asian Wall Street Journal*, 28 June 1989.
68 AI 1989, pp. 49–52.
69 *Asian Wall Street Journal*, 28 June 1989.
70 AI 1989, p. 53.
71 Ibid., pp. 53–4.
72 Ibid., p. 55.
73 Ibid., p. 55.
74 Ibid., p. 56.
75 Ibid., p. 57.
76 Ibid., pp. 57–8.
77 Ibid., p. 59.
78 Ibid., p. 59.
79 Ibid., pp. 59–60.
80 Ibid., pp. 60–61.
81 *New Yorker*, 9 October 1989, p. 95.
82 AI 1989, p. 64.
83 Ibid., p. 64.
84 Ibid., p. 65.
85 Ibid., p. 66.
86 Ibid., pp. 66–7.
87 *The New York Times*, 24 August 1989.
88 *The Times*, 29 July 1989.
89 AI 1989, p. 69.

90 *The Times*, 6 August 1989.
91 AI 1989, p. 70.
92 *Christian Science Monitor*, 14 August 1989.
93 Silverstein, this volume, p. 276.
94 Lintner, *Aung San Suu*, p. 28.
95 *Time International*, 11 June 1990.
96 Lintner, *Aung San Suu*, p. 28.
97 Amnesty International, 'Myanmar', 1991 (see n. 5 above).
98 European Political Co-operation, 'Statement on Burma', press release of the European Community, Brussels, 27 May 1991.
99 Foreign and Commonwealth Office, London, press release, 30 May 1991.
100 *The Times*, 8 August 1989.

28

The Spirit of Reconciliation

Aung San Suu Kyi read the following statement on 11 July 1995 at her first press conference after nearly six years of detention. She had been notified of her release the day before.

The official intimation of the end of my house arrest was conveyed to me verbally by Colonel Kyaw Win in the form of a message from Senior General Than Shwe which was signed and ordered. There were three points to the message apart from the ending of my house arrest:

- They would be happy to help me in matters of personal welfare.
- If I wished, the authorities would continue to take care of security arrangements.
- He would like me to help towards securing peace and stability in the country.

First of all I would like to say that I appreciate deeply both the tone and the content of the message. I have always believed that the future stability and happiness of our nation depends entirely on the readiness of all parties to work towards reconciliation. During the years that I spent under house arrest many parts of the world have undergone almost unbelievable change, and all changes for the better were brought about through dialogue. So dialogue has undoubtedly been the key to a happy resolution of long-festering problems.

Once bitter enemies in South Africa are now working together for the betterment of the people. Why can't we look forward to a similar process? We have to choose between dialogue and utter devastation. I would like to believe that the human instinct for survival alone, if nothing else, would eventually lead all of us to prefer dialogue.

You may ask: 'What are we going to talk about, once we reach the negotiation table?' Establishment of certain principles, recognition of critical objectives to be achieved, and joint approaches to the ails besetting the country will be the main items on the agenda.

Extreme viewpoints are not confined to any particular group, and it is the responsibility of the leaders to control such elements as threaten the spirit of reconciliation. There is more in common between the authorities and we of the democratic forces in Burma than existed between the black and white peoples of South Africa. The majority of the people of Burma believe in the market economy and in democracy, as was amply proved by the results of the elections of 1990.

Those of you who read the Burmese newspapers will know that it is the main aim of the State Law and Order Restoration Council to return power to the people. This is exactly our aim as well.

I would like to take this opportunity to urge the authorities to release those of us who still remain in prison. I am happy to be able to say that in spite of all that we have undergone, the forces for democracy remain strong and dedicated. I, on my part, bear no resentment against anybody for anything that has happened to me during the last six years.

This statement can only end in one way – with an expression of sincere thanks to people all over the world, especially to my countrymen, for all they have done to strengthen my resolve and effect my release.

Contributors

Philip Kreager is a Wellcome Trust Fellow in the Faculty of Modern History, Oxford University. He has been a lecturer at the London School of Economics, and a librarian and consultant to the Indian Institute in Oxford.

Ann Pasternak Slater is a Fellow in English at St Anne's College, Oxford. She is the author of *Shakespeare the Director* and the translator of *A Vanished Present: The Memoirs of Alexander Pasternak*. Her mother was the sister of Boris Pasternak, winner of the Nobel Prize for Literature in 1958. She is married to the poet Craig Raine and lives in Oxford with their four children.

Josef Silverstein is Professor of Political Science, Rutgers University, New Jersey. He is the author and editor of several books on Burma, including *The Political Legacy of Aung San* (Cornell University Southeast Asia Program monograph), *Burma: Military Rule and the Politics of Stagnation* (Cornell University Press) and *Burmese Politics: The Dilemma of National Unity* (Rutgers University Press). He was a Fulbright Lecturer at Mandalay University in 1961–2 and Director of the Institute of Southeast Asian Studies, Singapore 1970–72.

Ma Than E is a retired senior staff member of the United Nations Secretariat whom Aung San Suu Kyi has long referred to as 'my emergency aunt'. After the Second World War she came to know her parents well and has remained a close friend of the family ever since. While Ma Than E pursued a varied career as an international civil servant in many countries, in Burma she is widely remembered as a much-loved popular singer who performed under the name of Bilat-Pyan-Than ('Than Who Returned from England'). She now lives in retirement in Austria.

Index

Discover more about our forthcoming books through Penguin's FREE newspaper...

Penguin
Quarterly

It's packed with:

- exciting features

- author interviews

- previews & reviews

- books from your favourite films & TV series

- exclusive competitions & much, much more...

Write off for your free copy today to:
Dept JC
Penguin Books Ltd
FREEPOST
West Drayton
Middlesex
UB7 0BR
NO STAMP REQUIRED

READ MORE IN PENGUIN

In every corner of the world, on every subject under the sun, Penguin represents quality and variety – the very best in publishing today.

For complete information about books available from Penguin – including Puffins, Penguin Classics and Arkana – and how to order them, write to us at the appropriate address below. Please note that for copyright reasons the selection of books varies from country to country.

In the United Kingdom: Please write to *Dept. EP, Penguin Books Ltd, Bath Road, Harmondsworth, West Drayton, Middlesex UB7 ODA*

In the United States: Please write to *Consumer Sales, Penguin USA, P.O. Box 999, Dept. 17109, Bergenfield, New Jersey 07621-0120.* VISA and MasterCard holders call 1-800-253-6476 to order Penguin titles

In Canada: Please write to *Penguin Books Canada Ltd, 10 Alcorn Avenue, Suite 300, Toronto, Ontario M4V 3B2*

In Australia: Please write to *Penguin Books Australia Ltd, P.O. Box 257, Ringwood, Victoria 3134*

In New Zealand: Please write to *Penguin Books (NZ) Ltd, Private Bag 102902, North Shore Mail Centre, Auckland 10*

In India: Please write to *Penguin Books India Pvt Ltd, 706 Eros Apartments, 56 Nehru Place, New Delhi 110 019*

In the Netherlands: Please write to *Penguin Books Netherlands bv, Postbus 3507, NL-1001 AH Amsterdam*

In Germany: Please write to *Penguin Books Deutschland GmbH, Metzlerstrasse 26, 60594 Frankfurt am Main*

In Spain: Please write to *Penguin Books S. A., Bravo Murillo 19, 1° B, 28015 Madrid*

In Italy: Please write to *Penguin Italia s.r.l., Via Felice Casati 20, I–20124 Milano*

In France: Please write to *Penguin France S. A., 17 rue Lejeune, F–31000 Toulouse*

In Japan: Please write to *Penguin Books Japan, Ishikiribashi Building, 2–5–4, Suido, Bunkyo-ku, Tokyo 112*

In Greece: Please write to *Penguin Hellas Ltd, Dimocritou 3, GR–106 71 Athens*

In South Africa: Please write to *Longman Penguin Southern Africa (Pty) Ltd, Private Bag X08, Bertsham 2013*

READ MORE IN PENGUIN

POLITICS AND SOCIAL SCIENCES

National Identity Anthony D. Smith

In this stimulating new book, Anthony D. Smith asks why the first modern nation states developed in the West. He considers how ethnic origins, religion, language and shared symbols can provide a sense of nation and illuminates his argument with a wealth of detailed examples.

The Feminine Mystique Betty Friedan

'A brilliantly researched, passionately argued book – a time-bomb flung into the Mom-and-Apple-Pie image . . . Out of the debris of that shattered ideal, the Women's Liberation Movement was born' – Ann Leslie

Faith and Credit Susan George and Fabrizio Sabelli

In its fifty years of existence, the World Bank has influenced more lives in the Third World than any other institution yet remains largely unknown, even enigmatic. This richly illuminating and lively overview examines the policies of the Bank, its internal culture and the interests it serves.

Political Ideas Edited by David Thomson

From Machiavelli to Marx – a stimulating and informative introduction to the last 500 years of European political thinkers and political thought.

Structural Anthropology Volumes 1–2 Claude Lévi-Strauss

'That the complex ensemble of Lévi-Strauss's achievement . . . is one of the most original and intellectually exciting of the present age seems undeniable. No one seriously interested in language or literature, in sociology or psychology, can afford to ignore it' – George Steiner

Invitation to Sociology Peter L. Berger

Sociology is defined as 'the science of the development and nature and laws of human society'. But what is its purpose? Without belittling its scientific procedures Professor Berger stresses the humanistic affinity of sociology with history and philosophy. It is a discipline which encourages a fuller awareness of the human world . . . with the purpose of bettering it.

READ MORE IN PENGUIN

POLITICS AND SOCIAL SCIENCES

Conservatism Ted Honderich

'It offers a powerful critique of the major beliefs of modern conservatism, and shows how much a rigorous philosopher can contribute to understanding the fashionable but deeply ruinous absurdities of his times' – *New Statesman & Society*

The Battle for Scotland Andrew Marr

A nation without a parliament of its own, Scotland has been wrestling with its identity and status for a century. In this excellent and up-to-date account of the distinctive history of Scottish politics, Andrew Marr uses party and individual records, pamphlets, learned works, interviews and literature to tell a colourful and often surprising account.

Bricks of Shame: Britain's Prisons Vivien Stern

'Her well-researched book presents a chillingly realistic picture of the British sytstem and lucid argument for changes which could and should be made before a degrading and explosive situation deteriorates still further' – *Sunday Times*

Inside the Third World Paul Harrison

This comprehensive book brings home a wealth of facts and analysis on the often tragic realities of life for the poor people and communities of Asia, Africa and Latin America.

'Just like a Girl' Sue Sharpe
How Girls Learn to be Women

Sue Sharpe's unprecedented research and analysis of the attitudes and hopes of teenage girls from four London schools has become a classic of its kind. This new edition focuses on girls in the nineties – some of whom could even be the daughters of the teenagers she interviewed in the seventies – and represents their views and ideas on education, work, marriage, gender roles, feminism and women's rights.

READ MORE IN PENGUIN

A CHOICE OF NON-FICTION

Bernard Shaw Michael Holroyd
Volume 3 1918–1950 The Lure of Fantasy

'An achievement of the highest order that no one interested in the dramatic, social and cultural history of the time can afford to neglect' – *Financial Times*

In the Fascist Bathroom Greil Marcus

'More than seventy short pieces on "punk", its fall-out and its falling-outs. They are mostly brilliant . . . much of this book is hate as love, spite as well as delight. But when the professor does fall in love . . . he is a joy to behold' – *Sunday Times*

Visiting Mrs Nabokov Martin Amis

'From the wahooing triumphalism of the 1988 Republican Convention to darting drama in a Bishopsgate pub, from toplessness in Cannes to hopelessness in the snooker-room, Amis is a fantastically fluent decoder of the modern age . . . he is also one of its funniest' – *Independent*

Eating Children Jill Tweedie

'Jill Tweedie re-creates in fascinating detail the scenes and conditions that shaped her, scarred her, broke her up or put her back together . . . a remarkable story' – Glyn Maxwell in *Vogue*. 'A beautiful and courageous book' – Maya Angelou

Journey into Cyprus Colin Thubron

This is the account of a unique journey – a six-hundred-mile trek on foot around Cyprus in the last year of the island's peace. 'Purchased by blistered and bleeding feet, this picture is extraordinarily detailed and vivid . . . An accomplished linguist and historian, his passionate concern for antiquity in all its aspects lends weight and warmth to every chapter' – *Financial Times*

READ MORE IN PENGUIN

A CHOICE OF NON-FICTION

The Time of My Life Denis Healey

'Denis Healey's memoirs have been rightly hailed for their intelligence, wit and charm ... *The Time of My Life* should be read, certainly for pleasure, but also for profit ... he bestrides the post war world, a Colossus of a kind' – *Independent*. 'No finer autobiography has been written by a British politician this century' – *Economist*

Far Flung Floyd Keith Floyd

Keith Floyd's latest culinary odyssey takes him to the far flung East and the exotic flavours of Malaysia, Hong Kong, Vietnam and Thailand. The irrepressible Floyd as usual spices his recipes with witty stories, wry observation and a generous pinch of gastronomic wisdom.

Genie Russ Rymer

In 1970 thirteen-year-old Genie emerged from a terrible captivity. Her entire childhood had been spent in one room, caged in a cot or strapped in a chair. Almost mute, without linguistic or social skills, Genie aroused enormous excitement among the scientists who took over her life. 'Moving and terrifying ... opens windows some might prefer kept shut on man's inhumanity' – Ruth Rendell

The Galapagos Affair John Treherne

Stories about Friedrich Ritter and Dore Strauch, settlers on the remote Galapagos island of Floreana, quickly captivated the world's press in the early thirties. Then death and disappearance took the rumours to fever pitch ... 'A tale of brilliant mystery' – Paul Theroux

1914 Lyn Macdonald

'Once again she has collected an extraordinary mass of original accounts, some by old soldiers, some in the form of diaries and journals, even by French civilians ... Lyn Macdonald's research has been vast, and in result is triumphant' – Raleigh Trevelyan in the *Tablet*. 'These poignant voices from the past conjure up a lost innocence as well as a lost generation' – *Mail on Sunday*

READ MORE IN PENGUIN

A CHOICE OF NON-FICTION

My Secret Planet Denis Healey

'This is an anthology of the prose and poetry that has provided pleasure and inspiration to Denis Healey throughout his life ... pleasurable on account of the literature selected and also for the insight it provides of Denis Healey outside the world of politics ... a thoroughly good read' – *The Times*

The Sun King Nancy Mitford

Nancy Mitford's magnificent biography of Louis XIV is also an illuminating examination of France in the late seventeenth and early eighteenth centuries. It covers the intrigues of the court and the love affairs of the king, with extensive illustrations, many in full colour.

This Time Next Week Leslie Thomas

'Mr Thomas's book is all humanity, to which is added a Welshman's mastery of words ... Some of his episodes are hilarious, some unbearably touching, but everyone, staff and children, is looked upon with compassion' – *Observer*. 'Admirably written, with clarity, realism, poignancy and humour' – *Daily Telegraph*

Against the Stranger Janine di Giovanni

'In her powerfully written book Janine di Giovanni evokes the atmosphere of the Palestinian refugee camps in the Gaza Strip ... The effect of the Palestinians' sufferings on the next generation of children is powerfully documented' – *Sunday Express*

Native Stranger Eddy L. Harris

Native Stranger is a startling chronicle of the author's search for himself in Africa, the land of his ancestors. 'Since Richard Wright's *Black Power*, there has been a dearth of travel narratives on Africa by black Americans. *Native Stranger* picks up where Wright left off, and does so with both courage and honesty' – Caryl Phillips in the *Washington Post*